W9-AJO-236

# Face to Face

*Also by Lynne Sharon Schwartz*

NONFICTION

Ruined by Reading: A Life in Books

A Lynne Sharon Schwartz Reader: Selected Prose and Poetry

We Are Talking About Homes:
A Great University Against Its Neighbors

FICTION

In the Family Way: An Urban Comedy

The Fatigue Artist

Leaving Brooklyn

The Melting Pot and Other Subversive Stories

Acquainted with the Night and Other Stories

Disturbances in the Field

Balancing Acts

Rough Strife

FOR CHILDREN

The Four Questions (Illustrated by Ori Sherman)

TRANSLATION

Smoke Over Birkenau (Il fumo di Birkenau), by Liana Millu

# Face to Face

## *A Reader in the World*

Lynne Sharon Schwartz

BEACON PRESS
BOSTON

BEACON PRESS
25 Beacon Street
Boston, Massachusetts 02108-2892
www.beacon.org

BEACON PRESS BOOKS
are published under the auspices of
the Unitarian Universalist Association of Congregations.


Printed in the United States of America

07 06 05 04 03 02 01 00 8 7 6 5 4 3 2 1

This book is printed on recycled acid-free paper that contains
at least 20 percent postconsumer waste and meets the uncoated paper
ANSI/NISO specifications for permanence as revised in 1992.

Text design by Anne Chalmers
Composition by Wilsted & Taylor Publishing Services

Library of Congress Cataloging-in-Publication Data

Schwartz, Lynne Sharon.
Face to face : a reader in the world / Lynne Sharon Schwartz.
p. cm.
ISBN 0-8070-7220-6 (alk. paper)
I. Title.
PS3569.C567 055 2000
814'.54—dc21
99-051799

# Contents

# Face to Face

# Only Connect?

IT WAS tall, erect Miss Mulcare, in the seventh grade, who introduced me to the nuances of telephone etiquette. Lesson one: Never phone a friend and say, "Hello, is Claudia there?" Instead say, "This is Lynne. May I please speak to Claudia?" If we knew the parent answering, she enjoined with a flash of cerulean eyes, we must say, "Hello, Mrs. Jones. This is Lynne," and perhaps even add, "How are you?" depending on our degree of acquaintance and of aplomb.

Miss Mulcare was austere, and with age the rosy skin of her face had grown softly tufted, like certain pillows. Her hair was speckled gray and white. We, her students, were smooth of cheek, young enough to remember the aura of power and privilege attaching to the phone, the infantile thrill of burbling a few words and hearing, by magic, an answering voice. We had longed to grow big enough to dash for its ring, a prerogative of grown-ups.

We had phone privileges now, but they came with obligations. Lesson two: Never, under any circumstances, open with, "Who is this?" The caller, the invader of privacy, rather than the callee, must declare herself. "Reach out and touch someone" was plainly not Miss Mulcare's motto. In her civil code, the phone was an intrusion, and the person intruded upon was entitled, at the very least, to a smidgen of courtesy. She was so austere that she might have regarded any social overture as an intrusion.

Today, a shamelessly mercenary promotional flyer urges, "Go ahead and talk, talk, talk." I'll give you a ring, a buzz, a call, we say, and do it on a whim. The evolution of this most casual gesture—picking up the phone or, nowadays, whipping it out—has been swift.

In old movies, or new movies and TV shows that portray olden times, we see phones used in a cute, self-conscious manner, as vital elements of the story rather than as narrative aids of no interest per se. I'm thinking of the telephone that entered the lives of the young generation in the televised version of Galsworthy's *The Forsyte Saga.* Or the telephone in *Upstairs, Downstairs,* handled with cautious deference by the impeccable butler, Hudson. These phones are clumsy affairs, a tubular receiver and a box-like speaker on the wall into which the characters shout: sweet campy objects that make us laugh. (Affectionate, condescending laughter at things never intended to be laughed at is the essence of camp.) The Forsytes hardly took their phone for granted; if it rang, both they and we knew something noteworthy was afoot.

Later, yet not so long ago, the aim of the personal call was usually to arrange a meeting where, in the words of the smarmy slogan, we might indeed reach out and touch someone. The conversation itself might cover every topic under the sun, even ascend, or descend, to intimacy. Still, it was only a prelude, a snatch of delights to come if we signed on for the full experience, like a coming attraction for a movie. Nowadays the phone call *is* the visit, as though nothing essential or significant would be added were the speakers to meet.

Physical presence, the sensory awareness of others, counts for little. What does count is abstracted—hearing a disembodied voice and receiving its data. It's no accident that the phone call as a form of social life has flourished in an era of minimalism and conceptual art, when bare allusions are accepted substitutes for the real thing.

With my obvious bias, how come I'm a devotee of radio, where people exist through voices alone? I have no yen to meet my radio friends, or even to know what they look like. I avoid any opportunity to see them on a screen or in the flesh. I'm not convinced they exist materially, off the radio, just as in school we couldn't visualize lives for our teachers—certainly not for Miss Mulcare—outside of the classroom. They might as well have been locked in the metal closets at three o'clock and released the next morning.

Radio is an art form that distills immediate presence into the voice—all gross matter purged away—and its best practitioners can make the voice, with its variables of tone, pitch, rhythm, and inflection, as rich a bearer of sensibility as silent dancers can make of the body. Just as speech would not enhance a ballerina's performance, a radio voice needs no face or body.

Phone conversations are not quite an art form yet, though

they're evolving in that direction. Someday soon we may label people as good on the phone, just as we call them good company or good listeners or good dancers or good in bed. In fact I label them so already. There are moments when—too surfeited with work, too restless to read a book—nothing will serve me so well as a long chummy talk, curled up in a chair, analyzing the day's events with an absurd yet regenerating minuteness and concentration. That's when I seek out friends who blossom on the phone. I can feel them settling in, summoning their resources of clarity and empathy, calling forth my own best flights too. (Other friends, equally dear, are no use at all on the phone; they hurry off, saving themselves for the reality of our next meeting.)

So perhaps I've been hasty. Perhaps what phones offer is not so much a fraudulent and reduced version of human contact as a different kind or quality. After all, pen pals know each other only by letter and have rich connections, are even loath to meet for fear of disturbing the fragile bond so carefully nurtured. (E-mail is a whole other matter, on which I'm not ready to theorize.)

Likewise, with certain friends who live too far away for a visit, we talk so well and so thoroughly on the phone that we don't ever long to see them. If they do hit town periodically, we feel a discrepancy, a slight jolt when we meet. We're so accustomed to the unfleshed voice that we have trouble compounding and compacting it with the body it issues from. By the time our neural circuits have wedded the voice and the body so that we can speak as naturally as on the phone, the visit may be over, the critical moment passed. We part looking forward to the next phone call; we go home unsatisfied, as if we haven't really enjoyed the friend we know so well. Something was missing. What was missing was the physical absence, the fertile vacuum in which our friendship thrives, a vacuum that bathes our words in its delicate emptiness and suffuses them with a pure floating grace.

If certain friendships are best cultivated over the phone, certain things are more easily said, too. Asking favors is easier over the phone. So is refusing them, especially for those who find it hard to say no; the phone removes the awkward sight of the other's disappointment. (That kind of vicarious discomfort, of course, is less the sign of a kind heart than the dread of being the object of ill will.) Anger, a sharper way of saying no, is also easier over the phone, at least for the timid, who can hang up when the rising temperature begins to crackle the wires. (The brave and belligerent may relish the heat of confrontation.) The timid, again, profit by the phone when encountering someone for the first time, particularly someone in a position of power, a prospective employer, say. They can sit quaking and unkempt in their bathrobes, attending only to voice and words, heedless of facial expressions, gestures, and all the rest. Apologizing is easier over the phone, though without the sight of a forgiving face, one tends to apologize for too long, hoping to make an abstract absolution palpable. A telephone encounter can be a great equalizer for those who for one reason or another feel unpresentable. (Unless pride makes them flaunt their appearance: Take me as I am or not at all.) And none of these maxims applies if you're phonophobic, an ailment more widespread than is generally recognized; perhaps it will soon have its flurry of media attention and support groups, in which phoning fellow sufferers will be the first step in recovery.

Finally, saying good-bye is easier over the phone.

Easier. Easier to avoid the emotion that attends direct experience. One of phone culture's many results—ominous or convenient, depending on your outlook—is to dilute strong emotion, often to the vanishing point. To make everything personal feel, to some degree, like business. The phone makes us businesslike; it makes us conduct our lives like cottage industries, with appointments, calendar juggling, quick jottings of memos, names, and numbers.

In the world of business there are no interruptions. Or rather, interruption *means* business—action, transaction, goods and money flowing. A business with silent phones is on the path to doom. So with our lives, we want the phone to ring. It means we have a life, we're in business. And the ways we conduct our little businesses—from hello to good-bye—illustrate what the late social philosopher Erving Goffman so happily termed the presentation of self in everyday life. Some people feel they must greet the world with a steeled formality. They pick up with an officious, off-putting "Hello," then relax immediately into a colloquial tone.

Others, never having known the likes of Miss Mulcare, dispense with "Hello" altogether and launch into breezy narrative, confident that they're uppermost in my thoughts. How mistaken. Besides, though I have a good ear for music and speech rhythms, I can't readily identify phone voices. More times than I care to remember, I've had to reply to an exuberant rush of anecdote—"So who do you think just resurfaced in my life? That guy from . . ."—by asking, "Yes, but who *is* this?" And certain eccentrics baldly adopt the business mode for personal life—"John Doe speaking"—and in the space of a breath reshape the borders of public and private.

I've been told my "Hello" sounds a world-weary, "What now?" note—if not expecting the worst, then at least something pretty bad. This doesn't surprise me. Our every gesture shows how we anticipate that the world will impinge on us—for impinge it must, and more and more often right at home, assaulting the open gate of the ear. The world's approach, for me at any rate, is an interruption of the inner dialogue, at once fantastical and mundane, in which I'm forever absorbed. The call that summons me has about as much charm as a stranger bursting in on a rendezvous. Sometimes I even answer with an intimidating "Yes?," trying uselessly to forestall whatever is about to be demanded. I wouldn't want to be greeted by a "Hello" like mine, and luckily I'm not. The great majority, whose comfort in the universe I can barely imagine, pick up with a tone of merry preparedness: what delightful new event is about to befall me?

Endings tell as much as beginnings. The conversation draws to its natural close, but some people cannot hang up. They cherish the long good-bye. Either they dread the silence awaiting them or, less pathetically, they can't stop whatever they're doing, whether pleasant or painful. The longer they've been doing it, the harder it is to switch gears. A long conversation becomes incrementally longer until the good-bye resembles the drawn-out conclusion of a Romantic symphony. I, on the other hand, am restless to move on once "Well, it's been good talking to you" has been mutually sounded. I begin to hang up, but then I hear the dimming voice come from the lowered receiver. "Sorry, what was that?" Nothing, usually. Except in cases where the speaker leaves the most salient item, the real purpose of the call, for last—"I forgot to mention, I'm getting married and moving to Spain"—and what might that signify?

---

The simple contraption into which Don Ameche—as Alexander Graham Bell—so memorably shouted has become a wildly complex global network whose evolution could fill volumes. And the more varied its options, the less human contact. In a *New York Times Magazine* article of a few years ago by James Gleick, "The Telephone Transformed—Into Almost Everything," technical wizardry is amply documented and justly marveled at. Moreover, a Bell Communications Research representative is quoted as saying, "All this accumulated technology and accumulated vision is like a volcano waiting to erupt." What effects will this volcano inevitably spew on the human spirit? On our ways of being with each other?

One of the first jarring omens, which in our innocence we didn't properly read, was losing our beautiful and evocative exchanges, our Butterfields, our Murray Hills, our Morningsides. Obliterated overnight as if by an act of God and replaced by digits. One may not feel attached to a social security number or a zip code, but Plaza, Riverside, and Chelsea were no mere syllables or clues to location on a map. They were treasured possessions, tokens of identity. Trafalgar, Cloverdale, and Esplanade conferred traces of their multisyllabic glamour on us all, but there is no glamour to living in the 468 neighborhood. Despite the monotheistic solidity of 1 or the Christian symbolism of 3, the architectural satisfaction of 4, the Satanic connotations of 6 and the fabled luck of 7, numbers will never have the poetry of letters, whose magic conjunction makes names—music on the tongue—and conjures the winds of association and memory.

We accepted the deprivation meekly; we were taken aback, unprepared, unprovident. We should have seen the loss as political as well as aesthetic and fought for our exchanges, kept using them in nonviolent defiance. A handful of numbers in my address book are in fact still listed by their exchanges—sweet nostalgias, bitter reminders. Perhaps their owners have been tenacious, or else I never bothered to make the change. When I'm using state-of-the-art phones from which letters have been banished, I need to translate carefully, letter by luscious letter, into vapid numbers. Inconvenient, but a small price to pay. Total defeat would come only if every letter disappeared from every phone.

And this, it appears, is not about to happen. Ironically, letters—of a different sort—are making an unforeseen comeback. In the present global village, or global mall, of 800 numbers, they're replacing digits in part or entirely. Billboard and bus advertising teems with examples. To feel more at home in your chosen land, call 1-800-English. For help getting into college or graduate school, dial 1-800-Kap-Test. Trouble sleeping?

1-800-Mattres (*sic*). For therapy, 1-800-FEELING. Better still, to reshape your life and prospects, 1-800-55Blemish. The letters, presumably, are easier to remember. Thus the wheel, newly reinvented, comes round again.

In those days of Axminster, Baring, and Shore Road, my parents' friends would unexpectedly ring the doorbell—"We were just passing by"—and be invited in for coffee. The hour might be inopportune, but these were friends, after all, and they were made welcome. With scheduled appointments the order of our day, doorbells are silent but phones clamor. You're settling into the tub after worrying all day about a loved one who's sick or in trouble. What will the blood tests reveal? Will he get the job he needs so badly? The phone rings. You could let the machine take it but no, love propels you, dripping, toward the news. Hello? you pant. It's Planned Parenthood and they need your help.

The dinner hour has become a free-for-all. ("Courtesy calls"!) Hosts of strangers prod us to become a charitable point of light. Or to take out a new credit card. Or invest in land in Texas. (During the recent phone wars, competing firms called not to beg but to offer money, in exchange for your naming names, that is, suggesting future customers, as in the witch-hunts of the fifties. If the good-cause callers are irritating, these glad-handed ones are sinister.)

The voices give them away: unctuous, bright, a tad edgy, prepared for your hostility. Naturally they do all they can to avert it, and the worst thing they do—reading from their scripts—is greet you by name and ask how you are. For me, that "How are you this evening?" is the clincher. I don't do phone solicitations, I reply in the flat tone cleaning women use to say they don't do windows, or prostitutes that they don't do cuffs and chains. It usually suffices for all but the most avid. "I understand, but just let me tell you how worthy our cause is, and how dire our need."

Hanging up is the only solution. But hanging up, like breaking up, is hard to do—almost as hard as slamming the door in someone's face. I know people who'll hear out the whole script before saying no. True, there've been complaints about telemarketing, and yes, there are ways to keep your name off the lists. But since being a good citizen has come to mean being a good consumer, I shouldn't wonder that such cruel and unusual practices are by and large accepted passively. (Though they have their occasional uses. A recently divorced friend developed a warm long-distance relationship with a charming real-estate salesman. Good practice, no strings attached. She enjoyed the distraction and solicitude, along with the power to say no endlessly without discouraging her suitor.)

One step beyond the hypocrites who pretend to care how we are leads to a twilight zone: calls from no one. You're expecting your mate just stepping off the plane, and instead a voice severed from its owner says, You are the winner of a three-foot rubber raft, suitable for water sports. Or, This is the principal's office at Urban High School. Are you aware that your child did not attend classes today? Or, This is your telephone company. Press one if you still need service, two if the serviceman has already visited, three if the problem has disappeared. . . . (Don't *they* know?) Those virtual voices intoning virtual sentences jar our notions of what qualifies as talk. Is there perhaps something barbarous about using precious ordinary language—and extraordinary technology—to mimic actual communication? Maybe this other, profoundly offensive thing should have a different name.

I can't imagine ever being pleased to be addressed by a virtual voice. (My ear still holds an eerie echo of the voice in the Atlanta airport tram warning that the doors are closing. How does she know? She's not there. She's not anywhere.) Yet there are times, lonesome or bored or worse, when a stranger's live voice does for us what we cannot do for ourselves. We cannot interrupt ourselves, we are too much with us. I remember fondly a nuisance call that transcended nuisance-dom, on one eternal Sunday afternoon when isolation gripped me like a clamp. Release came through the voice of a cordial, motherly woman conducting a survey about insurance companies. Would I participate? What I might have resented on a good day became a link to the glistening world beyond. Sure! Ask me anything! Okay, how would I rate the probity of the following firms on a scale of one to ten? Which of the following words or images would I use to describe each? A good game, even though, as I freely confessed, I knew nothing about insurance companies. My caller didn't care. Maybe ignorance made me a better subject. It was a long survey, lots of questions. I made it even longer with little comments and jokes that she seemed to appreciate. I hated to part with her. I imagined going out and meeting her for coffee, but I was not so far gone as to suggest that; anyhow, she was probably miles away, a different time zone, different weather. Sadly for me, it ended. But I was not so sad as when it began. I had been stirred from torpor and enlisted in the affairs of the world, no matter how inane. From that factitious dialogue I might make the leap to real dialogue. I could see a future.

Not long after the tragic fall of President, Trafalgar, and Buckminster came the demise of answering services. They were favored by doctors for after-hours emergencies, by actors for the crucial callback, and by those people, ahead of their time, who couldn't stand to miss a call. The diverse and idiosyncratic voices that manned the services are silenced now; also gone forever are comic movie scenes of wires being hastily jabbed into switchboards by rows of operators whose antic garbling of messages drove the helter-skelter plot. Instead we have the answering machine. We wonder how we managed without it, yet manage we did. We must have lived more patiently. We had, perforce, the capacity to wait. But machines shape our nature as much as anything else, and the answering machine has wrought the need to reach out and touch someone—or someone's echo—into a craving that demands instant gratification.

The messages that greet callers are another Goffmanesque presentation of self. Early messages had a naive transparency, as in any new craft or art; in hindsight they seem touchingly ingenuous, like the great primitive paintings. Some were arch and self-conscious, others gracious—"I'm so sorry I can't get to the phone," or as one friend more elaborately put it, "I'm sorry to greet you with a recorded announcement." One of my favorites, showing a rare existential precision, declared, "This is the voice of John Smith."

How fast we've moved beyond all that. We're sophisticated, adaptable, ready to explore the possibilities of the form. Greetings range from friendly and functional to bare-bones terse: one close friend simply states her phone number—the ultimate in Mondrianesque. I get the point—this is, after all, only a machine—yet I feel a chill through my bones each time. Must she be quite so stark? It's not the world at large who's calling. It's me!

In the middle of the spectrum are the playful—snatches of popular songs hinting at the greeter's passing mood, the most famous bars of Handel's "Hallelujah Chorus," the daily changing homilies from Ecclesiastes or enshrined poetry—and what can only be called kitsch: the family's youngest member piping out a rehearsed sentence, sometimes assisted by a pet.

What a jolt it was, hearing my very first machine greeting. What was this eerie artifice, this absent presence? Did it actually expect me to say something in return? Over my dead body. I was so boggled by the prospect that I just hung up. Later I was told that hanging up mute is a form of rudeness. I didn't feel rude. How could you be rude to a machine? But apparently you could. How odd Miss Mulcare would have found that: machines legislating manners, expecting all the courtesy due to their owners.

I made judgments of character, in those frontier days, based on who had answering machines. But as they sprang up like weeds, my categories broke down. It was not merely the trendy, the anxious, or the self-important, but just plain folk. A select few, though, would surely never succumb: too old-fashioned, unimpressed by novelty, temperamentally ill-suited. How wrong I was. In the end, in a revolution that changed forever the nature of human connection and conversation, everyone succumbed.

Me too. I spent hours poring over the manual. Within a couple of weeks I was able to use the machine adequately, although tricks such as fast forwarding and selective erasing still strike me as risky. After some months, I learned by trial and error how to pick up my calls from outside. One day soon I may even feel ready to erase calls from outside.

I used to come home each day eager to check my mail. Now I have a double desire. I look for the flashing red bar, I count its flashes. I don't feel especially neglected or unloved if there are none; in some ways it's a relief to be left alone. What I do miss is the *frisson* called forth by news, happenings, change. Even in the absence of the flashing red bar I sometimes listen anyway, to be quite sure.

And what do I find? Styles of addressing machines are as varied as voices themselves. Most callers keep their usual patterns of diction and pace and inflection, and their usual personalities too. But a few are curiously altered, the kindly becoming imperious, the reserved loquacious. Romantic, volatile souls turn lucid and precise, and vice versa. Who can say why? Art is a mystery. Listening to one's messages is a study in the varieties of human response to a vacuum. We eavesdrop on a voice alone yet not alone, on a soliloquy played into the dark, in an empty house.

Gone are the amateur days of fumble and stammer. Now, when we make a call, we're prepared for the canned greeting; we have our speeches set. We talk freely, maybe even more freely than had we reached an actual person. Sometimes we even prefer to reach a machine and are startled by a real voice—What are *you* doing at home! And we're inhibited, as once we were inhibited by the machine; we need to revise our words to make them fit for live consumption.

Certain coy messages hint at, but never give away, the essence—"I just found out something really shocking about X"—a transparent ploy that ensures a quick call back. The efficiency-minded rattle off information, sending us scurrying for a pencil, while purists leave austere names and numbers; they wouldn't dream of confiding anything to a machine. I appreciate their Spartan aesthetic, but their opposites are far more entertaining. I mean the callers who make an imaginative leap and address my recorded voice as if it were my receptive presence, telling it everything they would tell me. With those messages, I settle in to listen awhile, chuckling or frowning as I would at any amazingly lifelike performance. Paradoxically, I'm in no hurry to call back, for it seems I've already had the zesty human exchange, and in so undemanding a fashion, too.

As a rule I return most of my calls promptly and willingly. But what of the others? The machine, with its demand for a response, makes the nuances of connection pitilessly explicit. We can gauge our feelings for people—feelings once serenely vague—by how soon we find ourselves calling back and how eagerly. Even worse, our caller can do the same. In the early days of ineptitude you could say the message was lost or the machine broken, but that excuse won't fly anymore. No, we are fated to discover all there is to know about our attachments, and to those who prize self-knowledge this may be a boon. Not such a boon, maybe, is discovering how keenly others feel attached to us.

But not all unreturned calls mean we're unloved. Lots of people, never having been schooled by Miss Mulcare, simply take advantage of a new way of being rude. Is not returning calls the same as not answering letters, or is it worse because the human voice—mightier even than the pen—is involved? If we're overlooked do we call again? How soon? More than once? I'm irritated by the nonreturners, and yet I secretly envy them. I wish I had that blithe and awful freedom.

Until recently, the only mail I received from the phone company was a monthly bill. Now they write constantly—clogging the mailbox, raising the rates, toppling the trees—to persuade me that some cunning new phone game would improve my life. Don't I want Speed Calling, Call Forwarding, Reminder Call? Three-Way Calling sounds piquant, a near relation of the *ménage à trois*. It might eventually supplant more traditional gathering places such as coffee shops, bars, and park benches. If one of the phone companies' aims is indeed to make human contact superfluous, it had better be planning alternate arrangements for procreation in the brave new world: phone sex can't yet go that far.

An undeniable aim is to ensure that the sound of the busy signal is heard no more in the land, since more completed calls mean more revenue. Success is imminent. The busy signal has all but died without the proper obsequies. Brought down by what a 1994 *New York Times* article calls "the demands of a frenetic society that increasingly sees the busy signal as a symbol of failure and lost opportunity, a vestige of the past that is no longer tolerable." Lost opportunity? Symbol of failure? What harsh words! The busy signal could be irksome, yes, but it was reassuring too. The object of desire was nearly within our grasp—tantalizingly there but not there. The preconditions of story, of romance. (Are they, too, a vestige of the past?) A little while longer and our efforts would be rewarded. Granted, we might suffer some jealousy and resentment meanwhile, but they were manageable, tempered by anticipation.

Uncertainty gives ordinary life the fine edge of suspense. Just so, the chance of a busy signal spiced the banal act of phoning. Now, with all the automated means of circumventing the busy signal, there's almost always success, of some sort or other. These semi-successes offer a restless semi-satisfaction which, as with sex, food, and sleep, is arguably worse than none at all. Moreover, alleged aids like Memory Mode or Redial, which require only one stroke rather than the arduous seven, not only glorify sloth and impatience but create a false sense of urgency. In time they make us less able to recognize true urgency, the way advertising distorts the true nature of need.

If the busy signal has not been properly mourned, its most common stand-in, Call Waiting, has been too naively welcomed, like the stranger of legend who knocks on the door in a storm and is given a place by the hearth, then makes off with the family heirlooms or worse. Call Waiting titillates the basest of impulses—greed and opportunism. (So sorry, a subsequent engagement, as Oscar Wilde prophetically said.) It plays on our anxiety—the nasty little need to know what or who might be better than what we've got now. More than a need: a fear, tantamount to desperation—given the Pavlovian alacrity with which people respond to the click—that something might be missed. The chance of a lifetime? Or an exciting emergency that requires our participation? And yet no one who's shunted me aside—after having phoned me!—has ever returned saying, I've got to go, my child has taken ill, or, Hey, I won the lottery.

For the interrupting caller, Call Waiting means being swiftly weighed in the balance. Are you more alluring than the person you innocently broke in on? If so, you feel gratification but also a small tug of guilt, as at any impure victory. If not, you're summarily dismissed. The busy signal avoided such minor abrasions to the spirit; it acted as an anodyne.

In the end, whatever role we play in the unholy Call Waiting triad, we talk on tenterhooks. Impending interruption, judgment, and competition hover over our words, draining the bloom of the present moment. The exchange is vitiated, the implicit premise of conversation overturned. The goal of the telecommunications wizards might as well be to unravel the social contract.

A half-dozen other examples of phone acrobatics confirm that our lives, our small going concerns, are important. They must be, mustn't they?, to warrant such high-tech attention as Voice Dialing, Wake-Up Call, or the customized Ring Mate Service—"Why rush to the phone . . . only to learn the call is

. . . for someone else in your household?" Pay for a distinctive ring that's all your own. Or Call Answering, the "revolutionary" message recording service touted as a lifesaving device, the EMS of phone life: "Imagine being in the middle of a call when another call comes in. . . ." Or Call Return, which by the touch of button reconnects the call you missed while racing from the shower.

One and all, they not only reveal unsightly fault lines in human nature, but widen them. There's something authoritative about a ringing phone, and the new devices encourage us to leap like good soldiers to the sound of authority. Even more, they appeal to latent desperation, rubbing at the sore need to feel connected, though to whom seems immaterial. How, they collectively needle us, can we afford to miss news that might change our lives? The implication is that our present lives are not quite enough, not quite right. And existentially speaking, that may well be. Insufficiency and imperfection are built into the human condition and are the impetus for art and science, love and crime. But they will not be remedied, or at least only temporarily, by a phone call.

In the past, it wasn't uncommon to ignore a ringing phone, provided you didn't have aged parents or young children on the loose. It was an impersonal act, or personal in the deepest sense—an assertion that privacy matters, that the uninterrupted flow of consciousness is our true life, maybe our only entitlement. But even if we have the strength of character to let the phone ring, the gesture is no longer the same. What was once a refusal has become a mere deferral; the answering machine will take the call. And as we all know, standing by while a plaintive voice addresses our machine makes us feel not private but roguishly perverse—a perverseness tinged with an unsavory sense of power.

That same power is the appeal of the insidious Caller ID, which "makes sure *you're* in control." The caller's number appears on a little box near the phone: if you don't want him or her, don't answer. (This is quite different from ignoring an anonymous ring—no tribute to privacy but an out-and-out snub.) Obviously Caller ID might be useful in deterring heavy breathers and dirty talkers, as well as children playing phone games: As kids, we'd call the local funeral parlor just for the pleasure of saying, "I'm dying to give you my business." And control of any kind can be a heady feeling. Except in this case the gift of control, along with the theft of privacy, is mutual. Never again would I be sure whether my own unanswered call means no one's home or I'm being forsaken.

Besides sowing the seeds of doubt, Caller ID spoils the surprise of a phone call. The ring may be intrusive, yet it can't help but set off a tiny thrill. Someone wants us. Who can it be? And for what? We must take what thrills we can get: In return for the interruption, grant us at least our shiver of suspense.

Like entropy, technical ingenuity is unstoppable. The impish new options, embraced not wisely but too well, are here to stay, and already their effects on social life are being felt. Call Forwarding, for example, ensures that your caller doesn't know where you are. He imagines you harmless at home while you're at the racetrack or in a hotel room. Wives and husbands can chat about picking up a loaf of bread amidst any kind of betrayal; marriages remain intact and children undisturbed—a contribution to family values. A boost for privacy, at any rate. Not so Redial. Was your daughter talking to the boy you warned her off? Your son hobnobbing with a drug dealer? Your boss hiring your replacement? Press Redial and see who turns up. TV mystery plots have already incorporated these fertile twists, and since life imitates television, our daily rounds should soon be laced with phone intrigue. As a matter of fact the *New York Times* ran a rueful little article about a woman who was "humiliated by a telephone." Pleading tiredness, she called to cancel a brunch date, only to find that her would-be host, equipped with Caller ID, knew immediately that she was calling from a mutual friend's home. "Even though he said he wasn't mad," she lamented, "I haven't heard from him for two weeks."

Notwithstanding all of the above, I must confess I have great affection for one clever phone game: the Conference Call. Conference Calls are festive—a regular little party, only you don't have to stand on your feet balancing drinks and paper plates, or worry that your skirt is too short or your hair frizzing up in the humidity of a crowded room. Conference Calls make you feel important. They must be set up in advance; your convenience is considered, never the case with ordinary calls. They arrive promptly, at least in my limited experience (I hope my future holds more Conference Calls). The operators are polite—they too must think the parties are important simply by virtue of engaging in a Conference Call. There's something amiably civil about the whole process. "Are you there, Lynne?

Good. We've already got Bob on the line. Please hold as we get Sue and Jim and Carol. . . . Are you there, Sue? Please hold as . . ." While you wait for the others to be lassoed from their far-off venues and pulled into the auditory corral, you can chat with the early arrivals, the kind of spontaneous freewheeling talk of people off on a giddy spree. Suddenly a new voice is heard. Welcome, Jim. Hi, Carol. The operator, like a suave *maitre d'*, bows out and the fête can begin. The habits of group discourse undergo a slight shift, becoming more democratic. The shy are encouraged to speak, for when a voice is the sole sign of our presence, an absent voice is notable. Those who talk too much are cut off more readily than if they loomed two feet away. Time is money, so matters are settled nimbly, without awkward silences or show-offy wrangling. No travel time is involved. All in all, the Conference Call is a far more natural outgrowth of the original telephone, the functional phone of Hudson and the Forsytes, than the grotesque mutations of Call Waiting or Call Return.

Or of Voice Mail, the dread labyrinth; I shudder to think of Miss Mulcare ensnared in it. Voice Mail is reshaping the dynamics of daily trivia. Humble though they are, trivia form the armature of our lives. We may curse them, yet we lean on them for comfort, as well as for relief from more serious pursuits. And we relied on the anonymous voices whose answers, sullen or friendly, helped us dispatch life's errands. Well, no more.

Voice Mail, whether its architects know it or not, has an august history. It derives from no less than Plato, who in his *Dialogues* used a process of dichotomizing and categorizing to generate the endlessly forking, ramifying answers to philosophical questions. Centuries later the Neoplatonist scholar Porphyry gave so astute an analysis of the method that it became known as a Tree of Porphyry. As a mode of inquiry, the Tree could provide instruction and delight, if you had the time. But Plato would be the first to agree it was never intended for the mundane. For one thing, it takes too long. (If Voice Mail is saving time for anyone, it's certainly not the humble citizen.)

You can't even leaf through a magazine, as in a doctor's office, while you wait—you have to keep a keen ear for your category. Hearing the relentless data drone by might be borne if you could trust that eventually a category would turn up that suits your need. But it doesn't. Your need is *sui generis:* either the Voice Mail daimon never thought of it, or else it was too singular to merit a slot. Uniqueness is gratifying, yet in this case it cannot mitigate despair. A despair not lost on the telecommunications experts: "I suppose," one speculated in Gleick's article, "in the future we could have devices on the lines that detect the caller's stress level and, based on that, access a prerecorded library of celebrity personalities designed to achieve maximum rapport and manipulate the hell out of us."

Until that day arrives, you wait with mounting panic and frustration, hoping for a human being as a last resort. You place your waning faith in the kindness of strangers. But more and more, the human option is omitted. The litany is over; you face the auditory equivalent of a brick wall.

Voice Mail is our latter-day Castle. Were Kafka alive he would write a book about it: *The Phone Call,* or more likely *The Phone Kall,* and the call would never go through. Like all evil empires, Voice Mail seeks to restrict and define the choices of the citizenry. The authoritarian spirit serves only itself; it sets the terms of discourse and proscribes dialogue. It shuns the ragged edges of the unclassifiable. It renders its victims impotent and passive, ultimately ensuring that there is no discourse, which is what happens when all we can do is obediently press buttons or hang up (flee the country). When all business, great and small, can be completed without any live interchange, when proliferating buttons supplant open-ended question and answer, then the dehumanization will be complete.

Well before our age of wonders, the phone supplied adventures in automation, but they were never so unnerving. Quite the contrary. My childhood fun with phones included dialing a number to get the time (with the lovely exchange of Meridian) or the weather report. How delicious to hold the receiver without uttering a word and hear: "At the tone, the time will be . . . 1:45 A.M." There couldn't be a woman, could there, sitting by the phone day and night repeating that sentence? No, you could sense a shift in the air, a hollowness, before the time was announced, so that even as a child I knew it was a recording played till the crack of doom with only the number alive and changing, just as the moments on a wall clock tick by unvaryingly, but the lived quality of each has a fresh taste and texture.

No longer can you get your time or weather pure, without a string of commercials. The spirit of free enterprise is alarmingly inventive and wriggly as a chameleon, finding its way into any vacant nook. It makes our opportunities for solitary phone adventure quite fantastic. Some years ago, the *New York Times* reported on the case of a Russian immigrant, alone and unable to afford English lessons (1-800-English), who spent hours every day calling 800 numbers, not only for language practice, but for whatever frail sense of connection they supplied. Happily, the article flushed out many volunteers willing to help him with simple English conversation.

For more banal needs, the hours of movies, the real-estate listings and the help-wanted ads may be useful, but how bland compared to soap opera updates, tips on homework, crossword puzzle answers, abbreviated religious sermons and, last but not least, sex. Phone sex is safe sex in unsafe times, but I think it would have thrived in any case, in keeping with telecommunications' shrewd ways of helping us avoid each other. Not that it's brand-new. It's probably been around ever since phones themselves, the crucial difference being that those who were so inclined were far from strangers engaged in a commercial transaction. Rather, they used the phone as a stopgap measure when they couldn't meet. Or sought diversion. (I can't picture the Forsytes or Hudson indulging, though, and as for Miss Mulcare, perish the thought.) I haven't investigated commercial phone sex, partly out of inhibition but mostly because I have a strong feeling it would lead to junk mail. Anyway, if I must have sex without another person present, I prefer to have it with a book.

Fun *with* the phone prompts the question of what you might do while *on* the phone. A question Miss Mulcare never broached, and for good reason: there wasn't much you could do. (Unless you had that enviable Look-Ma-no-hands ability to tuck the receiver in your neck and hold it there with a raised shoulder, leaving both hands free. I never figured out what sort of neck—short or swanlike—worked best for this trick, but either way I lacked it. Nor was I built to use the arc-shaped plastic gadget that hooked onto the receiver and nestled on the shoulder.)

My options increased exponentially when I became the proud owner of a cordless phone. It took only a few hours to read the manual, and after a day or so I was adept. Within my four walls, I can take my phone anywhere I want, like a snuggly pet. Hugging it close, I gaze out the window at passersby, mute strangers whose physicality complements the disembodied voice addressing me. Now and then I have the feeling I'm trailing a long cord or leash behind me, but I expect that will pass. Most of the time I feel liberated, untethered.

But always, new freedoms bring new dilemmas. Alone in our rooms, we claim all the rights of privacy and mobility, yet on the phone we're engaged in a social act too, a form, however bastardized, of being with another. A few open-hearted souls will welcome us to any sort of intimacy. I called someone in Hawaii and heard the sound of rushing water in the background. "You sound like you're near a waterfall," I said. "I am," he said. "I'm in the shower." On the other hand, I can testify that while my friends—also cordless—might have felt shielded by solitude, I've heard the sounds of dishes being washed, food chopped and stirred, a pencil doodling and, yes, even the muted tapping of computer keys. Hey, I want to shout. Listen to me!

Have we a right to expect someone's complete attention, as

we would over a cup of coffee? We haven't set up an appointment (though some people do make dates for phone calls); we've rung up out of the blue with a demand for talk. I'm no better than anyone: I've hunted for lost objects, checked the contents of the fridge and scribbled shopping lists, as well as done things I'd rather not talk about. I don't relish the day when videophones (or whatever they'll be called) display us all on their little screens, like a come-as-you-are party.

Cellular phones are still enough of a novelty to make us laugh at people ambling down the street all alone, chattering or arguing. You dismiss them as run-of-the-mill lunatics, until you catch sight of the small companion pressed to their ears. And they engender an obscure irritation. Walkers in the city should play their part in the street scene—strangers in a tacit community. But these defectors are both present and absent, split souls not giving themselves fully to either experience. Even more irritating are cell-phone addicts who insist on conducting their private lives in restaurants and department stores, or on trains and buses. Already, morning commuters on New York's Long Island Railroad have complained that their seatmates' ringing phones and intimate blather are disturbing their precious sleep. I myself have an ambivalent response. Who wants to know? I think when the diner at the next table assures the baby-sitter she'll be home in fifteen minutes. On the other hand, when the half-dialogue I'm forced to overhear sounds intriguing—"Impossible. I buried it under a tree on the outskirts of Mexico City"—I feel I've earned the right to hear the other half.

A cell phone must be a comfort on solitary drives through

uncharted territory, and yet it's a pity that the car, once one of the few places out of reach of the phone, couldn't remain chaste. No purist myself, I've called people in their cars, in California, and felt a vicarious thrill, as if I were traveling with them. As in a metaphysical sense I was—ear to ear though we moved through different hours, under different stages of the sun.

Suitable hours for calling were a key feature of Miss Mulcare's phone etiquette. Perhaps she began her career in a hospital or reform school, for she warned us never to call anyone past nine o'clock in the evening. Life in general seemed to take place earlier back then; whenever the phone rang at ten-thirty at night my mother, yawning over her two-cents-a-day rental novel, would groan wearily, "There's Uncle George again," as if he were violating a curfew. Beyond knowing Uncle George's propensities, though, she happened to have a near-infallible phone instinct, a kind of sonic ESP. "That's your sister," she'd inform my father at the first ring. Or, "Oh, good, it's the plumber," as if hearing his individual timbre (the opposite of today's Ring Mate), or sensing incipient vibrations from a voice not yet dancing on the air.

Even in adolescence I was a night person and broke Miss Mulcare's rules. The day's winding-down hours, ten to twelve, still feel like happy times for social phoning. This preference (maybe I share a gene with Uncle George) has naturally irked people who keep infantile hours, or infants. So I tend to favor friends who are willing to be phoned late at night—as sound a basis of affinity as any other: it means we're sharing the same diurnal round.

For much as we'd like to think of ourselves as a human family, brothers and sisters under the skin, the disparity in phoning hours points up what far-apart galaxies we inhabit. Lots of callers, for instance, feel that eight A.M., a savage hour, opens the official phoning day. And I must pick up, for what but disaster could seek me out so early? "So sorry, did I wake you?" they address my sleep-clogged voice. The proper reply is, "Oh no, it's quite all right." But it's not all right. I'm still tangled in dreams, while they've dressed and had their coffee; their every cell is alert, carrying forward the affairs of the world. I can accept that this is true for Australians, but when it happens right across town my sense of community is shaken.

Calls during working hours are problematic. Because the flow of work in offices, stores, and elsewhere is unpredictable and sporadic, businesses claim their employees' entire days, as in the age of indentured servitude. And those who spend their days out in the great world receive a certain respect for the seriousness of their labors. That is, their friends hesitate before interrupting. Yet often there's nothing to do at work except read, write letters, take care of personal business (on the phone), and generally try to appear busy. Personal calls can be a lifesaver, with the added advantage of leaving the evening free for more palpable pleasures.

For people who work at home, the situation is different. The world, for its own murky reasons, does not believe anyone working at home is really working, and so friends have no qualms about interrupting. They're even doing us a favor, or so they think, bringing welcome diversion. And, though I hate to expose a well-kept secret, they're not far from the truth. Our first indignant thought on hearing the ring is, "Don't they know I'm working?" The next instant, reaching out eagerly: "Thank God I can stop working for a while."

Making a long-distance call was once a major procedure, undertaken only in unusual circumstances—dire news or grand news. It meant placing yourself in the hands of a long-distance operator, specially trained like an intensive-care nurse, who appreciated the gravity of the act. She would patiently ask for data and offer a choice of treatment—collect, or maybe the more elite person-to-person.

Depending on your temperament, getting a long-distance call was cause for either alarm or joy. (In my childhood household it was commonly alarm. "Long Distance calling. I have a call from so-and-so. Will you accept the charges?" My mother turned pale as she breathed an assent.) Apart from announcements of death or disaster, though, long-distance calls were a brief exotic treat, like some delicate morsel. And similarly expensive. You didn't chat or loll but stuck to the matter at hand. Duration was not so important in any case. A small helping might be even better than a large, lest the richness begin to cloy. You made sure to savor every mouthful. That unique flavor seeped away, of course, with the advent of direct dialing, a treat in its own right. Even a small miracle—getting through all alone, no operator required! But very quickly it became commonplace.

Not yet so commonplace is the international call, the only phone experience that can duplicate the savor and intensity of yesteryear's long-distance. An international call requires planning and forethought. First of all, you have to figure out what time it is in another country, and the arithmetic can be daunting. (Why can I never remember time's direction—backward to the west and forward to the east—but have to look it up with each call? It's the same sort of riddle and ritual as the semiannual shift of the clock, and my resistance to both, I think, is a resistance to the artifice of turning time into numbers, as well as to the intractable fact that the earth moves, not the sun.)

Patterns of life in other countries are mysterious, and of individual lives even more so: we don't easily picture the daily routines, the comings and goings. Reaching a voice oceans away—hearing it live and palpitating—comes to seem a victory over nearly insuperable odds. Sometimes we don't reach the voice directly but an operator, and find ourselves embroiled in bureaucracy in a foreign tongue. Or we reach a machine offering what must be the usual message. How odd it sounds in those foreign syllables, yet it gives a warm flush of recognition too: Aha! So their lives are like ours; this is what their friends hear all the time.

At last the goal is reached. We speak. And until recently there would come that puzzling little time lag between our speech and the reply, the half second it took for each voice to stretch its way across the waters. We would speak, but every reply was preceded by a minuscule delay. The faraway person seemed to be hesitating ever so slightly, the sort of hesitation that in ordinary talk means disapproval or detachment or some ambiguous feeling barring the way to a willing response. The conversation had an awkwardness, moving as it did in tiny fits and starts. We felt our words were not being well received, or not being received in the way we intended them. We quickly grasped that this was an electronic, not a personal, lag, but the blight remained. And the feeling was surely mutual: our response never quite satisfying, our timing off.

This small lag embodied the true and broad meaning of distance. However wonderful the magic of electronics, it hadn't closed the gap entirely. Time and space were between us, claiming their reality. You may feel close, they told us, but you are not close. Now that small gap has been spanned, thanks to more efficient magic. At least I didn't hear it while talking to Italy last week. I missed it. The artisans of Persian carpets, we're told, left a small error in the weave to signify human imperfection. In the same spirit, it was good to be reminded of our separateness and of the uncrossable spaces, not merely between our bodies but between our voices and the words they tenderly, mutually, wistfully bear.

# Absence Makes the Heart

A CLOSE FRIEND goes away. Someone important. Say your life is a soup, then she is a vital ingredient. The soup will still be nourishing, appetizing, but different. Something's missing, you'd say if you tasted it. She too feels the loss: how will she manage without your conversations? she says. Still, she goes, for reasons of necessity. Quite far, to the other end of the earth. And she doesn't write. Nothing but a card, that is, giving her address.

You think of what it was like having her around. Around the corner, actually, so that often you'd run into her on the street, going to her car, maybe. A huge mustardy-green sedan, one of those ancient boat-like cars. She was very particular about having passengers fasten their seat belts even in the back seat, which was out of character—she wasn't especially cautious or finicky. Or only in certain ways. She maneuvered the car through the city with deft grace, with moderate aggression. She was good with machines, though she seemed, deceptively, the sort of gentle, elegant, sometimes even ethereal person who wouldn't be. She was one of the first people you knew to use a computer and used it with delight, long, long ago when it was a novelty; when you asked her what something typed on a computer would look like, she sent you a very brief letter that read, This is what it looks like, then signed her name. That was in character.

You would sit in her fifth-floor apartment with the French doors open, the breeze blowing in. The living room was cool and airy and colorful. You sat on one of several second-hand couches covered with print throws in muted colors, amber, lemon, mustardy colors. The room was filled, though not cluttered, with odd and distinctive objects you find now, regrettably, you cannot recall one by one, as well as with piles of books and papers. On the verge of messiness but not quite. Neatly messy. And paintings she had painted herself, in chalky tones, of flat disingenuous figures in rooms with mirrors and double images.

On a table in front of the couch she would set out neatly arranged snacks, wedges of cheese, crackers, small clusters of grapes. She would snip clusters of grapes off the bunch with a scissors—this you watched, sitting on a stool in her narrow kitchen while she prepared the snacks, poured the wine or made the tea. She was fussy about tea the way she was fussy about seat belts: the water had to be boiled. Very hot was not good enough, she said. It tasted right only if the water came to a boil. In restaurants, she said, she would ask specifically that the water be boiled, but could always tell when her request had not been honored.

Back in the living room her gentle voice murmured sly, hilarious, bitter words. Your topics of conversation were men, children, work, books, clothing, food, travel, parents, money, politics, mutual friends, pretty much in that order. She spoke so softly that it took a moment to grasp how outrageous and rebellious her words were. There was this unexpectedness in her, the subversive words belying a compliant surface. Also, unexpectedly, she was often late. Not insultingly, just mildly late, but always unexpectedly because her precision and considerateness suggested the habit of promptness.

You miss all of this. You wait for a letter about her new life. Finally you write; after a while she answers. You don't know her handwriting well—there has been no need for letters before—and studying this new representation of her, you feel puzzled. The handwriting is clear and fairly conventional, quite out of character. You write back, she doesn't answer. You are beginning to revise your naive notions of in character, out of character.

A year later she sends a card announcing she'll be back for a few months. She resumes your close friendship as if there had been no absence, and no absence of letters. You bring up the subject of her not writing. She explains that things have been difficult. In some ways. While in other ways, things have gone very well. She is so far away, she says, so stunned by the move and the distance, that in order to keep her equilibrium in the far place she cannot allow herself to think of anything or anyone from the old place. If she did, she would feel her feet were rooted on different continents and she might very well topple over or split down the middle. Therefore she cannot stay in touch. But on her intermittent returns, you can resume your close friendship just as before.

This is odd and puzzling. But, very well.

A year passes and again she returns for a while. Another year, another return, the close friendship once more resuming as if there had been no absence. You try to "catch up." But many things happen in a year, many changes. Every few months your own outlook on life shifts, you learn some hard and required lesson that makes you a slightly different person. The soup that is your life has a different taste, different ingredients, is thicker or thinner. Presumably the same is happening to her. How to take account of these shifts, let her know who you are now? You cannot sum up each lesson like a homily; you can, if you try, recount the events that led to the lessons, but that takes time and her time is limited; there is the present to enjoy; and it is tedious to narrate a series of small events whose vividness and importance are bound to the moment they took place. The pacing is what matters. The organic accumulation that is change. Had she been present to witness the small events succeeding each other, there would be no need to present the lessons in a package—they would be self-evident.

There is of course the telephone. You can call anywhere now, easily, even the other end of the earth. But you feel she doesn't wish to hear from you. She said it pains her to think of people from her old place. The fact that she does not wish to think of you, that she chooses to forget you for long periods and is able to do so, is painful and makes you angry. Naturally, you have passed permanently out of existence for many people, as many have for you—this is not troubling. But you cannot understand the shift taking place in her mind that enables her to banish you from existence for a year at a time, then to return and feel as close as before. This process you cannot understand shakes your sense of solidity: how odd to move in and out of existence in her mind while you feel so strongly your continuous bodily existence. This process she is capable of is what places distance between you, even more so than the actual expanse of land and ocean.

You have, of course, other friends who live far away. But they always did. They were never part of the soup but rather a snack, a special treat. Moreover, with other faraway friends you exchange letters, even phone calls. Or not, as the case may be. With other faraway friends, there is a tacit agreement on how to keep in touch. They do not put you out of their minds; they call or write now and then, saying, I was thinking of you and thought I'd call, or write. Or, Something important is happening that I must tell you. In this case, anything might be happening and she feels no need to tell you.

On the next visit, when she calls to announce that she is back, happy to hear your voice and ready to resume as if there had been no absence, you respond with anger. How can she expect, and so on and so on. She cries. She has no excuse. Things have been very hard, complicated, almost indescribably so. She repeats that she cannot think of anyone or anything here, she would be in two places at once, and so on. At her weeping, your anger dissipates. Very well, you will resume as if there had been no absence. You try to tell her some large things that have happened to you and how you are a different person because of them. But you are also the same person, the person who can tell her such things and have them understood. She listens and responds in the same gentle, sly, comprehending manner, as satisfying as before.

Still, you come away unsettled, confused about the continuity of identity, about the nature of friendship, of existence, even—the way, in her view, we can slip into and out of existence for each other. Not a congenial notion for you, though it apparently works for her.

When she leaves this time you try with, yes, a touch of vindictiveness to do as she does, not think about her, but you do not readily succeed. You wonder about her difficulties, what her house looks like, what kind of car she drives, who are the new people she thinks about daily. She has told you some and you imagine the rest; what is missing from your imaginings are things like snipped grapes, thoroughly boiled tea, and furniture. The details that do not, by their nature, get spoken of when time is short, and without which our images of people are wan.

After a while, though, you realize you are succeeding in your effort. You do think of her occasionally, but with an alien detachment. You think, but you do not care. It is as if she does not exist. She is not on the other end of the earth at all, she is nowhere, her life static, in abeyance until she returns next year to resume her existence. You do not especially look forward to her return or miss her anymore—the soup changes all the time, and that old soup of which she was a vital ingredient is a thing of the past—but when she returns you will be happy to see her and to care anew, as deeply as always, to take up your close friendship as before, as if there had been no absence.

This is a lesson. This is how you are different now.

# On Being Taken by Tom Victor

You could usually find Tom Victor, camera in hand or slung on his shoulder, darting about at a literary event, a reading or awards ceremony or publishing milestone. He would pause midflight to say an exuberant hello in his swift, smiling fashion, and then, as he slipped away—"Talk to you later!"—his face would change, and the sober, hermetic face of the man at work would show.

The secretive face intrigues me, the face of the man taking the measure of things. To see it again, I sometimes look at my pictures, the dozens of photographs he took, for they invoke him as much as they represent me. In every good artist's work the sensibility is immanent; in Tom's it is practically tangible, in the way the light sculpts the face.

I don't like having my picture taken. I am not one of those people who is "photogenic"; I don't even come out looking like anyone I care to acknowledge as myself. So I did not go to Tom Victor with enthusiasm. I was sent, for a book jacket, and apparently it was something of an honor, for he was one of the semi-official chroniclers of the brazen yet soulful world of books. Consciously or not, American readers know his work well; it is through his eyes that they see many of their writers.

You'll like him, I was told, everyone likes him—which made me immediately suspicious. (I didn't dare admit I was a trifle excited. And curious: I might even get a good picture out of the ordeal.) I called him first and suggested he come to my apartment—to get it over with quickly, for I imagined it would take fifteen or twenty minutes: set the stuff up, size me up, press the buttons. But I lived pretty far uptown, and Tom didn't want to haul his expensive equipment around the city. He urged me to come to his studio, which at that time was just south of Lincoln Center.

Very well, but how long would the session take? I had somewhere to go afterward. That was hard to say, he replied, a couple of hours, maybe. The idea of being scrutinized so closely for so long filled me with dread, yet goaded that keen, obscure, semi-erotic anticipation. Since he sounded friendly and forthcoming, I risked a nervous question: What should I wear? Anything, he said, anything you like. Getting bolder and sillier, I said I had several possible getups, each showing me in a different way. Bring your costumes along, said Tom. Bring whatever you like, jewelry, things to fix your hair. . . . Here was a man who knew about women, I thought, and who knew about vanity and anxiety, and accepted them with good cheer.

I went with my little bag of props, all set to impersonate my various selves. I found him to be small and dark and full of motion. He had a quick smile, an ingratiating voice, and a midwestern accent, and I liked the way he lingered on the liquid consonants of my name. He moved like those great blue translucent flies we used to call darning needles, which skim along the water's surface speedily and unobtrusively. Tom was a slender shape skimming in total ease amidst large black mystifying paraphernalia with which he would do something to me. My part was to yield. I felt as you do when abandoning yourself to a dentist or hair stylist or makeup artist or psychiatrist, someone for whom you are raw material, who readies you for presentation to the world—a genre of experience I avoided as far as possible. But I was here for my work. I had to do it.

I barely remember the studio—my memories of it have been erased by or merged with memories of his later, better studio, farther downtown—but I know it was spacious and white and fairly empty except for the lights and cameras and photos of familiar faces on the walls. It seemed to take him forever to set things up, and as he did, he talked. Talked and talked. Funny, I thought, that he wasn't trying to "draw me out," which I'd expected. On a desk piled with books sat a telephone, which intruded frequently. Tom would dash over and, pacing about in small arcs, hastily say a few friendly, firm words of the No, I can't or Yes, I will variety, then resume where he had left off.

He talked about his family and his childhood in a small town in Michigan. No matter how many celebrated people he met, he said, or how often he saw his work in newspapers and magazines, he still felt like a small-town kid making his way in the big city. (Yet his telephone manner was distinctly urbane.) He mentioned a number of writers and poets he had photographed and told what they had been like; so many seemed to have become his friends that I was skeptical, for name-droppers can use the word "friend" rather loosely. But they had indeed become his friends, I found out later. And I found out why, when I saw how he had rendered their faces in the extraordinary collection, *Preferences: 51 American Poets Choose Poems from Their Own Work and from the Past*, on which he collaborated with the poet and critic Richard Howard.

He talked about his various apprenticeships: years spent writing poetry, editing a literary magazine, and training as an actor at the Yale Drama School—though he later found acting too confining a discipline for his temperament. He also studied stage movement with the dancer and choreographer Pearl Lang, which led him to photograph dancers, a subtle task. A dance critic friend of mine saw in Tom's dance photos a curious quality of stillness.

I imagine he came to prize that stillness. It was perfect, in any event, for showing writers, maybe an even more subtle task. Unlike dancing, their act is undramatic, impossible to locate visually; the drama is within, a dilemma which suited Tom's gifts beautifully. He cared less for the outward act than the sensibility behind it, and its transformations: he knew all about that, about the way art happens, since it was his way too.

Meanwhile he kept on talking: about his work and the photographers he had learned from. August Sander, who had undertaken to document the faces of twentieth-century Germans, was one he revered; he showed me some of his photos. About books—poetry and fiction, particularly Katherine Anne Porter, the work and the woman herself, whom he had known and loved. He was a reader, which was rare in itself, many artists having little time for arts other than their own, and he made it a point to read the books of the writers he photographed. To my surprise, he had read mine, and since it was my first I was especially delighted.

By this time he had gotten to work—clicking, that is—though I know now he had been at work from the instant he opened the door. Soon I was talking quite a bit too, and more intimately than I generally do with strangers. How was he getting these anecdotes and memories out of me, these very private observations, attitudes, tastes? But I was having such a good time, moving about in the large space as he casually suggested, that I didn't draw back. Now and then I would change clothes or play with my hair, put it up, put it down, make it wild or austere. Very silly, no doubt, but he didn't seem to think so, which made it just fine. He understood the nature of every small change; he took me in all my guises.

And kept talking. His travels: Paris, where he had lived for a few years, and Greece, and Italy, where I had lived too. Health foods: he joked that if we ever had lunch he'd drag me to his favorite health food restaurant (which later on he did, full of half-serious apologies, recommending the soba noodles, "not so bad").

We must have talked for several hours, that first meeting, just as if he weren't clicking away all the while, a steady background of clicks, just as if we were making friends and finding all sorts of affinities, saying, Yes, yes, and Me too, every few moments. At some point he told me about an old friend and showed me pictures he'd taken of her. "She's beautiful, isn't she? Women never think they're beautiful. They don't know how beautiful they are." Typical seducer's lines. Couldn't be more calculated if they were a parody. Indeed, thinking it over later I grasped, as you always do later, that he must talk this way to everyone, fickle fellow.

Well, he had to. How else could he get it all out of us, men and women both, it didn't matter, sex, age, nothing mattered but the face and its play of spirit. Somehow, he had to find the means to induce the recalcitrant, impalpable thing out of hiding and at play in the lineaments of the face, to coax forth the mysteries of flesh and spirit and make them visible, incarnate. He was very good at it, a genius. He knew what the best seducers know: the trick is to talk. The trick is to give something. Not to coax or to wheedle, but to extend.

To link art and the erotic, in thinking of Tom's work, is inevitable. The process was, for him, a kind of love, both spiritual and exploitive in the highest sense: he could turn the love on, for his work. He didn't love his subjects, he loved the process, or rather, each subject as it took part in the process, which couldn't exist on its own. Of course he had to seduce, to fit himself so cleverly and naturally to our contours that we would stop guarding the borders. What he was asking of us was everything, yet in a sense nothing: none of the trappings of self, only what Borges has called "that kernel— . . . the central heart that deals not in words, traffics not with dreams and is untouched by time, by joy, by adversities."

Like so many other writers, I came away from an anticipated chore having had a lark instead, a kind of fantastic voyage behind the surface face. He led people to become, in his presence, the people they are in their best solitudes. No wonder everyone liked him. It happens he was indeed both good and charming, but that is not the point. If he hadn't been amiable by nature he would have learned to be, I am quite sure, as an obligation of his craft.

In the end, you didn't know how far you had gone till it was too late and you had shown him everything, given him exactly what he needed, the kernel. The pictures tell: I look at them and realize, My God, anyone would think we had spent the day in bed or something, they are that naked, I am that free, that present.

He died of AIDS on February 7, 1989, still young, long before his work was completed. When he got sick he left New York to stay with a sister and went into seclusion, toward the end not even communicating with close friends. He never acknowledged his illness; it was a different era then, as far as AIDS was concerned, though not very long ago. Perhaps he wouldn't have in any case. For all his surface verve, he was profoundly private. Like other casual acquaintances, I never figured out his mysterious illness and disappearance until after his death. At the memorial service, many who got up to speak recalled his eyes. It is difficult, when describing eyes, not to fall into clichés—only a limited number of adjectives apply. His eyes were unsually black and velvety, as everyone said; glittering and warm and animated and intense were other words his friends used. But they were hard, too, almost metallic. The best thing about them was not what they gave but what they withheld. What was behind the velvet: a quality of vision that had nothing to do with amiability.

His eyes held his craft, and they were crafty eyes. When I

caught him off guard (seldom), when the concentration outwitted the charm, I glimpsed their hardness—a cold formidable focusing, as if he were peering through me, which was unsettling. But I think he wasn't peering through me or any of us; he was not a portrait painter who spends hours, days, probing. He made his search quickly, like a raid, looking for the pictures we could become, imagining us as photographs—eventually, as part of his gallery, his life's work.

The hard thing screened by the eyes, the thing withheld, was the art. The scrutiny, the penetration, the sizing up, the shaping. The skill of the Zen archer so thoroughly at one with his craft that he can hit the target with eyes closed, taking inward aim, and at the spiritual peak of his skill hits not only the target but himself.

All of this, the unique part, he had to keep back. He was a truth seeker, a truth giver: the art was not warm or friendly but had truth's utter indifference. Even, in a way, love's utter indifference—he was indiscriminately loving to dozens of captured faces. But in the end, unlike habitual seducers, he kept nothing for himself except what was rightfully his, the work. He gave, in the end, the greatest gift, and the rarest. I look at his pictures—at my own faces—and find there what I know best in the world but never imagined I could see or hold in my hand.

# Found in Translation

STRENUOUS. Grim. Resolute. Blithe. Alluring. Cringe. Recoil. Admonish. The words come from a long list scrawled in my handwriting, four or five at a time in different colored pens, on the blank front pages of an Italian book: *Smoke Over Birkenau,* by Liana Millu. The author, a writer and journalist born in Genoa, spent four months of 1944 imprisoned in Birkenau, the women's part of Auschwitz. When she went home to Italy after the war—one of 57 people to return out of her transport of 672—she wrote her memoir of daily life in the women's camp, in the form of six stories which Primo Levi praised in a 1947 review as "human dilemmas in an inhuman world."

After that first edition in 1947, *Smoke Over Birkenau* went out of print until 1957, when it was reissued, half-heartedly, it appears, by the prominent Italian publisher, Mondadori, and went the usual way of unpublicized books. In 1979, the author recounts in a letter, she felt something had to be done. "I have no family. I am alone. I realized I couldn't neglect the future of my book." With the help of a friend, Daniel Vogelmann, proprietor of a small publishing firm in Florence called La Giuntina, she brought out two editions. In 1986 La Giuntina published a very successful fifth edition, and a sixth in 1991. Since then the book has been translated into German, French, and English.

I spent most of 1990 working on an English translation of *Smoke Over Birkenau*. When I recently opened the Italian edition I worked from, I found the list of words scrawled in the front, in my handwriting. Not long ago, I must have known how they got there and why, but now they were a mystery. Insouciant. Astounded. Hordes. Routine. Perfunctory. Fervent. Vitality. Interminable.

I did the translation in a kind of dream, or nightmare, mentally living four or five hours a day in the extermination camp I conjured up from words on the page, first the Italian, and then my own English words, which made the camp seem closer and more vivid, seen directly rather than through a screen. I didn't think much about why I was doing it. First, why was I doing a translation at all, something bound to be strenuous and difficult, especially as my knowledge of Italian was not as thorough as it should be. Even more, why had I chosen a book which would plunge me into so grim a setting—for more months, as it turned out, than the actual author spent in the actual camp? Only lately have I begun to think about how the work intersected with my life and with my own work, which was writing fiction.

In the fall of 1988 I had finished a novel, and for the next six months I didn't know what to do with myself. The novel was out of my hands, moving through the various stages of getting printed and bound, for which I was no longer necessary. I tried starting another one but couldn't find any more words. It was as if, in that novel, I had used up all the words I knew, although it was quite short, as novels go. I wrote an unsuccessful story. I was asked to do a few essays and reviews; as always, when writing on demand, I felt I was resolutely completing term papers. I had always wanted to write a musical comedy, so I did the lyrics for several songs which I still keep in a folder and hope to return to some day; they were funny songs but I couldn't think of a plot in which they might be set.

I wasn't teaching; there was no place I had to go each day. I would not be missed anywhere since no one expected me. In the morning I would sit down at my desk as a writer should, but that was as far as I got, sitting there and maybe writing a few more blithe verses for my songs. It got so that I would cringe when I woke and opened my eyes to the light, knowing that yet again I'd have to confront my desk. There were times my body actually recoiled from the desk, and no matter how I admonished myself I could not produce any useful words.

It was then that I got the notion of translating. I had done some translation years ago and recalled it as serene, absorbing work, wonderful work. It had all the alluring intricacies of writing, the playing with words and phrases and rhythms, except you didn't have to make anything up. That was the best part. You felt you were writing and in a way you were, but the part of the mind that made things up could rest, and obviously that was what my imagination needed. Of course writing—real writing—is also translation, that is, transferring something into one's native tongue, except the language from which one is translating isn't a verbal, audible language.

An astute friend once told me that when you need any of the

basics in life—a job, an apartment, or a mate—the first thing to do is tell everyone you encounter that you're looking. I did that. I told everyone who crossed my path that I wanted to translate something from Italian. And sure enough, an Italian friend, a professor of American literature at the University of Florence, soon wrote to say that at his urging, the Jewish Publication Society had acquired *Smoke Over Birkenau* but had not yet settled on a translator.

I was sent a copy of the book—I remember it was in July of 1989—and read it while on vacation in Westhampton. It was a strange routine indeed, passing the days in the insouciant ambience of the Long Island beaches and the evenings reading of the atrocities of the Nazi extermination camps. I found the book enthralling. More important, it was a tangible thing I could do; as I held it in my hands I felt its shape and bulk could release me from the limbo where I was adrift.

I developed a yen to do it, coupled with apprehension. The language was simple and direct, but I knew how inadequate my Italian was. I would have to look up so many words, even words I was pretty sure of, to be absolutely sure. On the other hand, I had an affinity for the language and its rhythms. I understood the inner shapes of the sentences, their movements and their routes. I almost felt as if Italian was my native tongue, except that I lacked the vocabulary. I had its forms in my head, in the Chomskyesque sense, but not the words. I also had a feeling for how the book should sound in English.

There was still another reason. The subject—the Nazi death camps—was something I thought about a lot, as do many writers, perhaps all thinking people. But it would probably not find a path into my writing except in the most oblique way, since it existed in my life only in an oblique way. Even if I knew what to say, even if I had the skill and imagination, I would still hesitate; I would worry about my ignorance, my possible arrogance in attempting it. The translation would be a way of writing about the camps without actually writing, just as I had not actually lived in them. It would be taking part in some way, doing a small service. It would also be an escape from the need or desire to write about the subject, just as my having been born when and where I was was an escape from the reality.

Haggard. Cantankerous. Imploring. Dreary. Plucky. Banter. Superb. Vivacious. Snarling. Prattled.

There ensued a lengthy period of correspondence and cantankerous negotiations with the publisher, again, a period longer than the time Liana Millu spent in Birkenau: The endless delays were galling, especially as the project was a modest book of one hundred sixty pages, involving a sum of money in the middling four figures.

Toward the end of July I wrote a letter from the beach saying I'd be interested in doing the book. A few months later, in early fall, I was invited to submit a sample translation of five pages, any five pages I wished. I chose a passage in which a prisoner sneaks out to the camp's black market in the evening to trade a bit of bread for a carrot or piece of onion she could smuggle to her thirteen-year-old son, whom she has discovered, scrawny and haggard, working in the garbage detail in nearby Auschwitz. It was a passage which made the despicable outrage of the camps quite clear, as the imploring mother bargains with fellow prisoners over miserable scraps of food.

It took me two weeks to get the five pages in good shape. If five pages took two weeks, I figured that one hundred sixty pages would take about thirty-two weeks or eight months.

Early in December, winter coming on, the beach a distant memory, I received a written offer to do the book. I set myself a goal of five pages a day in very rough form—a literal, not yet literary, translation. As anticipated, I had to look up many words. I had a fat, excellent Italian-English dictionary, and I became so intimate with this dictionary that I could turn automatically to the correct page for the first letter of the word I sought, and soon to the correct page for the first two or three letters of the word. This is no mean feat with a dictionary, particularly one so thick.

But help was not always to be found in the dictionary—for instance in the story of Bruna, the prisoner who one day spies her half-dead son in neighboring Auschwitz. The narrator, Liana, wonders how she can help Bruna smuggle food to the boy to keep him alive, as well as to make his coming birthday a bit less dreary. She recalls how on her own recent birthday in the camp, a friend with an unquenchable sense of style presented her with a "small slice of salted bread and a tiny curl of margarine," procured by saving up crusts and trading them on the camp's black market. This plucky friend, elegant and freckle-faced, she calls "*la mia amica fiumana.*"

*Fiumana*, that adjective describing the friend, was a puzzler. It obviously derived from *fiume*, "river," and indeed there it was in the dictionary, right above *fiume*, in the "*f*'s," to which my trained finger turned unerringly. But it was listed as a noun meaning "broad stream" or "large stream"; another meaning was "flood." Figuratively, *fiumana* could also mean a crowd or stream of people, as in "a stream of people came out of the theatre." "My streaming friend?" No, that wouldn't do.

I spent some time pondering this freckled, stylish *amica fiumana*. She must have had a generous, vivacious nature, since in such straitened circumstances she'd managed to give the narrator that gift of bread and margarine. "My generous friend?" No, the author would simply have called her *generosa*. There was more to it. "My bountiful friend?" I was leaning towards "my exuberant friend," trying to keep the riverlike, overflowing sense contained in the word. But I wasn't satisfied. I happened to mention my problem on the phone to the Italian professor who had gotten me involved in the project to begin with. "*Fiumana?*" he repeated, amused. "From Fiume."

Fiume is a Northern Italian city and *fiumana* was a simple adjective of location like *romana* (Roman) or *fiorentina* (Florentine). What threw me off was that in Italian, adjectives derived from proper nouns are not capitalized. Of course I knew this elementary fact, but because of my geographical ignorance—not having heard of the city of Fiume—I never thought to apply it to the situation at hand. Meanwhile, being a novelist, I had developed a whole identity for this friend who exists in a mere four lines—bountiful, exuberant, with long flowing hair and moist, brimming eyes and an undulating way of moving. A common practice of fiction writers is: When you don't know something, make it up. But it clearly wasn't going to be the proper strategy for a translator.

In the end, the narrator decides to emulate her bountiful friend from Fiume and persuades the other women in the barrack to put aside a morsel of bread each day for a week. By this means they amass enough bread to trade on the black market for a clove of garlic for the boy's birthday; his mother is overcome with gratitude.

For all I knew, people from Fiume might be noted for their generosity and exuberance, their lush features and fluid grace, the way, for example, people from New York are noted (mistakenly) for their brusque manners and haste and snarling speech. At any rate, I realized that to avoid similar errors, I needed help. A translation therapist, so to speak. For a year or so there had been ads on the New York City buses for psychological services. "Let's face it," the ads said. "Emotional problems don't go away by themselves." Well, neither do translation problems. I needed someone to elucidate turns of phrase, offhand jokes, and references that are clear only to native speakers or insiders. I had lived in Italy for a year, long ago, but that wasn't enough.

I thought immediately of Francesco, a language teacher I had lately made friends with. Francesco was thirty-two years old then, and a polyglot. True, he was not a native speaker of Italian—he was from the Bronx—but he had grown up speaking it with his Italian father, as well as speaking Spanish with his mother, who was Dominican. Along the way, at Cardinal Spelman High School in the Bronx and later at Cornell, he had picked up Latin, French, and Portuguese. When it came to matters linguistic, Francesco was the ultimate authority. During his first few years out of college he had worked for a bank, where he was a most valuable employee since he could be sent anywhere in the world. If he didn't already speak the language he'd pick it up in a few minutes.

It was plain to see that Francesco was not born to bank. He was slender and sprite-like, full of vitality, with quick, lithe movements—rather like the friend from Fiume. He had darkish skin, straight coal-black hair, and a gap between his teeth; he had huge dark soulful eyes, and he was warm and ebullient, full of laughter and banter. He read religion and philosophy and was a fervent believer who went to church regularly—a Protestant church, not the church of his parents. He had also studied history, and knew the dates and names of everything that had ever happened in Western Europe and perhaps elsewhere. After a few years in a business suit he'd quit the bank and begun giving language lessons; that way he could wear jeans and his superb and colorful silk shirts.

I imagined bringing the translation to him for help: we would sit in the tiny living room of his fifth-floor walk-up, or else climb the spiral staircase to the room with the birds. He kept two finches in a cage, and if they made too much noise when he had friends or students over, he would spread a towel over the cage to make them think it was night, and the gullible creatures would immediately shut up. Or we might go out on the roof terrace, which he'd decorated with thriving plants and colored banners—red, purple, green, pink, blue, and yellow—and look out over the city as I told him my translation problems and he listened with sympathetic nods.

But Francesco said regretfully that he was too busy with students and suggested someone else, a young Italian woman across town. Her name sounded familiar. I remembered I had known a couple by that name when I lived in Rome in the 1960s. There might be no connection at all, but then again it was an unusual name. I went to her apartment and asked her if her parents' names were Dora and Ruggiero. Yes, they were. "I knew your parents in Rome," I said in astonishment. "We were friends. I knew your mother even before that, back in Philadelphia. In fact I think I even baby-sat for you once or twice. Were you a year or two old in 1964?" "Yes," she said, "that must have been me."

She was pleasant enough, but she didn't seem astounded at the coincidence as I was, or even terribly interested. Her interest was perfunctory, as I prattled on about how I'd stayed at her parents' beach house at Fregene and looked after her and her sister as a favor—I was hardly more than a girl myself then. I grasped that while it was for me indeed an astounding coincidence to be referred to the daughter—living unaccountably in New York—of friends I'd known almost thirty years ago in Rome, for her it was simply running into an old friend of her parents, ho-hum.

Insipid. Puny. Taunt. Rejoinder. Seethed. Rancid. Drab. Halting. Surly.

I had met the young translation therapist's American mother, Dora, shortly after I graduated from college: she was the personnel director who interviewed me for a typing job at the American Friends Service Committee in Philadelphia. I had just married and was to be the breadwinner while my husband went to graduate school.

Typing for a Quaker social service agency was not my first choice. Since I'd been an English major, I had initially looked in the field of publishing, specifically Curtis Publishing Company, whose headquarters were in Philadelphia and which published the *Saturday Evening Post* and other popular magazines of the day. The interviewer at Curtis—I remember her still, a bony woman in a narrow, insipid little dress with a cap of dark hair that clung to her puny head—raised her eyes from my resume and said, as if it were a taunt, "I see you are married." In those days such information was included on resumes. "Yes," I acknowledged. "If you're married," she countered, "you might get pregnant." That was definitely a rebuke.

I could hardly dispute the bare statement. "But I don't plan to get pregnant for a long time," I said. "The best laid plans of mice and men go oft astray," was her rejoinder.

Fresh from college and steeped in English literature, I might have told her that the line she misquoted was actually, "The best-laid schemes o'mice an' Men, Gang aft a-gley." But I didn't have the presence of mind. I seethed with outrage. In 1959 we didn't know that what she was doing was a form of discrimination, of sexism, as well as intimidation. Or was it? Is injustice abstract? Does it exist before it is officially recognized as such? Well, that is a metaphysical question, like the tree falling in the forest. In any case I felt very badly used, but at the time there wasn't anything I could do about my rejection. It's possible that enough of those encounters might make a young woman go out and get pregnant in a fit of spite, to fulfill the prophesy. I left the Curtis building with the rancid taste of injustice on my tongue.

I wasn't too successful at hunting up jobs. Another I applied for was in a laboratory, removing the legs from fruit flies, the kind you swat in the kitchen. The man who interviewed me was a drab person with halting speech. "You know about fruit flies?" he mumbled. "*Drosophila melanogaster.*" As a matter of fact I did know, even though I was an English major. I remembered from high school biology that because of certain physical properties, and perhaps also because of their ubiquity, fruit flies were commonly used for experiments in genetics. Not only had Mendelian genetics been one of the few topics in biology that interested me, but I liked the fruit flies' Latin name: *Drosophila melanogaster.* Perhaps they are still used, though with recent discoveries about DNA and the Genome Project under way, they may have been superseded.

Despite a certain repugnance, I was considering taking the fruit fly job with the mumbling scientist, when I was offered the typing job at the American Friends Service Committee by Dora, future mother of the translation therapist. Typing was not what I'd had in mind all those years I pored over English literature, but it seemed preferable to fruit flies. I had tried to rationalize the fruit fly job by telling myself I'd be contributing to genetic research, and now I tried to rationalize the typing job by telling myself I'd be contributing to peace in the world, for the Quakers who ran the AFSC were doing a variety of good works in trouble spots such as Algeria and South Africa and Harlem. But I think what clinched it was the vision of myself interminably plucking the legs from fruit flies—after all, who knew how long it might take my husband to finish his graduate studies?

At the AFSC Dora was kind to me. She saw to it that after six months as a typist I was promoted upstairs to the Foreign Service Section as a secretarial assistant. I worked for a man who administered a work camp program in Europe; we processed the applications of hordes of American college students who hoped to spend the summer living in Spartan conditions while digging wells or building schools or libraries in poor European towns, some still feeling the devastation of the war. I was barely older than the students going to the camps, and my boss—a gentle, innocent Quaker I thought of as elderly but who was probably about fifty-five—occasionally asked if I wouldn't want to try a work camp myself.

I said no, I didn't care to sleep in a sleeping bag and eat cheap starchy food cooked communally in enormous pots and dig ditches for six weeks. I was an English major through and through and, innocent though he was, he soon came to grasp this. "Oh, but a human being can stand anything for six weeks," he would tease. "I'm not so sure," I retorted.

It was 1960. Little by little over the past decade, details about the extermination camps had begun seeping into the public consciousness. When he said, "A human being can stand anything for six weeks," I immediately thought of Auschwitz and Dachau. I couldn't foresee that in later life, once I had escaped being a typist and become a writer, I would learn Italian and one day translate a book about Auschwitz. But I would sometimes imagine myself imprisoned there, in those hellish conditions, and did not think I'd be among the ones who endured. I was too hot-tempered and impatient—I would anger a surly guard, who would shoot me. Now I am no longer so hot-tempered, and when I imagine myself there, I think I might have the patience but not the physical stamina to endure. They'd take one look at me and, with a perfunctory wave of the hand, send me off to the bad side.

In one of the six stories in *Smoke Over Birkenau*, which I was to translate long after I typed for the AFSC, an eighteen-year-old Dutch prisoner named Lotti understands quite well that some human beings can't bear certain conditions. Watching her sister sicken and wither in the camp, Lotti volunteers to work in the Nazi brothel. When her dying sister disowns her in shame, Lotti justifies her choice in an ardent speech about her passion to stay alive by any means. She quotes from the Book of Job: "'As the cloud is consumed and vanisheth away; so he that goeth down to the grave shall come up no more. He shall return no more to his house.' Well," Lotti protests, "I refused to be consumed and vanish like a cloud. I wanted to return to my house. I'm eighteen years old—I don't want to die. I know, no one wants to die, you'll tell me. But maybe I don't want to more than the others. Maybe that's the difference."

I was not only moved but alarmed when I came across this passage. It was hard enough to translate a contemporary Italian author. Must I tackle the Bible as well? What grave misgivings I suffered, until it dawned on me that the Bible had already been translated into English. All I had to do was locate the passage and copy it.

The act of copying felt sneaky. Fiction writers store many beloved snatches from other writers in their heads, often for so long that we feel we've written them ourselves. We learn to be wary about what we appropriate. Even though it was perfectly legitimate in this case, I lifted from the Book of Job with unease.

Meanwhile, when my Quaker boss teased me, back in 1960, saying, "A human being can stand anything for six weeks," I replied, "I'm not so sure." He looked perplexed; he really thought a human being could stand anything for six weeks—a tribute to the innocence of his imagination—and I did not enlighten him. He was a mild man; I wasn't sure he could stand my fantasies about concentration camps for even a few minutes.

I worked listlessly at the AFSC for two years and because of the innocence I perceived there, was probably the only employee who never attended the optional silent meeting held every morning before work. I also liked to sleep late. Toward the end of my tenure I did finally attend a few silent meetings at Pendle Hill, a Quaker retreat outside of Philadelphia, where our work campers came for a week of orientation and where I was permitted to use some of my college education in teaching rudimentary French classes. The silent meetings were fine, a curiosity, and I regretted my two-year intransigence, but I was disturbed by an evening talk given by one of the high-ranking AFSC executives. (As a Quaker group, the AFSC wasn't supposed to have ranks but it did nonetheless, and everyone tacitly understood and observed them, for example in the company lunchroom where one was invited to sit anywhere, but the executives always sat at certain tables and the secretaries at others.)

The talk was about pacifism. It was a very nice talk—Quakers and pacifism can be appealing—but during the question and answer period one of the students asked, as people invariably do, about Hitler. What would you do about Hitler? "Hate the deed and not the doer," the high-ranking executive replied in his rasping voice. He said it as if he had been asked that question many times and was tired of it, even rankled—Why do they keep harping on that? I imagined him thinking—and had his answer prepared to deliver by rote. As if on cue, I walked out and strolled through the pleasant suburban grounds in the warm evening.

After I left my secretarial assistant's job at the AFSC I went to graduate school. What else, if typing and fruit flies were my only career options? I needed two languages for a master's degree and decided to study Italian on my own. Languages had always come easily to me, and all I needed was enough to pass a reading comprehension exam. It was a happy choice, for two years later I found myself living in Rome. There I looked up Dora, who had also left the AFSC, married a Roman, moved to Italy, and had two babies, whom I would take care of a few times in gratitude for her invitations to the beach house in Fregene, and one of whom, decades later, would become my translation therapist.

I couldn't stop thinking about the convoluted trail of coincidence leading me back to Dora and her Italian daughter. It nagged at me with mounting intensity, the way a story idea nags. It wasn't the coincidence as such that I found so compelling, after my initial surprise, as the discrepancy between my reaction to it and that of the translation therapist. It was interesting, in the Jamesian sense of the word, that the same situation could be so striking to one party involved, evoking whole chunks of the past, and so negligible to the other. And yet in this situation the discrepancy was natural and understandable.

Misgivings. Listless. Rasping. Harping. Wary. Capitulate. Cue. Immersed. Mounting.

As I got deeper into the translation and could navigate in the author's idiom, the English version emerged, and with it the sensation that I myself was writing the book. I had familiar urges to cut, to revise, to sharpen and expand dialogue, move paragraphs around and make verbal links. I would see an opportunity for a metaphor or analogy, or an opening where characters from earlier stories might reappear speaking new words. I had to keep myself from capitulating to such urges. The text came to seem a constraint. What felt most peculiar was not the urge to cut but the opposite urge to expand. Maybe just another phrase or so here, . . . I'd think, and, on the verge of inventing something, would suddenly remember I wasn't the writer. I wasn't allowed to invent. Moreover, the book wasn't really fiction, or fiction only in the loosest sense; it was a memoir, no doubt adorned and enhanced, but the events had really happened. Besides being only the translator, I couldn't expand because I didn't know any more than what was given on the page. I hadn't been there. It wasn't my memoir.

While I was immersed in the translation, I went to the Mac-

Dowell Colony in New Hampshire. Now, writers go to these colonies to write, not to translate, and even though no one checks your daily output, you do feel an obligation at least to try to write. I even wanted to write. It was almost spring, and I finally had words; I had a new novel in mind. But I had contracted to do the Birkenau book, and so I established a routine: I would spend the mornings on my alloted five pages of the translation, which was coming to feel interminable—the roll calls, the brutal labor, the hard crusts of bread and watery turnip soup, the beatings, the selections, the smoke rising from the crematoria—and the afternoons on my novel.

But something happened to disrupt my well-laid plans. They went astray, as the prim interviewer at Curtis Publishing might say. A part of my mind that was not routinized stealthily came up with a story idea parallel to my situation with Dora's daughter, the translation therapist. What other pair of people might have similarly polar reactions to a chance connection? I imagined a man, a diffident, unformed young man, going to Italy, having a brief unforgettable love affair, returning home to resume his humdrum life, and years later meeting a young Italian woman who he realizes is his daughter. Francesca would be her name. He doesn't tell her the whole truth, only that he knew her parents years ago in Rome. To him, the coincidence is astounding and impels him to review his entire life. To her, it's nothing much.

Bemused, I began pacing around my chilly MacDowell studio as the story took on vitality. I dropped my routine to write it and called it "Francesca." It turned out, as stories do, to be about many other and more complex things than the discrepancy in two characters' perception of a coincidence. And any of its other strands might be traced back through my life in a meandering quest much like this one.

Stealthy. Bemused. Upbraided. Pacing. Predicament. Gasp. Runt. Deserted.

Beyond its fictional offshoots, the translation generated scores of problems, all of which I had to work out myself. For a translation therapist is like any therapist—she cannot do the difficult thing for you; she can only offer information and a disinterested view, maybe setting the problem in a more auspicious context.

The problems began with the very first sentence. A raw literal translation would be: "There was a bit of confusion that morning because there had been a medical check the night before, and many girls had been sent to the sand block." Those "girls," for openers. The book had been written in 1946, a time when men were men and women were . . . girls. People like the interviewer at Curtis did their damage unchallenged. But no longer. There was no way I could refer to a group of women doing hard labor and facing imminent death, many grieving for the husbands they'd left behind and the children torn from them, as girls. Yes, quite a few were in their late teens, but most were in their twenties and thirties, and one major character and several minor ones seemed around fifty. The real girls—

children—had been destroyed before they ever reached the camp or else at its gates.

I agonized over the word, trying to be true simultaneously to the author's vision, to the idiom of the contemporary reader, and to my own convictions. Generally, when seeking the right word, my principle had been to imagine how the writer would express herself were English her native tongue. But I had no idea how Liana Millu, over seventy now, felt about American feminism or the politics of language; perhaps at her age any woman under thirty or even forty seemed a girl.

I tried it both ways—"women" and "girls"—and in the end took a liberty. Whenever "girls" didn't sit right with me—and by extension, with my imagined readers—whenever it felt distracting or alienating, I used "women." I also used "women" when referring to the characters in groups. But I kept Millu's "girl" when the character was a teen-ager, as in, "Two rows away stood a very young, pretty girl with a friendly smile," and in the case of the two sisters, one of whom dies of hunger while the other goes to the well-fed Nazi brothel: not only did "girls" seem all right given their age, but the poignancy of the word heightened the pain of their predicament.

Also in that first sentence, the girls or women "had been sent to the sand block." On receiving my manuscript, the editor wrote and asked, What is this sand block? Well, I replied, it says exactly that, "*block della sabbia.*" "Block" was the German word used throughout for the barracks where the women slept. Many prisoners worked in the sand pits, pointlessly hauling truckloads of sand back and forth. I could only assume "the sand block" referred to the barracks housing those women who worked in the pits. I agreed, though, that the phrase was vaguer than Millu's usual style. And in English it had an auditory suggestion of "sandbox," which was very inopportune.

Imagine our surprise when, the book already set in galleys, a letter arrived from Daniel Vogelmann, the Italian publisher. I wonder if I mentioned, he wrote, that in the 1986 edition there were two typos. It wasn't the "*block della sabbia*" at all, but the "*block della scabbia.*" "*Scabbia*" (I had to look it up in my fat dictionary) means "scabies." That is, after "the medical check of the night before," many women had been sent to be disinfected for scabies, and thus the confusion in the barracks. Who would have thought it?

A reference to scabies was a fine opening stroke on the author's part, almost lost to something blander and ambiguous. It makes one wonder about all the enduring works passed down through centuries, painstakingly copied by hand—or maybe not so painstakingly—and what similar misreadings might be serving as the pillars of Western thought.

The other typo was the same perilous, just possible, kind. A young woman in the camp tries to conceal her pregnancy—a forbidden condition in Birkenau—by binding up her stomach with rags to make it look flat. Unwilling to submit to the required abortion, she fervently hopes the war will end in time for her to have her baby at home. She tells the narrator how hard it is to carry the heavy loads assigned to her: "*i sacchi di acqua, i sacchi del pane, i sacchi della paglia*"—sacks of water, sacks of bread, sacks of straw.

Water is not carried in sacks. Yet given the camps' surreal absurdities, the fact that idiotic and impossible tasks were demanded simply to destroy morale, it might just be. I don't recall what I was planning to do about those sacks of water; one mediocre way out might have been to have the character complain of "loads" of water, bread, and straw.

Not "*sacchi,*" Vogelmann wrote, but "*secchi.*" Buckets. A single letter made the difference between the absurd and the ordinary. And yet the notion of carrying water in a sack is less absurd than the actuality of being forced to conceal a pregnancy and haul buckets of water all day for being born into a race scheduled for extermination.

More trouble arose when the narrator and Lili, the "young, very pretty girl with a friendly smile," visit the barrack of an exotic Tunisian prisoner, Madame Louise, the camp's fortune-teller. For a slice of bread or a few leaves of cabbage, the enigmatic Madame Louise will read the tarot cards. She predicts a long journey for Lili, so long that she can't even see the end of it. Lili is overjoyed: she imagines going home to her mother. I managed the intricate laying out of the cards—hearts, spades, the wicked queen of spades. But I was stumped when Madame Louise laid out an ominous card she called the *stella,* or star. It wasn't clubs or diamonds. The dictionary was no help. Even the translation therapist was baffled. I thought of Francesco, my polyglot friend who knew everything.

"Pentagram," he said over the phone, without hesitation. Pentagram. I'd never have gotten it. I would have committed a worse blunder than sacks of water. And I envisioned his fifth-floor walk-up apartment, the crowded living room, the spiral staircase, the birds, the roof terrace with the lush plants and brightly colored streamers, and wished he were helping me, bounding about the room as he liked to do, talking of history and politics and books and movies in his exuberant way, his dark fluid eyes ever attentive.

Whisked. Piteously. Incorrigible. Reprisals. Gaping. Gross. Furtive. Chide.

*Smoke Over Birkenau* reflects a polyglot world, dotted with phrases from the various languages spoken in the camp—what we'd call today a multicultural text. In keeping with the author's choice, I left such phrases as they were, now and then giving their meaning unobtrusively in parentheses or a footnote where I feared American readers might be puzzled. For instance, the story about the two Dutch sisters, one dying in the infirmary and the other working in the brothel, is called "*Scheiss Egal*," a German phrase equivalent in English to "the same old shit."

It was easy enough to explain that title in a note. But when the phrase appeared in the story, used by a middle-aged SS man visiting the brothel, I hit a snag. Liana, the narrator, has just told Lotti, the young prostitute, that her sister is dying. As Lotti weeps, the SS man, hurriedly unbuckling his belt to get down to business, grumbles, "Her sister is sick? Who gives a shit? Always the same old shit!"

"That atrocious, despairing phrase," the narrator comments, "that they would repeat day in and day out, as if to confer on Cambronne's words the dignity of a philosophy."

Who was this Cambronne whose name is dropped so casually, as if every reader ought to know? And what were his words? I tried the encyclopedia. A French general who served under Napoleon. Present at the defeat at Waterloo. So? I called a French friend, who had a good laugh when she heard my question. General Cambronne earned immortality, she told me, by his famous response at the battle of Waterloo: *Merde.* Since then every French schoolchild has been scolded at one time or another for uttering what is called *"le mot Cambronne."* I hadn't thought of asking Francesco, and I wonder now if he would have known.

Cambronne became a small but, to me, crucial footnote to the text. Whenever I succeeded in solving some such tiny problem I felt a great delight, the same delight I knew from my own writing when things suddenly fell into place. An instant later I felt a twinge, resembling guilt, at the bizarre discrepancy of my response. I was so tickled to be able to get it right, so transported by the gifts of language that I lost sight of the dreadful subject—in this case the German officer's unbuckling his belt to make use of the grieving girl—a scene for which language was only the means, the translation.

The author quoted songs, too, in several languages, for despite their wretchedness the characters would occasionally sing as they worked, or sing to cheer each other up, or sing during the few hours' rest on Sunday afternoons. One musical woman even sleeps with a German *kapo* in exchange for a harmonica, along with a few slices of bread. But when the songs were translated into Italian, they needed to be rendered in English, as in the story of Lili, who is nicknamed for the familiar

German war song, "Lili Marlene." It was Lili who, according to the tarot cards, would be taking a long journey, so long that Madame Louise couldn't even see the end of it.

The pungent lyrics of "Lili Marlene" become emblematic of the characters' situation. After the Bible episode, I realized right away that these lyrics existed in an English translation. Hunting for them took me to the Library of the Performing Arts at Lincoln Center in New York, where I waited in a cozy armchair while the librarian whisked off behind locked doors to fetch my request. She handed me a mound of tattered old sheet music from the 1940s and I whiled away the afternoon, transported back half a century and enchanted by the songs printed in innocent old typefaces with period illustrations.

The other songs in the text were originally Russian and Dutch, and since it wasn't feasible to visit the Russian and Dutch versions of the Lincoln Center Library of the Performing Arts, I translated them as best I could. This was a treat; I was growing nostalgic for my own work, and almost felt I was back in the lyrics for my nonexistent musical comedy.

Consorting with the *kapos* wasn't unusual; the women prisoners did it not only for bread, but to snatch a few moments of pleasure in a doomed life, or to have a possible ally during a selection for the gas chambers. Because of their desperation, I needed to know the proper declensions—masculine, feminine, singular, and plural—for the Polish word *kochany*, meaning lover, or more informally, boyfriend or girlfriend. A Polish-English dictionary was no help, so I went to the Slavic languages department at Columbia University, hoping a kind professor might come to my aid. I was so disappointed to find no one in that I moaned piteously to the secretary, a plump blonde woman who seemed a tolerant sort, "All I wanted was the right spelling for a few simple Polish words." "Is that all?" she said. "I'm Polish. What do you need to know?" The experience not only corroborated but extended my astute friend's maxim: Tell everyone you meet what you're looking for, even if it isn't one of the basics such as a job, an apartment, or a mate, but merely the word for mate.

My last foray away from the dictionary was to the Yivo Institute in New York to find the English terminology for the different work groups in the camps—*commandos*, as they were called in Nazi military argot. The Yivo Institute, a center for the study of the Holocaust, is housed in a stately Fifth Avenue mansion with marble walls and a magnificently curving wrought-iron staircase in the lobby. It contains endless shelves of documentation—war reports, statistical breakdowns of prisoners by nationality, age, and sex, as well as by how they died, with photographs. Here too I spent an afternoon mesmerized by old books and papers, though not so happily as in the Library of the Performing Arts with the sheet music.

I didn't find what I needed and ended up fudging it, but I found something else: a chart showing the Nazis' division of prisoners into categories with distinct identifying marks. A red triangle sewn on the uniform meant political prisoners, a purple triangle meant Jehovah's Witnesses, green was for criminals, pink was for homosexuals, black for "antisocial" types, blue for immigrants, and yellow for Jews, though in this last case an additional triangle was superimposed to form a six-pointed star. A Rainbow Coalition.

I've thought a great deal about the list of words scrawled in my handwriting in the front of the book in different colored pens, signifying that the entries were made at different times. Interminable. Outrage. Stampede. Rancid. And so on. It's true many of the words suit the text and appear in my English version, but others do not. I think they weren't simply suggested by the Italian, but were also words I liked and hoped to find an opportunity to use, like an heiress seeking social occasions to display her collection of jewels. That sounds a trifle frivolous, I know, especially for a translator. How can words come first? What about the truth of a piece of writing, its meaning or content?

Well, a writer's real allegiance is to language, words and their proper placement, without which there is no truth or meaning. The list reminds me that along with the given of Millu's stories, the translation is built out of the English lexicon, the way bricks and mortar make walls to house life.

Just a few months ago my polyglot friend Francesco died of AIDS at thirty-five years old. He would have worn a pink triangle. When he was sick and I visited him in his fifth-floor walk-up apartment with the caged finches and the plants and colored banners on the roof, I saw lying on a table the copy of the translation which I'd given him. Only he had known the name for the pentagram in the tarot deck, the card Madame Louise said meant a long journey, so long that she couldn't even see the end of it.

Visiting the Yivo Institute, I knew immediately that the information about the colored triangles, the rainbow of prisoners, would become a poem. Sometimes the form of a piece of writing or the images by which it will travel hit you before anything else. I haven't yet written it but when I do, it will become another instance of the finite time during which I worked on the translation stretching out and arching, bending as physicists tell us time does when viewed under the aspect of eternity, reaching its tentacles back and forth over my life to encompass it all in a vast and flexible hand.

# The Spoils of War

HE ALWAYS sat in the back row, as far away as he could get: long skinny body and long face, thin curly hair, dark mustache. Sometimes his bony shoulders were hunched as he peered down at his notebook lying open on that bizarre prehensile arm that grows out of college classroom chairs. Or else he leaned way back, the lopsided chair balanced on two legs and propped against the rear wall, his chest appearing slightly concave beneath his white shirt, and one narrow leg, in jeans, elegantly stretched out to rest on a nearby empty chair.

Casual but tense, rather like a male fashion model. Volatile beneath the calm: someone you would not want to meet on a dark street. His face was severely impassive in a way that suggested arrogance and scorn.

He must have been about twenty-seven years old, an extremely thin young man—ascetic, stripped down to the essentials. His body looked so brittle and so electrically charged that I almost expected crackling noises when he moved, but in fact he slipped in and out silently, in the wink of an eye. His whole lanky, scrutinizing demeanor was intimidating. He would have no patience with anything phony, I imagined; would not suffer fools gladly.

About every fourth or fifth class he was absent, common enough for evening-session students who had jobs, families, grown-up lives and responsibilities. I was a trifle relieved at his absences—I could relax—yet I missed him, too. His presence made a definite and compelling statement, but in an unintelligible language. I couldn't interpret him as readily as I could the books on the reading list.

I was hired in the spring of 1970. It was wartime. Students were enraged. When I went for my interview at Hunter College I had to walk past pickets into a building where black flags hung from the windows. I would use the Socratic method, I earnestly told the interviewer, since I believed in the students' innate intelligence. To myself, I vowed I would win their confidence. After all, I was scarcely older than they were and I shared their mood of protest. I would wear jeans to show I was one of them, and even though I had just passed thirty and was married and had two children, I would prove that I could be trusted. I was prepared—even eager—for youthful, strident, moral indignation.

Far from strident, he was totally silent, never speaking in class discussions, and I was reluctant to call on him. Since he had a Hispanic name, I wondered whether he might have trouble with English. Bureaucratic chaos was the order of the day, with the City University enacting in microcosm the confusion in the nation at large; it was not unusual for students barely speaking English to wind up in an Introduction to Literature class. His silence and his blank arrogant look could simply mean bewilderment. I ought to find out, but I waited.

His first paper was a shocker. I was surprised to receive it at all—I had him pegged as the sullen type who would give up at the first difficult assignment, then complain that college was irrelevant. On the contrary, the paper, formidably intelligent, jarred my view of the fitness of things. It didn't seem possible—no, it didn't seem *right*—that a person so sullen and mute should be so eloquent. Someone must have helped him. The truth would come out in impromptu class papers, and then I would confront him. I bided my time.

After the first exam he tossed his blue book onto my desk, not meeting my eyes, and, wary and feline, glided away, withdrawing into his body as if attempting a disappearing act. The topic he had chosen was the meaning of "the horror" in Joseph Conrad's *Heart of Darkness*, the novella we had spent the first few sessions on.

He compared it to Faulkner's *Intruder in the Dust*. He wrote at length about racial hatred and war and their connection in the dark, unspeakable places in the soul from which both spring, without sentimentality but with a sort of matter-of-fact, old knowledge. He knew Faulkner better than I did; I had to go back and skim *Intruder in the Dust* to understand his exam. I do know that I had never before sat transfixed in disbelief over a student paper.

The next day I called him over after class and asked if he knew that he had an extraordinary mind. He said, yes, he did. Close up, there was nothing arrogant about him. A bit awkward and shy, yet gracious, with something antique and courtly in his manner.

Why did he never speak in class, I asked.

He didn't like to speak in front of people. His voice and his eyes turned evasive, like an adolescent's, as he told me this. Couldn't, in fact. Couldn't speak.

What do you mean, I said. You're not a kid. You have a lot to say. You write like this and you sit in class like a statue? What's it all about?

He was in the war, he said, and he finally looked at my face and spoke like the adult that he was. He was lost for a long time in the jungles of Vietnam, he explained patiently, as if I might not know what Vietnam was, or what a jungle was, or what it was to be lost. And after that, he said, he couldn't. He just found it hard to be with people. To speak to people.

But you're so smart. You could do so much.

I know. He shrugged: a rueful, devil-may-care, movie war-hero shrug. Can't be helped.

Anything can be helped, I insisted.

No, he insisted back, quietly. Not after that jungle.

Hunter had a counseling service, free. Go, I urged.

He had already gone. They keep asking me questions about my childhood, he said, my relationship with my parents, my toilet training. He grinned quickly, turning it on and off. But it doesn't help. It's none of that. It's from when I was lost in that jungle.

You must work, I said. Don't you have to talk to people when you work?

No, he was a meter man.

A what?

He went around checking on cars, to see if they had overstayed their time at the parking meters.

You can't do that forever, I said. With your brains?

Well, at least he didn't have to talk to people, he said sweetly. For now. Maybe later on he would get braver.

And what would he do if I called on him in class? If I made him talk?

Oh no, don't do that, he said, and flashed the wry grin again. If you did that I'd probably run out of the room.

I never called on him because I didn't want to risk seeing him run out of the room. But at least we stopped being afraid of each other. He gave up his blank look, and occasionally I would glance at his face, to see if I was still making sense or drifting off into some seductive, academic cloud of words.

I've thought of him a lot over the past twenty-five years. I think of him every time I see young men entering an Army recruiting office. I think of him every time I hear presidents announce plans to send troops to some faraway jungle or desert, the prefab, endlessly recyclable phrases billowing from their lips: "solemnly pledging," "protecting," "upholding commitments," "defending," "taking every measure to ensure." Not one yet has pledged himself to the defense of this country's young men, "taking every measure necessary" to "ensure" that their genius does not turn mute and their lives become the spoils of war.

# Help

My edgy feelings about maids go way back. As a child I lived next door to the only family on our all-white block to employ a black maid. Not a "colored girl" appearing once a week, which was not quite so uncommon, but a "live-in" maid. Roselle, who was about twenty, cleaned, cooked, and generally catered to the family's every domestic need, and they in turn made a point of telling the neighbors she was "just like one of the family," a piece of unexamined hypocrisy that irked me even before I could say why. I knew in some way that her work in the house and her color, both of which made her distinctly not like one of the family, were connected. The lady of the house boasted of how they had "gotten" her from the South when she was still in her teens, while I also knew that was not how any other family member had been gotten. Moreover, though Roselle did sit on the small brick porch on warm evenings, chatting with neighbors taking the air, she came out later, once she had cleared the remains of the dinner she had prepared and served.

Above all, claiming her as part of the family seemed to obliterate any family Roselle might possess on her own, a family evidenced by a grandmother who occasionally traveled north to visit her and sat out on the porch chatting and gossiping too, yet for all I knew helped with the housework in exchange for hospitality. I suspected that had Roselle or her grandmother or any black person bought a house on our block, my neighbors would have been among the first to flee.

As I grew up and perceived the way things were, I was certain I could never be so insensitive, patronizing and disrespectful as to boast of friendship with an employee, especially one so intimately placed. It would be a point of honor not to mistake the civility of common interests for true friendship, not to appropriate someone's private life along with her labor. Certain relationships existed, I reasoned, because of deplorable inequities; every connection based on economic necessity was shaped and warped by it. To pretend otherwise was to exploit still further, adding personal insult to social injury.

I was young. I thought in terms of abstract principle. I hadn't learned there are times, crucial times, when you find yourself doing in good faith something you have scorned in others on principle. The act sneaks into your life like an infiltrator, confounding, unnerving you: how did it manage to get past the border guards? Not very effective guards, after all. No sooner do simple instincts present themselves than principles are bared as straw men, scarecrows that scare no winged impulse.

In any case, it seemed I needn't worry about being tempted or tainted, since I would never be in a position to have a maid or cleaning woman. During the early years of marriage, while

I held various jobs and went to graduate school, my husband and I did the minimal housework together, with the feeling of playing House. No doubt we ate real food, not the airy food consumed in childhood games of House, but though I remember marathon shopping trips and bulging bags of groceries, what those groceries turned into and by what means has sunk into oblivion. Then as soon as our first daughter was born we slipped unthinkingly into the ready-to-wear habits of working husband and stay-at-home wife, for lack of imagination and with no other visible model. It was the early 1960s. We instituted some enlightened variations—I worked part-time doing writing and public relations for a civil rights agency in neighboring Harlem, with my mother filling in at home—but not so as to make a significant difference in the standard pattern. Three and a half years later our second daughter was born.

I did not take easily to the grown-up version of House—quite the contrary. One day I announced that either we found someone to take care of the children so I could get out and work, or I went to Kings County. Kings County was the Brooklyn hospital now called Downstate, but for those who grew up in its shadow, the label was generic: as Kafka's castle has come to signify state bureaucracy and, more broadly, the hopeless intransigence of the human condition, Kings County meant the psycho ward, the terminus.

My husband replied earnestly, without irony, as if, like the wife on the TV commercial, I had proposed a choice between stuffing or potatoes: "In that case we'd better find someone to take care of the children." Strictly speaking, this meant I must find someone, since besides my mental health, the children too were apparently my responsibility. Naturally whatever money I earned would go to pay for the maid, who represented my sanity. With luck I would break even. Sanity, in any event, is beyond measuring in dollars and cents.

Nothing had been stopping me from making this move on my own, but one didn't, then. At least I didn't. Besides—or as a result of—my distaste for the maid situation I had observed as a child, I didn't believe in having servants altogether. I believed, and still do, that people should clean up after themselves. My rudimentary social philosophy went as follows: if people tended to their own needs, pernicious hierarchies of class and race would be abolished (I was not yet keenly aware of those of sex), the artificial ranking of different kinds of work would fall away, the power-hungry would be kept from making trouble. Everyone would stay close to the elementary, necessary tasks of maintenance and child care, which would engender respect and reverence for the essentials—family bonds, children, useful work, a salutary life on earth: all sorts of unquestionably fine goals would be accomplished. I still believe this, though I have not found or created a setting in which I can live by it.

Now suddenly, with my quaint beliefs lost in eddies of boredom and despair, what stood between me and collapse was a maid. She, this person I didn't even know yet, was my lifeline, my life. I called the New York State Employment Agency and they sent Mattie Lou Colton to be interviewed. The children and I liked her and she appeared to like us. I telephoned her previous employer, one Mrs. Zimmerman, who sounded a bit high-handed but gave an excellent reference. As we came to an agreement, Mattie noted that I needed to pay social security and unemployment benefits, something the maids of my childhood had either not demanded or not known about, nor had their employers enlightened them. The bargain was struck and she was hired.

I had a cleaning woman. That was the term I used in my mind, where it was fraught with the discomfort and unease soon to be diagnosed as liberal guilt, a widespread affliction in the sixties: the civil rights movement, over and above its specific achievements, was forcing whites for the first time to take the existence of black people seriously. In my childhood, women who were paid to do housework and who were invariably black—as was Mattie—were called "girls," which had struck me as absurd even then and was now scandalously incorrect. (As a matter of fact Mrs. Zimmerman had sounded like the sort of woman who might call her cleaning woman a girl.) "Maid" felt upper-crust and demeaning, while "Nanny," with its Anglo and aristocratic associations, was out of the question. (Nowadays the word "Nanny" has become democratized but is still, I think, used self-consciously by the middle class.) "Babysitter" overlooked the household chores and had girlish overtones. "Housekeeper" seemed pretentious—the employer of a housekeeper should be a more grown-up and established member of society than I felt myself to be. In the end, cleaning woman seemed the most straightforward and dignified, though it omitted the crucial task of child care. As time went on, Mattie, in referring to her position, used the term "maid."

Mattie was about thirty-three, a couple of years older than

I, and was tall and heavy, with straight glossy black hair, huge liquidy dark eyes, dark skin, full cheeks and lips. She would arrive at work dressed as if for a casual lunch date or a shopping expedition, usually in a pants suit or slacks and a sweater, and then change into a white uniform—a short-sleeved polyester dress that suggested a nurse's costume. The uniform made me uncomfortable, advertising that I was undeniably the employer of a maid, but I felt it hardly my business to dictate what she wore.

She lived in the Bronx with her husband, Charles, who worked downtown in the garment center. They had been childhood sweethearts in rural Alabama, where her family had farmed, and Mattie kept a strong Southern accent—a true drawl—which I had to strain to understand, the first few weeks. Her body language was a drawl as well: large, soft, and bulky, she moved with a sense of consciously transporting her weight, yet at the same time managed to appear calmly dextrous; her movements had a luxuriance which I came to see concealed an inner turbulence very familiar to me, very much like my own.

Mattie had diabetes, childhood diabetes, the more serious kind—this she told me when she began work. She said I needed to have orange juice around the house in case she ever started slipping into a diabetic coma. Only a couple of times in the four years she worked for me did she ever need the orange juice. I was ignorant, then, of how serious diabetes could be, and thought her something of a hypochondriac for dwelling on it as she did. She was meticulously careful about her diet. In the course of time, as we sat around talking, I once or twice offered her a drink, but she said she couldn't touch it; it would kill her. This categorical refusal set off ironic reverberations, for in the local lore of my childhood, black or "colored" "girls" were reputed to rifle the liquor cabinets when the lady of the house was out. "See, she doesn't!" I wanted to hurl out to the ladies on my old block, now mostly dispersed to the outer boroughs in the wake of black neighbors. "They don't all do it!" Then my own voice retorted indignantly, "What do you mean, *they?* Who are 'they'? You sound just like *them,*" "them" in this case being the ladies. I hated my own smugness: caught between fixed, generic "theys" on either side, I alone seemed to occupy the mediating ground of reality, made unsteady by bad faith.

The plan was that I would work temporarily in my husband's office, editing and writing reports, and use the phones and typewriter there to find a teaching job: at home I could hardly make a business call or type a resumé without interruption. I postponed starting until I was certain Mattie had learned the routine and the children were used to her. For several days I stayed at home along with her and the girls, who were one and a half and five, doing the usual chores—lunches, diapers, shopping, trips to the park. There was an awkward excess of authority, two grown women tending two small girls, but I needed to feel sure. Maybe I was reluctant to take up my new independence, such as it was. Mattie evidently thought so. After the third day she turned monumentally to face me in the kitchen, hands on her hips, a Maillol in nurse's garb, and asked in an ironic tone I would come to know intimately, "Well, are you going to keep hanging around here forever?" I was mortified. The children seemed to be getting along fine, possibly even better than with me. I left.

During those first few months, Mattie alluded often to Mrs. Zimmerman, her East Side apartment, her personal habits. Though I knew it was foolish, I felt jealous. It seemed Mattie's loyalty and engagement remained over on the East Side with Mrs. Zimmerman while I, as the new employer, could never claim such attachment. I didn't know if there was a Mr. Zimmerman and was too proud to ask; clearly there were no little Zimmermans. From Mattie's allusions, Mrs. Zimmerman appeared to lead a leisurely, privileged life, staying in bed late into the morning, then going out to shop or play cards. I imagined Mattie was very fond of the indolent Mrs. Zimmerman and missed her, and that I could never hold an equal place in her affections. It seemed inconceivable that she would ever reminisce about me with the same zeal. Of course I didn't want that blighted attachment, I reminded myself, but the reminders did little to change my feelings.

After a few months I found a teaching job for the fall, which meant that on two nights a week I wouldn't get home until seven o'clock. I wondered if I might ask Mattie to cook dinner. So newly and unexpectedly an employer, I didn't know the rules of the ruling class, wasn't even sure what I was permitted to ask Mattie to do. Besides, she was moody, sometimes unperturbed in the face of domestic chaos, other times irritated by trifles. Her moodiness made me uneasy because it was so like my own. Knowing the vagaries of moods, I also knew that Mattie's might have nothing to do with me or my household, but they intimidated me nonetheless, and then irritated me, for I knew at the very least that a member of the ruling class shouldn't be timid in the face of an employee. I could tell when she walked in the door what kind of mood she was in, depending on whether she said a brief hello and went off to change into the distressing white uniform, or started talking right away about some curious scene she had observed on the bus, or what was in store for the day, or what she had cooked for Charles's dinner the night before. Cooking Charles's dinner, or "fixing his plate," as she called it, seemed the key event in her day, a ritual of near-sacred proportions in which she was the high, the only, priestess and he the boy-god. After I got to know her better she would say, in the bad moods, what was on her mind: something to do with her health or Charles or her family, some real or imagined slight from a friend or a stranger—for she saw slights everywhere. Whatever it was, it was a relief to know. I wondered if people had to pussyfoot around me in the same way.

With trepidation, I raised the question of her cooking on the nights I taught. Mattie took my humble request in her imperturbable mood. She said she was a good cook, which was soon borne out by Southern-style dinners of hush puppies, greens, fried chicken. My older daughter, just past six then, commented that Mattie's chicken was better than mine. Crisper. Or "crispier," she probably said. I felt a faint pang, but mostly I was glad, secure in my new dignity as a college teacher. Here was one more thing I didn't have to do. The same thing happened with laundry. Gradually I realized Mattie would do most reasonable household tasks, and I thought how silly I had been to hesitate with the cooking and laundry.

I got bolder: one night when friends stayed very late, I left the dirty dinner dishes. When Mattie found them heaped in the sink the next morning she was angry, and when she was angry she not only sulked but also spoke her mind, which seemed oddly redundant: in my case, one usually precluded the other.

"How you expect me to do all this and get them out to the park and everything else?" She had never bargained for dirty dishes from the night before, she said. I said I didn't see, under the circumstances, how dirty dishes were different from other chores. But I never left them again. Thinking it over now, I suppose dishes from the previous night's dinner party are different from the ordinary demands of daily life—they are the leavings of a sort of indulgence, and Mattie defined her work as dealing with necessities. The issue was not dishes, really, but who was doing the defining.

Insofar as Mattie or I had any formal ideas about raising children, on the other hand, they were identical, except mine were edged with anxiety mounting to a kind of panic over whether I could do it properly. While Mattie was anxious about a number of things—primarily health and money—she was serene with the children. She would stop any kind of housework to play games or read books or listen to them read to her; this was as I would have wished, but never thought to say. After she began cooking twice a week, I would come home from work to find her at the stove, the children dancing around her and chattering as they did with me; unlike me, she could both cook and be thoroughly engaged in their whimsy. Other days she would be sitting on the floor playing Chinese Checkers or coloring pictures or building fantastical structures with blocks, nor did she look abashed to be found at these pursuits, as I might have done in her place. She simply glanced up, said hello, and continued playing. I envied her certainty that whatever she was doing at the moment was the right thing to be doing. She never jumped up to rush home either, even though there was Charles's plate to fix and, more important, Charles himself.

For she talked about Charles all the time, never saying what he was like exactly, just weaving his name in and out of conversation, making him an abiding, immanent presence. He was good, she said. "Charles is *good*," she would say emphatically. "He's *good!*" which might have meant all sorts of things but meant, I think, the simplest. I nursed an enormous curiosity to see this good man.

Just as I was prepared—or so I thought—to show Mattie the respect of not claiming or expecting to be her friend, I was prepared for her to regard my children as no more than a job, to be handled with care and sympathy, but a job nonetheless. Still, every mother secretly hopes the person watching over her children will love them. Mattie did. She came to regard them as hers to such a degree that had I been a different sort of person, I would have been jealous. But while I was jealous of her presumed affection for Mrs. Zimmerman, I was not jealous of her possessive love for my children, nor of theirs for her. On the contrary, it was a kind of relief. I didn't have to be a mother all alone any more. My children knew quite well that I was their mother; meanwhile I was glad they had someone they could love as another mother in my absence, the capacity for love not being finite, like energy or patience. And since Mattie was so like me in the way she treated them, I felt it was not very different for them, whether they had her or me around. In a sense she was more like me than I was, for often I became too anxious to act on my enlightened attitudes and generous feelings, and reverted to old jittery ways.

It may seem unconvincing, and very likely politically incorrect, to say she loved them almost as a mother—as dubious as my old neighbors' "just like one of the family" line. Nevertheless, she recognized exactly who they were, and recognition is the yeast of love. Each day she would report in detail on their doings and the fluctuations of their spirits in the same proud, sagacious tone my husband and I or their grandmothers used, thoroughly aware of and intrigued by every illustration of character and habit, every like, dislike and inclination, every virtue and flaw. And miraculously, she found all of this as noteworthy as I did. I had an ally of the most intimate sort, someone to share not merely the work but the secret, succulent pleasures of motherhood, and this alliance was my private and delectable comfort, like my older daughter's blanket or the younger one's thumb.

As I came to know Mattie, I found our likeness uncanny. I was hardly a drawler, but I too moved calmly and gave off an aura of ease, I had been told: only I knew the turbulence beneath. Yet in both of us, beneath the turbulence lay another, deeper calm, a sanity dependable as bread, which helped hold it in check. (I wouldn't have gone to Kings County, only suffered and fretted and grown embittered.) The turbulence was sandwiched between the surface and the more sustaining calm; it swelled or lay dormant depending on our moods or situations, but the bread remained.

Since the children were not one of Mattie's anxieties, her turbulence never invaded her feelings for them. When I was exasperated at my younger daughter's stubbornness and burst out, "What are we going to do with her?" Mattie said, "I guess we just going to have to let her be." This jolted me, not because the words were wise but because they were self-evident. I should have known that. I did know it, but my painful and tortuous anxiety about being a mother screened it from view.

Perhaps Mattie saw so clearly about letting things be because she had borne a child once, a boy named John, who died at birth as a result of complications from diabetes. She talked about John often, almost as if she had seen him grow and develop, gotten to know him. In her visions she did know him—he lived as a complete person, arrested forever at a few hours old. She noted his birthday and referred to him from time to time, dating events by his birth—before John was born, after John was born. I found this odd at first, even a little eerie, but once I got to know her it didn't seem odd at all, and there was nothing eerie or mystical about it. John was important, that was the point; he was not to be dismissed or forgotten because he had not lived as long as other children. It came to seem natural to refer to him and I did too, asking whether certain events in her life had happened before or after John was born. And as my family got to know Charles, first in legend and then in the flesh, as we grew a connection as two families, John was part of the connection.

She often talked about the rest of her family too: her older sister Thelma, serious and steady, who worked in an office and lived in Mattie's apartment building, and younger sister Lila Jean, barely twenty, who had recently come up from the South to live with Thelma. Mattie considered Lila Jean potentially wild and, now that she had hit the big city, in need of constant supervision. Lila Jean took the Broadway bus to her job downtown, and according to Mattie, indulged a regrettable tendency to make friends with bus drivers. Every few days Mattie would report ruefully, yet with a kind of pride, on Lila Jean's escapades. Not far from my house was a diner where the Broadway bus terminated and the drivers congregated, and one day while we were taking a walk, Mattie pointed out this diner. "That's where Lila Jean found out about life," she said. Her younger brother, George, whom she described as handsome and irresistible, got married, and when the couple had a baby a year later, Mattie paid doting visits to Boston and brought home Polaroid snapshots to show me.

Over the years I met the family one by one, always with that curious stirring of anticipation you feel when people have been described in such detail that you know them already—their physical presence will merely touch up the picture. Thelma was indeed a homebody, huge and phlegmatic, Lila Jean was attractive in a snappy sort of way, George was smooth and charming. There was another brother down South whom I never met. Mattie's sisters and brothers called her Sister, and they called their mother Miss Lucy. They portrayed Miss Lucy, still living in Alabama, as difficult, egotistical, and exacting, though when I met her years later she seemed a mild, harmless old lady. Mattie told me that was her public manner, I shouldn't be fooled.

Mrs. Zimmerman's name hardly ever came up now, which was highly gratifying; on the rare occasions when it did, I realized Mattie had not liked Mrs. Zimmerman at all. The zeal expressed in her reminiscences was the zeal of disapproval. She had found Mrs. Zimmerman lazy, demanding, inconsiderate, and generally disagreeable. I was very pleased. Since we felt the same about many people we knew in common—neighbors, children in the nursery school and their parents—I felt sure I would have shared her feelings about Mrs. Zimmerman.

By this time, Mattie always tacitly defined her own role, which beyond the routine housework included dealing firmly with repairmen as well as with the social life at nursery school. Rather than being "like part of the family," she wished to take us as part of her family. She kept urging me to bring the children over so she could "keep" them for the weekend and have Charles meet them, and we finally arranged this—I wanted to meet the famous Charles the Good myself. I was curious, too, to see where Mattie lived, and how. She spoke pridefully of her apartment and furniture, and I suspected everything would be alarmingly neat and orderly.

We brought the kids up there on a Saturday morning: not the notoriously ruined South Bronx as, with a native Brooklynite's geographical ignorance of the Bronx, I had imagined, but the East Bronx, a poor, slightly shabby but not slummy neighborhood. The three-room carpeted apartment, filled with puffy furniture, knickknacks, and framed, glassed-in family photos, was even more orderly than I anticipated: it made me wonder what her secret judgments about our household must be, for she had firm judgments about everything and everyone she encountered. No doubt she would have been as skeptical as I am about the current injunction to be "nonjudgmental."

She would have considered it a sacrifice of her best qualities of discernment.

Mattie's furniture was more like real furniture—heavy, solid, and enduring—and more carefully chosen than our haphazard graduate school items. The bedroom was dominated by an enormous king-sized bed piled with soft fluffy pastel-colored quilts matching the floral window drapes. I was startled to see her living room furniture covered in plastic, just as the furniture in my parents' house had been shielded through most of my childhood. That felt familiar, to me if not to the children.

There, at last, was Charles, the well fed and much beloved: tall, athletic looking, and mustached, a soft-spoken man of few words, who smiled a lot. We all felt we knew him already, and I imagined he felt the same. He greeted the children by name and immediately began talking to them, more, in fact, than he talked to my husband and me. Perhaps he was shy, or perhaps he knew us so well by proxy that there was no need for small talk. Whenever we met him afterwards he was quiet, not a chilly but a placid, benign quiet. Perhaps he let Mattie do the talking for him, as she did so many other things.

We returned Sunday evening, having relished our rare solitude, to find the children in no hurry to be reclaimed, but hovering around Mattie in the kitchen as they did at home, while Charles watched a ball game on television. Besides Charles, they had made the acquaintance of Mattie's sister Thelma, and of Cora, a friend, as well as several neighbors. Mattie showed us Polaroid snapshots of the girls posed with Charles, with her, with both of them, in the living room, the bedroom, the kitchen. Some of these eventually got hung up alongside photos of a niece down South and the baby in Boston.

That outing emboldened us: we decided to go to London for a real vacation alone, something we hadn't had in recent memory. Mattie and Charles came to stay in our apartment for the week so the children could keep going to school, and we flew away. From across the ocean, I reveled in images of Mattie and Charles sleeping in our bed, eating in our kitchen—Charles's plate being fixed right at our table—hearing the creakings of the floorboards and the hum of the refrigerator, watching "our" sunsets from the front window, grumbling over the slowness of our elevator—in short, being us, taking over our children and our domestic lives. It made me feel I could be in two places at once.

There were times when I did need to be in two places at once, such as the long day I spent in a hospital lounge, waiting for the outcome of my father's operation for cancer. It had begun at noon and six hours later was still not over, with no word of its progress. I had lurid fantasies of the doctors and nurses going out for a snack and forgetting my father, his innards bared on the table—nothing in their manner indicated this was impossible. Mattie had gotten to know my parents and was fond of them; still, I knew she would be wanting to go home and fix Charles's plate. When I called and explained, she said, sure, she'd stay another hour. An hour later—no report yet—I called again, to find that my in-laws were in town and had dropped in. How fortunate, I thought. "Mattie has to leave," I told my mother-in-law on the phone. "Could you stay with the kids at least until I know whether my father is dead or alive?"

"Oh, I don't think so," she said. "We're supposed to go visit Aunt Rose."

Mattie had of course overheard half this exchange. Back on the phone, before I could speak, she said with a steely indignation that exceeded even my own, "Don't worry, I'm going to stay." When I got home—my father survived and was to live another seven years—she announced with a sniff and a toss of the head, "I told them they could leave and they did."

I can't remember whether she accepted money for those extra hours. Perhaps my memory has tossed out the fact because it is unimportant; perhaps the transfer of money is not as decisive a factor in human relations as I once thought. Surely that day was one of the many instances when the unlovely categories of employer and employee—always tenuous in our case—fell away to leave a fluid connection responsive to simple need. For more and more I see that far beyond running the household, our shared endeavor—half unwitting and only half successful—was to have our relations shaped spontaneously by nature and circumstance rather than by predetermined roles, to leap past the chafing strictures of class and race into a free state.

Later that year my father-in-law died suddenly. We had, in our shock, less than a day to organize a funeral and prepare food for a large group at our house afterward. Mattie said not to worry, she would take care of everything. When we returned from the funeral, the table was laden with the foods Jewish families like to eat after funerals and on less momentous occasions as well: bialys, cream cheese, lox, whitefish, baked salmon, sable, radishes, tomatoes, cucumbers, tea, coffee. . . . Perhaps she had learned all this from Mrs. Zimmerman, who was finally serving some purpose in my life.

Generosity of spirit was not in Mattie's job definition as it might have been formulated by either of us. No, I thought, this was done out of friendship. For friends we were, at least it is the closest word for what we were. In fact my musings at this very moment arise because there is no satisfactory or ingenuous word to label what we were, just as it was not a satisfactory or ingenuous condition. Because even as I was overwhelmed at how a burden could so easily be lifted, in a more callous part of my mind I was finally appreciating the age-old allure of having servants, something my high-minded social theories had not let me imagine. So this is how the rich must feel! So this is what money can buy!

Bought or not, it was friendship as I felt it. And it wasn't Mattie's competence or generosity that made us friends; she was generous *because* we were friends. Nor was it the gratitude on either side, mine for having someone to be a mother with, hers for having children to mother. No, what made us friends was what makes any two people friends—emotional affinity or some great passion shared. Our great shared passion was the children. As for the emotional affinity—we felt the same way about many things. We told each other, as friends do, about our parents, our past, our present, our plans. We trusted; we knew what the other was likely to say or do or feel, and we knew what irritated each other—often the same things: dirty dishes, lateness, incompetence, injustice, too many simultaneous demands. We liked peace, but we also liked speaking our minds, being righteously indignant about people who didn't meet our standards, who didn't try hard, didn't almost wear themselves out with effort for the things they cared about, as we did and as we recognized and esteemed in each other.

Would she so readily have called us friends? I sometimes wonder. Yes, of course: she was no casuist, she would not have indulged in finicky analyses to define the obvious. But at other times I think, of course not: she knew better than I, knew in her bones, the palpable boundaries drawn by class and race and money, cutting mercilessly across the landscape of delicate feelings. Maybe as Mattie saw it, she had simply landed a good job in a household where she could feel genuine affection for her employer and her charges. Or maybe she would have comfortably felt yes and no—she was clear eyed and worldly enough for that. People in her situation learn to be, of necessity.

We did not, as ordinary friends do, go to the movies or arrange to meet on the weekends, but we did do what was ritualistic among friends in those days, which was to get high together, though we did it inadvertently: on a patent medicine aptly named Cope, advertised to relieve what was euphemistically called premenstrual tension—the periodic inability to Cope. I was home that afternoon, wandering around fretfully, and announced I would give Cope a try. "Let me have some too, would you," said Mattie. "I have the same thing." We popped a couple of Copes, sat around in the kitchen, and within twenty minutes were buoyant with hilarity, floating above our chairs, light and loose and dreamy. No one cooked dinner that day, or did any dirty dishes, only laughed and floated, the neglected children watching in wonder. "This stuff sure does work," Mattie remarked with a throaty laugh, as we sat at the table giggling and telling raunchy anecdotes and sipping tea. When it began wearing off we were a bit flustered at its power. Maybe we should take it one at a time, at least when the kids were around.

Besides the fact that she was my paid employee with all the attendant uneasy nuances, there was something more bothersome, almost shameful, about our friendship, and this was that she persisted in calling me Ms. Schwartz while I called her Mattie. We had started off this way, unthinking. (Today it sounds appalling even to me, but it was the way things were done in those distant days.) Though I quickly asked her to call me Lynne as soon as I had an inkling of how things would be between us, she never did. (I partly blame Mrs. Zimmerman for this.) I asked her several times, but she would only nod and look uncomfortable and end up calling me nothing at all, so I gave up.

To make matters worse, Mattie had begun working a couple of mornings a week, while the kids were in school, for a friend of mine downstairs, who also had two young children. Since our kids played together, Mattie had often had to deal with Dale, and since the kids and I called her Dale, Mattie did too. Now that Dale had begun employing Mattie, it galled me that they were on a first-name basis, especially as they were not friends, which I well knew from Mattie's detailed reports. It seemed inconsistent at the very least, even unjust. I mentioned it to Dale, a person with a rather strong will, who said, "Yes, well, when she started working she suddenly switched to Ms. Lambert. But every time she said it I stopped short, stared at her, and repeated loudly, '*Dale!*,' until I got it through her head."

"Mattie," I confronted her. "You call Dale Dale. So . . . ?" "Uh-huh," she grunted, and got busy with something. I had a pretty powerful will too, but I could not force Mattie to call me something she didn't want to call me. I couldn't stop and stare every time she said Ms. Schwartz, and say firmly, Lynne, until she succumbed. It would feel like appropriating her as part of the family; it would be worse than her calling me Ms. Schwartz.

Much as she loved and depended on Charles, whom she spoke of and cared for as though he were a large child, buying his clothes, speaking for him, whipping up delicacies and fixing his plate, Mattie fell into frequent conversation and soon flirtation with a cop pounding the beat in our neighborhood. She would run into him coming to and from work, going to the park, taking the kids to school. At first they merely passed the time of day, and then it became clear he was keeping an eye out for her. As their talk gradually slipped into a kind of teasing banter, she gave me periodic progress reports: it soon reached the point where the cop was urging her to meet him somewhere, indoors.

"Well, are you going to do it?" I asked. "I don't know, maybe." But nothing much happened. "Did you see him today?" I'd ask when I got home. Yes, in the park, or near the bus stop, and she would recount their conversation. Things moved at such an imperceptible pace that I was convinced the affair was going nowhere and stopped asking. One day when I returned from work she sat me down at the dining-room table while the kids were in another room. From her gravity I assumed she was about to relate some troubling incident—maybe the girls had quarreled and she had had to adjudicate, or one of the mothers in the cooperative nursery school had looked at her sideways, for she was sensitive to every shade of behavior and there were several mothers whom she judged were "not stitched together too tight."

Instead she said, "Well, I went to the hotel with him." "You did? So what happened?" She wouldn't say right away but kept up the suspense with her hemming and hawing; she had me itching with anticipation. "So we got undressed and laid down." She paused. "So?" "So that was it." "What do you mean, that was it?" "There was nothing there," she said. "It was like a pencil." "A pencil?" "A pencil, I'm telling you." It was like a re-enactment of the Cope episode, but without Cope this time. "You mean small," I said. "I'm not talking 'bout small. Small's not the issue here," she said with haughty indignation. "I said a pencil." It seemed the cop had not developed properly, had had some illness or injury that left him physically like a young boy. "So what did you do?" "I said to him, You drag me all the way up here for *this!* I swear, what some mens won't do."

This was her foray into infidelity, and I suspected she was glad it turned out as it did. For weeks after, all she had to do was mutter, "Like a pencil," to set us tittering like adolescents. All the same, here was another bad-faith trap, like a little patch of quicksand in a cheerful stretch of meadow. I knew that had anything like that happened in my own life I would not have told Mattie. I could not have given her that power over me, while her information, in my hands, was no power at all.

One day Mattie came to work limping in pain: a woman on the crowded bus had stepped on her little toe, crushing it. She went to the doctor and continued to complain about the toe for a long time—excessively, it seemed to me, for a toe, and a little one at that. I didn't know then what she knew all too well—the many and dire ramifications of diabetes; a common one is the danger of gangrene. In the end, Mattie had to go to the hospital to have the toe amputated. Though she wasn't as naively incredulous as I, she couldn't quite get over the nonchalant malice of fate: that some stranger's misstep could have such a grotesque result. We went to visit her in the hospital, which happened to be in Brooklyn and quite near where I had grown up, next door to the people with a maid just like one of the family.

Soon she returned to work. Knowing Mattie, I figured she would want to show me her toe, or the place her toe had been, and I dreaded it. When she did, I held my breath as she slowly removed her shoe, prolonging the action, I was sure, for dramatic suspense. But it wasn't so bad—the little toe wasn't there, that was all. The foot didn't look deformed; it merely had a longer arc ending at the fourth toe. From then on she wore closed shoes—for safety, not vanity. I could not foresee, as perhaps Mattie did, that the lost toe would be the first of a series of side effects of diabetes coming to plague her.

When the children were about five and eight Mattie mentioned now and then that Charles was talking vaguely of moving to Los Angeles, where he had family and thought he might find a better job. She was determined not to go and swore she'd refuse if it came to an actual decision, but I saw she was worried. She loved New York—as Charles did not—and liked her apartment, liked being near her sisters and her friends, liked her job, and loved the children. She couldn't possibly leave them, she said. But I knew she could; of course she'd go with Charles if it came to that. Still, to myself I tried to dismiss it as idle talk—who, in the course of a bleak New York winter, has not had fantasies of moving to California?

She talked more often of the possible move—first it was maybe, then someday, then some time next year. The talk became specific: Charles's mother and stepfather were there, as well as a married sister. They had a job lined up for him in a Ford assembly plant.

Much as I tried to ignore the inevitable, it was upon us in no time at all. Mattie was very depressed over the move. She didn't like California, she said, and it did no good to point out she had never been there. I have completely forgotten her last few days. Repressed them, I suppose. One morning, despite all her vows to the contrary, she was gone. Ten o'clock came—her hour—and I was alone. It was almost four years that she had been helping me raise the children. I have no memory of how they responded, whether they were deeply upset or only mildly so. I have no memory of any good-byes. We promised to keep in touch, that I remember.

The girls were about five and a half and nine now. I was teaching and writing a novel. Reluctantly, I looked around for another housekeeper and found a Haitian woman who seemed able and good-natured. The children liked her well enough; she was not Mattie, needless to say, but they no longer required a mother around constantly—they were in school all day, had their friends, the beginnings of independent lives. The new woman did her job but was hardly enthusiastic about it. I reminded myself that I wouldn't be enthusiastic about taking care of someone else's household either—Mattie was an exception.

For several days in a row I came home to find the new woman sitting at the kitchen table with her head in her hands. I asked what was the matter and she said, Oh, nothing. The children, when I asked, said she habitually sat that way when the housework was done. I felt sorry for her, but apart from being sympathetic, I couldn't help her—we weren't friends—and I equally couldn't bear thinking of the children home alone with a despairing stranger sitting at the kitchen table with her head in her hands. Probably it hinted at what I might have become had I not found Mattie. I asked her to leave.

I never hired another cleaning woman. At that point I could manage on my own, with my husband's "help," a bitter word for working women. Over the years that followed, it would have made life considerably easier to have someone take over a goodly portion of the household tasks, but I could never get around to hiring anyone. I said it was my old principles about having servants, but that was a pretty transparent excuse.

We kept in touch. Mattie and Charles settled in one of the towns clustered around Los Angeles, and though she kept saying, over the phone, that she didn't like California, things seemed to be working out all right. Charles had his new job, they had a small house with a yard, and Mattie found work as a chambermaid in a hotel, where very soon she was promoted to head chambermaid. Still she complained, vigorously at first, weakly later. Like me, she had a complaining streak, and it showed most strongly in new situations and in adversity. To begin with, she wasn't crazy about Charles's family; back in the Bronx they had been surrounded by her family, whom she much preferred. And the house was in an all-black area—she liked New York, where there was a great mix of people, she said, and you didn't feel so insulated or segregated. She had come up from Alabama partly to get away from that sense of separateness. Her job was all right but she missed the children painfully. I would call them to the phone for long conversations about school and games and friends and whatnot. She wrote them a few brief letters—correspondence was clearly not her medium, physical presence was—and they wrote back.

One thing I accomplished through her absence was persuading her to call me Lynne and not Ms. Schwartz. "You're not working for me anymore, okay? Will you do it, do me a favor, once and for all?" So she did, over the phone. She'd call and say, "Hello, Lynne?" But she never sounded happy saying it, and I felt some remorse for, perhaps, forcing her.

Little by little things began to be not all right for Mattie. Charles had frequent layoffs at the plant and finally lost his job and spent a long period out of work. There were petty quarrels with his family. Worst of all, the diabetes began to torment her—minor symptoms at the beginning, and then she had go to the hospital several times for kidney problems. Her eyes began to get bad, until soon she had to give up her job at the hotel. A year or two went by. The girls had to write their letters in large block print. Mattie wanted a job working with children but was afraid she couldn't manage it—her eyes were so bad she could hardly see.

Charles found another job, eventually. Though Mattie still

managed to take care of the house, she said, she didn't feel well at all. They got a dog so she could have company, alone at home all day. She didn't like the neighbors. She still didn't like California. Then there were money problems—the ever more frequent hospital bills were ruining them. It took me longer than it should have to realize what I must do. Because of my old notion of respect, of not patronizing her precisely because she was an employee—though she wasn't my employee any more—I hadn't thought immediately of money. Had she been an ordinary friend, a friend in the untrammeled sense of the word, I would have thought of it sooner. I asked if I should send some. She said, "Yes, that would surely be very good," in her faintly ironic way, as if to say, why didn't I think of that earlier.

One day Mattie announced over the phone that she was coming East for a visit, at long last. We were both very excited and arranged to meet at Thelma's apartment, where she would be staying. She couldn't wait to see the children. Even though they were too old by now to be brought for display—about nine and twelve—I was determined to do so anyway. But it wasn't necessary to drag them. They hadn't seen Mattie in four years and were eager to go. They knew she was sick and blind, and I took pains to explain that she might look different, so they wouldn't be shocked.

In Thelma's apartment, also neatly furnished and carpeted, we found Mattie sitting in an armchair like someone who didn't move about very much. She had never been one to move breezily, but now she seemed attached to the chair. Beside her sat her mother, Miss Lucy, visiting from Alabama, a slight, docile-seeming old lady who said very little. She was dressed in a narrow, prim, flowered dress, and it seemed incredible that she should have borne such large, luxuriant daughters. We were not shocked at Mattie's appearance. Apart from her stillness, she looked almost the same, though heavier. I was relieved. I had tried to prepare the children, but no one could prepare me. She couldn't see, but she ran her hands over the girls and talked to them. It was tearful and awkward. They still loved her, but hadn't seen her in so long that they didn't know exactly what to say—their conversation had been rooted in dailiness, not generalities and certainly not pleasantries. They told her about school, brought her up to date on friends she'd known. Mostly Mattie sensed what they had become. Thelma called Mattie Sister, as she had always done; even Miss Lucy called her Sister. It was not a satisfying visit for me, maybe because there were so many people in the small room and we couldn't swap stories or gossip and laugh as we used to.

Back in Los Angeles, she spent long periods in the hospital; I wouldn't hear from her for months at a stretch, and no one answered when I phoned. During those silences I would call Thelma for information, to learn invariably that Mattie was in the hospital again. When she got out she would call, her voice sounding thinner and more subdued each time. Her mother, Miss Lucy, died, and besides the sense of loss, she had all the mixed feelings that go with losing someone you have loved and resented for decades, who has loved and resented you as well. She told me her niece, a daughter of the brother down South, who had just finished training as a nurse, was coming out to stay and take care of her. She couldn't be left alone all day. I was glad Mattie would have the niece for company, but alarmed that she needed her. She was also getting upsetting crank phone calls and suspected various acquaintances. There were troubles between her and Charles because of her illness. He was still *good* and looked after her, but it was hard on him, she said; he couldn't help feeling frustrated sometimes. She couldn't cook for him anymore, or fix his plate.

Feeling frustrated myself, I sent more money. The unfairness of things brought me down. That was one of Mattie's expressions—things would "bring her down," and now I knew how she meant it. When my life had been crumbling around me, she had appeared so I could put myself back together, but there was nothing I could do against diabetes, no more than against the army of inequities which sent us to lead our lives in such different, distant territories.

I didn't hear from her for a long time and got no answer when I called. I tried every couple of weeks, knowing it would be useless—only the formality of dialing. I put my thoughts of her to one side in an attitude of half-acknowledged waiting, almost glad to have no news. When many silent months went by, I even tried to imagine it might all miraculously be coming right: she was thriving, as in our younger days, and hadn't a spare moment to call.

One afternoon the phone rang and the voice announced, "It's Thelma." She had never called me before. I was surprised just for an infinitely small instant. I didn't need to hear the words.

"Sister died," she said.

Sister died.

It seems strange to me now that I didn't tell anyone for quite a while, not the children, or my husband, or Dale downstairs. But at the time, I think I wanted to cling to the loss all alone, to embrace it in private and give it full weight before it became a public fact. All the more so as there was nothing I could do, not even a funeral I could attend, where grief becomes the great cathartic leveler, for tears are all alike, untinged by class or race or social role. I did write a brief note to Charles, which helped neither me nor, probably, him.

Most losses can be weighed fairly accurately; you can locate the gap in your life, probe and measure its depth and breadth. I could never even locate her properly when she was alive. She haunts me because I cannot place her still; she falls in no easy category, or has a shifting place in several—family, friend, person defined by function or need. Her memory will not be pinned down, will not rest, is pervasive. She was more important than she was supposed to be, more than I bargained for when first we struck our bargain. What was clumsy between us crystallizes, now, all that is wrong with our human arrangements in this place, in this time, and what was good mirrors the strivings of the heart, pushing against the meanness of barriers to rise into a pure clarity.

# Drive, She Said

THERE IS NOTHING so nice as being whisked somewhere in a car, very fast. There is nothing so not nice as having to drive yourself.

My father was to the motor born. He drove for pleasure when he was happy, and drove for catharsis when he was in a rage, and drove for the sake of driving. "Come," he'd beckon when I was a child, "let's go for a ride." I hopped in and we were off.

The car was his natural habitat. He drove rashly and aggressively but with perfect control, and I always felt perfectly safe as well as excited to be his passenger. Excited because, beyond the daring eccentricities of his moves—cutting across lanes of traffic to make a turn, or driving in lanes blocked off for construction—we were playing the game of life: driving was competition and triumphing over others, getting there quicker and with more panache. Long before I was born he had driven a taxi, moonlighting, and he still drove like a taxi driver, that is, with offhand flair, yet with serious and Darwinian intent: driving was not simply a means but an end in itself, the driving force. At the same time, his driving had an aesthetic dimension: it was a performance that answered to the most rigorous technique; he might have been dancing in a *corps de ballet*, except the other members of the corps were not his fellows but his adversaries. You might say he wanted to steal the show. Buses and trolleys, other cars, pedestrians, even street furniture like lampposts or mailboxes were impediments to his progress and were treated as such. He would keep up a running commentary on these impediments, a commentary so rich with scorn and derision that anything moving less nimbly than we were seemed too inept and contemptible to exist, never mind occupy the road. I must be exaggerating of course; memories plucked from childhood tend to be exaggerations. But so his driving seems in retrospect. He had no major accidents and just a few minor ones with larger vehicles like buses or trucks—David-and-Goliath-type fender benders, born of hubris.

This all held me spellbound, and for some reason I assumed driving talent was an inherited trait and I would be the same sort of bold, virtuoso driver as my father. My brother is, though not quite with such incensed and ostentatious defiance. In fact my brother was born with cars in his blood—from the age of two he could identify the make and name of any car in the advertising pages of glossy magazines, a feat he was often called on to display. My sister learned to drive under my father's harrowing tutelage. He would have her maneuver through heavily congested lower Manhattan while he dashed in and out of the car on business errands. "Drive around the block," and if she demurred, "What could happen?" he would say. She turned out an excellent driver too, though in a far more temperate mode—a good, easy, reliable driver. I am not. My driving is not bad, but it is far from easy.

Nor have I inherited my mother's driving genes. My mother learned to drive in her fifties, when she and my father moved to the suburbs, where you must drive in order to have a life. She was not uneasy but plucky and confident, a confidence quite misplaced, since her driving was the stuff of farce. For a good while into her driving career she believed the rearview mirror was for powdering her nose. She could go out of her way for miles before she found an opportune moment for making a left turn. She managed to enter the Palisades Parkway, a four-lane divided highway, going in the wrong direction and, new to the suburbs, believed the madly waving drivers she encountered were exhibiting rural friendliness. She talked her way out of endless minor traffic tickets with a totally artificial and deplorable kind of wide-eyed, dumb-blonde appeal in which she took great pride.

I learned to drive in my twenties, in Boston, a city known for its anarchic traffic. Unluckily, around that time I read somewhere that whenever you step into a car you're taking your life in your hands. Often it doesn't become clear for years why, of all the casual bits of warped advice we come across, certain ones lodge themselves in the mind forever—anyhow, this bit did in mine. I was distressed by the presence of other cars on the road. I wasn't afraid they would kill me. No, I would kill someone. Failing that, I would do something clumsy and gauche and be mocked for it, as my father had mocked the drivers in his path, for I assumed every driver must feel the same tortured antagonism as he did. I'm not sure which fear, killing someone or being mocked, was the stronger. Being mocked, probably. My driving fear was a species of social anxiety, the anxiety of an inexperienced person at some formal event, afraid of committing a ghastly blunder, or more aptly, the anxiety of dreams in which one becomes the laughingstock of a hooting crowd.

On foot, I had no special fear of social blunders; I trusted my savoir faire, and in any case people were usually oblivious, or tolerant, and if not, what did it matter? But the road, ah, the road had its grown-up male rites, the ignorance of which could bring undying shame: how to merge, how to get gas, how to rent a car; what was the custom of the country if, Heaven forfend, I had a flat (fixing it myself was unthinkable), or a minor accident (in a major one I'd be unconscious or dead and the police would take care of everything). The road was the real game of life, and I was not convinced I knew its rules. Beyond the basic rules in the driving manual, surely there were secret rules, known only to an inner cabal, not for the likes of me.

Despite all this nonsense, I got a license, but I rarely drove. I walked, or took public transit, or slid into the passenger's seat. Later on I learned all over again, in New York City. This time, I vowed, I would become a happy driver. Driving was my birthright. I owed it to my bloodline.

But I did not become a happy driver. I drove only intermittently, when I couldn't avoid it. I was assured that were I to drive regularly I would get used to it and do it without thinking. But the thought of getting behind the wheel filled me with dread. I strove to adopt my father's devil-may-care outlook: What could happen? Plenty. The steering wheel could lock in place and the car would run amok. The gas pedal could get stuck, or maybe the brake; one way or another, I would be unable to stop. Should I drive till I ran out of gas? That might take me to Canada or beyond. Surely situations would arise where I would need to stop before Canada, tollbooths or the border-crossing itself. As I drove, these fantasies swirled into ever more elaborate patterns, scaring me with the morbid self-torture of children conjuring up ogres in dark closets, a torture that in some inadmissible way is a grim delight.

In New York, again I seldom needed a car to get anywhere; when I did, there were usually others who could do the driving and I willingly, though with secret chagrin, let them. My reluctance to drive felt shameful, as if I were not living up to some family tradition, and stupid, for when I did get behind the wheel I handled the car well enough in spite of my lurid fantasies; at times I even felt the elation of power, of controlling this large and menacing and mysterious machine. I even got in the habit of cursing other drivers as my father did, but more for the ritual, without his passionate conviction. But though I believed driving was my birthright, I contradictorily felt I was sneaking some privilege, was not truly entitled to this elation and power: what's a girl like me doing in charge of this powerful machine? On foot, meanwhile, I took all the other perquisites of adulthood for granted.

For brief periods, I lived in places where I had to drive to get to work or stores or friends. I forced myself. I would get used to it. I liked the feeling of unlocking my car and climbing in, breezy and grown-up, looking like any ordinary driver, my shameful fear—taking my life in my hands—invisible. And I drove adequately. I was a decent, if dull, driver, I kept telling myself. No one sitting beside me would notice anything amiss. Yet for hours before that breezy gesture of unlocking the car, a cloud of dread hung over me, dense and black, or else gray and sparse, depending on the nature of the trip. And I knew the nature of each trip intimately. For short routine runs I could summon something approaching nonchalance. Anything more complex I would plan over and over in advance, reviewing every turn, every traffic light, every lane change. Then, once I got behind the wheel and started the engine, the cloud of dread would lighten faintly: what a relief to be driving and not anticipating.

The anticipatory dread and the driving, I realized, were two distinct phases of any trip. And dread by its very nature is something you never get used to. I was dreading a highway full of drivers like my father, only now I was no longer his thrilled ally and accomplice, but his adversary, the object of his scorn. Somehow I never imagined a highway full of happy-go-lucky drivers like my mother, which might have been more perilous, and more realistic, too.

Yet strange to say, what I anticipated most vividly was the eruption of my father's driving genes lurking within me, the ugly duckling: I suspected that if not for my fear I could and would drive as boldly as he did. I yearned to do this and I dreaded it, and I despised myself for my fear.

By now I have made countless uneventful trips: I've shared the driving halfway across the country; I've driven through rain and sleet and hail and dark of night, on dirt roads and bracing freeways. Alone, I am most prey to my bold secret self, and self-loathing. With a passenger beside me I am soothed, even inspired to drive with unaccustomed grace. I know I wouldn't risk a passenger's life by letting my father's lurking genes run rampant. Also, if my right to occupy the road is dubious, my passenger, unburdened by my history, has every right to get somewhere: I gain legitimacy behind the wheel by proxy. I especially like driving with my children—I would never endanger them. And in their presence I'm unquestionably adult, entitled to sit in the driver's seat.

Still, a police car rolling into view means they're coming to get me for some foolish infraction—something I never feel on foot. The impatient, threatening blare of a horn means it is I who have given offense: "Ask not for whom the bell tolls. . . ." I can hear the other drivers jeering behind their closed windows: she's not her father's daughter. I writhe with analogies: he was the glamorous movie star and I turned out the timorous wallflower, he the brilliant composer and I the tone-deaf clod, he the great poet, I the dyslexic.

I once told a therapist a bit about my driving anxieties, though I must admit that in this telling I didn't mention my father, not quite playing by the rules. Maybe this omission could be classed under "resistance"; it was surely, among other things, perversity. In answer to one of the therapist's questions, I told him quite truthfully that while driving from New York City to see a friend in a nearby suburb, I had the curious and exhilarating feeling, when nearing her exit, that I need not exit there at all: I was free, I had a car, I could go on and on for as long as I wanted and to wherever I wanted. Naturally he tried to make something metaphorical and psychologically significant out of this, and for a few moments I was caught up in his elaborations on flight and freedom, which were reasonable, in fact pretty astute, given the incomplete raw material I'd supplied. But I was convinced that to follow him along this route would come to nothing. I might have unacknowledged longings for flight and freedom, but they were not at the heart of my driving dread. If those longings became urgent enough I would probably hail a taxi to the nearest airport, something I did extremely well.

No, talking about driving would be useless, I decided: words spoken from a firm chair were light-years away from the swift, heady unreeling of the road. What I really would have liked was for the therapist to come out for a spin and reassure me that I was doing everything right, but I never managed to make that suggestion. Perhaps I thought that after what I had told him, he might be reluctant to drive with me—I certainly would be, in his place—and it would be unfair to ask something so clearly beyond the call of duty.

He did say something I was able to take to heart, though. He said with a shrug, as if it were the most natural thing in the world, that I had the right to drive at whatever speed and in whatever manner I found comfortable. The car was a means of getting me somewhere, and that was that. It was plain from the way he spoke that as a driver himself, he had no contempt for other drivers; he had no interest at all in other drivers. Here was a new way of looking at the game of life as played on the road. The road was a community in which we all pursued our goals in our own way and at our own pace; naturally we obeyed the same set of rules—the social contract—and accorded each other communal rights and courtesies, and it was tacitly understood that we must cooperate for our common good and safety. But essentially we were following our individual paths.

This, I know, is a most banal piece of news, so banal that I was amazed it had never struck me before. It described ordinary life—idealized, for sure, yet recognizably life as I lived it on foot. It had never occurred to me that the social contract might prevail on the road as it does, or should do, on foot. To my father, and to me when I was his passenger, the road was the state of nature. And the allure of that state is overpowering. To move with such arrogance, such abandonment, such self-interest, such predatory skill! But I cannot bring myself to yield to its allure. No doubt it is better so. Yet I know what it feels like to sit, small and excited, beside that yielding. Ah, to go for a ride with my father again!

You might think that after this great yet banal revelation, my dread would vanish and I would drive with ease. At least I thought so. Almost as alluring as the myth of the state of nature is the myth of instant transformation: the scales falling from the eyes, the paralytic striding away from Lourdes, the frog, having done penance, turning back into the prince he really was all along. And it does happen—not every great change must be attended by long patience and a tedious accumulation of incremental efforts. Was there not Saul becoming Paul on the road to Damascus, or the unexpected collapse of the Berlin Wall? Yes, I had served my time in darkness and reached the light of truth. Now I would come into my inheritance.

But this, alas, didn't happen. Sometimes on long trips everyone agrees to share the driving. Pride makes it impossible for me to refuse. I pray that when my turn comes it will be an easy stretch. But at heart I know it doesn't matter what kind of stretch it is; every stretch—crowded or empty, fast or slow, pitted, slick, or under construction—offers its own ordeals, and they do not appreciably alter my dread. At the appointed moment I take my turn gallantly at the wheel, stomach clenched, will taut. I build up speed—I may be scared, but I'm not slow. I relish the power, the breeze, the swiftness. I try to anticipate what's ahead and plan for it, but on the road this is impossible. I mutter curses when some nearby driver does something clumsy or inept. Aside from that harmless indulgence, I observe the social contract, but I long to be in a state of nature. That tension is grimly exciting. I am terrified and elated. Anything might happen. Joy, power, and dread swirl and contend in my every cell. The road of life.

# Being There

AT ABOUT eleven in the morning on March 2, 1983, the Greek men working on the roof of Diana Angel Stamoulis's apartment building banged on her door to tell her, speaking in Greek, that they saw smoke. "Stop making fun," she said, and closed her door. They banged again. This time she went out into the hall and opened the window. She saw smoke coming up from the fourth floor below. She climbed the stairs to the sixth floor, where she saw smoke coming from under the door of one of the apartments.

Mrs. Angel phoned her daughter, Adrienne, an actress who lived in the building next door. Adrienne came right over, and together the two women left the building, walking down the five flights of stairs. Once outside, where fire engines were already gathering on the Manhattan street, Mrs. Angel decided to go back to save some of her possessions. She had thousands of dollars' worth of stamp collections, knickknacks, jewelry, a trunk full of fabrics—she had been a dressmaker like her mother before her—as well as valuable papers and correspondence with New York's Mayor John Lindsay, Governor Nelson Rockefeller, and President Lyndon Johnson. Apparently no one saw her reenter to climb the four flights.

Back in her seven-room apartment, Mrs. Angel felt intense heat coming from next door. She heard the crashing of windows exploding from the heat, and when she looked out her kitchen window she saw flames. She sat down on her living room sofa and spoke to God in Greek. "You're not going to let this building burn," she said. "But if it's time for me to go, I'll go with the building." At that moment, the large mirror behind her, above the sofa, crashed and splintered, the glass flying right over her without hurting her. Mrs. Angel knew then that God felt it wasn't time for her to go.

Hot water coming from the ceiling fell on her left shoulder. She thought the building's boiler must have burst, and wondered how water from the boiler in the basement could have gotten so high up. She soon realized it was water that had been hosed into the floor above and heated by the flames. Mrs. Angel walked to her front window, facing Riverside Park and the Hudson River, thinking the falling water couldn't reach her there. Up on the hill across from the building, a small crowd of people who had gathered to watch the fire noticed her and waved at her to come down, but she shook her head. She was not afraid. She was "in a sort of trance," watching the colors of the flames, hearing the loud crashing of glass. She stayed there listening and gazing at the gorgeous black and gray smoke, at the reds and blues and greens. "People don't realize how beautiful fire is," she recalled.

A fireman saw her standing at the front window, and very

soon two firemen, along with Adrienne, came up the stairs to get her. Mrs. Angel didn't want to go, but they led her out of the building. About a half hour later the roof of the apartment above collapsed and fell through to her apartment.

Diana Angel was eighty at the time. She was my downstairs neighbor. Together with the people in the other twenty-two apartments, we had been making a kind of urban history, though we didn't know it then—it was just our daily lives. Nor could we have known that this very local, very intimate history would be suddenly erased.

A year and a half later, living in a place that didn't feel quite like home, I went back to look at our former apartment, now partially restored. There were light squares on the grayed walls where pictures had hung, and light circles on the blackened floors where chairs had stood. The huge old windows with their elaborately molded frames, through which we had seen the world, were gone, replaced by nondescript square black metal frames. The place was alien, blank, nobody's. Smaller without the furniture. I remembered the day I arrived there twenty years earlier, pregnant, and we set to work to make it a place we could live in. It had had a future. This place didn't even seem to have a past. It didn't seem possible that this was where I had sat watching, far across the river, the lights of the roller coaster of Palisades Amusement Park, itself now vanished. But if not here, where?

It began in 1964, when my husband and I returned from a year in Rome, where Harry had had a Fulbright grant to study urban history and planning. We had no money, no jobs, no place to live, and I was pregnant. We camped at my parents' house in Rockland County, and Harry would go into the city every day to look for an apartment. One day he came back pleased: six rooms in a nice old building on Riverside Drive, near Columbia University, where we had both been students. I went with him to have a look. I saw mostly that it was big, and that its wide front windows overlooked the green of Riverside Park and the Hudson River. Soon after, Harry got a job at the New York City Planning Commission. It wouldn't make sense for me to get a job, we agreed, since I would be having the baby in November, and it was almost September.

The day we officially moved in I took a good look around. The ceilings were very high, the walls all brown, and in the long hall, especially, they pressed in with a feeling of hushed desolation. I felt suddenly desolate too, and I cried at the prospect of living in such desolation, especially after the glories of Rome. We began painting; my family came to help. My brother and my nephews painted the hall; my brother, who is very tall, could paint all the way up to the ceiling, past the molding, without a ladder. As he moved smoothly along the hall with his roller, turning it from brown to white, I stopped crying. It would be a place to live, for a while at least. We were nomadic. Before Rome we had lived in one apartment in New York, three in Philadelphia, and two in Boston, in the space of six years, so I expected we would keep moving. Because I was quite pregnant, I painted that segment of wall which could be reached without much bending or stretching. Sometimes I would sit on the floor and creep around the perimeter of a room to do the lower moldings.

Among his many endeavors, my father, by profession a tax lawyer and CPA, had a furniture store in Chinatown. Since we had no furniture, it seemed natural to him that we should go to the store and pick out what we needed. Others like us, young people brought up in provincial sections of Brooklyn, would buy furniture when they set up house: bedroom suites, living room suites, and carpeting to match. But we wanted never to "set up house." We wanted to be the opposite of the way our families were, and to play house. Wherever we went, we made bookcases out of shelves and bricks and had big pillows in the living room instead of chairs. Our bed was a mattress on a frame. To placate my parents we did go to the store and pick out a few things—a round white kitchen table and four red chairs, a kitchen cabinet, and a couple of simple lamps. I remember my father looking with some contempt at one simple red lamp and saying, "That's all you want?" What we lacked in furniture we made up for on the walls—lots of posters, prints, and odd hangings; over the years we added works of art done by our children and some real works of art loaned by friends who were painters. Harry also cultivated eighty-two plants, so the place was a bit like a greenhouse.

Towards the end of the pregnancy I would sit at night in a red and white flowered wing chair we had gotten at some thrift shop and look out over the river at the bright lights of Palisades Amusement Park over on the New Jersey shore. I could see the outline of the roller coaster, all its snaking figure eights, and the cars swooping around them. I watched the moving letters on the park's huge marquee, advertising products I no longer remember, till I had memorized all the slogans in a trance of lethargy and muted panic over having a baby. The baby was late. Thanksgiving came and I called my mother to say I hadn't the strength to come to Rockland County for her big dinner. She had a solution. Hours later my mother and father and brother, my sister and brother-in-law and their two sons marched in carrying the Thanksgiving dinner and set it up on paper plates, the first of many parties in our apartment. When they left I sat in the dark and watched the lights of Palisades Park, wondering when I would ever have this baby.

Rachel was born two days later. When she was a few months old my mother began coming over one day a week to stay with her so I could, in her words, "get out of the house." Soon I hired baby-sitters so I could get out some more. I found a part-time job writing publicity material for an open housing program in Harlem, which was close enough to walk to, and my mother remarked, "I always thought a woman should stay home with a baby, but in your case I see you can't. Go."

During six years of marriage, I had gone to work, and we had done the housework infrequently and together. Suddenly I found myself in a spacious, solid apartment with a baby it was universally assumed I should take care of, and wondered how on earth this had come about. I suppose my parents were relieved I had married at all, since I had always threatened to do bizarre things with my life, and relieved that I had gone so far as to have a baby and do the conventional things for it like buy a crib and a playpen, dress it and feed it and take it to the park in a carriage with a hood and a row of plastic balls strung across the front. My mother told me things I ought to do for the baby; one was to give her a lamb chop for lunch when she got old enough to hold a bone. My mother believed in lamb chops the way later on people came to believe in yogurt and tofu. And once a week she arrived at around nine-thirty in the morning (my father dropped her off on his way to work) and I would fly out of the house to my job in Harlem.

When we first took the apartment, the real-estate agent told us another couple just back from Rome had moved in on the third floor, both artists. Coming out of the elevator one day, I saw a young man who looked like he might be an artist, and who looked as new to the place as I did. I inquired and he said yes, he was the one, Bob Birmelin. We invited him and his wife, Blair, over for coffee. I tried to heat a frozen Sara Lee banana cake in the oven and ruined it—the frosting melted and dripped and I was embarrassed serving it. Nevertheless we became very good friends, especially Blair and I. I discovered she read Proust and Henry James and liked to sit and talk about books just as I did. Amidst our marathon talks, periodically there would be a new baby. I had a girl, and a year and a half later she had a boy. I visited her in the hospital, bringing books, and when she came home with her baby we talked about childbirth and about the books. Two years later I had another girl, and a year and a half later Blair had another boy. We went to the park together, Riverside Park across the street, and in the course of an afternoon shifted our equipment from the benches near the slide to the benches near the jungle gym to the benches near the sandbox, along with other local mothers, women whose husbands were studying at Columbia or at Union Theological Seminary or Jewish Theological Seminary. I have a photo of Blair and me in heavy wool sweaters and jeans, playing hopscotch in the park. We look intent and defiant, as the children stand by and watch.

In our early years the park had a sprinkler for hot days, but one year it disappeared. Too much vandalism, the park man said. And the kids took water into the sandbox. I never understood what was wrong with taking water into the sandbox, but the park man, a jovial, short, dark man who liked to flirt with the mothers, was adamantly against it. He would sit and talk to any woman alone, as if part of his job for the Parks Department was to keep young mothers company, and it was in fact pleasant to be flirted with at a time when babies and sandboxes constituted so much of the once variegated world. When he hurt his leg and disappeared soon after the sprinkler, I missed him.

After the park, Blair and I would take the children back to one of our apartments and have drinks while they played and fought. We would be talking about books, drinking and smoking, feeling like grown women, when one of the children would rush in insulted or injured, and we would have to mediate. I tried to settle disputes by reason and fairness, but in her house, I remember, she gave the children apples. Blair seemed to have an unlimited supply of McIntosh apples, which soothed all injuries better than sweet reason. The children, especially as they got older, made so much noise that it was a wonder we could manage to keep talking about books, but manage we did, and like my mother she helped rescue me; perhaps I did the same for her.

At night the four of us grown-ups would get together to eat and drink and play games like pick-up-sticks; it seemed all right to leave the children alone on the sixth floor or on the third, and dash out from time to time to check on them. We were all very competitive, and so the games of pick-up-sticks were tense. Especially we women were competitive, for the men were out working at their chosen professions while we had little outlet for our competitiveness. Probably we would have been competitive in any case. On and off we played with a Ouija board, which predicted the date of the birth of Blair and Bob's first baby, the results of the 1968 presidential election, and later on spelled out the name of Rachel's nursery school teacher.

After a few years of babies and, for me, graduate school, we began to write fiction, Blair downstairs and I upstairs. She started first, after her second child was born. She had always been the painter and I the writer, at least in my mind. But there she was, writing. If a painter could write, I thought, surely I, a writer, could write too. When I had no private place to work she let me use a room in her apartment, so that sometimes we were both writing there, in different rooms. Years later, what we were both writing was in books and in bookstores, which seems miraculous.

Meanwhile, once a week my mother kept coming over to take care of the children while I got out. When I returned home I would find she had done some laundry and ironing too. She bathed the first baby, but with the second she said she couldn't anymore—she was older and this baby was heavier; her arm ached. But she took both out to the park, for she believed in fresh air as in lamb chops, and sometimes on her return she would rest for a few moments in the lobby on one of the old high-backed, velvet-cushioned chairs that flanked a large oak breakfront. One day these pieces of furniture vanished. Stolen, our building superintendent, Mrs. Flanagan, said in amazement. The mystery of how and when these massive items could have been stolen was never solved. After that there was no furniture in the lobby.

My father would come by after work to pick my mother up, and we would sit and talk for a while, my mother enumerating what wondrous things the baby, and then babies, had done and said that day. During one of these talks the lights suddenly went out. First we thought it was our building alone, but out the window, up and down our side of the river as far as we could see, was blackness. Across the river New Jersey's lights were bright. We sat in the dark bemused. I unearthed a few candles. Our neighbor from across the hall rang the bell to offer us a huge Christmas candle, and she sat with us for a while. She said she kept a lot of candles around for emergencies. She had the reputation of being eccentric, and indeed she had a touch of the Ancient Mariner about her, stopping us in the hall occasionally when some far-fetched topic seemed to weigh on her mind. She didn't have a glittering eye, but she did have a pale, waxy-looking face, as if she never went outdoors, and her hair was done in two long braids wound about her head like an Edwardian heroine's. She wore strange dun-colored shabby clothes that also seemed never to have seen the light of day—there was an overall mustiness to her—and those who had been in the building longer than we had told fantastic tales about primeval chaos in her apartment; and she had some strange habits as well, like reading late at night on the hall steps, to save electricity, she explained when we jumped back, startled, at the elevator door. She was often seen carrying shopping bags in and out, and she drove a repainted mail truck, which took up more than its share of precious street parking space. But with all that she could be pleasant to talk to, and she was intelligent. She was a public school teacher. And so we sat there bemused by the blackout—none of us could remember this happening in New York City before.

Soon my parents groped their way down the stairs. When they got home my mother called to describe to me how strange New York had looked from across the river, black and empty like an abandoned city. All evening, people in our building roamed the stairs and halls with flashlights, seeing if everyone was all right, if everyone had candles. It felt like a great adventure. But later on I was frightened, alone in the dark with a year-old baby. Even when the lights were on I was often afraid that something terrible would befall the baby and that I would not know the right thing to do. How much worse in the dark. It must have been from my mother that I had the notion that for every eventuality—particularly in the case of children—there was a right thing to do, as opposed to any number of wrong things, and that the acquiring of wisdom was learning all those right things in advance. Harry got home around midnight. He had walked all the way from the Lower East Side in stages, stopping off at friends' houses along the way, resting and gathering strength in the various darknesses. He brought news of the outside, like a courier in the Dark Ages.

Around this time Harry's family—mother, sister, cousins, and all—decided to have a surprise party for Harry's father's seventieth birthday in our apartment. Well, fine, except we hardly had suitable furniture. We felt we should dignify the occasion with a couch, at the very least. We did have a couch of sorts, but it was ragged and falling apart, having traveled to

Philadelphia and to Boston and languished in storage for a year. Harry went to an auction in Brooklyn on the day of the party and found an elegant, old-fashioned tufted couch for eleven dollars, plus twenty-five to have it delivered the same day. The couch was white, which I thought beautiful. I was very proud of it when all the family arrived. Later my mother informed me that, beautiful or not, the white was merely the muslin that belonged under a covering. I didn't doubt this; she knew all about such things. She said we ought to have it covered. "Slipcovers," like "bedroom suite" and "carpeting" was a word connoting things Harry and I did not want any connection with. We kept it white for a long time. At last—perhaps our principles began to lapse or perhaps it was simply the dirt—we had it covered (though not with slipcovers) in blue velvet, which, even with my father's upholstery liaisons, cost many times more than the couch itself and the delivery. Blue velvet was beautiful too; that became the couch our children and our friends' boys from downstairs jumped on and off for many years. It was destroyed in the fire. Not burned: the living room window frame collapsed on it, doing more damage in one instant than four children over twelve years.

The feeling of having one's things desecrated was not new to us, though. Twice, while the babies were small, I came home to find the apartment had been burglarized. Drawers emptied onto the floor, a typewriter my father had given me when I was in high school gone, a watch, cufflinks, jars of pennies, gone. Both times I rang our next-door neighbors' bell and they came over to commiserate. George and Nena O'Neill, with their sons Michael and Brian, had moved in the same week we did, and we had become friendly comparing notes about painting those fine high-ceilinged rooms with their interminable moldings. George said if I was ever home alone and burglarized, I must bang on his door and he would come with his machete. As anthropologists, he and Nena had traversed jungles in Mexico and South America, and besides the machete had brought back Latin American rugs, wall hangings, and masks that decorated their apartment. Late one afternoon as I was stirring sweet-and-sour chicken in an electric frying pan, I heard footsteps in the hall. Harry was at work, Rachel with a friend down the street, and Miranda in her crib. The sweet-and-sour chicken was for a Barnard College freshman for whom I was a Big Sister, and her visiting parents from Cleveland. I advanced into the hall armed with my vegetable spoon and saw a skinny boy in a porkpie hat coming towards me. My face froze, a prefiguring, for I recognized my end. We both stopped moving at the same time, as in *High Noon*. After an eon I asked what he wanted, though I thought I knew. I was wearing a striped minidress. Too much of me was exposed, I felt; certainly he would want to rape me and then possibly kill me. He said he came to tell me the house was on fire and the hall was full of smoke. I walked past him to open the door and see. The hall was not full of smoke—he had climbed through a bedroom window. He walked past me and out, turned back to jeer, then went up the steps to the roof. I banged on George's door. Wearing a bathrobe, he ran for his machete and chased the boy. Buddy Maggart, an actor who lived on the fifth floor, joined in, but they never caught him. The police arrived to do their everlasting paperwork, and I finished cooking the chicken—it seemed pointless not to—and everyone came and ate it. For a year I was nervous about being in the apartment alone, then it passed.

The O'Neills' best-selling book on contemporary mores, *Open Marriage*, was reviewed in the *Village Voice* in 1972 by a critic who fantasized about the authors holding group orgies on Mexican rugs with their next-door neighbors. We all had a laugh over this, since all we ever did with the O'Neills was talk lengthily in the hall, and visit now and then for drinks; also we went to their Christmas parties and George came gallantly to my aid with his machete. We were both couples who argued a lot, in loud voices, near our front doors. We never took each other's arguments very seriously, but we were well aware, tacitly, of their styles and contents, and that knowledge established an intimacy very different from the kind that would have existed had we had group orgies on Mexican rugs. The uncanny thing about the *Voice* reviewer's fantasy was that the O'Neills did in fact have Mexican rugs.

For sixteen years we watched their sons and they watched our daughters grow up. I admired Nena's elegance. She had left Akron, Ohio, years earlier to attend Barnard College and loved New York so much that she stayed to become a warmly earthy, glamorous woman: dark hair streaked with gray, olive complexion and soft, pensive features, tinted glasses and flowing, colorful clothes. She had a distinctively low voice which seldom veered from its mellow composure. A reasonable, tolerant, yet dashing middle-aged woman—everything I had no hopes then of ever becoming. Assiduous, too. Early one morning, when I opened the door to investigate the rapid rhythmic sounds coming from the hall, I found her jumping rope. She seemed faintly abashed to be discovered, but kept on jumping. After that, whenever I heard the morning sound of her rope slapping against the linoleum, I felt the sense of security that rituals—even those of other people—afford.

Then one September evening I met Nena coming into the lobby. I hadn't seen her all summer and so we fell into each other's arms. She started to cry and said George was dying. He had septicemia and was in St. Vincent's Hospital in Greenwich Village. I tried to encourage her, but people are usually right about such things, and George died in October of 1980. At the funeral, Jerry Silverstein, an actor and broadcaster who lived just across the hall, spoke long and eloquently about his friendship with George, their late-night talks, their seeing each other through hard times. Jerry and his wife, Selma, had been closer to the O'Neills than we had—though neither had they had orgies on the Mexican rugs. Just long friendship.

This was not our only loss. Ben Irving, an assistant executive secretary of Actors Equity and unofficial mayor of our building—he had lived there since 1956—had also died. Ben used to take care of everyone's problems, large and small. Particularly if you were having trouble with the landlord, you called Ben. He was universally available and loved for his wit and generous spirit—a big robust man with a ruddy face, a booming voice, and thinning honey-colored hair.

Ben and Inge, his wife, used to give large parties, stretching over afternoons into the late evenings, where food overflowed and neighbors and friends, many of them theater people, drifted in and out with children of all ages. And then one day in 1968, when the Irvings were returning from a vacation, Ben had a heart attack in our lobby. Inge called for help and did mouth-to-mouth resuscitation until the ambulance from St. Luke's Hospital arrived, too late. He was forty-eight. At his funeral, so crowded that people had to stand at the back, the actor and folk singer Theodore Bikel said the Kaddish. Bikel said that though Ben may not have wanted a religious service, he himself wanted Kaddish said for his friend and so he was going to say it.

I went down to Inge's the morning after Ben died to offer to buy some groceries. She was sitting in a chair looking weak, surrounded by family. Inge was always a forceful, highly assertive person—it was unsettling to see her weakened. Assertive she still was: she said I could not only get the groceries but also over the weekend perhaps Harry and I could take Victor, her youngest son, out somewhere for a change of scene. We took Victor, who was seven, on a boat ride to the Statue of Liberty, along with Rachel. It started to rain on the ferry, a chill, stinging rain; Rachel cried and we had to take turns carrying her; I was pregnant again and the climb up to the torch was arduous. Later I thought we might have come up with something better. To this day I sometimes think, why, of all places, the Statue of Liberty, which Harry and I had seen before and Rachel was too young to appreciate and Victor, in his state of grief, probably didn't care about?

A year or so after the Statue of Liberty, Rachel began attending a free nursery school run by the Parks Department in Morningside Park, ten blocks away. Lots of kids from the neighborhood went. On Riverside Drive, Tiemann Place, and Claremont Avenue flourished the oldest established permanent floating cooperative walking pool: each parent made only two trips a week but they were epic—half a mile with six four-year-olds. I took Rachel and Julienne Maggart from the fifth floor, and pushed Miranda in a stroller. Picking up the third and fourth kids was tolerable, but the fifth and sixth stops were harrowing, what with heavy front doors, timed buzzers, stairs, stroller, elevators, traffic, and the nature of children. There existed two imperfect strategies for getting the children safely across wide and heavily traveled Broadway and Amsterdam Avenue—in one mighty swoop or in shifts. I chose the swoop, never daring to let them get behind me. One of the mothers, an experienced one with four children, took a shortcut on snowy days through Cherry Park up on the Drive. Its attraction was an enormous flight of stone steps completely obliterated by snow. She let the kids slide down one by one, then slid down herself.

Julienne's father, Brandon, or Buddy, as we called him then, did the nursery school trek with the nonchalance of a father of five, and at first my children, each in turn, were thrilled since they saw him daily in the Buddy and Jim comedy skit on *Sesame Street.* Also, any time Buddy appeared in a television commercial—touting the softness of a baby's diaper or twirling pizza dough—they would call us to come and watch. But very quickly they grasped that Buddy, however nonchalant, made them hold hands and not run in the street like the rest of us, and the experience became far less thrilling. Soon they would even stop calling us to the TV screen but lackadaisically, hours later, let fall the news that Buddy was now doing wine or chocolate.

Accidental gatherings in the halls, the lobby, or at the elevator door propelled the life of the building like the conjunctions that take place at nerve endings. With the Silversteins, we held long and rather grandiose conversations at the elevator door, all about our lives and aspirations. The Silversteins were two of the most energetic and bouncy people I had ever met. They were always jogging or playing tennis, and would turn up at the elevator in their various sporting costumes, with their reverberating actors' voices and beaming faces, and sometimes they would scold me because, with my babies trailing after me and my vague dreams of being a writer in abeyance, I wasn't lively enough for their high standards of joie de vivre. They were a wonderfully matched pair, Jerry dark and earnest and cheerful, Selma fair and wry and practical—even their squabbles were entertaining, like a performance. They had married way back in 1947 and spent their early summers acting in summer theater.

But at the time I knew them, Selma was already bouncing on to something new; she was studying for a master's degree in social work and planned to become a therapist, and naturally she recommended therapy for everyone, in her energetic, wry way. And Jerry was now on TV every week, doing a news program for children, which won countless awards; at the elevator he would stop to tell me the topic of the week—the death of Nasser, or New York City's water shortage. If I had time I would watch and marvel at the way he conducted panel discussions with kids, inquiring into their opinions with the greatest respect and attention. And always, at the elevator, one of us would finally say, How silly to stand here at the door, let's get together for an evening. The evening would arrive: we would eat and drink; Jerry would tell jokes and Selma would tell anecdotes about Jerry's large and forthright family, especially his brother the rabbi, whose pithy pronouncements she rendered so vividly that when I finally met him at one of the Silversteins' family parties I felt I already knew him. And so these evenings would laugh themselves by, with little said about our grander aspirations. Soon we would meet at the elevator again. . . .

The Silversteins' son Kenny was our baby-sitter, and the O'Neills' son Brian, and Inge's three children, Debby, Jonathan, and Victor in turn, and Annie from the third floor, and Yvonne from the first floor. To this day, our children, now grown, can rate them all on the various aspects of baby-sitting. We know which ones slept on the job and which foraged for food and which talked on the phone all evening, as well as their varying degrees of patience and imagination. Jonathan was a favorite because he would let the kids stand on his big shoes, facing him and gripping his hands, then walk them around with giant steps; this they found irresistible. Jonathan wrote a story for Rachel about the adventures of an umbrella, and bound it and presented it to her with a flourish; she still has it. Years later Rachel baby-sat for Joan Regelin's three children, on the second floor, and doubtless they can rate her too.

Joan was my unemployment companion. When New York City underwent its fiscal collapse in 1975, I lost my job teaching English at Hunter College, and would take the subway to Washington Heights every Monday to claim unemployment insurance. I stood in line in an enormous dingy green room that made everyone in it look dingy. There were about twelve lines stretching the length of the room, and about seventy or eighty people on each. Naturally I looked for the shortest line, but in the end it never made much difference. Joan, then a sporadically employed singer, sometimes collected unemployment at the same hour—three o'clock—and she offered to drive me up. She was a large, dark-haired, dramatic-looking woman of around thirty, with, like many singers, a rich, sensuous, persuasive speaking voice. While she zoomed a tortuous path up the West Side Highway, she told me about growing up the oldest in a family of five children in North Carolina. She told me, too, how her grandparents used to live on our block, three buildings down, in the building that was taken over by Union Theological Seminary and became a dormitory for married students—her grandmother was the last holdout tenant. And she told me some of the adventures and idiosyncrasies of her car, which she spoke of as a member of the family. The car, a plucky 1971 Volvo which for many years had borne North Carolina plates, was something of a local legend, its adventures with crime and bureaucracy making it seem almost human. It had been stolen and retrieved, it had been towed away, it had weathered near-terminal illnesses. On weekends, Christian, Joan's husband, would often be in front of the house, washing it or applying first aid. (Little did we know then that before long the car would suffer the ultimate indignity of being stolen for good.)

Joan took me to claim unemployment and I gave her outgrown toys and down jackets, and we sent the kids back and forth endlessly for cups of sugar and milk. After a year of standing in line I got my job back, and then the following year lost it again. But this time my unemployment depot was changed to Fifty-fourth Street. I missed the rides with Joan, not least the skill and verve of her driving, the energy with which she hauled that stick shift through its paces.

There were no longer as many children around when Joan's three were small. Columbia University had bought the building in 1966 and from then on rented mostly to graduate students and junior faculty. But in the early years our daughters were part of a troop, the Maggarts' five, Blair and Bob's two boys downstairs, a girl named Carla on the first floor, and Yvonne's younger brother, Gregory. Traipsing about on Halloween, they could never comprehend how Mrs. Lurier on the first floor, who gave the best treats—individually wrapped packages of homemade cookies—could be the same Mrs. Lurier who the rest of the year yelled to scare them off when they played in the lobby or in the courtyard right under her window.

Mrs. Lurier's sister, Mrs. Angel, on the fifth floor, was reputed to be strange as well, since, as she let everyone know, she was writing to President Lyndon Johnson, among other leaders, about the disability case connected with a portion of ceiling having fallen on her arm in 1963, aggravating an injury sustained at work two years earlier and making it difficult for her to continue as a dressmaker. She would talk about the evils of bureaucracy to whoever would listen. But I liked her and shared her feelings about the evils of bureaucracy, and given my verbal and vociferous and large family of Russian Jewish immigrants, I saw nothing strange about people expressing themselves in forceful and extreme ways; indeed, it made me nostalgic for my childhood, when stately people like Mrs. Angel—aunts and uncles—sat around oilcloth-covered tables dotted with glasses of amber tea and shouted at each other warmly. I also liked her because she admired my children and said so whenever we met. Since I had long ago given up broiling lamb chops for lunch, her pronouncements were reassuring. And I liked the way she looked, big and squarishly built, a square unlined face, high cheekbones and clear eyes, dark brown hair close to auburn pulled away from her forehead to show a widow's peak and done in a knot. Stern and formidable, she used to walk erectly down Riverside Drive with the gait of one who has business abroad in the world. I often imagined her up on an outdoor podium, exhorting crowds to justice and righteousness, and in fact she once told me she might have gone into politics like her father, had she been a man, and thought she would have done well, but that now, after three turbulent marriages—one arranged when she was sixteen, one "the love of her life," and one to an excitable Greek naval officer—and a lifetime crowded with incident, it was too late.

As a matter of fact it was politics that brought her to this country. In 1904 her father, George Dalianis, ran for office in his hometown of Amalias, population 26,000, and lost. "In America," she said, "when they lose they shake hands and make up, but in Greece they could shoot themselves." To help Mr. Dalianis get over the pain of losing, the family set off on a trip to America.

When Diana Angel spoke of these things, alternately laughing and scowling, her voice would traverse the scales, penetrating the air. She might well have been addressing a group—her narration had that sweep and force of one born for public oratory. But when she laughed she became suddenly girlish and I could see she must have been a beauty. Eventually I even found out what the correspondence with Lyndon Johnson was all about. Because Mrs. Johnson's private secretary was a girlhood friend of Diana's daughter Adrienne, the president had actually responded to the pleas about the disability claim as well as sent Diana New Year's and other greetings, plus a book containing the laws he drew up while in Congress, plus a flag.

One Sunday afternoon Diana got stuck in the elevator. Getting stuck was not unusual; ours was a highly capricious elevator. Among its whims was a periodic refusal to sort out the numbers above 4. During those spells, if your destination was 5 you pressed 6, and if it was 6 you pressed 7, which was the roof. People who got stuck pushed the alarm button, setting loose a loud and terrible clanging which those of us on the top floor had learned to distinguish from the loud and terrible clanging set off when the roof door was illicitly opened. At the sound of the elevator alarm we would stream out in the halls to shout encouragement to the prisoner until Mrs. Flanagan or her brother, Tom Kelly, either fixed it or called the elevator men.

Diana Angel was not a patient victim; invisible, she shouted furiously about her nerves and her stress—everyone of course understood she had been tried to the limit by the ceiling falling. Finally Tom Kelly induced the elevator to come within a foot of our floor, and, even more difficult, induced Diana to climb out, shaken, trembling, and vociferous. She came to our apartment for a cup of tea. Calm at last, her stalwart self emergent, she pronounced as usual that my children were very well brought up.

Tom Kelly lived in the basement apartment with his sister,

Anna Flanagan, and helped her out with chores in the building. I was put off by him at first because when he drank he was silent and sullen. He would answer the door looking irritated beyond measure and quickly get his sister to deal with the complaint. But when he wasn't drinking—and for long periods he would stop, till he stopped altogether—he was wry and witty, with a fund of mordant comments on life in its most grand or petty manifestations. During his dry spells he would often get jobs in other buildings around town as a doorman or elevator operator, and set off for work very well dressed and very brisk. But these jobs never lasted long.

From May to October, Tom and his sister, and the super from next door and her daughter, would sit out on the ledge in front of our building every evening, taking the air. We never had a doorman like more elegant buildings farther south: the party of supers, sharp-eyed and vigilant, was for a long time the closest we got to any sort of guardianship. Comings and goings provided the raw material for their criticism of life. Boyfriends and girlfriends of our teenagers were duly assessed, and reports to the parents submitted promptly, though unsought. Passing by, I would stop to catch up on local news delivered in Tom's trenchantly satirical style. He liked children and would tease mine, when they were small, asking them to take him along to school or to camp—perhaps he had fantasies of escape from the basement into a life of youthful capers—and at first they were leery because he was gruff, with a low, snarling voice that sounded like it had snaked its way through a wringer, besides which he had an ailment that made his head lean permanently to one side. But once they got past these traits they grew fond of him too. When Tom brought plumbers or plasterers to our apartment, he would hang around diverting me with his snarling opinions on everyone in the building, and also cadge cigarettes, since he had to have a cigarette dangling from his lips at all times. He was a thin, white-haired man with a caved-in chest and a squarish face: rheumy blue eyes, pinkish cheeks, full lips, and a dangling cigarette. While plumbers probed, we would discuss the atrocious state of the apartment across the hall, to which the tenant refused to give Mrs. Flanagan a key, and to which she admitted no repairmen. Yes, Tom would grunt bitterly, it was a terrible fire hazard.

Tom knew I was a writer; in the fall of 1981 he asked if I would write a letter for him to a *CBS News* commentator who had broadcast a segment about a chewing gum that supposedly helped people stop smoking. He snarled that it was only fair I should do this since I had rung his bell with a complaint while he was watching the TV news, and because of my interruption he hadn't caught the name of the gum. I wrote to *CBS News* a few times and finally telephoned. The name of the gum was Nicorette, I reported back to Tom, but it wasn't yet available in the United States, only in Europe. He accepted this news ruefully, his cigarette drooping. A few months later I was in Italy, where I'd promised him I'd look for the gum, but I didn't find it. Tom developed lung cancer and would go for what his sister called X-ray treatments. He was glum and resigned about his disease, and when we all tried to encourage him with visions of recovery, he would nod sarcastically and snarl. He grew weak. His chest caved in even more. He kept smoking. He said he might as well, now. Before I left for Iowa in the summer of 1982, where I had a temporary teaching job, he asked me to ring his bell and say hello when I came home for vacations, which I did. He never asked me in—that was not part of our friendship—but at the door he brought me up to date on which elderly neighbors were growing eccentric and exactly how, who was moving out to greener pastures, whose children were getting married or going away to school, and the observable love life of the recently divorced; also how his disease was progressing, and how hard it was to stop smoking. After the fire, Columbia University, the landlord, moved Tom and his sister to a tiny apartment ten blocks south on 113th Street, which they hated. He died about a month later, in the spring of 1983. I was still away and was sorry I could not go to his funeral as a final tribute, but even more sorry that I never got to hear what he would have snarled about the fire. Soon after he died, the gum was approved for sale in the United States.

Our apartment had a big living room and dining room joined by an archway, both rooms facing west, graced by large windows overlooking the park and the river with its boats going by. We painted that windowed wall red, and it framed the outdoors. North, we could see all the way up to the George Washington Bridge. In spring and summer the trees in the park were so lushly leaved we could barely see the water through them, but in winter and fall the view was broad and clear. On windy days there were whitecaps all along the river so that it looked like a printed fabric billowing about, or the wet fur of a large beast with the shivers. Often in winter ice would clog it for weeks at a time, huge chunks of jagged ice like cold driftwood, and for those weeks no ships could pass. Sometimes a ship got stuck and stayed there for days at a time, till the ice melted. Most of the ships we saw were barges or small cargo ships or the Circle Line taking tourists on a pleasure cruise around Manhattan Island, but now and then a good-sized ship would float by, and when the children were small I would call them to watch. Even when they were older, I still sometimes called them for a truly spectacular ship.

Also out the living room windows, across in Riverside Park, was the big hill all the neighborhood kids and their parents used for sledding. Early on, Harry and I would go out sledding with the kids; in later years we could keep an eye on them from the window as they skimmed down and trudged up, dragging the sleds behind them. But the finest things we watched from the window were the sunsets, especially the late ones, June through October. We abandoned cooking, eating, or homework to rush to the window, for once it began, each instant's configuration of clouds and color above the Palisades, of light and shadow on the surface of the water, could vanish in a trice. Irreverent, we even rated them—better than yesterday's, not so fine as last Sunday's—and sometimes on summer evenings we were lured out to walk along the Drive, to get closer up. We grew to be connoisseurs, knowing from the way each sinking began whether it would be drawn out or abrupt, magnificent or humble, whether it would start out splendid and dissipate, or start out nondescript and turn splendid, whether the best part would be just before or just after the sun went down. We could tell from the formations of the clouds and the color of the air, pink or violet or amber, and sometimes even a pale weird lime green.

Off the once-desolate long hall were three bedrooms, medium-sized, small, and very small. The advantage of the very small one was its own private bathroom—it must have been a maid's room in the days when the building housed the rich. Harry and I always had the small back bedroom as our own, but the other two rooms went through countless changes of role over nineteen years, mostly depending on the phases of our children. When they could live and sleep peaceably together we used the tiny room as a study, two desks crowded in. When they couldn't we moved our desks elsewhere: in the end, I wrote three books under our loft bed. But way back in the sixties, I don't remember what I expected to do at a desk—I don't remember any plans except a vague notion that somehow I would become a writer, as if it happened to a person like puberty or gray hair. Eventually I went to graduate school, then dropped out to write, because being a writer showed no signs of happening to me like puberty or gray hair. In the tiny bedroom I wrote my first published article, a Watergate satire, in June of 1974 and Harry made a big party with all our friends to celebrate; there was a feeling of buoyancy abroad over the climax of Watergate, with its satisfying cast of heroes and villains.

That party took its place in the annals of parties held in the vanished apartment, parties like the snows of yesteryear: the New Year's Day party thrown together that morning, where Rachel at a mere twelve years old concocted a triumphant eggnog; and the surprise party for Harry's father which occasioned our getting the white couch; and then the party for Harry's fortieth birthday, when he got piles of presents like a child; and the July 4 party in the bicentennial year, when friends gathered on our tarred roof to watch the glorious procession of tall-masted and bannered ships parade up the Hudson all that long sunny summer afternoon. Parties the children cannot remember, Halloween parties where guests masqueraded as their secret selves, a frog, a toad, Lolita and Superman and Al Capone. Not to mention the two children's birthday parties a year with the requisite balloons and whistles, parties I smiled through because I poured Scotch—which can pass for apple juice—into my paper cup.

Like a person, the apartment had a few chronic ailments. The bedroom doors never closed completely. The closet in the largest bedroom had no door. We never got around to asking the landlord for one, and hung up a curtain instead. The shower didn't drain properly—one stood ankle-deep in water. The plumbers who came to remedy this once and for all were a merry troop who stayed for days, creating chaos out of order, but in the end nothing much was changed. In the tiny bathroom in the erstwhile maid's room, a leak in the pipes in the wall would spring mysteriously every New Year's Day. We had no evidence of it, but Inge, downstairs, would call to report that water was pouring from the ceiling. Eventually Inge had only to call on New Year's, say hello in a certain wry tone, and we would know. After a few years the plumbers didn't bother to plaster up the wall when they were finished, but simply put in a wooden panel that could be easily removed the following New Year's.

I knew every person in every one of those twenty-four apartments until the last few years, when Columbia began housing students there, and the students, just passing through, were not interested in knowing their neighbors. But for most of the nineteen years I knew the feel of people's apartments, the furnishings and the quality of the light on the different floors, people's relatives—Jerry's brother the rabbi, Inge's sister Eva and Ben's sister Esther—and their children, what schools they went to and how they turned out. I watched as Yvonne, our baby-sitter, a slender, shy, soft-spoken girl, became a beauty at fifteen or sixteen; for a year or so we all endured crowds of boys mooning outside on the front step waiting for an appearance, a word, a glance. Together we also endured the summer Columbia replaced our ever-ailing boiler, when those of us with no vacation plans learned how to take cold showers, which is not so hard once you get used to it. Worse to endure was the collapse of the wall separating our back courtyard from the opposite building, on Claremont Avenue—a mighty and prolonged roar on a still Saturday afternoon. We were in the papers, notorious. For weeks our gigantic heap of rubble was a place of interest for the locals, less historically evocative than Riverside Church or Grant's Tomb, where tourists went, but more dramatic for those in the know. Apparently Columbia had been aware of the tremulous wall for some time, but had been haggling with the Claremont Avenue landlord over whose responsibility it was to fix it. At last workmen arrived with cement trucks and sacks of sand and gravel. They began their dragging and drilling at six in the morning, which incensed Buddy Maggart most of all since he worked nights and slept mornings. When the wall was rebuilt months later, Mrs. Flanagan and Tom complained bitterly, since the courtyard they had used to hang out wash and grow plants and cool off in on hot nights was a third of its original size.

I knew when Mrs. Flanagan's son had a heart attack and exactly how overweight he was. I could even remember the days when Mrs. Flanagan, a talkative kind of super, complained that her son and his wife had no children; then, overnight it seemed, there were four, and her talk switched to anecdotes of the grandchildren. When they visited she brought them up to display them. I knew when Joan's son hurt his head and she feared there might be serious damage but there wasn't, and when Jerry Silverstein suffered from tennis elbow. Likewise everyone knew when Rachel tumbled off the back of Yvonne's bike in the park and I rushed her, holding the torn ball of the bleeding finger in place with a towel, to the emergency room at St. Luke's Hospital in the back of a passing police car. Police don't like to take passengers, but they didn't refuse. Everyone knew, too, when a man in the building next door was killed by a speeding car at the corner, and then finally the city put up the traffic light we had long been asking for, with a pedestrian button as a bonus.

I had been inside Grant's Tomb and climbed to the top of Riverside Church during the ringing of the carillon bells, and ridden my bike in Riverside Park; I knew who played tennis there and who ran, and who, like us, had picnics. Where people walked their dogs, who cleaned up after them and who didn't. Who walked around late at night and who was afraid to. Who was mugged, when and where and how. Mrs. Lurier of the Halloween cookies, beaten up in her apartment and no one heard her scream—an empty Saturday afternoon in spring. Inge, coming home from work, by a boy with a knife. Joan, bringing home groceries. Nena, on the subway steps. We organized a tenants' association on the block. Harry was the chairman. With money from those willing to pay, we hired a uniformed guard to patrol at night: genteel Mr. Crawford, who reported for duty in a shiny black Cadillac. The supers taking the air resented his presence, as if it impugned their ability to keep the street safe; still, they included him in their nightly conferences on the ledge.

It was hardly possible to get down that street without stopping to talk. Over the years we came to know people all up and down the block, and when the old ones stopped appearing we knew they had died. I didn't like everyone equally, but it was scarcely a question of liking. They came with the territory, and when they moved or died I missed them. It is possible to miss even people you don't like.

I never liked the apartment that much either, or never thought I did. I found it cramped. Despite its six rooms there never seemed to be enough privacy, though perhaps it was the way we lived, with no clear boundaries and turfs, that deterred privacy. And the neighborhood wasn't safe, especially at night, even during the years Mr. Crawford patrolled with his reassuring black Cadillac. I also never quite forgot the three dreadful spells when we had mice, and how Jonathan Irving of the big shoes came up and baited our traps with chocolate—he claimed mice preferred chocolate to cheese and judging from the results he was right. Yet now it strikes me that I lived in that apartment longer than any other place in my life, and the placement of the furniture and the pots and pans and the pictures on the walls seems fixed and preordained, the only way we could have lived.

There are times, opening my eyes in the morning, when I am astonished to find myself in alien surroundings; I close my eyes, not yet fully awake, and imagine taking my old route through the morning, first to the front windows to look out at the park and river and see what kind of day it might be. Not until long after the fire could I bear to remember in detail how it was to move through those rooms in patterns developed over the years; how, when it rained, I whisked from room to room in a well-worn path closing windows, then stood in the front watching it pour into the abundant river; how we put speakers in the kitchen so I could hear music while I cooked; how I was lulled to sleep watching old movies on TV up in the loft bed; and how, as I talked on the kitchen wall phone, my eyes panned every plane of the room, so every square foot is now forever printed on my retina—yellow walls, dark green cabinets, striped curtain, the arrangement of pots and pans on a dark red board; the plastic magnetic letters on the refrigerator that our grown children still fooled with, messages like Happy Anniversary or Good Luck on SATs, or messages from their friends—Julie Was Here; and the round white table which, to my father's gratification, we bought at his store, and the orange chairs. For after my father's red plastic chairs gave out we replaced them with wooden ones bought for a dollar each from a local synagogue that was clearing out old furniture. I made covers out of bright printed corduroy for their ugly plastic seats, covers that looked like shower caps, and the children, aware of my limitations in the domestic arts, laughed at them, but when stretched out they fit perfectly.

I remember most of all being pregnant with my first baby in that apartment, and toward the end, when it was an effort even to move, sitting in the old wing chair looking out over the river, watching the moving lights over Palisades Amusement Park advertising things I cannot remember now but which twenty years ago I knew by heart. I would watch the letters slide by again and again, wondering what it would be like to be a family in that apartment, wanting the pregnancy over but fearing the birth, and falling into a trance induced by the glitter of the far-away roller coaster. Maybe I might live in that static condition, pregnant forever, a permanent trance. Years later they tore down Palisades Amusement Park to replace it with two high-rise apartment buildings which were nothing at all to look at. But on clear nights we could still lean out the window and see the strand of lights that was the George Washington Bridge looping above the water.

We were ignorant then, our lives full of vast and unformed possibilities that narrowed and congealed to specifics. In that apartment we raised two children, and I made myself into a writer instead of dreaming it, and I learned that the getting of wisdom is something other and more fruitful than finding out the right things to do on every occasion. By the end, we were four grown people, two of whom had never known any other home.

# Two Fashion Statements

## The First Dress

THE DRESS was satin, off-white, the color of heavy cream pouring thickly from a spout. It even smelled creamy. Rich. Sweet on its tangy, inevitable way to sour. It hung aloofly in my closet like an aristocrat mingling with the populace yet maintaining an aura, almost a halo. No banal cotton blouse or corduroy jumper dared rub shoulders, crowd, or crush.

It was a mandarin-style dress, my mother said when we found it in a store we frequented only for special occasions. I forget the occasion for the dress. Maybe none at all. Maybe an act of charity on my mother's part, as she sensed my vague, restless need for something, anything, hinting at a future more adventurous than the past. I wore the dress, as it turned out, on my first date. I was twelve and a half.

Mandarin meant sleeveless, form-fitting, quilted, with a round stand-up collar resembling a priest's and a narrow skirt slit on either side. Eloquent, understated, the most seductive dress ever to have embraced my waiting body. In it I became the girl I was meant to be, a worldly, pleasure-seeking F. Scott Fitzgerald girl.

The boy component of the date was a dull-witted, amiable sort, whose invitation came as a surprise. Still, I leaped at the chance to embark on what I envisioned as my date-studded life. When he announced we would be going to Radio City Music Hall—Christmas stage show, Rockettes, and movie—I thought instantly: The Dress.

After the subway and a trudge through snowy streets, I shed my winter coat to bare the dress, enhanced by nylons and pumps with Cuban heels. I sank back in a velvet seat in the chandeliered theater to bask in the dress's splendor. And my own in it. Could this boy of clay appreciate our symbiotic beauty? Surely not.

The movie, no doubt panoramic, is long gone from memory. What I do recall is the boy's hand inching along the back of the seat to attain my shoulder, which he stroked. This was an integral part of the date, arguably its purpose. The goal of my vague longings. Now that it was happening, I found it monotonous and distracting. A far greater thrill was the caress of the dress: satiny, clinging, transforming.

The date came to an uneventful close. At school the boy and I behaved as if it had not taken place. No matter. In memory the date reposed amid crystal lighting and ruby carpets, in a dark hush. It had been a grand and fulfilling success: a date with my dress.

# Brief Encounter

I THOUGHT they were extinct, done in by changing times as surely as bustles and crinolines, doublets and jerkins—until the breezy morning when a rack of unpretentious dresses fluttering in the air caught my eye. I slowed down. It was a cut-rate shop of a kind I remembered from my childhood, its cornucopia of homey wares and wear spilling onto the sidewalk. High above, the dresses seemed pretty on first glance. For a split second I idly pictured myself in them. Then, the shock of recognition: Housedresses!

Could they be making a comeback?

Housedresses, for those too young to remember, were what women put on each morning to do housework, until jeans swept them aside decades ago. Light-colored, with a floral print (small modest flowers, never big flamboyant ones), the boxy housedress was utilitarian and sadly charmless: A-line, which made for easy, girdle-less movement, short sleeves or cap sleeves, a hem just below the knee. Their coarse cotton grew soft with frequent washing; frequent ironing would restore crispness and prepare the dress for a new day of housekeeping.

Plain, sturdy buttons marched down the front, and ribbons in the same floral pattern drooped from either side of the waist to tie in back. It was those buttons and those ribbons, as well as the A-line cut, that distinguished the housedress from the muu-muu, a related garment but very different in character.

The round-necked muu-muu had no buttons or belt but was a huge ballooning sack that completely obliterated the shape of the woman within it. Nevertheless the muu-muu, a Hawaiian import, had more character than the housedress. True to its Polynesian origins, it was brightly colored and gaily printed with big lush flowers. There was something flashy and devil-may-care emblazoned on the muu-muu, a feeling distinctly absent from the housedress, which stood placidly for common sense and housewifely propriety. You could imagine women in muu-muus laughing loudly and dancing, the sack-like dress whipping almost ribaldly about their knees. Muu-muus were what Gauguin's gorgeous nymphs might have worn in late middle age, their erotic sinuosity still lurking beneath pads of fat.

In their housedresses, big women resembled upright mattresses, and small women, limp pillowcases on wire hangers. You can still see them in old postwar movies; Shelley Winters, the housewife of *The Night of the Hunter,* wears one as she's stalked by evil Robert Mitchum in suit and hat: she looks soft and puffy, like a pinprick might crumple her. It is hard to imagine what else she might have worn, in her humble station. Women of the leisured class in movies of the same period, Barbara Stanwyck or Bette Davis–type women, or dowagers with uniformed maids, were portrayed lounging idly at home in floor-length satin evening wear or, in intimate moments, a negligee, another rarely seen but more lamentable loss. There was apparently nothing in between.

The housedress was not designed to venture far from home. But for an expedition to the local shops, a fresh one, not yet faded, would do. The same could not be said of another kindred garment, the duster. Occupying a sartorial rung between the housedress and the bathrobe or nightgown, the duster was paler and flimsier than the housedress. It had buttons, but never a belt. Its A-line cut was ampler, but the real giveaway was the sleeves, wide and shapeless and reaching to the elbow. Somehow those big pathetic sleeves made it plain that the duster would not be leaving the house.

But the housedress could go out and did. On the streets, with pocketbooks dangling from one hand and a small child from the other (I was one such dangler), the housewives were readily identifiable, like uniformed soldiers in wartime—and it was wartime. On the march, ready to assault the shops and gather booty for dinner.

Those dresses billowing aloft were not quite the classic models of my childhood. Some were sleeveless, or short, or V-necked, or beltless. The colors were darker and richer—bold splotches, jagged stripes, even African prints. The housewives of yore would no sooner have been caught in an African print than on safari. I wondered who wore them now. Old women who had never stopped wearing them all those years when the rest of us were snug in our jeans? Or newly arrived immigrant women who were oblivious to their symbolism? Or maybe women who simply liked them. Was it possible to feel affection for a housedress?

Granted, the housedresses had marginally improved, yet they were unmistakable. I guess no style, however styleless, is ever quite extinct. They looked comfortable and safe, but I knew better. I didn't dare go any closer. No, I stepped up my pace, as if the beckoning folds might reach out and seize me, swaddling me from head to foot.

# Face to Face

THE CAT was of no interest to me—I am not now and never was a cat lover. When cat lovers' cats made their advances, I sat in frozen courtesy. But for reasons also of no interest, I had to spend four months with the cat and I determined, on principle, to make something interesting out of our enforced sojourn. I studied the features of catness that cat lovers go on about with such ardor: the rippling undulations of flesh and fur, the ingenious forays into high and low places, the fabled inscrutabilities. I was impressed. The cat lovers were right about all that. On the other hand, the cat was not aloof, as cat lovers had led me to expect, but affectionate: like an infant, he craved attention.

I studied catness in stages, and soon I felt I had thoroughly witnessed its famous mysteries. Which is not to say that I plumbed those mysteries or that they were not worth plumbing, only that I had had enough: they were familiar now, and they were finite.

I might have passed the remaining time indifferent to the

cat, but there came upon me an unfamiliar sense of freedom and power in his presence. Alone with the cat in this singular situation—not quite solitary, not quite social—I was free to do anything at all. He would never tell. The cat would not reveal any bursts of temper, peculiar lapses, eccentric habits or rituals, vexing flaws. If by any chance it judged, it would keep those judgments to itself and soon forget, or so I assumed; it would not bring old grudges to the next encounter as a person might.

Alone, we know who we are. In company our certainty is blurred. Other presences, like surgical lasers, penetrate and work subtle changes and adjustments on our innards. Also, in the company of others we hide our faults as best we can, or, failing that, tinge them with a whimsical, quasi-charming light, often deluding ourselves in the process. There is no need to hide our failings with a cat: the cat will never tell. With the cat I was not accountable, or not to anyone but myself. How I behaved with the cat would be a uniquely accurate reflection of character: rather than penetrating and altering me, the cat would serve as my mirror.

Being with a baby comes to mind. Babies cannot tell either. But with a baby we are constrained to behave decently since, after all, it is a baby, and more often than not our own; moreover, if we behave badly with the baby we may suffer the ill effects later on. We need not bear the ill effects of our behavior with a cat: if it becomes unmanageable or neurotic as a result of mistreatment we can give it away, which is not ordinarily the case with a baby. So with a cat we see ourselves not through a gloss of social behavior but face to face, mirrored: who we really are in relation to the Other, who we might be in a situation of impossible freedom.

Under the unexpected aspect of mirror, the cat became infinitely fascinating, and my stay with him became an exercise in self-scrutiny—part of my routine in any event, and now accomplished while I cared for the cat. Killing two birds with one stone, as they say, only nothing like killing was involved. I was kind to the cat, for the most part; I had little urge to be cruel, even when he was intrusive or irritating. That was a happy discovery. I was willing to stroke and give the affection he craved, even willing to play a bit. But only when I was in the mood. I was utterly free, with the cat, to indulge my moods, which were many and various, a freedom I had not felt with babies. You cannot ignore babies when you are not in the mood, or rather, you can but you will suffer guilt or worse. You can ignore cats without suffering guilt, at least I could. Did I hold myself to a higher standard of behavior with babies because babies are the same species and thus compel allegiance? Or was it simply greater love for the babies? I do not think greater love, though it surely existed, is the answer. Great love has never held anyone to a high standard of behavior, quite the contrary. At any rate, I was kind to the cat when I felt like it and ignored him when I felt no kindness, and these alternations were arbitrary.

Maybe not totally arbitrary. The moods of moody people do have causes, tangled but not beyond unraveling, should we care to unravel. Mine, though, had nothing to do with the cat. They were strangely arbitrary. And when the cat seemed puzzled or dismayed at my arbitrariness I didn't care, as I would have with a baby; I would have cared what a baby thought of me, aside from caring for the baby itself. Faced with a baby's dismay I would have mustered a show of congeniality. With the cat I rarely made such efforts.

At first I was playful with the cat, and it loved to play. After a while I noticed that while I didn't mind having him curl up warm against my body, I no longer was inclined to play. I ought to play, I thought: the cat needed, or was entitled to, or at least would have enjoyed, play. But for various reasons I no longer felt playful, and after some moral struggle I decided I need not force myself to play with the cat as I surely would have done with a baby, who needs play for its civilized future.

So this cat would have to do without much play. He would be an infrequently played-with cat, and if his mood became somber in consequence, like mine, so be it. Failure to play was not mistreatment. Anyway, the cat would never tell.

If I was not obliged to play with him, I was even less obliged to sleep with him. Yet when he took to sleeping in my bed at night I liked feeling his ripply warmth nearby. I could even imagine myself a great-hearted cat lover, which I knew I was not. When he walked up my back and pawed at my face, though, I had no qualms about pushing him away. Qualms arose when he settled in the precise place at the end of the bed where I wanted to move my feet. The cat could not be faulted, yet my feet longed for that very spot. Why not just shove him over? The cat was sleeping. I have a keen reverence for sleepers; they seem so trusting and vulnerable, so touchingly benign in a near-sacred way, that I hate to disturb them. Still, it seemed overly scrupulous to sacrifice the comfort of my feet merely to avoid disturbing a cat, especially when in all likelihood he would promptly fall back asleep. On the other hand, who was I in the hierarchy of creatures, and of what importance were my feet, that this minuscule comfort should take precedence over the cat's sacred sleep? Wakeful and distracted, I pondered whether the need to move my feet might be born of a perverse, unconscious urge to cross the cat. No, I thought not. At last, overcome by the absurdity of self-denial, I would nudge him over. He looked innocently aggrieved and sometimes went away altogether. I wished I could explain and persuade him to return, only not to that precise spot. And his catty inability to grasp this explanation was frustrating and came between us.

Cat lovers say cats are a comfort but I rarely found this to be so. Though his warmth at my side was pleasant, like a living pillow, the cat did not relieve loneliness or grief or frustration. Nor was he company: his cat silence, his very inability to tell, which conferred such freedom, was a drawback when it came to being company. The cat was more a burden than a comfort. As cat lovers are always saying, cats require little in the way of physical care, far less than infants. The burden was not physical care. The burden of the cat was its presence. It was there, inexorably, and as such demanded a response, whether attention or indifference. Even ignoring a fellow creature requires effort, and for the conscientious and scrupulous, possibly more effort than attention. But I made this effort. Now and then I regretted my inattentiveness and tried to make amends, treating the cat as I treat people, following the moral imperative that the needs of others have some claim on us, as we strive to believe. But only now and then, in an arbitrary way.

Physical care aside, the cat was a burden as infants are burdens and not company, except with infants we bear the burden as an investment in expectation of future return: a baby will grow to be company, a comfort, while a cat, though it ages and endures, never outgrows catness. Besides, we are responsible for raising the babies, not only for their future good but for our own, since if we do not raise them properly they will continue to be a burden. Also, people will readily see we have not raised our babies properly. Would people censure a cat's behavior and judge us to be poor cat raisers? I think not. The cat would be thought to have a bad nature: we would claim we had made every effort to raise it properly but its bad nature defeated our efforts. This excuse, rightly or wrongly, would not work with a child. The parents are held responsible. Nurture is more in vogue than nature.

Once, as I tried to nudge the cat off my desk—for he had the habit of leaping up to sit on my spread-out papers, a habit that was cute once or twice but soon palled—he slipped and landed not on his feet, as I had heard cats always do, but on his back. He looked stunned and distressed. I was distressed too, not only because I had had no intention of hurting him, but also because if he were maimed for life, I might be suspected of cruelty or violence. True, the cat could not tell—even if he could, my nudge had been gentle, not violent—but the vet might harbor suspicion. Mistakenly. Luckily, after a tense moment the cat rose and sauntered away.

On a few occasions I spoke harshly to the cat, but speaking harshly did not give the relief—often a false relief—that speaking harshly to a person might have given. In a moment of pique, I even smacked him lightly. And once, when the cat persisted in climbing on the kitchen counter, pawing and sniffing at food, knocking over containers, I screamed loudly, Get away. Get away! Twice, and louder than I had screamed at anyone or anything in years. My scream must have expressed a resentment stored up for some time, all the time I was learning the fabled mysteries of catness, a dormant resentment ready to spring awake and pounce. And then I shut up. Maybe I had gained a measure of self-control since my screaming days, or maybe I grasped, even in my rage, that screaming would do no good: the cat could not understand a surge of bilious words as children would have done. Though now that I think of it, maybe they hadn't understood either, back then. Anyhow, no satisfaction could be gotten from scolding the cat, not that there is ever much satisfaction in scolding anyone, but somehow the opaque catness of the cat, the way it slunk away as if ashamed not of itself but of me, made that very clear.

I grasped that the presence of any living creature would be a burden to me, except maybe a plant. The least burdened state would be solitude, where I could indulge every arbitrary mood without the slightest thought for its effect on others. But solitude too has its burdens and demands. There is really no easy way to be conscious; that must be why I revere sleep.

I was cool toward the cat after the kitchen counter incident. Not cruel, only cool, again indulging my nature with all its moods. The cat would never tell. The cat might even be seen as practice for indulging my moods in society, for not straining to offer more in the way of kindness or engagement than I am inclined to give. Cat therapy. I was almost afraid to envision how I might behave with people, were I to master too well the lessons of being with the cat. I would rarely consider how others felt or what they needed, until I was abandoned by everyone, left all alone to indulge my arbitrary moods.

After a day or so, I decided this coolness was unworthy of me. The cat was just a cat; it could not help climbing on the counter. (Or could it? Was it purposely provoking me? This is one of the unplumbed mysteries of catness.) It had no moral nature and apparently did not learn from experience; its feelings could be hurt, yes, but it was unwilling or unable to behave well in order to avoid having its feelings hurt. I had no illusion that cause and effect was operative, that shouting would deter him from pawing at food; I did not credit the cat with that much logic or self-control. Even babies do not have that much logic or self-control, though we tend to forget that when rearing them. Anyhow, the cat need not be prepared to get on in life. There were no crucial or obligatory lessons. Treating it well was in no way an investment in the future.

Treating the cat well was a gratuitous act. Living with the cat was living in an eternal present—no history, no patient shaping of connection through accommodation, nor any call for anger and forgiveness. The cat was a cat. I might as well end my coolness and give him the affection he craved. But I felt constrained giving affection I didn't feel, reasoned affection, so I waited a day or so until my annoyance dissipated and I could give affection in good faith, and we resumed our life in the eternal present.

In the end, I liked the cat best when he sat quietly on my lap and consented to be stroked. But while seemingly contented, he would abruptly leap up to pursue his mysterious business, as arbitrary in his way as I was in mine. Maybe he didn't like me at all, only used me as a provider of food and strokes. (Or as a mirror?) He must like me a bit, I thought. Probably he both liked me and used me, in very human fashion. We may love others, but they are useful all the same as providers, and it is wisest for both user and used not to measure comparative degrees of love and utility.

I remembered I loved my infants with most ease when they too lay docile on my lap, showing no will and making no abrupt movements. They were safe. Passive receptacles for my affection. I was safe. As soon as they stirred, perhaps to demand of me something unknown, I would feel a faint irritation which only years later I recognized as the mask of panic. As soon as a creature shows itself distinct and self-willed, it begins to determine and shape the nature of the love it seeks. And in turn, the love you give becomes something not entirely of your own shaping and thus dangerous. Was I unable, then, to love anything that had its own being, could I love only an utterly passive creature? If so, my love was arbitrary and self-serving, not so much love of something distinct from me as love of my own act of loving, which is easy, natural, and demands nothing. Self-love.

The cat was becoming a fun-house mirror, alarming me with its unlovely distortions. I turned away. His usefulness was finished. Even so, when our sojourn was over, I missed the cat from the heart. I study photographs of him. In the photographs, there are no reflections of me. I see only the cat himself, large, orange, and beautiful. At last, with him far away and requiring nothing, I can revel in his beauty.

# Listening to Powell

YEARS AGO, working at a temporary job in some godforsaken place, bored and friendless, I spent a while on the phone complaining to an old friend about my plight. When I was finished I paused, hoping for some Delphic utterance about how I might endure until my term came to an end. In the past she had been occasionally oracular. The pause lasted for some time, growing weighty with her anticipated wisdom. Finally she said, "What you need is . . ."

I waited, taut.

"A VCR."

Like other oracular utterances, this was puzzling, even disappointing at first. But it turned out to be very smart. I remembered it much later when I found myself again working in exile—luckily not bored and friendless this time, but in a place I didn't want to be, in a life that didn't seem my own. My sublet house had a VCR but I had no time to sit in front of it. I needed something for short, intermittent flights from reality. A colleague mentioned listening to books on tape while pacing the treadmill in the gym. Portable. Controllable. Soon I had in my eager hands tapes of the opening volumes of Anthony Powell's epic twelve-volume novel, *A Dance to the Music of Time.* The entire work took up six boxes of tapes, each box holding some ten to a dozen tapes. It was winter. I trudged through the snow in heavy gear and came home to the warm house, the cat that was part of the sublet deal, and the tapes. When I finished listening to one box, I'd seal it up, drop it in the corner mailbox, and phone an 800 number to order the next.

*A Dance to the Music of Time,* hailed as a twentieth-century British masterpiece, was something I had always intended to read, but I had been daunted by its Proustian magnitude. I thought I had to wait for some endless summer, like the long-ago summer of my youth that I spent with Proust. Anthony Powell's book turned out to be like Proust in other ways as well: its submission to the rigors and caprices of time, its reliance on memory as a magnetic field, its enormous cast of recurring characters. The comparison has been noted often enough by readers and critics and is alluded to more than once by Powell himself, most memorably when the narrator, serving as an Army liaison officer, realizes that the French seaside town where he's quartered for the night is none other than Proust's Balbec.

> I had been standing on the esplanade along which . . . Albertine had strolled into Marcel's life. Through the high windows of the Grand Hotel's dining room . . . was to be seen Saint-Loup, at the same table Bloch, mendaciously claiming acquaintance with the Swanns.

But even though he capitalizes "Time" much of the time, Powell is a Proust minus the fluid poetry and minus the soul. Proust made pragmatic, stripped of metaphysics. Or more precisely, the novel is Proustian with the social world in its broadest sense—lineage, tradition, the tangled web of relationships—inflated and elevated to occupy the place of the metaphysical. Whether society can be successfully made to occupy this place is one challenge of the enterprise, whose true genre is wry social comedy, frequently edging into satire and burlesque.

Proust or no, *A Dance to the Music of Time* was fine for my purposes. I wanted something to see me through, something I couldn't see the end of. In the very first moments of listening, as I heard the words of the second paragraph (though of course I couldn't know it was the second paragraph), I knew I'd found my salvation:

> For some reason, the sight of snow descending on fire always makes me think of the ancient world, . . . of human beings, facing outward like the Seasons, moving hand in hand in intricate measure, stepping slowly, methodically, sometimes a trifle awkwardly, in evolutions that take recognizable shape.

Here was an alternate world in which I could live, and for a long time indeed.

I shouldn't give the impression that those opening paragraphs were what I heard first. No. Presumably to ensure that the listener misses nothing a reader would be privy to, the producers of the tapes were excruciatingly thorough. The reading opens with a recitation of the copyright page, followed by the jacket copy, even the blurbs. When opening a book, I find this material a nice aperitif; when listening, it's a delay, like an actor clearing his throat before the great soliloquy. It also has a greater influence than it should, read as it is in the same voice and tone as the text itself. I tend to read jacket copy in a skeptical mood. "The most important fiction since the war," says Kingsley Amis? We'll see about that!

Powell's gargantuan and hugely funny novel is narrated in the first person by Nicholas Jenkins, himself a novelist, who begins as a late-adolescent British schoolboy and progresses through the twelve volumes to early old age; it sweeps through the century from the First World War to the social antics of the 1960s and 1970s, chronicling the strivings and connivings of a generation bent on making its mark, while the old order collapses to be replaced by a new kind of anarchic, aggressive pluralism, many of whose manifestations—student activism, bizarre utopian cults, and shoddy clothes among them—the author clearly finds appalling. In "real" life, I was later distressed to learn, Anthony Powell has been a lifelong Tory and recently an admirer of Margaret Thatcher. Also, one of his passionate interests is genealogy, which was not surprising given his patient tracings of the histories and labyrinthine connections of invented families that go back centuries, in a few cases to the time of the Norman conquest.

*A Dance to the Music of Time* sweeps across social classes too, as Nick Jenkins moves through archetypal institutions like the public school (Eton), the university (Oxford), and the Army, and through London literary and social circles where the aristocracy, politicians, artists, lowlifes, and gay theatrical types mingle with more ease than one might expect. Powell's life seems in broad outline to have followed the same paths as his narrator's, and like Jenkins, he was acquainted with the major literary figures of his day. In fact, to informed British readers the novel is doubtless a roman à clef, but on this side of the Atlantic and far from home besides, I was not in possession of the *clef*, nor did I seek it. My whole desire was to be transported to an imaginary realm that would welcome me without any passkey.

Had I been reading, I would have made the automatic effort one does to distinguish between the narrator and the author, especially in a novel that appears autobiographical to some degree. But listening, I found an intermediate character muddling my efforts, and this character was the reader, identified on the tape as David Case. Since David Case was so proficient and convincing a reader, I couldn't help imagining he was Anthony Powell himself, or possibly Nicholas Jenkins himself, confiding his gossip to my ear alone. (Gossip, in its most exalted mode, is what I was hearing and relishing. Much of the dialogue consists of characters, by the dozen, reporting on each others' love affairs, marriages and divorces, career moves, war records, all the assorted high jinks of lives crowded with incident, in a tumultuous century.) Yet paradoxically, Case's skilled reading also established him as a strong presence distinct from author or narrator: the transmitter of the story. Someone new was added to the cozy intimacy of writer and reader—the proverbial third who makes a crowd. And as in any sudden threesome, the positions of the original intimate pair undergo subtle shifts. Where, in the presence of this newcomer, was Anthony Powell? Where was I?

Hearing fiction read aloud by actors, either on tape or in

public performance, is a mixed blessing. It would take a heart of stone not to be entertained by their virtuoso displays. Still, while I grin and groan along with the rest, I always feel suspicious. Something is being betrayed. We're all having a wonderful time at the expense of . . . what? The words themselves. The actors, by voice and gesture, illustrate the meanings of the words literally, act them out as in a game of charades. On the page the words neither have nor need any such assistance: they present themselves and we do the rest. Nothing is lost, or added, in translation. Even though performances give color and vivacity to the words—bring them to life, as we say—these translations into another medium are a trifle patronizing, as if the words themselves can't be trusted to deliver the emotion they bear, as if they were mere lifeless nothings before actors got their vocal cords around them.

Again, had I been reading the book, it would have been my own voice silently taking on the roles: schoolboys and masters, marriageable society girls, business tycoons, military men from private to general, innkeepers, servants, musicians, royalty-in-exile, demimondaines, editors, spiritualists, communist agitators, plus Welshmen (Powell himself is from an old Welsh family), Europeans and Americans (South and North, from a charming military dictator to a filmmaking playboy). Of course David Case played them better than I ever could, but they lived in his impeccable and variegated accents, not mine. If reading is simultaneous interpretation, then David Case was doing the interpreting for me. Either I accepted his version whole, or did a simultaneous translation of my own, a translation of a translation. But how could I? I had no text, only his voice! I was enjoying a command performance, an unattainable—for me—accuracy of diction; the price was giving up my own voice, the sonic prism of literature.

Now and then I'd wonder in confusion, Would the "real" Nicholas Jenkins sound like this? *A Dance to the Music of Time* is not quite a *bildungsroman*, certainly no *Education Sentimentale*. Even more than the object of our observation, Nick is the point from which we observe—at once a character in formation passing before us and the window through which we regard the passing scene. The trouble is that the window is not quite transparent.

At first, Nick Jenkins seems a self-effacing narrator, even ingenuous—or it disingenuous? In dialogue, Case-as-Jenkins's tones are bland and reactions to him temperate, with only a few exceptions as clues to his nature. "Why are you so stuck up?" the raucous, vulgar communist agitator Gypsy Jones asks "truculently." "I'm just made that way." "You ought to fight it." "I can't see why." But Powell has such obvious scorn for poor Gypsy Jones that her judgment is not to be trusted. A smug middle-aged do-gooder remarks that Jenkins does not "seem a very serious young man," no doubt because at that early stage he shows no evidence of what we'd call "career goals," and his conversational style is terse and marked by levity. A canny fortune-teller (the story is spiced by devotees of the occult) says that Nick is "thought cold but has deep affections."

Apart from the dialogue, he poses as the unobtrusive chronicler of his ill-fated contemporaries (alcoholic, depressive, womanizing, killed in battle or in the Blitz), with his own ups and downs mentioned almost as modest afterthoughts. In truth, Jenkins has us firmly in his grasp, calibrating the viewpoint with his unrelentingly ironic commentary. At least David Case's cultivated voice and accent gave every word an ironic edge. (He could sound supercilious even while instructing the listener to "slap the cassette smartly on a hard, flat surface" if it gets stuck.) Whole clauses might have been set in quotation marks; indeed, I can't imagine a better example of audible quotation marks than Case's description of a benefit concert for a "good cause." Of course most British social novels cohere thanks to irony—that's one reason we read them. Jenkins himself, brooding on "the complexity of writing a novel about English life," notes that "understatement and irony—in which all classes of this island converse—upset the normal emphasis of reported speech."

But just how sarcastic did Powell intend to be? To find out whether so pungent an irony were built into the novel and not simply built into David Case's voice, I would need to read it later on. The voice itself, while making me laugh and ponder, was also making me passive, lulling my critical faculties to sleep. For now, though, I had no choice but to accept the faint sneer rimming the words, an audible equivalent of the faint sneer on the face of the cat who took to listening along with me.

Besides, it would be most ungrateful to criticize David Case, who gave his all through countless hours of taping. Which raises a question that often nagged at me: Did he study all twelve volumes first, planning the dozens of accents and voices he would use? I could picture his text, the dialogue marked with his own private code for the characters, according to social class, gender, age, and nationality. Or could he possibly have read extemporaneously? He'd have to be something of a genius to manage that, but maybe skilled actors can sight-read as well as musicians. A rare slip now and then suggested he might have been sight-reading, for instance, when he adjusted the accent midway through a speech, or missed the stress of a sentence. But as a rule he was faultless and unstinting. (Was he ever bored? Tickled? When once in a while his voice began on a new pitch, had the tape been turned off so he could laugh or grunt?)

In the unlikely event that he read off-the-cuff, he couldn't have known that the clumsy schoolboy Widmerpool, at first so Uriah Heepish in his creepy false humility, "the embodiment of thankless labour and unsatisfied ambition," would turn out to be a monstrous and dangerous hypocrite. Must David Case have known Widmerpool's future in order to give an accurate reading of his youth? How remarkable, in general, that actors manage to hint at the seeds of the future lurking in the present, while pretending to be as innocent as the audience itself. How unlike "real" life, where we don't know where our natures will lead us, yet must play our roles perfectly, and usually do.

As the novel's villain, finally brought grotesquely low, Widmerpool begins as a comic oaf who's frequently the target of projectiles—a ripe banana, a canister of sugar, and in his late years, a can of red paint. He soon becomes chilling, though no less oafish: "an archetypal figure, one of those fabulous monsters that haunt the recesses of the individual imagination, he held an immutable place in my own private mythology." In Jenkins's mythology, Widmerpool represents exorbitant egotism, will unhampered by any semblance of heart, wild ambition, and a narrow bureaucratic intelligence immune to shame, perpetually rising "from the ashes of his own humiliation," rather like Richard Nixon. As an army major and later a member of Parliament with Stalinist leanings, Widmerpool wreaks havoc, destroying lives and provoking a murky international incident. But beyond his mythic aspects, Widmerpool's periodic and unwelcome reappearances in Jenkins's life carry with them the novel's favorite and unifying theme: a rhythmic recurrence that gives shape to the dance of the title, "the repetitive contacts of certain individual souls in the earthly lives of other individual souls."

Eternal return as a strategy for fiction makes *A Dance to the Music of Time* especially apt for hearing aloud. Everything in the early books is foreshadowing, no detail arbitrary or forgotten. Every hint and anomaly, every nuance of character will blossom into incident, anecdote, drama, or disaster, even if it takes two or three or six volumes—or in my case, weeks of listening. The season changed; the snows melted; the cat stared out the window at budding branches instead of icicles. As I changed my heavy coat for a light jacket, characters I remembered from the winter tapes kept reappearing, altered by Time. By the middle volumes, they were even echoing each other exactly as they might in life—those strange reincarnations when a woman met at yesterday's party recalls your algebra teacher, or the new pharmacist moves with the same gestures as your bygone Uncle Joe. Jenkins's brother-in-law evokes his old school friend, the languid, doomed Charles Stringham, dead in a Japanese prisoner-of-war camp; the adolescent look-alike daughter of a once-loved woman stirs Jenkins's erotic memory more than the aging woman herself.

It would be a mistake to imagine me as resting quietly, taking these meaty matters in. No. I listened mornings while I did a half hour of dance exercises, puttered in the kitchen, and prepared to set off for work, and then early evenings, again in the kitchen. Normally, when an author is a stylist, I linger over the sentences I like. Aside from his glittery dialogue, Powell's sentences range from juicily aphoristic ("Though love may die, vanity lives on timelessly") to gorgeously baroque. Nick's speech may favor brevity, but his narrative style, like Henry James's, often takes lengthy circuits. At their best, such sentences are brilliantly hyperbolic, at their worst merely tendentious. In any event, to linger over passages on tape, athletic feats and prestigiditation were required. I'd be flat on the floor with my feet over my head when something came along that I must stop and think about: "There is no greater sign of innate misery than a love of teasing." Right on! Or some spectacular gossipy and/or philosophical bit, such as,

> Establishing the sequence of inevitable sameness that pursues individual progression through life, Flavia had married another drunk, Harrison F. Wisebite, son of a Minneapolis hardware millionaire, whose jocularity he had inherited with only a minute fragment of a post-depression fortune.

There was nothing for it but to unwind my body, rewind the tape, and play the passage again. Over and over this happened, in the middle of stirring a soup, or packing my briefcase, or folding laundry. It was vexing to me and perplexing for the cat, who perhaps was caught up in the narrative and resented the interruption. Other times, I'd turn off the tape to stew a while at some gross generalization, as when Jenkins passes the site of a bombed-out café where he used to meet an old friend, and muses, "In the end most things in life—perhaps all things—turn out to be appropriate." Or, when a show of paintings by a friend of his youth makes him

> think of long forgotten conflicts and compromises between the imagination and the will, reason and feeling, power and sensuality; together with many more specific personal sensations, experienced in the past, of pleasure and pain,

how could I not pause to do the same? After two or three hearings, or after a reflective silence, the rhythms of the phrases would be set in my mind as they could not be from ordinary rereading. And it was in David Case's voice, not my own, that these rhythms lived and continue to live in my ear. Eerie.

Daffodils finally popped up all over my neighborhood. I shed my jacket and dug out my sandals. Soon my job was over; time to leave the rented house and cat and return to my life. Sadly, I dropped the last box of tapes in the corner mailbox and packed up. I felt like Nick Jenkins at the close of an unexpectedly intimate talk with a mellow old retired general:

> The change in his voice announced that our fantasy life together was over. We had returned to the world of everyday things. Perhaps it would be truer to say that our real life together was over, and we returned to the world of fantasy. Who can say?

Either way, I had had a fine time, the book was majestic and delicious and irritating, but had I actually read it? How much of its majesty and delight and narrow-mindedness was due to the reader, David Case, rather than the author? How much to my own desperate need? Would my responses and judgments be the same had I "really" read it? Did I underestimate, overestimate, grasp the relative weights of things? Get the characters right? The sense and texture? Would it stay with me, or had it literally floated in an ear, soon to drift out the other?

Back home, I got hold of Powell in the flesh, so to speak. I read the twelve volumes in a fever of curiosity, one after the other, a swift two and a half weeks compared to four months of sporadic listening. I wasn't surprised at the rush of familiarity, but it was not the familiarity of rereading. An unfamiliar familiarity. The airy sounds that had been, for me, the book, were collected in one place, tethered to printed words. And speaking of printed words, the first thing that struck my eye was a matter that may seem trivial but in fact was not. Here were the characters, my companions in exile, whose names I had heard daily over a stretch of months lived more intensely in their world than in my own, and I had been misspelling many of them in my mind. Precisely because they were made-up characters, their names were as important a feature of their identity as any other data. Besides, I am a spelling fetishist: the look of words is as crucial as their sound, and misspelled is as jarring as mispronounced.

The florid, ageless fortune-teller who rhythmically reappears to read palms, tarot cards and the future at large (always correctly, despite Jenkins's skepticism) was not Mrs. "Erdly," as

I had been labeling her, but Mrs. Erdleigh. On earth, a rose by any other name may smell as sweet, but in fiction a Mrs. Erdly is not the same as Mrs. Erdleigh. My vision of her changed entirely. She became someone to be reckoned with; a trifle ramshackle before, she took on dignity. Another transformation struck the racy (and racing buff) Dicky Umfraville, whom I'd been seeing as Umpherville—unaccountably, since David Case's diction was flawless. The delectable comment, "Like many men who have enjoyed a career of more than usual dissipation, he had come to look notably distinguished in middle years," is truer of an Umfraville than an Umpherville. And Jenkins's commanding officer in the army, Roland Gwatkin, a Welsh bank clerk who harbors fantasies of battlefield heroics, was deromanticized by proper spelling. "Gwatkin" is the squat, sad truth about a character whose first name echoes heroes of chivalric times—*La Chanson de Roland* as well as Ariosto's *Orlando Furioso*.

The spelling jolt once passed, the book was the same—yet different. Not as much unadulterated fun. More than a touch melancholic. (Jenkins, as it happens, writes a book about Robert Burton, seventeenth-century author of *The Anatomy of Melancholy*.) Certain characters who had seemed engagingly lightweight on tape took on density and sobriety. Others became more sinister or more outrageous—audible voices had tempered them to a less threatening mode. Complex passages—the frequent descriptions of paintings, the historical analogies—naturally proved more lucid on the page. Just as naturally, dramatic or comic dialogues had shone more brilliantly on tape. Reading took less time, but was more painstaking and precise. At first David Case's voice accompanied me, a simultaneous sound track, but as I read on, it faded, replaced at last by my own.

Majestic and delicious it all remained, and even more irritating without the mitigating appeal of its reader. Irritating above all in its wholesale contempt for all efforts at liberal political change, a contempt which might reflect Powell's horror at Stalinism, or just plain snobbery and orneriness. Or, to be reluctantly fair, conviction. (Or "conviction," as David Case might sarcastically pronounce it.) Powell seems closest to the character who declares, in true Orwellian spirit, "The people who feel they suffer from authority and oppression want to be authoritative and oppressive." (He was well acquainted with Orwell.) Irritating also for the continual cavalier generalizations about women as an alien and troublesome species, some kind of beautiful and necessary, but regrettable, pest.

David Case could be exonerated from adding his own irony. The irony is all Powell's, shielding each page like a scrim. Even the neutrality of Nick Jenkins's conversation, as rendered on tape, was actually a dryness wrought, or wrung out, to the highest degree, an arch, self-protective detachment so suffusing that it comes to be taken for granted, like London fog, maybe. On the page, it's clear that what Jenkins, and presumably Powell, loathes most is hypocrisy and pomposity. What he admires is character, restraint, style, and panache—the aristocratic virtues. He rarely finds them among the aristocracy, however; they are distributed democratically, if sparsely.

But "irony, facile or otherwise," Jenkins acknowledges, "can go too far." Even in comedy. With very few exceptions, Powell is unable or unwilling to say anything with a straight face—what today's thirty-somethings call fear of commitment, in the moral or philosophical sense. This might be acceptable: no one demands earnestness of Swift or Wodehouse. But Powell solicits our allegiance to what is behind the fixed mask of bemused urbanity—an equally fixed piety.

No one could quarrel with what Powell holds sacred, only with his discomfort in presenting it: first, the sufferings, both military and civilian, during the Second World War. His most "sincere" passage occurs at a ceremony of General Thanksgiving held in St. Paul's Cathedral at the end of the war, when for a brief moment, after some initial squirming in the toils of cleverness, Jenkins finds a simple statement of feeling manageable:

> The sense of being present at a Great Occasion—for, if this was not a Great Occasion, then what was?—had somehow failed to take adequate shape, to catch on the wing those inner perceptions of a more exalted sort, evasive by their very nature, at best transient enough, but not altogether unknown. . . . Perhaps that was because everyone was by now so tired. The country, there could be no doubt, was absolutely worn out. That was the truth of the matter.

Almost as sacred is genuine friendship as opposed to the utilitarian camaraderie of literary and upper-class life. After seeing his dying friend Moreland in the hospital, Nick says, "It was . . . the last time I had, with anyone, the sort of talk we used to have together." Finally, married love, at least the kind we must infer Nick enjoys with his wife, Isobel, daughter of a large family of eccentric aristocrats. On this theme, restraint nearly catapults to sentimentality, the satirist's lurking danger.

About his devotion to Isobel and about her perfections, Nick is reticent to the point of perversity. Before she ever appears, she's called "rather different" and "a bit of a highbrow when she isn't going to nightclubs." Perfect for him, in other words. When she turns up, it's love at first sight, on Nick's part at least:

> Would it be too explicit, too exaggerated, to say that when I set eyes on Isobel Tolland, I knew at once that I should marry her? . . . It was as if I had known her for many years already; enjoyed happiness with her and suffered sadness. I was conscious of that, as of another life, nostalgically remembered. Then, at that moment, to be compelled to go through all the paraphernalia of introduction, of "getting to know" one another by means of the normal formalities of social life, seemed hardly worth while. We knew one another already; the future was determinate.

Marriage, a miscarriage, and an unspecified number of children ensue. (At one point Nick alludes to Isobel's having "her" baby; later on he leaves town for an "arrangement about a son going to school." Otherwise his domestic life is discreetly elided—safe from Powell's acidic pen.) Isobel appears maybe eight or ten times over the twelve volumes; her remarks could fit on a couple of pages, and their tone is uncannily close to Jenkins's own—wry, knowing, understated. Of her tastes, her activities, her predilections, we hear nothing but that she has, like Nick himself, a "knowledge . . . of obscure or forgotten fiction."

Sketched with such pious reserve, Isobel is a generic, idealized presence; one suspects her voice, like Cordelia's, is "ever soft, gentle, and low, an excellent thing in woman." How different from the treatment of Jean Templer, with whom Jenkins has an affair in his mid-twenties. Nowhere near as perfect as Isobel, Jean is a far better character, rich in subtleties and surprises and sex and shrewdly drawn betrayals. The subject of sex does not graze Isobel. Powell must be aware of some great lacuna, for he tries several times to explain it away. When asked about Isobel, Nick eludes the question: "It is hard to describe your wife." Elsewhere he resorts to literary casuistry:

> It is doubtful whether an existing marriage can ever be described directly in the first person and convey a sense of reality. Even those writers who suggest some of the substance of married life best, stylise heavily, losing the subtlety of the relationship at the price of a few accurately recorded, but isolated, aspects. To think at all objectively about one's own marriage is impossible. . . . Objectivity is not, of course, everything in writing; but even casting objectivity aside, the difficulties of presenting marriage are inordinate. Its forms are at once so varied, yet so constant, providing a kaleidoscope, the colours of which are always changing, always the same.

A poor excuse from a writer who manages to present, without much worry about objectivity, the broad spectrum of postwar political hues, or the finest nuances of social class, or the changes in attitude toward homosexuality, or the psychic toll of alcoholism, depression, and thwarted affection. Beyond misplaced piety, the reason for Powell's constraint with Isobel is not hard to fathom: her virtues undermine the novel's presiding view of women as willful items of merchandise passing themselves from one man to another. Even in her absence, Isobel defies one character's view that "The minds of most women are unamusing, unoriginal, determinedly banal." She couldn't possibly be treated as another suggests: "Why discuss your work with her? . . . Tell her to get on with the washing-up." Perhaps she conforms to the type Jenkins describes approvingly as a suitable companion for a writer, "unusually pretty, . . . also to all appearances bright, good-tempered and unambitious." No wonder Powell has more to say about eccentric, foolish, promiscuous, and downright awful women than about the classic helpmeet. Dreadful Pamela Flitton, a brittle, predatory avenger, is, in literary terms, the best of women, drawn with zest and esprit.

In the end, reading brought no great shocks. I found I had already absorbed the book through the ear and through the pores; I had heard its music, tripped to its rhythms, joined in its dance. Its prejudices I had passed over more easily than I would have on the page, or rather had let them pass over me as I stirred my soup and the tape rolled on. I suspect I might not have loved it so much had I first encountered it in print. Enjoyed, yes, but not loved. Cold, austere, and supremely amusing, perfect tonic for my apathy, it is not lovable in the manner of Jane Austen or even Ivy Compton-Burnett. Probably it was the faithful performance of David Case that I loved. His role was paramount. And enduring: because of it, I'll never know what I might have felt or thought about the novel as a "mere" book.

Of course, on the page, *A Dance to the Music of Time* is its own grand performance too, exquisitely choreographed and staged with the deep genius of a Balanchine and the deft direction of a Busby Berkeley. And because of the limits of ear and of memory, I couldn't appreciate the grandeur of its design until my marathon weeks of reading.

Powell's dance comes full circle to end where it began. I missed that the first time around. Forgot in May the words that had so enthralled me in January. That early passage, "For some reason, the sight of snow descending on fire always makes me think of the ancient world," refers to a group of workmen huddled around a bucket of flaming coke, taking a break from fixing the pipes beneath a London street as Nick Jenkins happens by. His musings on the ancient world lead in turn to memories of school, and so the story begins.

At the close of the twelfth volume—I'm only a season older, while Nick is nearing seventy—he visits a gallery showing paintings by a long-dead friend: in keeping with Powell's notion of periodic recurrence, the artist who had barely been taken seriously in his own time has been rediscovered as an example of what we'd call "outsider art." On the way, Nick notes offhandedly "the street in process of being rebuilt." Afterward, having seen the paintings (and coincidentally run into his old faithless lover, Jean Templer), he walks out into the starting snow: "The men taking up the road in front of the gallery were preparing to knock off work. Some of them were gathering round their fire-bucket."

The attentive reader is ready to begin all over again, to think again of "the ancient world," and then of school and the long life and long century that followed, "of human beings, facing outward like the Seasons, moving hand in hand in intricate measure, stepping slowly, methodically, sometimes a trifle awkwardly, in evolutions that take recognizable shape."

# At a Certain Age

When I was young I was a fairly good judge of age. No longer. Everyone between twenty and forty looks more or less the same to me, and so does everyone between forty and sixty. But for some reason I can tell the ages of children very accurately: I can see the difference between three and a half and four, or eight and nine.

Also, my friends do not age. They all seem around forty-five. Some are in fact around forty-five and some are less: over the years I've made several young friends, partly with selfish calculation—in case I live long, I won't find myself friendless, the friends of my age having died off. But even the older ones seem around forty-five. If I make a serious effort to recall their age, I always come up with the age they were when I first learned it, as if our friendship has persisted in a timeless medium. This is true even of the friends who are what is called "a certain age"—the women, that is, for it is invariably women who attain a certain age; men have a number.

"A certain age." As if the actual number were too shameful

to utter. A phrase rich with contempt in the guise of deference. A condescending phrase. Cancer was spoken of that way not so long ago. People didn't want to embarrass the poor sufferer by speaking the word. And they were superstitious — it might happen to them, if they let the word so much as float over their tongues. "He has a growth," they would say. "It's malignant," if they were brave. A certain age is malignant too. I will surely die of it in time.

Now that I myself may be a certain age — I'm not sure when it starts, since it is never specified — I think about age all the time. I think about age the way younger people think about sex. I haven't stopped thinking about sex, but its mysteries no longer tease me. I know a lot about sex at my certain age. But age is still a mystery, so I think about it. I watch for its signs. Not so much the tangible signs, though those are appalling in their sneaky gradualness and irreversibility, and I work hard at staving them off. I imagine a contest between my efforts and age's incursions. I know, of course, who the winner will be; the thrill of the contest is seeing how long I can delay its victory. The signs I watch for more closely are not the obvious ones but the negative ones, the little things I can no longer do, or do as well. The diminishments. So far they are few and I would not, at this point at least, dream of naming them.

Thinking about age has borne prejudices, alas. I have preconceptions about people depending on their age; I like to ascertain people's ages so I can judge them properly. I favor the old. I have always had an affinity for the old, even when I was young. I like the way they look. I've never especially connected beauty with youth and am always surprised when someone says of an older woman, a woman of a certain age, She must have been a great beauty, since to me she still is. But then I'm not looking the way men look, with "beauty" meaning they'd like to sleep with her. I'm looking at the aesthetic object.

The old are more substantial, even when physically frail. Time has textured their nature and their words along with their skin and their voices. I tend to think the opinions of people under thirty-five are negligible; by the time they're forty or so they may be worth paying attention to. People over fifty are trustworthy; over sixty, they're either wise or they should be. All this is very wrong, I know. Older people tolerated me and listened to me when I was young. I appreciate now how tolerant they were. And yet, like racists or sexists who also should know better, I cling to my prejudices as truth.

Even worse, I feel the only people who can understand and properly appreciate me are around my age. I used to allow a ten-year range for this understanding, then a five-year range. Now I feel the most kinship for people within two or three years of my age, and the time may come when I can speak freely and wholeheartedly only to people born in the same month as I was.

One of the many things young people don't know is that everyone no longer chronologically young is privately young, or at least younger; we all have an age at which, subjectively, we stopped aging. We were comfortable there and remained: perhaps it's the age at which we felt fully ourselves, or felt finally grown-up. But if we each have an optimum age, what happens when we pass it? We lead a kind of double life, one life in the actual world, where the numbers accumulate, and the other in a temporal no-man's-land.

I regret that in years to come my children will not often

think of me as I was at thirty-eight, say, or even forty-one, but most likely as I am just before death. That is how I most often recall my mother. It's hard to keep in mind, when picturing the dead, that they spent only a short time in that worn state in which we picture them, and that for most of their life they were younger and more vigorous, blessed with an uncertain future.

As a child, when I asked my mother her age she was coy and evasive: in our family, the ages of women were never spoken aloud. My father liked to boast of his age in company, as if the combination of his years and his vigor were noteworthy, and my mother would fret and try to make him stop, for if he announced he was sixty, could she be far behind? As an adult, I didn't dream of asking her age—it would have been an immense breach of courtesy. I figured I'd find out when she died. I didn't have to wait that long. At some point, she wanted us to open a joint bank account, and I saw her year of birth on the cards the bank had us fill out. Had she really cared about concealing her age, she could have had me fill out my section of the cards first, when they were blank. I took this oversight or perhaps nonchalance about her age as itself a sign of age: either she had lost the acuity to be devious, or else she was giving in, her vanity depleted. Her age surprised me—my guesses had been off by about six years; her past evasions had been successful.

I think I may begin lying about my age too. I can imagine times when it would be advantageous. Or just for the hell of it. I can probably get away with about five or six years, like my mother. For now, at any rate. But if I start now and later on begin to look my actual age, people will think I have aged prematurely or look old for my age. That is not desirable either. A dilemma to ponder—but not for too long.

Why lie? Despite the encouraging books on aging which proclaim its great gifts, old age is an embarrassment, both for those who have it and those who regard it. If its gifts were so great, there would be no need for books to proclaim them. The old, however beautiful and substantial, are disconcerting. They mar the *tableau vivant,* not by their appearance but by what they signify, the nearness of death. Mortality embarrasses us; the notion that notwithstanding all our efforts we must die is literally mortifying. The old, in all their gallantry, signify our common helplessness: the more gallant they are in the face of approaching death, the more vividly they denote our plight.

Thinking about age is thinking about death. Approaching death: how to parse the phrase? Is it approaching me, or am I approaching it? Either way, will we come face to face in ten minutes or ten months or ten years, and what, exactly, will be the form of our greeting? Which indignities are in store? Once, I thought I'd rather die than live with certain physical humiliations; now I'm more amenable. I could manage, given the alternative.

For the most part death seems an outrage, the rudest of interruptions. But at times it seems not so bad—a relief, even, to have the whole business over with. There are a few things I'd like to get done first, though. Also a few things I'd like to live to see. Still, it is some consolation to think that if I died in ten minutes, or even ten months, I'd be considered young to die, even if I'm not considered young to be alive.

I may not even be considered truly alive; I can't be sure. I recently had an intense, intimate, and mildly sexually charged conversation with a man I assumed was my own age. He had that nice, substantial, slightly worn look. Later I discovered he was quite a bit younger. Maybe I had mistaken the sexual charge; maybe he was talking so intimately because he felt the freedom of talking to an "older" woman. Not a happy thought. At this certain age, when I make such a discovery, I cannot say with confidence exactly what the air was charged with.

This is because a certain age engenders the famous invisibility. I've observed it, naturally: men digging up the street no longer stop eating their sandwiches to gawk at me. But I'm not invisible to everyone. Old men look at me, men over fifty, that is. We look at each other. There's an implicit and amused recognition along with the sexual flicker: Those kids must be blind! we say. Yes, it's not that we're invisible, but that they're blind! This is pleasant, especially as I've always been drawn to older, even old, men. Despite this penchant, I married a man who is a mere four years older, which at the time I married him was an appropriate and conventional age difference. I was incapable, then, of doing anything so unconventional as marrying an "older" man, and at this point it's a good thing I didn't, for he might well be dead. Out in the world, I would look at old men, then think, This is silly, why am I looking at these old guys when I have this attractive and virile youngish man right at home? Now, with time, he has become just the sort of older man I always liked. This is one of the unanticipated rewards of age. Not a reward that would be granted to old men who like young women, and if I had in fact broken with convention to marry one of those, as time passed he might have become increasingly disenchanted and left me for someone younger.

It's assumed that women who like older men are thinking of their fathers. This is true only in a very small way, like most psychological explanations. I loved my father, but he was not really my type. I enjoy seeing one of his features, a tone of voice or a gesture, turn up in some stranger, but apart from the little gust of nostalgia, the intriguing thing is how my father's familiar tone of voice or gesture meshes into the unfamiliar configuration of a stranger who is unlike my father in every other way. I would not like the stranger any better were he more like my father; I might like him less.

But this may be taking the psychological explanation too literally. Apart from their specific features, fathers, ideally, are people who take care of you, and perhaps women who like older men want to be taken care of. That would be appealing, I grant, but in fact at a certain age one no longer expects it to happen—one has become so accustomed to taking care of others—and besides, the ways I would enjoy being taken care of are not at all the ways—quite solid, honorable, and uninteresting—I recall my father taking care of me.

Obviously this could lead to further thickets of the psyche, but psychological explanations are among the many sets of beliefs I've shed with age. I hardly believe in anything any more except the brutality, greed, stupidity, and capacity for destruction demonstrated by the human race, and the need to counteract them by doing good. I'm not much interested in personal improvement either, as I was when young. I thought of myself and my life as a kind of giant sculpture I worked on patiently day by day, chipping away here, adding there, forever remodeling with a view to perfection. No longer. I may still chip and model, but more in a spirit of curiosity than of perfectability.

Age itself, in the encouraging books, is considered ameliorative, bringing wisdom, acceptance, and freedom from petty vanities. It's true that at a certain age a certain wise and philosophical acceptance settles over you, like a cloud. That is inevitable, considering all we've seen, and one should never scorn wisdom. Still, my own acceptance seems a loss of vitality. No doubt I'm obtuse in thinking so, but I would rather retain the qualities that need to vanish in order for wisdom, acceptance, and freedom from vanity to take their place, qualities like impulsiveness and struggle and energy and endless hope. The thing about fighting and struggle that philosophical and accepting people don't grasp is that we fighters and strugglers enjoy it. Luckily I can still struggle to accept my acceptance.

My mother, were she still alive, would be horrified at my setting down these thoughts. Not horrified at the thoughts themselves. No. She would say, You're telling the whole world how old you are. But now that I may be a certain age, it may be time to stop thinking about what my mother would say.

# The Page Turner

THE PAGE TURNER appears from the wings and walks onstage, into the light, a few seconds after the pianist and the cellist, just as the welcoming applause begins to wane. By her precise timing the page turner acknowledges, not so much humbly as serenely, lucidly, that the applause is not meant for her: she has no intention of appropriating any part of the welcome. She is onstage merely to serve a purpose, a worthy purpose even if a bit absurd—a concession, amid the coming glories, to the limitations of matter and of spirit. Precision of timing, it goes without saying, is the most important attribute of a page turner. Also important is unobtrusiveness.

But strive though she may to be unobtrusive, to dim or diminish her radiance in ways known only to herself, the page turner cannot render herself invisible, and so her sudden appearance onstage is as exciting as the appearance of the musicians; it gives the audience an unanticipated stab of pleasure. The page turner is golden-tressed—yes, "tresses" is the word for the mass of hair rippling down her back, hair that emits light like a shower of fine sparkles diffusing into the glow of the stage lights. She is young and tall, younger and taller than either of the musicians, who are squarish, unprepossessing middle-aged men. She wears black, a suitable choice for one who should be unobtrusive. Yet the arresting manner in which her black clothes shelter her flesh, flesh that seems molded like clay and yields to the fabric with a certain playful, even droll resistance, defies unobtrusiveness. Her black long-sleeved knit shirt reaches just below her waist, and the fabric of her perfectly fitting black slacks stirs gently around her narrow hips and thighs. Beyond the hem of her slacks can be glimpsed her shiny, but not too conspicuously shiny, black boots with a thick two-inch heel. Her face is heart-shaped, like the illustrations of princesses in fairy tales. The skin of her face and neck and hands, the only visible skin, is pale, an off-white like heavy cream or the best butter. Her lips are painted magenta.

Of course she is not a princess or even a professional beauty hired to enhance the decor but most likely, offstage, a music student, selected as a reward for achievement or for having demonstrated an ability to sit still and turn the pages at the proper moment. Or else she has volunteered for any number of practical reasons: to help pay for her studies, to gain experience of being onstage. Perhaps she should have been disqualified because of her appearance, which might distract from the music. But given the principles of fair play and equal opportunity, beauty can no more disqualify than plainness. For the moment, though, life offstage and whatever the page turner's place in it might be are far removed from the audience, transported as they are by the hair combed back from her high forehead and cascading in a loose, lacy mass that covers her back like a cloak.

In the waiting hush, the page turner lowers her body onto a chair to the left and slightly behind the pianist's seat, the fabric of her slacks adjusting around her recalcitrant hips, the hem rising a trifle to reveal more of her boots. She folds her white hands patiently in her lap like lilies resting on the surface of a dark pond and fixes her eyes on the sheets of music on the rack, her body calm but alert for the moment when she must perform her task.

After the musicians' usual tics and fussing, the pianist's last-minute swipes at face and hair, the cellist's slow and fastidious tuning of his instrument, his nervous flicking of his jacket away from his body as if to let his torso breathe, the music begins. The page turner, utterly still, waits. Very soon, she rises soundlessly and leans forward—and at this instant, with the right side of her upper body leaning over the pianist, the audience inevitably imagines him, feels him, inhaling the fragrance of her breast and arm, of her cascading hair; they imagine she exudes a delicate scent, lightly alluring but not so alluring as to distract the pianist, not more alluring than the music he plays.

She stays poised briefly in that leaning position until with a swift movement, almost a surprise yet unsurprising, she reaches her hand over to the right-hand page. The upper corner of the page is already turned down, suggesting that the page turner has prepared the music in advance, has, in her patient, able manner (more like a lady-in-waiting, really, than an idle fairy-tale princess), folded down all the necessary corners so that she need not fumble when the moment arrives. At the pianist's barely perceptible nod, she propels the page in the blink of an eye through its small leftward arc and smooths it flat, then seats herself, her body drifting lightly yet firmly, purposefully, down to the chair. Once again the edge of her short shirt sinks into her waist and the folds of her slacks reassemble beguilingly over her hips; the hem of her slacks rises to reveal more of her shiny boots. With her back straight, her seated body making a slender black L shape, once again she waits with hands folded, and very soon rises, quite silently, to perform the same set of movements. Soon this becomes a ritual, expected and hypnotic, changeless and evocative.

The page turner listens attentively but appears, fittingly, unmoved by the music itself; her body is focused entirely on her task, which is a demanding one, not simply turning the pages at the proper moments but dimming her presence, suppressing everything of herself except her attentiveness. But as able as she proves to be at turning pages—never a split second late, never fumbling with the corners or making an excessive gesture—she cannot, in her helpless radiance, keep from absorbing all the visual energy in the concert hall. The performance taking place in the hall is a gift to the ear, and while all ears are fully occupied, satiated—the musicians being excellent, more than excellent, capable of seraphic sounds—the listeners' eyes are idle. The musicians are only moderately interesting to look at. The eyes crave occupation too. Offered a pleasure to match that of the ears, naturally the eyes accept the offering. They fix on the page turner—pale skin, black clothes, and gold tresses—who surely knows she is being watched, who cannot deflect the gaze of the audience, only absorb it into the deep well of her stillness, her own intent yet detached absorption in the music.

The very banality of her task lends her a dignity, adds a richness to her already rich presence, since it illustrates a crucial truth: banality is necessary in the making of splendid music, or splendid anything for that matter, much like the pianist's probable clipping of his fingernails or the cellist's dusting of his bow, though such banalities are performed in private, which is just as well.

And then little by little, while the listeners' eyes yearn toward the page turner, it comes to appear that her purpose is not so banal after all, nor is she anything so common as a distraction. Instead it appears that she has an unusual and intimate connection with the music. She is not a physical expression of it, a living symbol; that would be too facile. More subtly, she might be an emanation of the music, a phantom conjured into being by the sounds, but her physical reality—her stylish clothes and shiny boots—contradicts this possibility, and besides, the audience has seen her enter minutes before the music began and can attest to her independent life. No, the connection must be this: though the pianist is clearly striking the keys and the cellist drawing the bow over the strings (with, incidentally, many unfortunate contortions of his face), it comes to seem, through the force of the audience's gaze, that the music is issuing from the page turner, effortlessly, or through some supernatural, indescribable effort, as she sits in her golden radiance and stillness. So that as the concert proceeds, the audience gazes ever more raptly at the page turner. By virtue of her beauty and their gaze, she has become an ineffable instrument—no longer a distraction but rather the very source of the music.

Though the concert is long, very long, the air in the hall remains charged with vitality, the seraphic sounds yielding an ecstasy for which the entranced listeners silently bless the page turner. But perhaps because the concert is long and the page turner is only human, not even a princess, she cannot maintain her aloof pose forever. Though not flagging in her task, without any lapse of efficiency, she begins to show her pleasure in the music as any ordinary person might: her eyelids tremble at a finely executed turn, her lips hint at a smile for a satisfying chord resolution. Her breathing is visible, her upper body rising and sinking with the undulations of the sounds swirling about her. She leans into the music, once or twice even swaying her body a bit. While undeniably pretty to watch, this relaxation of discipline is a sad portent. It suggests the concert has gone on almost long enough, that beauty cannot be endlessly sustained, and that we, too, cannot remain absorbed indefinitely in radiant stillness: we have our limits, even for ecstasy. Banality beckons us back to its leaden, relieving embrace. The ordinary, appreciative movements of the page turner are a signal that the concert will soon end. We feel an anticipatory nostalgia for the notes we are hearing, even for the notes we have not yet heard, have yet to hear, which will be the closing notes. The early notes of a concert lead us into a safe and luxuriant green meadow of sound, a kind of Eden of the ear, but there comes a point, the climax in the music's arc, when we grasp that the notes are curving back and leading us out of the meadow, back into silent and harsher weather.

And this impression of being led regrettably back to dailiness grows still stronger when now and then the pianist glances over at the page turner with a half-smile, a tacit acknowledgment related to some passage in the music, maybe to a little problem of page turning successfully overcome, a private performance within the public performance, which will remain forever unfathomed by the audience and for those instants makes us feel excluded. With their work almost over the performers can afford such small indulgences—a foretaste of the inevitable melancholy moment when audience and performers, alike excluded, will file out into their lives, stripped of this glory, relieved of its burden.

When the music ends, as it must, the page turner remains composed and still: unlike the musicians, she does not relax into triumphant relief. As they take their bows, they show intimate glimpses of themselves in the ardor of achievement, as well as a happy camaraderie—their arms around each other's shoulders—in which the page turner cannot share, just as she cannot share in the applause or show intimate glimpses of herself. She stands patiently beside her chair near the piano and then, with the same precise timing as at the start, leaves the stage a few seconds after the musicians, deftly gathering up the music from the rack to carry off with her, tidying up like a good lady-in-waiting.

The musicians reappear for more bows. The page turner does not reappear. Her service is completed. We understand her absence yet we miss her, as though an essential part of the lingering pleasure is being withheld, as though the essential instrument through which the music reached us has vanished along with the sounds themselves. We do not wish to think of what ordinary gestures she might now be performing off in the wings, putting the music away or lifting her hair off her neck with long-staved-off weariness, released from the burden of being looked at. We cannot deny her her life, her future, yet we wish her to be only as she was onstage, in the beginning. We will forget how the musicians looked, but ever after when we revisit the music we will see the page turner—black clothes, golden hair, regal carriage—radiant and still, emitting the sounds that too briefly enraptured us.

# Credits

"On Being Taken by Tom Victor," "Absence Makes the Heart," "The Page Turner," and "At a Certain Age," copyright © 1991, 1995, 1997, 1999, by Lynne Sharon Schwartz, originally appeared in *The Threepenny Review,* no. 44 (winter 1991), no. 60 (winter 1995), no. 68 (winter 1997), and no. 77 (spring 1999).

"Being There," copyright © 1985 by Lynne Sharon Schwartz, originally appeared in *We Are Talking About Homes: A Great University Against Its Neighbors* (Harper & Row, 1985).

"Alone with the Cat" ("Face to Face") is reprinted from *The American Scholar* 69, no. 1 (winter 2000), copyright © 1999 by Lynne Sharon Schwartz, by permission of the publishers, the Phi Beta Kappa Society.

"The First Dress," copyright © 1994 by Lynne Sharon Schwartz, was originally published as "True Romance" in the *New York Times Magazine*, October 23, 1994.

"Found in Translation," copyright © 1994 by Lynne Sharon Schwartz, originally appeared as "Time Off to Translate" in *American Literary Review* 5, no. 2 (fall 1994).

"Help," copyright © 1992 by Lynne Sharon Schwartz, originally appeared in the *Michigan Quarterly Review* 31, no. 2 (spring 1992).

"Only Connect?" copyright © 1996 by Lynne Sharon Schwartz, originally appeared in *Salmagundi*, nos. 109–10 (winter–spring 1996).

"The Spoils of War," copyright © 1980 by Lynne Sharon Schwartz, originally appeared in the *New York Times*, October 16, 1980.

"Listening to Powell," copyright © 2000 by Lynne Sharon Schwartz, originally appeared in *Salmagundi*, no. 126 (spring 2000).

## Evening Primrose (*Oenothera biennis*)

The winter fruits of Evening Primrose are one of its loveliest aspects. Almond-shaped, they split into four sections at their

*Evening Primrose seedcases*

unattached end, curling back like the petals of a woody flower. Each of the four sections is lined with two rows of loose seeds; they look like coffee grounds, being brown and irregularly shaped. Occasionally insect larvae will spend the winter in these cases. (Obviously any structure the plant produces to contain its seeds will make a fine winter home for insects. Many other fruits of winter weeds are used in this way.)

The name Evening Primrose comes from the plant's curious summer habits. The yellow flowers open usually at night and may be pollinated by a night-flying Sphinx moth. The moth hovers like a hummingbird in front of the flower, unrolling its long tube-mouth to suck the nectar. Each plant opens only a few flowers at any time.

Evening Primrose in its first year is a tight rosette of lance-shaped leaves. The roots of this rosette are a fine vegetable and, in fact, for best eating should be collected in winter. Just look for the new leaves near the base of a winter stalk

*Evening Primrose winter rosette*

and dig up the attached root. Boil the roots twice if they taste too peppery; then salt and butter them. Starting with the second spring, the root becomes woody and the plant produces the large stalk that lasts through the winter.

## Field Garlic (*Allium vineale*)

Shooting up from among grasses of winter meadows is Field Garlic, its tall lone stem topped with a tangle of dried flowers. Where there is one plant, there are usually others scattered nearby.

Field Garlic spreads primarily by two methods of vegetative reproduction. It grows from bulbs similar in appearance to fresh garlic bought at a supermarket. These bulbs produce new adjacent bulbs, which eventually split off and grow shoots of their own. Garlic's other method of reproduction occurs at the tips of the stalks. Instead of flowers, it

*Garlic bulb*
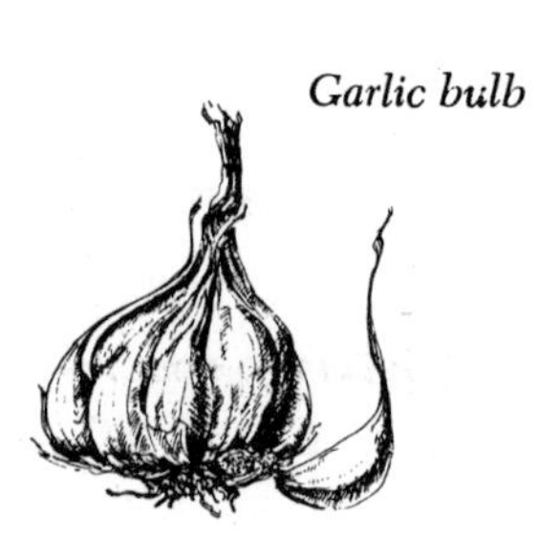

more commonly produces a tight cluster of small bulblike growths called "bulbets." These become hard, and throughout the winter they drop off the tip of the stalk, quickly growing into new plants in spring.

There are many plants in the same genus as Garlic — e.g., Wild Leek, Wild Onion, and Chives — all with similar physical characteristics: growth from bulbs, narrow leaves with parallel veins, and six-part flowers. The bulbs and bulbets of

*Field Garlic bulbets*

some varieties of Garlic are sweet and tender, but others, especially Field Garlic, are far too strong for us to eat. Even the slightest taste will stay on your breath for the day, regardless of efforts to cover or remove it. Perverse as it may seem, cows and livestock love this strong flavor and will eat Field Garlic whenever they can lay their mouths on it. Since it will flavor the animals' meat or milk, farmers try to avoid this situation, for although there may be some demand for garlic beef, there is no market for garlic milk.

## Goldenrod (*Solidago* species)

On the winter stalks of Goldenrod look for round or elliptical swellings about halfway up the stem. These are a com-

*Goldenrod with galls*

mon natural phenomenon known as "galls." Insects form them in summer by laying eggs inside young stems. With the eggs there is a chemical which causes the plant to form a tumorous growth around the eggs. When the eggs hatch, larvae use this growth for food and, after maturing, often winter over in the space they have hollowed out.

Three types of Goldenrod galls are commonly seen in winter. The Elliptical Gall and Ball Gall are both found on the stem and are made by moths and flies. The third, known as the Bunch Gall, is formed at the tip of the stalk and appears as an intricate woody flower. (See Chapter 4.)

In snow around the stalks you may find tracks of Sparrows, Finches, or Juncos that have been feeding on the seeds. The uneaten seeds are scattered by the wind, giving rise to patches of Goldenrod even in abandoned lots of the

*Shapes of Goldenrod stalks*

city. Goldenrod is a perennial and, once rooted, will continue to grow in the same area. It does not do well in cultivated land, and its presence is a sign that the ground has lain fallow for at least a year.

*Star-shaped flower parts of Goldenrod*

In late winter, when the small seeds and delicate star-shaped flower parts are worn away by the wind, Goldenrod appears dried and lifeless, but in fact, many of the winter stalks are holding deep within their galls the developing life of next year's insects.

## Heal-All (*Prunella vulgaris*)

Heal-All is a member of the Mint family but lacks any mint scent or flavor in winter. Its unusual flowerhead is

*Heal-All*

composed of tiers of hairy bracts topping a single stem. Two dried spines protrude from each tier. The small black seeds are probably shaken free by the wind and passing animals.

*Heal-All flowerheads*

The plant is a perennial and spreads by underground rootstocks, which periodically send up new stems; tolerant of a variety of conditions, growing in both shady and sunny areas. It does not form large stands or colonies, but is more commonly found as an isolated group along roadsides or in lawns.

## Joe-Pye Weed (*Eupatorium* species)

Joe Pye, an American Indian living in colonial Massachusetts, had a native weed which he used to help cure European settlers of various illnesses. The plant became known by his name, but sole recognition was not really deserved,

*Joe-Pye Weed*

for Joe Pye's people as well as many other Indian tribes had known and used the plant long before.

The weed is tall, usually growing near open water or marshy areas, and during late summer and fall it puts forth a cluster of showy purple flowers. It is a member of the Composite family, as can be seen by the similarity of its flowers to those of Goldenrod and Aster. The plant is a native of North America and in its genus, *Eupatorium,* has many close relatives, including the Thoroughworts, Boneset, and Snakeroot.

*Joe-Pye Weed flowerheads*

The last of these, Snakeroot, is poisonous and was the cause of what early settlers called "milk sickness." When

Snakeroot was eaten by cows, the poison was passed on in their milk, often causing the death of whole families. But this genus need not leave a bad taste in your mouth, for remember that it also includes Joe-Pye Weed, one plant that can do more to help than harm.

## Loosestrife (*Lythrum salicaria*)

Loosestrife, so prominent in summer with its purple flowers massing the edges of lakes and swamps, is deflatingly inconspicuous in its winter habit. Few people ever guess the real identity of this dried weed. In winter, Loosestrife's slender branches reach out and bend up beside the thin main stem. They are punctuated at even intervals by surrounding sets of flowerheads.

The plant is a strange mixture of geometry and numbers. The main stem tends to be hexagonal, the side branches

*Purple Loosestrife*

*Loosestrife branching*

square. The branches usually grow in whorls of three on the single main stem. Flower clusters grow in two's, three flowers in each cluster. Even more relationships between the plant parts exist, too lengthy to describe but easy to discover.

Purple Loosestrife, a native of Europe, is now the most widespread of its genus in North America. Look for the winter weed near lakes and by swamps; its upturned branches surrounded at even intervals by flowerheads are its characteristic mark. The generic name means "blood from wounds" and may be a reference to the plant's purple flowers or its bright red leaves in fall. The specific name, *salicaria*, means "willowlike" and refers to the shape of Loosestrife's leaves. Like Willows, Loosestrife grows near water, fulfilling much the same function as Cattails — slowly filling in sections of marshy areas.

## Milkweed (*Asclepias* species)

The most enticing plant among winter weeds must be Milkweed, for who can resist taking handfuls of its silken seeds and tossing them into the wind? But the way these seeds

*Milkweed pods and seeds*

disperse when not interfered with is a more ordered event than their casual appearance would suggest.

The process starts with the pod splitting open and exposing the seeds, which are arranged so that they are released only a few at a time. Next, a few seeds separate from the others while remaining attached to the top of the pod by their filaments. This is important, for if the seeds just fell, most of them would land at the base of the parent plant and have to compete with each other. Finally, the wind separates the seeds from the pod and carries them across open fields. If the parachute of hollow filaments becomes trapped by a thicket or among grasses, the seed will separate from it and fall to the ground.

Milkweed grows in open meadows and barren lots. Its widespreading shallow root system, extending to a diameter of fifteen feet, makes it good for areas susceptible to erosion. In summer the plant is a stalk three feet high with lush green leaves; its veins, when broken, release a white milky sap from which the plant gets its name. Although not eaten by many animals, Milkweed's spring shoots are among the tastiest wild vegetables to be found. They can be eaten cooked like asparagus, or raw if they are still young and tender.

Certainly the winter stalk and pods of Milkweed are an inspired sculpture, but unless you want a snowstorm of Milkweed parachutes throughout your house, be sure they are empty before bringing them inside.

## Motherwort (*Leonurus cardiaca*)

Motherwort is one of the tallest members of the Mint family growing in North America. Its strange name simply means "mother's plant" and may have been given because of an old belief that the plant could aid discomforts connected with pregnancy.

The fruits of the winter weed are particularly spiky; seeing these and its four-sided stem, it is impossible to mistake this plant for any other.

Motherwort is a perennial, for it lasts through the winter as a living rootstock which will continue to send up new stems each year.

The Mint family contains over three thousand species, most of which have square stems and glands in their leaves that produce odoriferous oils. Many of our cooking herbs are in this family, which includes Marjoram, Thyme, and Sage and other plants such as Rosemary, Lavender, and the familiar houseplant Coleus.

*Motherwort flowerheads*

Motherwort, although not native to North America, is nonetheless widespread throughout the Northeast, growing in the sunny areas of roadsides and undisturbed fields where so many of the winter weeds are found.

## Mullein (*Verbascum thapsus*)

Mullein is certainly a bizarre form in the winter landscape. Appearing either as a giant candelabrum or a lone staff

*Mullein*

stuck in the ground, it may grow to heights of seven feet or more. It seems to favor the poorest of soils, often growing even in unplanted gravel by the sides of highways.

Mullein tops are encrusted with cuplike flower remains for up to three feet of their length; below, long leafy ridges line the stems. If you give the weed a shake, hundreds of small black seeds will pepper the snow below. These dried plants were once used as torches in Europe; dipped in tal-

*Mullein flowerhead*

low, they burned long, each empty flowerhead holding the solidifying fat.

Rosettes of large woolly leaves that you may find in winter are the first-year stage of Mullein's biennial growth. Like velvet to the touch, they are described by the common name which comes from the Latin *mollis,* meaning "soft." These rosettes are a favorite winter home for many insects.

Remembering a plant's whereabouts in summer or winter enables you to come back and enjoy it during another stage when it might otherwise be hard to identify. Knowing the winter rosette, you can return in summer to see the large stalk of yellow flowers, so lovely that it is grown in cultivated gardens of Europe. Then later in the fall you can return again and enjoy the strange form of the winter weed.

## Mustard (*Brassica* species)

Mustard is an easy plant to identify in the snow-draped road edges and neglected fields, for its slim transluscent membranes point upward along each part of its stem, giving the plant an airy featherlike quality.

Seeds, appearing as small black discs, may still be at-

*Translucent pods of Mustard*

tached to some of these membranes. It is these seeds, dark-colored in Black Mustard and light in White Mustard, that go into the familiar spreads so prevalent at baseball games and Sunday picnics. Uusally ground-up Black Mustard seeds are sold as dry mustard, whereas the spread is made from seeds of both white and black varieties, to which there has been added a mixture of vinegar and spices.

The generic name for Mustard, *Brassica,* means cabbage or cauliflower and reflects the close relationship among the three plants. In fact, Rutabaga, Cabbage, Kale, Cauliflower, Brussels sprouts, Turnip, and Kohlrabi are all in the same genus as Mustard. This relationship is also reflected in the facts that spring leaves of Mustard make a good potherb, and that the flowerheads can be eaten in the same manner as broccoli.

Another genus of the Mustard family is *Barbarea,* or Winter Cress. In the fall, this plant grows a rosette of distinctive

*Mustard winter rosette*
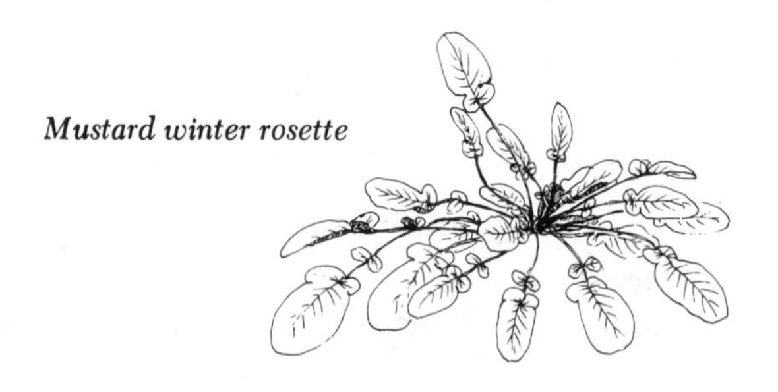

green leaves, which can be gathered throughout winter for use as salad greens.

## Peppergrass (*Lepidium* species)

Peppergrass is probably more common in the city than in the country, being a familiar inhabitant of that unused space between sidewalk and city street, where trashcans wait to be emptied and where cars pull up, people step out, and

*Peppergrass*

dogs pause. The plant, seeming to favor this hardpacked earth, sends its single taproot deep into the soil to gather what moisture it can.

When the seeds of Peppergrass are newly matured they are thrown from the plant by an expulsive reaction within the pod. Those that remain on the stalk are often dispersed like the seeds of Tumbleweed, for the winter stalk, being

*Peppergrass seed pods*

brittle, lightweight, and generally spherical, may break off from its roots and be blown about by the wind, scattering seeds as it goes. This is particularly true of the city species *Lepidium virginicum*, which is short and stout, compared to its country cousin, Field Peppergrass (*Lepidium campestre*), which is too tall to tumble.

The spring shoots of Peppergrass are a good salad green, and the plant's common name refers to its pepperlike taste. Caution should be used, however, when gathering plants in the city, because of the likelihood that they have been polluted by the waste products of cars and dogs.

The generic name, *Lepidium*, comes from a word meaning "a small flake or scale" and describes the two ochre-colored seeds. City sparrows seem to enjoy these seeds, as is evidenced by the numerous bird tracks you will find in the snow beneath the plant. Besides having interesting habits, Peppergrass is always pleasant to see, for the transparent membranes dot its gracefully branching stalk, giving the whole plant the quality of intricate lace.

## Ragweed (*Ambrosia* species)

Ragweed is known to most as the ubiquitous source of hayfever, but to birds it is a plentiful source of food. Its seeds,

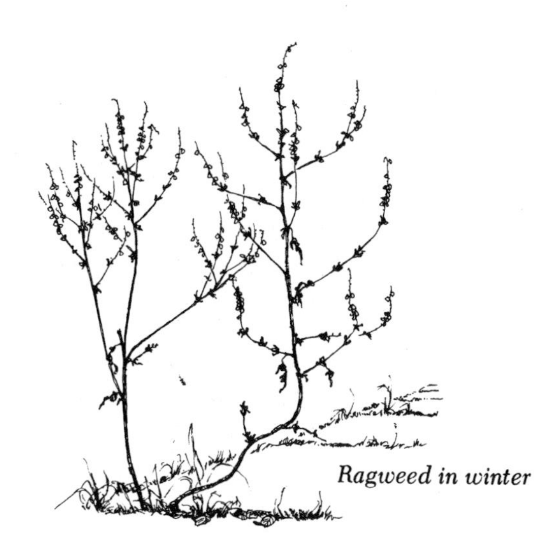

*Ragweed in winter*

present after autumn, are one of the most valuable winter foods for all ground feeding birds. Among its admirers are the Sparrows, Finches, Juncos, Redpolls, and Bobwhites.

As most people know, Ragweed thrives in the city. The hundreds of seeds it produces may lie dormant up to five years, waiting for the slightest turn of the earth. Any gouge in the soil, or some loosened earth allows them to sprout into a ridiculously healthy crop of plants.

Having sprouted, the plant produces two types of flowers: greenish male flowers at the tips of the stems, and inconspicuous female flowers at the leaf axils. There are two

*Ragweed's summer male flowers*

main species: Common Ragweed (*Ambrosia artemisiifolia*), which grows to five feet tall on dry soil, and Great Ragweed (*Ambrosia trifida*), which, loving moister areas, grows to a towering fifteen feet. The seeds of Great Ragweed are less useful to wildlife because of their tough outer coating.

The common name, Ragweed, comes from the ragged appearance of the plant's deeply cut leaves. The generic name, *Ambrosia,* was given by the Roman natural historian Pliny and seems to be a misnomer. One of its meanings is "food for the gods," which should be changed to "food for the birds," or for those who get hayfever, to just "for the birds."

## St. Johnswort (*Hypericum perforatum*)

An old country custom in Europe was to hang a special yellow-blossomed plant in your window on the eve of St. John's Day (June 24), in order to repel bad spirits and counteract the evil eye. In general, the presence of this plant was considered a good omen, and since it was thought that the plant warded off lightning and revealed the identity of passing witches, St. Johnswort was allowed to prosper around the farmhouse. It became known as St. John's Plant or St. Johnswort (*wort* meaning "plant" or "herb"). When

*St. Johnswort flowerhead*

the plant immigrated to North America it left its traditions behind, and although still as effective as it probably ever was against evil, St. Johnswort is now seldom used for that purpose.

The side branches of St. Johnswort grow in perfect pairs off the central stem. At the end of each branch there are numerous cupped seed containers, each of which holds over a hundred minute, shiny black seeds. As the plant is swayed by wind, the seeds fall out and are blown to areas nearby. It has no known wildlife use, but its red-brown stems are certainly a pleasant touch of color in the winter landscape.

## Sensitive Fern (*Onoclea sensibilis*)

Sensitive Fern often baffles winter plant enthusiasts, for it differs so from other weeds. It has no remains of leaves, it is

*Sensitive Fern spore cases*

never in bloom, it lasts over two years, and its capsules, when broken, contain only "brown dust." Knowing that the plant is part of a fern helps some people but confuses others.

Ferns reproduce by spores rather than by seeds. The brown dust in the capsules is actually hundreds of thousands of spores, which will be dispersed by wind in dry weather. Fern spores, when they sprout, do not grow into a

*Sensitive Fern summer fronds*

plant of the same shape as the one they came from, but each grows into a small heart-shaped leaf no taller than ½ inch. This new tiny plant reproduces sexually, growing both egg and sperm cells. The fertilized egg then sprouts tall, green, leafy fronds — what we normally think of as ferns. Along with the green fronds it grows the spore-bearing stalk. The fronds die back after the first fall frost, but the spore-bearing stalk remains standing through the winter and into the next summer.

Sensitive Fern is one of the few ferns with such a hardy spore-bearing stalk, and it is frequently found growing near wet areas. In late winter you may find the spore cases already broken open and emptied by the action of early spring moisture and warmth.

### Spiraea (*Spiraea* species)

*Spiraea* is one of the few winter weeds whose stalks remain alive in winter. Since it is a deciduous plant, it is often

*Spiraea flowerheads*

considered a shrub. It drops its leaves in fall, revealing a smooth reddish brown stem, which in spring puts forth new leaves. At the top of the winter stalk are jewellike minute flowerheads. Their five-part structure hints at the plant's membership in the Rose family, and their tiny beauty should not be missed.

*Meadowsweet and Steeplebush*

Steeplebush and Meadowsweet are the two species of *Spiraea* most commonly found. They are easily told apart even in winter, for the flowers of Steeplebush are arranged into a slender pointed steeple, while those of Meadowsweet form a broad rounded top. Both typically grow in little

*Meadowsweet with Sparrow's nest*

groves among the grasses of old open meadows. There are often sparrows' nests and occasionally hornets' nests built among them, because of the cover they afford in summer.

The generic name, *Spiraea*, means "herbs for garlands." It was probably given to the plants because their strong flexible stems lined with leaves and topped with showy flowers made them ideal for weaving into garlands and summer wreaths. Meadowsweet and Steeplebush are natives of North America and grow most commonly on rocky soil of northeastern coastal states and Southern Canada.

## Teasel (*Dipsacus* species)

Teasel forms an exciting design among the winter weeds. Covered with stiff thorns, it is hostile to the touch but fascinating to the eye. Look for the marvelous geometric arrangement of spines on the dried flowerheads. Woody

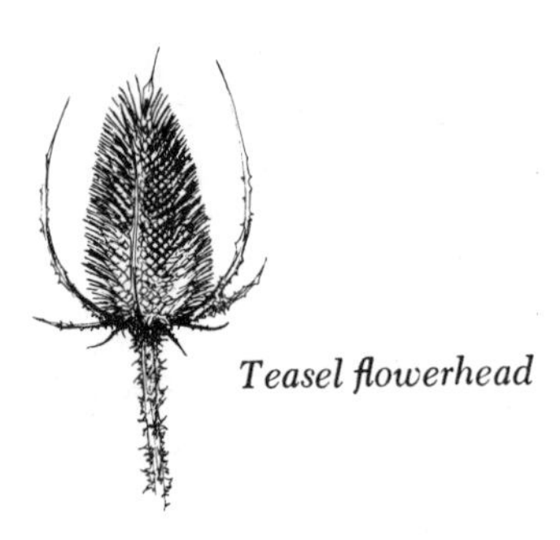

*Teasel flowerhead*

bracts encircling the flowerheads often bend into perfect curlicues at their tips. Also notice how thorns grow out of long ridges that line the branches and stem.

Teasel is a native of Europe and Asia and has long been used in wool processing. The dried flowerheads, split and placed on rollers, were used to card, or tease, wool, giving

*Teasel*

some of the common names for the plant: Teasel and Fuller's Teasel.

The plant is a biennial, growing a hardy rosette the first year and a zesty stalk the second. The plant, rare on the East Coast, is common from central New York to the Midwest. If you wear heavy gloves when picking it and have a floor vase to put the tall stalk in, Teasel's intricate designs can be a great source of visual enjoyment throughout the winter.

## Tansy (*Tanacetum vulgare*)

Tansy's rosette of leaves that lasts into winter is a real odoriferous treat. Dig down through the snow at the base of the winter stalk to get a small piece of one of the green fernlike leaves, crush it between your fingers, and smell it. The rich odor comes from an oil in the leaves that has been used for such varied purposes as baking, easing sunburn pain, and repelling insects. In large doses the oil is poisonous.

The winter stalk of Tansy has a group of small brown "buttons" at its top, arranged in a flat cluster. Take one of these buttons and rub its surface; the seeds will break off in

Tansy

your hand. They are thin and packed into a hemisphere on the flowerhead. From July to September these buttons are bright yellow, and if picked and crushed together, can be the start of a good yellow dye.

Tansy, a native of Europe, has been grown in European gardens for centuries, and herbalists have ascribed many cures to its use. Today we no longer use it — in fact few

*Tansy winter rosette* *Tansy flowerheads*

people even notice it — though it fills city lots and lines country roads with fragrant leaves and button-topped stalks.

## Thistle (*Circium* species)

Whatever you do, don't try to gather Thistles, for there is no way to come close to them without getting stabbed by sharp thorns. The stems, leaves, and even flowers are thorned. The thorns keep us as well as some grazing animals away from

*Thistle*

the plant. Just look across any well-grazed meadow and you will spot the Thistles, untouched and surrounded by close-cropped grass. Their protection allows the plant to mature unharmed, and leaves it basking in the sun without a leafy competitor in sight.

You might think this would be enough to insure the sur-

*Thistle flowerhead*

vival of any self-respecting plant, but the Thistle takes it even farther. First, it produces an average of 4,000 seeds per plant — seeds that are protected, while developing, by a spined container and that have their own parachute of filaments when they are released. The filaments are similar to Milkweed's except that each filament is lined with further small hairs, increasing wind resistance tremendously. A Thistle seed in still air will take 10 seconds to float just 6 feet to the ground.

Besides the seeds and thorns, Thistles have evolved a long taproot that grows 6 feet down. It cannot be pulled up, and if the upper plant is cut off there is enough stored food in the root to send up new shoots. In one common species, Canada Thistle (*Circium arvense*), lateral rootstocks grow off the main taproot. At intervals along these rootstocks there are nodes, which in turn send up new shoots above the ground. This is vegetative reproduction: one plant producing another without the seed state intervening. These rootstocks can grow as long as 20 feet in one season. If a cultivator runs over a rootstock and chops it up, each piece can then develop into a new plant.

No protection in nature is perfect, however, for some other organism will always evolve a way either to overcome it or to use it to its own advantage, like the Goldfinch, which eats the Thistle seeds and makes its nest with the filaments, or the beetle, which lays its eggs inside the flower, where its hatched larvae will be both safe and well-fed.

*Thistle thorns*

## Vervain (*Verbena* species)

Vervain's branches, all reaching toward the sky, are slender, and seed-coated at their tips, making the plant appear more delicate than most of its winter companions. Its appearance has led it to be used as an ornamental flower in cultivated gardens.

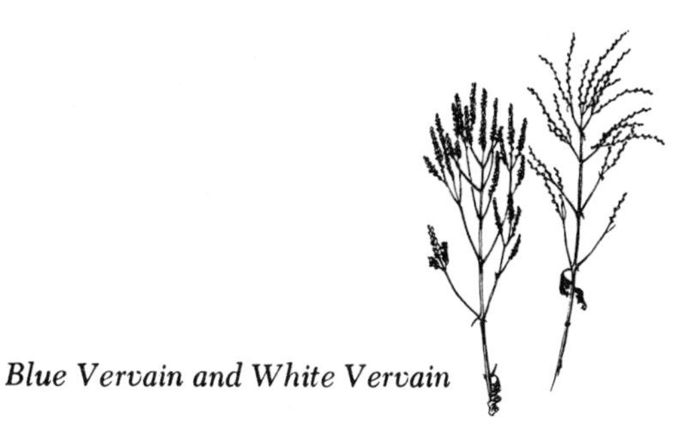

*Blue Vervain and White Vervain*

Two species of Vervain are common, and, unlike most other winter weeds, these two can be easily distinguished in their dried form. White Vervain (*Verbena urticifolia*) has seeds intermittently spaced along its branch tips, whereas the branches of Blue Vervain (*Verbena hastata*) are solidly

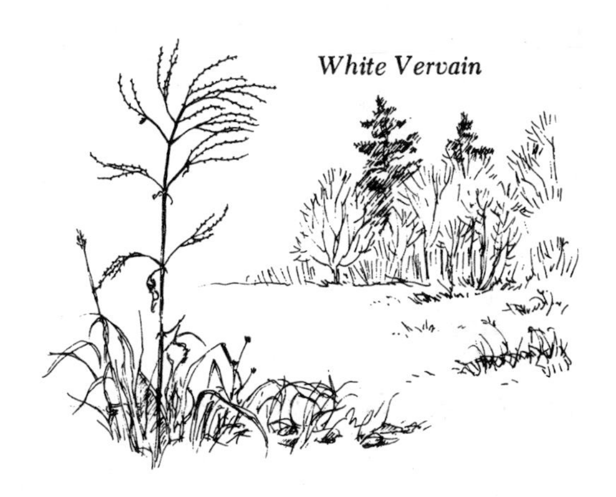

*White Vervain*

coated with seeds. Both species grow up to 5 feet tall in sun-filled habitats.

Vervain has a square stem but is not part of the Mint family, which also has square stems. Its numerous seeds are eaten only occasionally by birds, but the California Indians were known to gather, roast, and grind them for use in making breadstuffs. Vervain is a perennial and a native of North America. It rarely grows in colonies, more commonly being found as isolated plants in roadsides and waste spaces.

## Wild Carrot (*Daucus carota*)

Wild Carrot, better known to some as Queen Anne's Lace, is a close relative of our domestic carrot. This becomes clear

*Wild Carrot*

when you examine the plant's first-year stage, which can be seen usually near the base of the winter stalk. Its rosette of leaves is exactly like a carrot top and if pulled up will reveal a thick white taproot with both the shape and odor of a small carrot. Since the plant is a biennial, it is not until the second year that it produces a stalk with flowers.

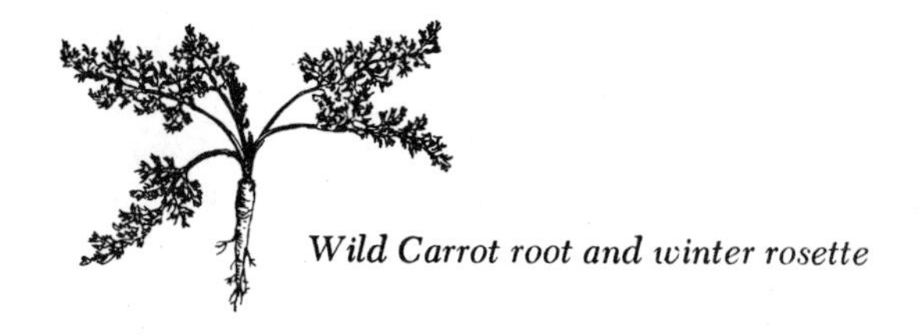

*Wild Carrot root and winter rosette*

The intricate lace quality of these flowers has earned the plant its other name, Queen Anne's Lace. The shape of the flowerhead is called umbellate, which means "shaped like an umbrella"; this is the characteristic flower shape of all plants in the order Umbellales. In summer the flower opens and closes in relation to the humidity of the surrounding air, and a similar mechanism may again be used in the fall, when the flower bracts close around the matured seeds, holding them in what is commonly described as a "bird's nest."

The seeds, small and lined with four rows of spines, are dispersed by animals, whose fur picks up the seeds as they pass by. Wild Carrot seeds can be gathered and steeped in hot water to make a good-tasting tea — fun to make after a winter walk. If you bite one of the seeds in the field you will find its flavor similar to that of cooked carrots. The seeds can be used as a spice; in fact, many plants from which we get spices are related to Wild Carrot, such as Caraway, Fennel, Coriander, Anise, and Parsley.

*Wild Carrot flowerheads*

After the first snowfall Wild Carrot's flowerheads again become white, this time not with lace but with puffs of fresh snow, giving the appearance of a cotton plant strangely out of place. Formerly a native of Asia, Wild Carrot is now thoroughly naturalized in North America, thriving in city lots as well as in country meadows.

## Yarrow (*Achillea millefolium*)

A Yarrow stalk broken off near the top makes a perfect miniature tree or shrub for the landscapes of train sets and model buildings. Its flat-topped cluster of flowers is a good example of nature grouping a number of small flowers into one showy bunch, more attractive to insects.

*Yarrow flowerheads*

*Yarrow winter rosette*

In some ways Yarrow's winter stalk is like a small version of Tansy; like Tansy, it has fragrant leaves. Brush the snow away from the base and crush one of the leaves that form a rosette around the stalk. They smell strong and spicy. Some people use them to make a tea that induces sweating.

The leaves are finely cut like a ragged feather, and Yarrow's specific name describes this: *millefolium*, or thousand-leaved. Its generic name, *Achillea,* refers to its association

*Yarrow*

with Achilles, who, as the legend goes, used the leaves to stop the bleeding from the wounds of his soldiers. Some herbalists go even further, claiming it will cure baldness and purge the soul (but not claiming any connection between the two).

Yarrow's success in populating the land is due in part to its growth patterns. Being a perennial, it comes up each year from the same widespreading set of roots, sometimes producing flowers in both spring and fall. In addition, each flowering produces thousands of seeds, which are small, light, and easily carried on the wind. It is no wonder that it is as common in the city as in the country.

*II*

# *Snow*

EACH YEAR SNOW RENEWS our sense of wonder. The first flakes are always magical, their slow whitening of the landscape drawing us irresistibly out of doors. Do other animals see snow as we do? They may wonder at snow, but above all, their instincts prepare them to deal with it as a

***Seeds being dispersed over the snow's hard crust***

physical force in their lives, a force that can freeze or warm, feed or starve, trap or free. We have to deal with snow for only as long as it takes us to shovel our walks and plow our streets, but animals have to cope with it constantly. Many animals must travel on a razor's edge between survival and death; snow, by its character or depth, can easily throw them to one side or the other.

Every form of life is affected differently by the depth of snow. Even as little as an inch hides the daily movements of Meadow Mice from the keen eyes of their predators; this same depth also hinders Bobwhites as they feed, because it covers seeds and insects from their view. Slightly deeper snow forms an insulating layer over the land, keeping dormant insects, plants, and small mammals protected from drying and chilling winds, yet allowing the sun's radiant energy to penetrate.

As the snow becomes deeper, it creates more problems for

*Under a young Spruce in deep snow is a shelter for Grouse or Rabbits.*

animals. A Red Fox can walk easily in six inches of snow, but when the snow is deeper, the animal must bound through it, expending more energy and catching its prey less often. A hunger-weakened White-tailed Deer can actually be immobilized by deep drifts, and even healthy deer will have more difficulty escaping a Bobcat attack. But for the Cottontail Rabbit, deep snow provides food; since it feeds on the winter buds of sapling trees, the deeper snow helps it to reach more buds.

The character of snow is as important as its depth. Snow can be fluffy, wind-packed, wet, thinly crusted, glazed, or dry and drifting. These qualities hurt or help each plant and animal in a different way, and the adaptations and instincts of different species determine whether or not they can use the qualities of snow to their own advantage.

The presence of snow over thousands of years has favored certain physical adaptations of plants and animals. Birches are small trees with fine branches; the weight of the snow and ice bends them to the ground, but their trunks are flexible even in winter, and the trees spring back up when the snow melts. The Long-tailed Weasel turns white in winter so that it is hidden from both predators and prey. The Ruffed Grouse grows combs on the sides of its toes to support it better on the snow. The Lynx and Snowshoe Hare, also, have large feet which support them on the surface, enabling them to live farther north than other cats and hares.

*Snow bending Birches*

Snow shapes the behavior of animals as well. Wolves travel on the wind-packed snow of northern lakes. Otters combine sliding and bounding to travel overland in late winter. Deer stay in the shallow snow under spruces, taking

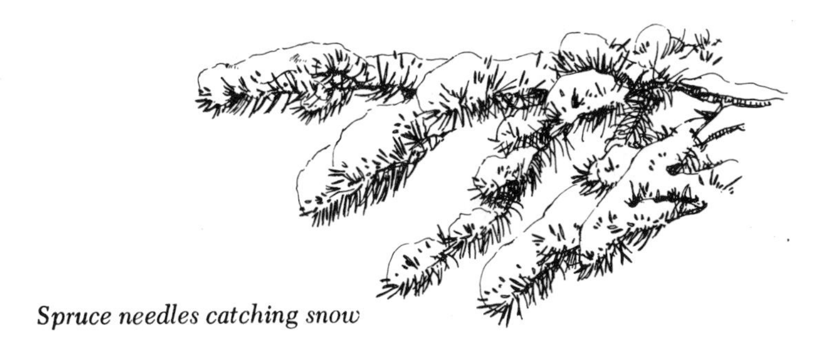

*Spruce needles catching snow*

advantage of the fact that a third of the snow accumulation is held in the branches above. Bobcats travel on the trails of humans and other animals to avoid the uncertainty of unaltered snow. And Ruffed Grouse dive into powdery snow to keep warm at night.

These are just a few examples of the hundreds of ways in which plants and animals specifically interact with snow.

*Shallow snow under a fallen log forms a runway for Squirrels and rodents.*

But snow affects nature on an even larger scale. By protecting insects from ground feeding birds, small mammals from predators, and green plants from browsers, it increases their populations and the diversity of their types in both winter and summer. And, on the other hand, by limiting the food of birds, predators, and browsers, it limits the populations and diversity of these animals. So, in a very direct way, snow controls the character and composition of life throughout the year, and learning its ways as well as how life is affected by it is essential to understanding the ecology of the north.

To some extent, the snow cover itself is influenced by the types of snow crystals within it. This influence is usually greatest at the time of a storm, for snow crystals, once fallen, tend to change into similarly shaped ice granules. But as the snow falls the crystal type will determine how much the snow adheres, packs, builds up, or drifts.

Snow crystals form in clouds where temperatures are anywhere from 32° to −39°F. These clouds are made up of water droplets so microscopic that thousands could fit on the dot of an *i*. We see them as a cloud only because such vast numbers are concentrated in one area. Along with the droplets there are minute particles of dust and salt from the surface of the earth and sea that have been carried miles up into the sky by prevailing winds.

These cooled particles have the physical property of attracting water molecules from the microscopic droplets in the cloud. As these molecules gather on the particle, they freeze and build ice crystals. This is the start of a snowflake or snow crystal.

As these crystals become larger they begin to fall, often hitting other crystals. The result is that part of the crystal breaks off and becomes the center or "nucleus" for another crystal. This occurrence often causes a chain reaction that in turn starts other crystals growing, and is believed to result in the sudden bursts of heavy snowfall we often experience during a snowstorm.

Which one of seven common shapes a crystal will be is determined by the temperature and humidity of the air in which the crystal is formed. If the air is cold and there is little moisture, then the very small column crystals are formed. If the air is warmer and there is lots of moisture, then the stellar crystals have a better chance of forming. Since it is also common for a crystal to pass through a number of atmospheric conditions before it lands, it may start off as a hexagonal plate, go through the conditions of stellar formation, and then go back through the conditions that will form a plate.

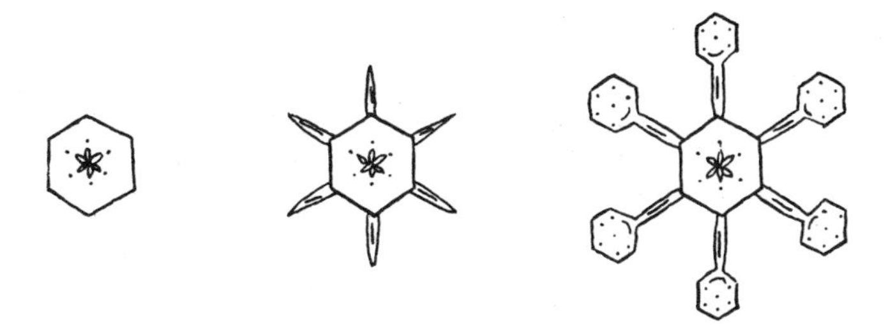

Another crystal might start out as a column crystal and then pass through the conditions that produce plate crystals.

Often snow crystals that are formed at warmer temperatures will collide and stick together. Then they fall as large

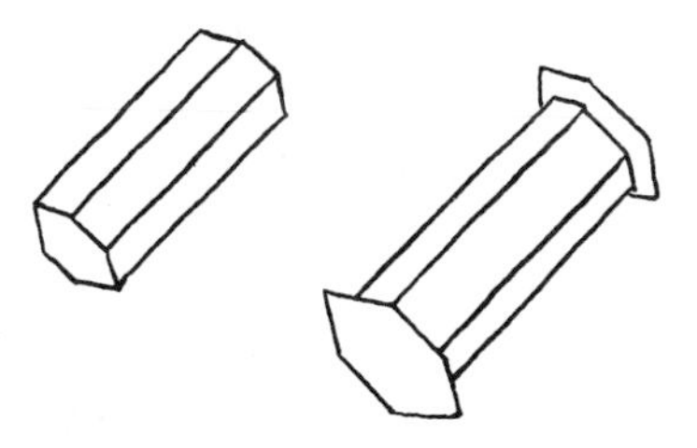

conglomerate flakes that may be as big as 2 inches in diameter. Conglomerate flakes also form when the crystal structure is intricate enough to interlock with other crystals.

Once snow crystals land on the ground, they start to lose their fine detail through a process called metamorphosis or sublimation. In sublimation the fine outer parts of the crystal evaporate and condense on the larger central part of the crystal. In this way, almost all fallen crystals soon change into small granules of ice.

### *SNOW, RAIN, SLEET, AND HAIL*

*Snow* starts as a nucleus of dust or salt that attracts molecules of water from cloud droplets. As these water molecules accumulate on the nucleus, they form ice crystals, which become larger as more water molecules are added.

*Rain* starts as the microscopic droplets in clouds that are so concentrated that they join together into larger droplets. They soon become so heavy that they fall to the earth.

*Sleet* starts as rain, then passes through a very cold layer of air on its way to the earth's surface. At this point the droplets freeze into solid icy raindrops and continue falling.

*Hail* starts as sleet but is thrown back into the raincloud by thunderstorm updrafts. In the raincloud the droplets pick up another coating of water and fall again. This process continues until the strong updrafts can no longer keep the drops in the air. Hailstones, which can be up to 3 inches in diameter, are the largest precipitate that falls from the sky.

## *Key to Snow Crystals*

Snow-crystal-watching opens up a world of discovery each time it snows. The crystals are not only a never-ending type of aesthetic enjoyment, but they also indicate the type of snow cover that will result — whether it will be good for tracking, will break limbs off trees, will form huge drifts, and so on. The crystals are usually variations on a small number of basic shapes. There are illustrations below of the shapes and their combinations, followed by more detailed descriptions of the characteristics of the crystals and the types of clouds they form in. By checking the snowflakes in a storm more than once you can see the progression of crystal types, for they usually change in the course of a given snowfall.

Crystal-watching is best done by catching snowflakes on a dark surface such as the arm of your jacket or sweater. Some of the crystals will be too tiny to appreciate without a small magnifying glass, but most are easy to enjoy with the unaided eye. As you bend close to see them, try to avoid melting them with your breath.

*SIMPLE CRYSTALS*

| *MAGNIFIED* | *LARGEST ACTUAL SIZE TO BE SEEN* | *NAME* |
|---|---|---|
|  |  | *Hexagonal Plate Crystal* |
|  |  | |

| *MAGNIFIED* | *LARGEST ACTUAL SIZE TO BE SEEN* | *NAME* |
| --- | --- | --- |
|  |  | *Stellar Crystal, or Dendrite* |
| 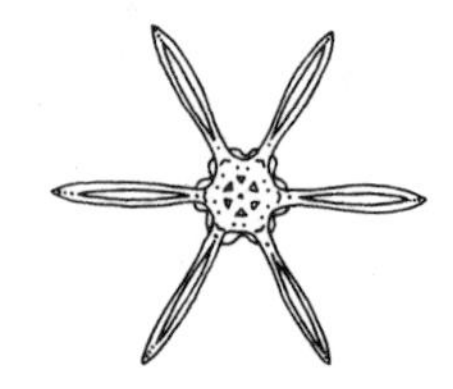 |  | |
| 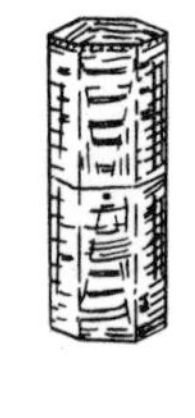 |  | *Column Crystal* |
|  |  | *Needle Crystal* |
|  |  | |

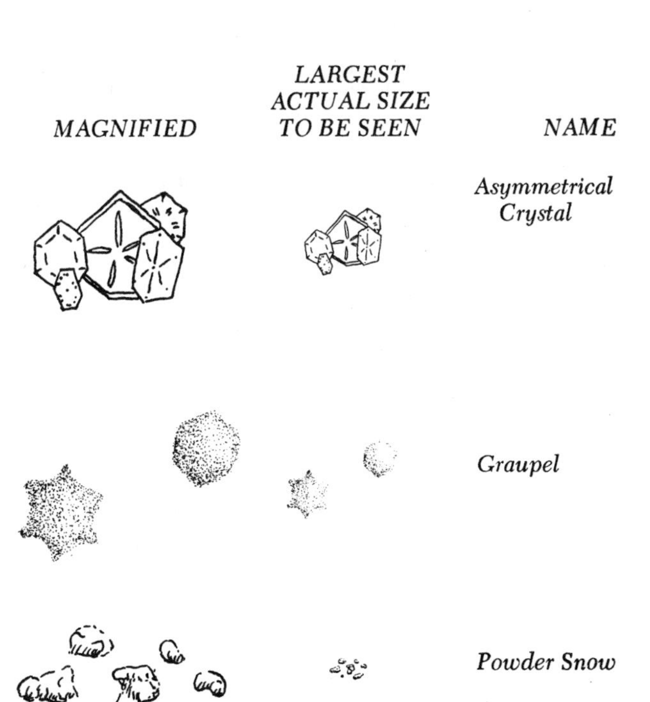


## COMBINATION CRYSTALS

These are crystals that are composed of more than one basic type.

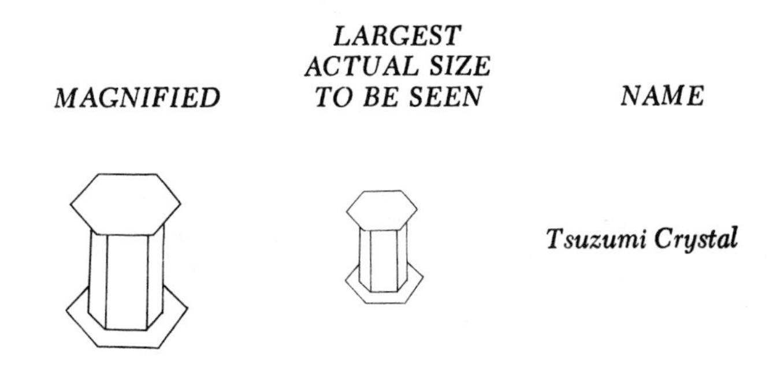

| *MAGNIFIED* | *LARGEST ACTUAL SIZE TO BE SEEN* | *NAME* |
| --- | --- | --- |
|  |  | *Bullet Crystal* |
|  |  | *Spatial Dendrite* |
| 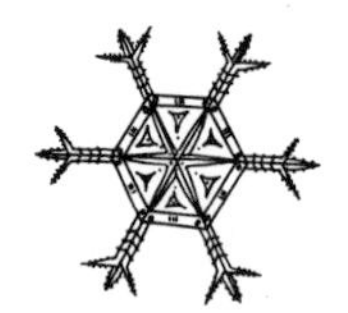 |  | *Hexagonal Plates with Stellar Formations* |
|  |  | *Stellar Crystals with Hexagonal Plate Formations* |

## *Natural History Descriptions*

### *SIMPLE CRYSTALS*

HEXAGONAL PLATE CRYSTAL This is a six-sided, flat crystal with varying degrees of design on its surface. The largest size to be seen is $\frac{3}{16}$ inch in diameter, but about half that size is more common. They are always only a small per-

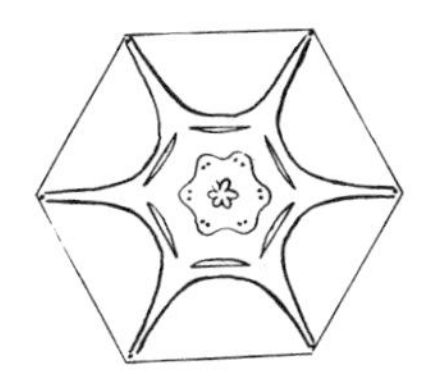

centage of all the snowflakes in a storm and often appear along with Stellar Crystals. Since they have no projections, they do not interlock, but drift freely.

I find these a particular joy to come across, because they represent a perfect hexagon in nature and they reflect light off their surfaces.

STELLAR CRYSTAL OR DENDRITE As the name indicates, this type is shaped like a star with six points radiating from the center. The points can be any shape, from a simple spike to an elaborate design. These crystals are what we typically

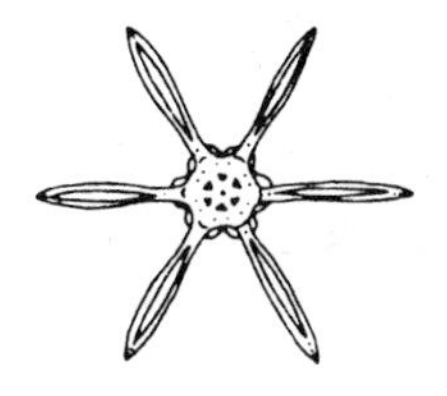

think of as snowflakes. The largest size to be seen is ½ inch in diameter. Stellar crystals form only a small percentage of any storm; they often occur with Hexagonal Plate Crystals.

Stellar Crystals form in low clouds where the temperature is not too cold and where there is plenty of moisture. Because of their intricate design, they often interlock while falling, ending as large conglomerate flakes, sometimes as much as 2 inches in diameter, that drift slowly to the ground. The flakes, since they will readily hold together, stack on the tops of branches and street signs. Because of their slow falling, Stellar Crystals create a peaceful effect during a snowfall.

COLUMN CRYSTAL Column Crystals are small six-sided columns with flat or pointed ends. The largest size likely to be seen is ¼ inch in length. These crystals often have hollow air spaces inside them, but this is hard to observe because the crystals are so small. They are not a common crystal.

They form in very cold clouds where there is little moisture. Extremely high clouds that appear like pulled wisps of cotton, called cirrus clouds or mares' tails, are made almost entirely of these crystals in winter. When clouds with these crystals pass in front of the moon, they create a beautiful colored halo around it.

NEEDLE CRYSTAL This is a long, slender, six-sided column with fine points projecting from either end. Extremely common crystals, they can account for much of a storm's accumulation. They range in length from ¼ to ⅜ inch and

often freeze together, forming conglomerate flakes. These conglomerate flakes fall slowly to the ground but seem to break into many splinters of ice when they land on a hard surface.

ASYMMETRICAL CRYSTAL These groups of platelike crystals, joined together in an irregular shape, are another

common type to fall in our snows. When they join to form conglomerate flakes, they can be mistaken at a distance for Stellar Crystals. The largest size to be seen is approximately ⅜ inch in diameter.

GRAUPEL Graupel are small pellets of snow, actually small Hexagonal Plate or Stellar Crystals that became coated with frozen droplets (rime) as they fell through

moisture-laden clouds. The shape of the original crystal is usually obscured or only partially visible. Graupel tend to fall in short concentrated showers within a longer snowstorm. When they hit the ground, they bounce off hard objects.

POWDER CRYSTALS This snow gets its name from its minute granular quality. It is known best by skiers, for since it does not pack, it makes good skiing. Although the crystals seem like small grains of snow, they are really minute col-

umns and plates connected to each other in irregular formations too small to be distinguished by the naked eye.

## *COMBINATION CRYSTALS*

The following are crystals that have started in one atmospheric condition and traveled through one or more different conditions before they land.

TSUZUMI CRYSTAL This is a Column Crystal with a Hexagonal Plate Crystal at either end; it is named after a type of Japanese drum that has a similar appearance.

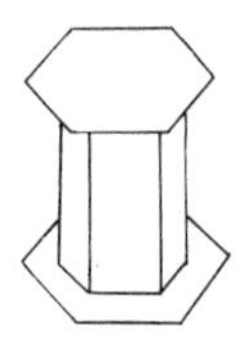

STELLAR HEXAGONAL PLATE CRYSTALS These are either Hexagonal Plate Crystals that went through Stellar Crystal cloud conditions, or Stellar Crystals that went through Hex-

agonal Plate cloud conditions. They are quite common and form some of the most spectacular crystal shapes.

BULLET CRYSTALS These are Column Crystals with hexa-

gonal pyramids at one end, joined together with others of the same type.

SPATIAL DENDRITE Spatial Dendrites are feathery Stellar Crystals with other points projecting at 90° angles from each of the six original points.

III

# *Wintering Trees*

Trees are plants that have evolved woody stems so that their leaves will be supported in the air, thus avoiding the competition for sunlight at ground level. As with all green plants, their first priority must be to place their leaves in sunlight, for the sun is the primal source of their energy. This striving to arrange leaves in light is most clearly shown in the winter trees. Here in the outlines of their bare branches hundreds of solutions are revealed, each species a distinct linear sculpture created jointly by the forces of light and life.

Two basic forms are immediately evident in the branching of trees. One is a single main trunk with branches radiating off it; the other, a trunk that splits above the ground into many smaller trunks. The first form is conical and pointed, like Cedars, Pines, and Spruces, the second spreading and rounded, like Oaks, Elms, and Sycamores.

Not all branches on a tree grow at the same rate. Some trees have two types of branches: long shoots, which grow quickly, forming large, long branches that create the basic pattern of the tree, and short shoots, which grow slowly, forming the smaller twigs that fill in the spaces between the branches and generally hold the leaves. The ratio of long shoots to short shoots and their placement determines much of the overall character of the tree; they make it seem full or open, heavy or delicate.

But the growth pattern of a tree and its particular arrangement of leaves in light is very elastic. It can be stretched, shrunk, pulled, or twisted, depending on its environment and the competition for sunlight. Trees in open fields may display their purest shapes in relation to light, but even there, a constant wind can stunt them. Forest trees are stretched tall, clear of branches until near the top, with a small flattened crown that carves a territory out of the forest canopy. Those at the edges of meadows, lakes, or rivers grow into the open space, leaning away from their competitors.

Besides this display of form, what is a tree doing in winter? How will it know when to put forth leaves in spring? Why did it drop them in the fall?

To plants, winter is a time of drought. Most water is frozen within the ground or above it as snow, and is therefore unavailable to them. Winter's drought lasts six months or more and is a serious condition to which plants must adapt.

Since the summer processes of food production and growth use tremendous amounts of water, they must stop in winter. These processes are centered in the leaf; therefore trees in temperate climates drop their leaves in fall and seal over the point of attachment with a corky layer. Even next year's leaves, neatly miniaturized in the winter buds, are covered over with moisture-conserving scales. Trees that keep their leaves, notably the evergreens, have adaptations which conserve water — thin or small needlelike leaves with waxy coatings.

But a tree doesn't just grow in summer and stop in winter; it continually alternates the parts of it that grow, channeling energy to some, withholding it from others.

For example, trees in summer have already grown their next year's leaves, neatly miniaturized and contained within scale-covered buds. In late summer the tree keeps these leaves from expanding and growing, while at the same time, maturing the present year's seeds and fruits.

Trees in winter must also control their growth. They must carefully time the opening of leaves and flowers in spring to avoid injury by heavy frost. To do this, they cannot rely solely on temperature or availability of water, for they might be "fooled" by late winter thaws. They must respond to more consistent measures, such as the timed break-down of chemicals within their cells, or the changing ratios of light to dark that reflect the solar season.

So the image of the wintering tree as a symbol of death and emptiness must itself die, for in reality, winter trees already contain the coming year's leaves and flowers, continually respond to light and temperature in the environment, and in their silhouettes, graphically represent the reaching out of life to absorb energy from the sun.

## *Key to Wintering Trees*

Trees are really not hard to identify in winter, especially if you concentrate on the most common ones first. When you have learned to recognize the six most common deciduous trees and the evergreen trees, you will know at least 80 percent of the trees found in most northern forests.

The first section lists the six most common deciduous trees and gives short descriptions and illustrations that will enable you to identify them. This is where to start; continue to find and identify these six and your ability to make distinctions between winter trees will keep improving.

When you know these trees well, pick a new tree that you often come across. Look at its buds, bark, and branching, and any other feature such as seeds or dead leaves. Then go to the list of remaining trees and find one whose important characteristics are the same as those of your tree. If for some reason you can't find it, don't despair; just remember the tree and try another.

When a leaf falls from a tree, a small mark, called the leaf scar, remains where the leaf was attached. Just above the recent leaf scars are small buds, which contain next year's leaves and flowers. These buds, called leaf buds or flower buds, are different for each tree, and are often used for identification in winter.

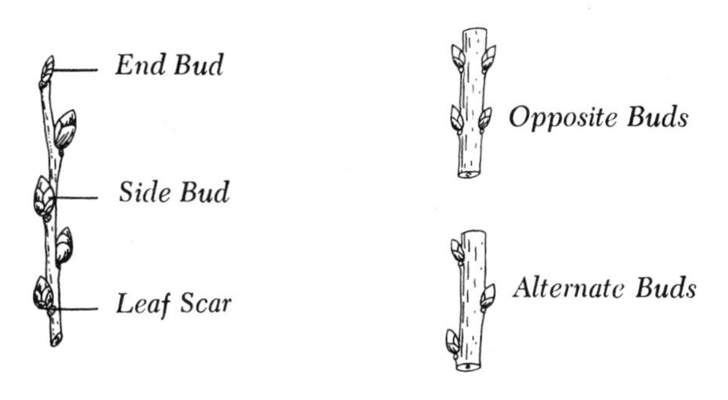


## *THE SIX MOST COMMON TREES*

OAK — Oak has clusters of four or more buds at the ends of its twigs. These buds usually vary in size. Oaks, especially younger trees, may also have brown, leathery leaves still attached to their branches all through winter.

MAPLE AND ASH — There are only four native trees in our northern woods with opposite branching — Dogwood, Buckeye, Maple, and Ash — and by far the most common are Maple and Ash. These two can be told apart by their distinctive end buds. Ash's end bud is dark and dome-shaped.

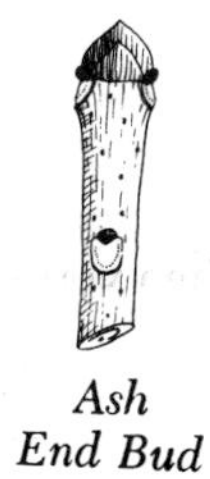

*Ash End Bud*

Maple buds are oval and between ¼ inch and ½ inch in length. No other opposite branching tree has buds that look like them except Buckeyes. Since Buckeye end buds are well over ½ inch long, it's easy to tell Buckeye and Maple buds apart.

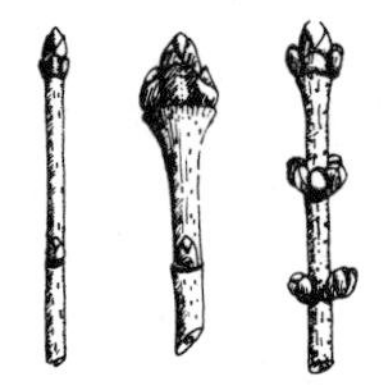

*Maple Twigs and End Buds*

BEECH — You can identify Beech by its buds or its bark. The buds are brown to beige, long, and pointed, unlike those of any other tree. Beech bark is light silver-gray, and smooth. Other trees may have smooth gray bark when young, but with age it splits and fissures, whereas Beech bark remains smooth even when the tree is old.

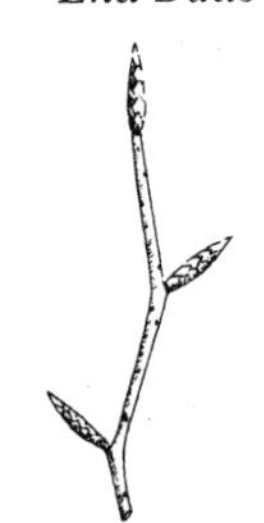

*Beech Buds*

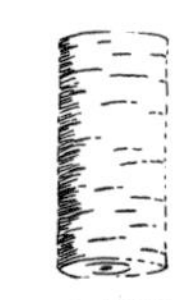

*Horizontal Lines on Birch Bark*

BIRCH — There are two ways to identify all Birches. One is by the long, thin horizontal lines that mark the bark; the other is by the catkins that hang from the tips of the upper branches. Some other trees have one or the other of these characteristics, but only Birches have both. The bark of some Birch trees is very white, that of others is silvery; still others have black bark.

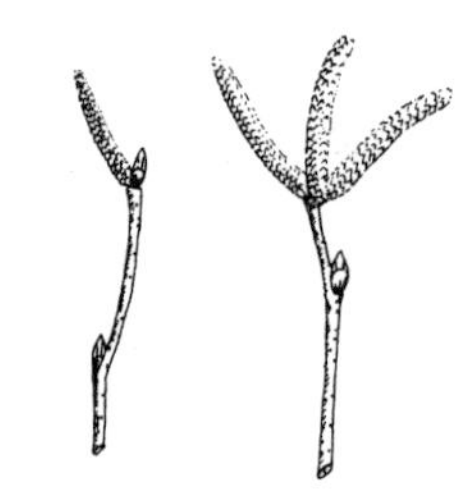

*Birch Catkins*

ASPEN — Two things will help you identify Aspens in winter. First, they grow as a group of small trees in a waste area or forest edge. Second, the smooth, light bark of their upper trunks has a greenish tinge. Where they grow is as important as what they look like, for Aspens typically like open sunny waste spaces such as old fields, the land along turnpikes, or old gravel pits and dumps. Here they quickly form small groups of short-lived trees, usually under 25 feet tall. Their light-colored, smooth bark with its greenish tinge, once recognized, is the most striking feature to help you identify them.

*Quaking Aspen Twig and Buds*

Aspen buds are variable in size, color and texture but always sharply pointed. Quaking Aspen has dark, shiny brown buds (see illustration), while Bigtooth Aspen has grayish downy buds.

## *TREES WITH NEEDLES OR CONES*

*Pine Needles*

*Cedar Needles*

PINE — Long, thin needles attached in bundles of 5, 3, or 2.

CEDAR — Small, scalelike needles arranged along twigs.

*Hemlock Needles*

HEMLOCK — Flat needles with two white lines on the underside. Short stem between needle and twig. Needles ± ½ inch long.

BALSAM FIR — Flat needles, slightly rounded at ends, with two white lines on the underside. No stem on needle. Needles ± 1 inch long.

SPRUCE — Generally, four-sided (not flat) needles. Needle sharply pointed.

LARCH — No needles on tree in winter, but small cones usually present. Stubby twigs on branches.

*Larch Cone and Branch*

The rest of the deciduous trees are listed in order, starting with the most common. Each of these trees has two characteristics listed next to it. To identify a tree, simply read the first characteristic listed next to each name until you find one that describes your tree. If the first feature given matches your tree, read the second also. If both match, then you have identified the tree. If a second characteristic is in parentheses, it means that the first clue is enough for positive identification.

## *TREES WITHOUT GREEN NEEDLES OR CONES*

ELM — Side buds placed off-center from leaf scar. (Trunk often divides into many other, smaller trunks.)

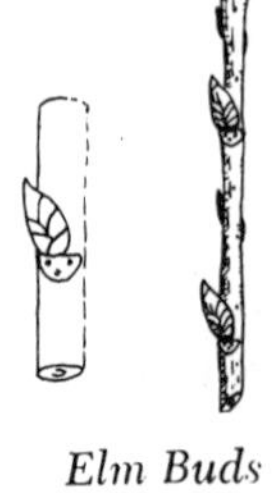

*Elm Buds*

*Branching of American Elm*

WILLOW — Single scale covers leaf buds. (Twigs colored yellow or orange.)

*Willow Buds*

CHERRY — Thick horizontal markings on dark bark of upper trunk and branches. Bark of young twigs tastes like stale cigars. (Just take a small taste.)

*Cherry Bark*

HICKORY — Large alternate leaf scars. End buds large and ovate (egg-shaped), or thinner and mustard yellow in color.

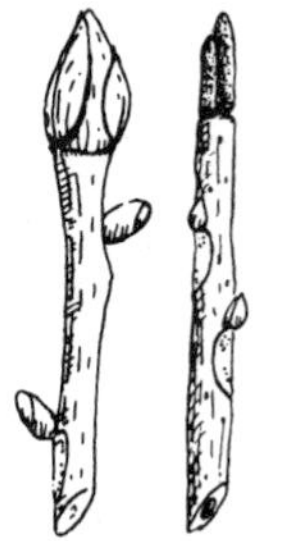

*Hickory End Buds*

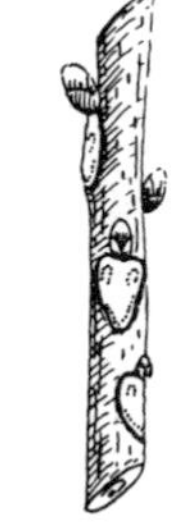

*Hickory Leaf Scars*

LOCUST — Thorns: small and paired on twigs, or long and branched on trunk. (Flattened bean pods on tree or on ground beneath.)

*Honey Locust Bean Pod*

*Black Locust Bean Pods*

BASSWOOD — Buds waxy red with only two scales covering each bud. (Seeds possibly still on tree.)

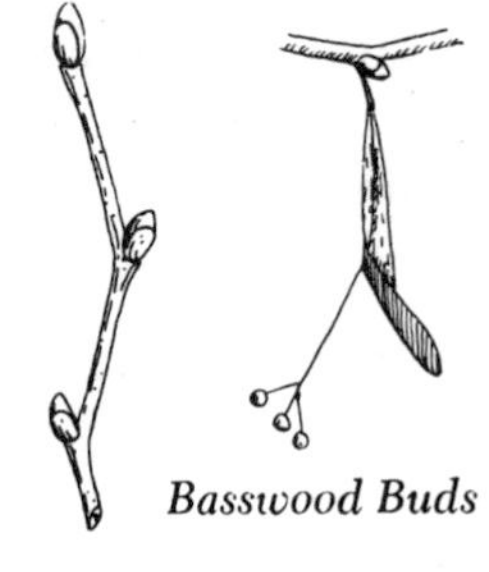

*Basswood Buds*

*Basswood Seeds*

SYCAMORE — Irregular patches of whitish bark under peeling, darker, outer bark. Seed balls handing off twig ends.

*Sycamore Seed Cluster*

POPLAR — Long, pointed end buds: sticky, or fragrant when rubbed. Alternate side buds diverge from twig.

*Poplar Buds*

TULIP TREE — Beige seeds arranged in flowerlike clusters on upper twigs. End buds dark green and flattened like a duck's bill.

*Tulip Tree Seed Cluster*

BUCKEYE — Opposite side buds. Large ovate end buds, more than ½ inch long.

*Buckeye Buds*

SASSAFRAS — Dark green twigs and end buds. Twigs have lemony odor when scratched or lemon taste when chewed.

*Sassafras Twig*

DOGWOOD — Opposite side buds and leaf scars. End buds shaped in either of two ways.

*Dogwood End Buds*

APPLE — Many 1-inch-long twigs that look like thorns. These short twigs have raised leaf scars or many lines encircling them.

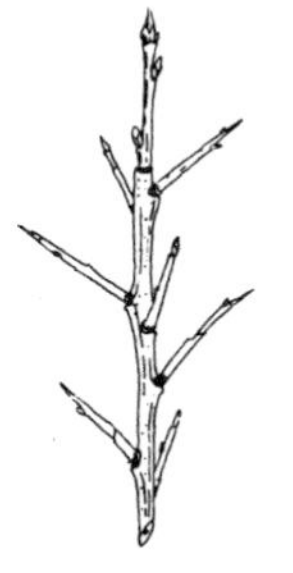

*Crabapple Twig* *Apple Twig*

HAWTHORN — Long, smooth, unbranched thorns. (Small, densely branched tree.)

*Hawthorn Thorns*

HOP HORNBEAM — Small catkins on upper branches, in groups of three. Bark has many thin, vertical, flaking strips.

*Hop Hornbeam Catkins*

HORNBEAM — Smooth, sinewy, dark gray bark on small tree; often more than one trunk together. Thin, polished, dark red twigs.

WALNUT — Large, alternate leaf scars. Furry moustache above leaf scar; or side buds downy, gray, and globular.

*Walnut Side Buds*

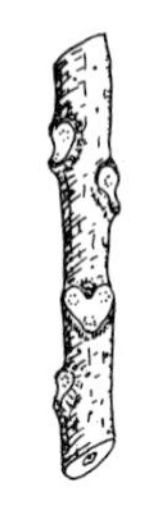

*Walnut Leaf Scars*

## *SHRUBS*

Although shrubs are too numerous to cover adequately in this guide, I have included Blueberry, Sumac, Alder, and Hobblebush because they are common in the North, and Witch Hazel because its fruit capsules are so outstanding.

High Bush Blueberry
*Vaccinium corymbosum*

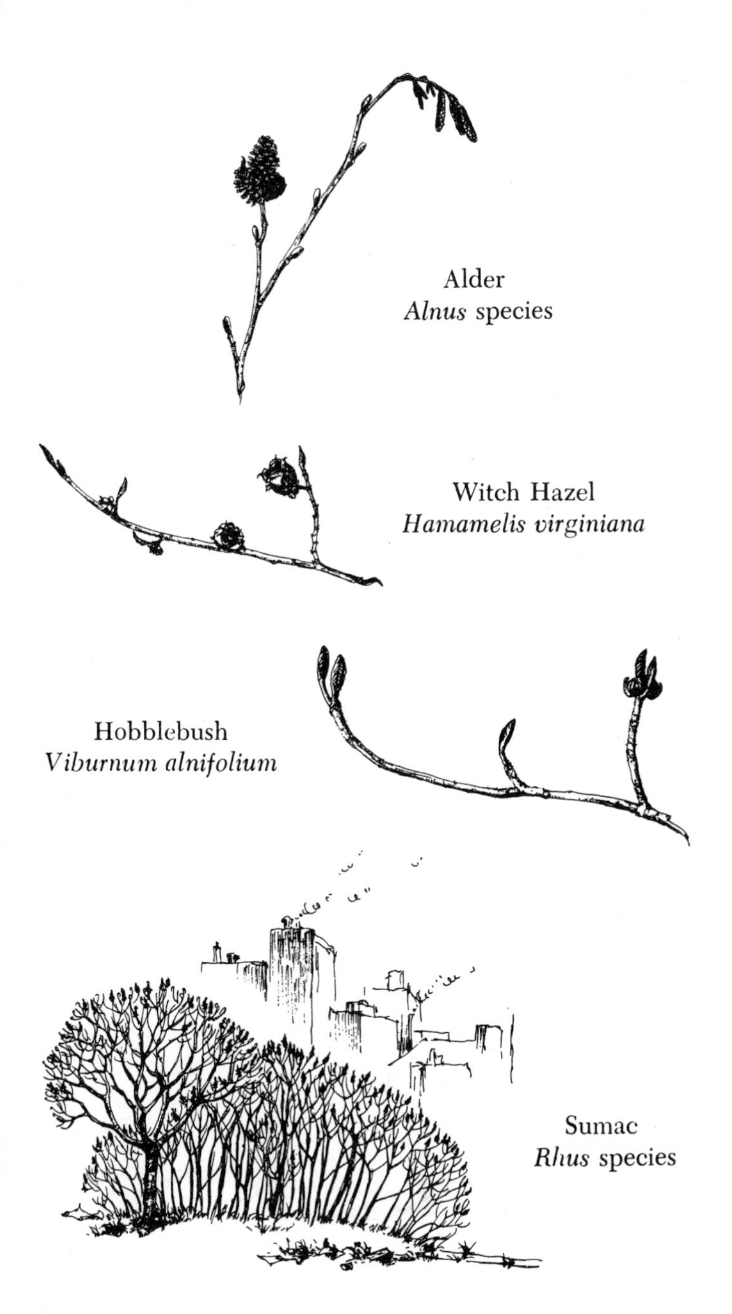
Alder
*Alnus* species
Witch Hazel
*Hamamelis virginiana*
Hobblebush
*Viburnum alnifolium*
Sumac
*Rhus* species

## Apple (*Malus* species)

Apple trees can be recognized by the short stubby twigs which line their branches. Called spurs, they grow only a fraction of an inch each year, providing sturdy support for

*Apple*

the heavy fruit. Lines closely encircle them, each one representing a year's growth. Cherry trees and other orchard trees also have spurs.

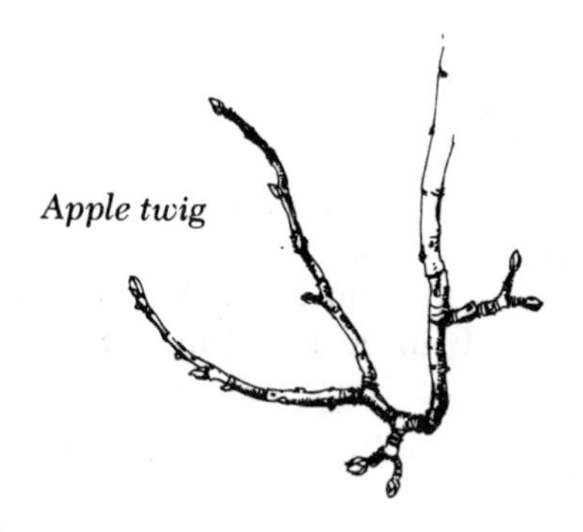

*Apple twig*

Our only native apple trees are the Crabapples. The trees that produce our market apples were brought from Europe by early settlers. Strangely enough, commercial Apple trees do not grow true from seed. In other words, if you plant a seed from a McIntosh apple, it will produce fruit slightly different from the McIntosh; they may be more tasty or, more likely, less so. Therefore, there are hundreds of varieties of Apples and Crabapples, only a few of which have worked their way into the stomachs of avid apple eaters. Many of these varieties have been discovered by chance, like the McIntosh Apple, which was discovered by John McIntosh in Ontario as he was clearing his forest. Other varieties have been produced through careful hybridization. When a good variety is found it must be continued by cuttings and graftings rather than by seeds.

Both wild and cultivated apples are enjoyed by wildlife.

*Crabapple with fruit*

When the fruit is ripe, Foxes, Deer, Raccoons, and birds come out of the woods to eat them. Insect larvae also feed on apples, and Yellow Jackets especially enjoy the rotting fruit.

Native Crabapples are small trees with fruit varying in quality almost always too sour to eat right off the tree, but always delicious when made into jellies. Sometimes their fruit hangs on the trees through the winter, and a Crabapple tree can startle the observer with its apparent abundance in the midst of the surrounding winter scarcity.

## Ash (*Fraxinus* species)

Ash trees, somewhat undistinguished-looking but extremely hardy, are one of the four common trees with opposite leaf buds and opposite branching. Their leaf scars are easily seen near the branch tips. Ashes grow well in average soils and usually grow scattered throughout a forest, rarely forming stands of more than a few trees.

Four species grow in the area covered by this guide, all very similar in appearance and each with a color name:

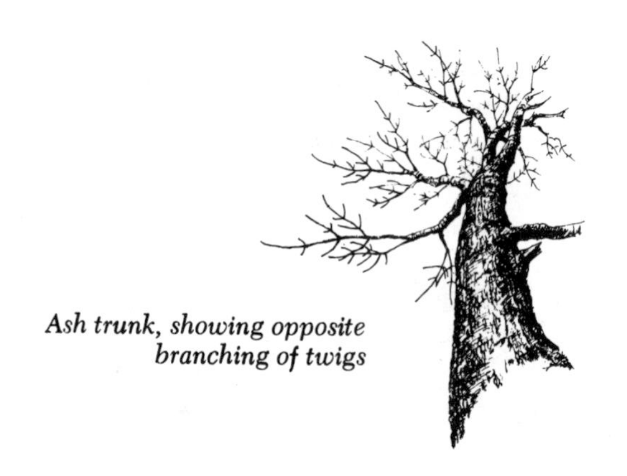

*Ash trunk, showing opposite branching of twigs*

White, Green, Blue, and Black Ash. Green and White Ash bear their male and female flowers on separate trees, whereas Blue and Black Ash often have both sexes on the same tree. The seeds, bearing attached wings, mature in the fall. They hang in clusters on the branches well into winter,

*Ash seeds*

and when falling twirl in the air like a one-bladed propeller. The wing slows the fall and allows more time for wind to disperse the seeds away from the parent plant.

Although abundant, Ashes have never been of more than

*Ash twig and buds*

moderate value to wildlife. However, Finches, Grosbeaks, and Cardinals do eat the seeds in fall and early winter; Beaver and Porcupine occasionally eat the bark, and Deer and Rabbits will chew a sapling's twigs down to mere nubs.

Where Ash comes closest to distinction is in the quality of its wood. Almost all wood sports equipment is Ash. Baseball bats, hockey sticks, tennis rackets, oars, snowshoes, skis, bowling alleys, and the handles of garden tools are all made of Ash. This is because Ash is light and strong, can take stress, and is just pliant enough to have some spring and resilience. Other woods, such as Oak and Hickory, may be stronger, but they are also heavier. Some of you may have Black Ash picnic baskets that belonged to your parents or grandparents. The American Indians taught the settlers how to pound Black Ash until it split along its growth rings, forming thin slats which could then be woven into strong baskets or backpacks. Ash grows quite rapidly, so the tree can actually be planted and harvested. This saves it from the fate of many other valuable hardwoods, which, being slow-growing and in great demand, do not replace themselves as quickly as they are methodically cut from within our forests.

## Aspen (*Populus grandidentata, Populus tremuloides*)

Eroded mountainsides, neglected fields, burned-over forests, and turnpike cloverleafs are among the areas Aspens regularly grow in. Over time, Aspens have evolved adaptations which enable them to claim lands too remote or too poor in soil for other trees.

In spring, hundreds of thousands of Aspen seeds mature on the trees, each seed weighing less than a millionth of a pound. Their light weight enables them to be blown to remote areas; their abundance increases the chances of survival. The seeds, dispersing long before those of other trees, land on wet and open soil of spring, easily germinating and getting a head start on the competition for sunlight.

*Aspen grove*

Aspens are a member of the Poplar genus, which is part of the Willow family. As such, they put forth the familiar furry silver growths in late winter, just like the Pussy Willow.

*Aspen winter buds and spring flowers*

These are actually flowers, the male and female flowers being borne on separate trees.

As young trees, Aspens grow rapidly reproducing by shoots from their roots as well as by seeds. The trees grow in dense stands that thin out with age. The stands rarely last more than eighty years, for the trees are very susceptible to attack by insects, bacteria, and fungi, and they do not thrive when shaded by taller trees.

Aspen wood is generally too weak and of small dimension to be useful as board lumber, but its abundance and rapid growth are in its favor. Today its main commercial uses are as pulpwood and as shredded wood to make fiberboard.

Aspen bark, though bitter, is the favorite food of Beavers, and after eating the bark they use the peeled, straight saplings in the construction of their dams and lodges. These

*Aspen bark*

peeled Aspen branches make light and sturdy walking sticks, and a beaver dam is a good place to collect one. Aspen bark and winter buds are also eaten by Grouse, Moose, Deer, and Rabbits.

Although Aspens in winter lack their refreshing summer leaves or their brilliant autumn color, they are still an inspiring sight, for the upper trunk and branches, now stripped of their foliage, reveal a light hue of green, which when increased by the dense stands, billows from forest edges like a spring haze.

## Balsam Fir (*Abies balsamea*)

A sure way to identify Balsam Fir is to crush a few of its needles in your hand and smell them. If they give off a rich

*Balsam Fir*

pungent odor that somehow reminds you of Christmas, then you are standing next to a Balsam Fir. It may in fact be in your living room covered with ornaments, it may be a single small green tree in a deciduous forest, or it may be just one of many kinds of conifers packed into the dense northern woods.

Tolerant of shade, Balsam Fir keeps many of its lower branches, forming one of the most perfectly symmetrical evergreens. This shape, along with the fact that Balsam keeps its needles well after being cut, has made it a favorite species for Christmas trees. Over four million Balsam Firs are cut annually, along with millions of Spruces and Pines, just for use during Christmas. But since most of these are raised on tree farms, the huge market does not deplete our natural forests.

Like those of Hemlock, Balsam needles are flat and have rows of stomata, appearing as two white lines, on the underside of each needle. The needles tend to be shorter on the top branches than they are lower down, and they stay on the tree for as long as eight years before being shed. Grouse sit on Balsam branches and eat the needles, whereas Moose and Deer browse the whole twig. The canopy of Balsam's lower branches forms a protected place for animals and birds to stay during severe weather.

Fir trees produce upright cones that are purple when young. Unlike those of other Conifers the cones drop their

*Balsam cones*

scales and release their seeds, leaving just a spike on the branch where the scales and seeds were attached. The seeds

have a single wing and are dispersed by the wind if the Crossbills, Squirrels, and Chipmunks don't eat them first. Firs occasionally reproduce vegetatively, when the lowest branches become covered with forest litter and send down their own roots.

If you get close to the trunk of a Balsam Fir you will see swellings in the young bark. They are called resin blisters; when broken by pressure, they release a clear fluid called Canada Balsam. This fluid is used commercially to mount microscope slides and to glue optical equipment, for when dry it has the same optical properties as glass. During forest fires these resin blisters burst into flames, adding to the rapid destruction of the trees.

As you go farther north, more and more gift shops try to sell you cushions and dolls stuffed with Balsam's fragrant needles, but these curios are only the merest hint of the natural odor which on a warm day can fill the air of the northern woods with its sunned fragrance.

## Basswood (*Tilia* species)

A feature of Basswood in fall and early winter is its ingenious aerodynamic seed. Hard and rounded, it is counterbalanced beneath a leafy wing which spins as the seed falls. As with the winged seeds of Pine, Ash, Maple, and Tulip Tree, its purpose is merely to slow the seed's fall, allowing

*Basswood seeds*

time for the wind to move it slightly away from the parent plant. This is in contrast to the parachuted seeds of Sycamore, Poplar, and Willow, which are actually caught up by the wind and carried great distances. In late winter, when the seeds are not present, Basswood can still be easily identified by its bright red waxy buds. The buds are each covered by two rounded scales. They are pleasant-tasting and produce a thick, syrupy mixture in your mouth.

*Basswood*

Many parts of Basswood trees are useful. The flowers can be dried and used for tea or for scenting bathwater. The inner bark, when soaked free from the outer bark, forms long fibrous strands, which can be twined into rope or woven into mats and fishnets. The wood is light in color and weight, and perhaps it's best known for its use in the forms that hold comb honey.

Basswood's tall trunk and arching branches create pleasant shade, and this property, along with its fragrant blossoms, has led it to be extensively planted in city parks and backyard lawns. In the wilds, the tree is most often an isolated one growing among other deciduous hardwoods.

## Beech (*Fagus grandifolia*)

Groves of Beeches are at their best in winter, when sunlight reflecting off their smooth silver bark illuminates the forest space. On the younger trees, dried leaves often remain; drained of their green, they no longer catch the light, but

*Beech trunks*

they brighten as it passes through. In colonial times they were used to stuff mattresses, for they are long-lasting, springy, and softer than straw.

You may see nut husks dotting the tree's upper branches, or littering the snow beneath. The four-part husk is prickly and, when young, encloses a delicious triangular nut. You can gather the nuts in fall, but you mustn't be late, for birds

*Beech buds, husks, and nuts*

and mammals soon strip them from the trees. A large crop of nuts is produced every two to three years.

Pure stands of Beeches are common. They are created because Beeches, like Hemlocks, are tolerant of shade and themselves cause shady conditions unfavorable to most other saplings. Also, mature Beeches send up shoots from their lateral roots, producing many saplings that take over when older trees die. Deer may also help create Beech stands, for they leave Beech saplings alone while heavily browsing the buds of other saplings, such as Oak, Maple, Ash, and Birch.

We are lucky that such a majestic tree as the Beech has proved itself relatively useless as commercial wood.

## Birch (*Betula* species)

Birches are best known in winter by the horizontal markings on their tight-fitting bark. These markings, called lenticels, allow air to penetrate the bark into the inner growing layer

*Birches*

of the trunk. As Birches grow their bark fits more tightly, then stretches; the lenticels become stretched, and soon the pressure makes the bark peel off. The bark on each species of Birch peels differently: White Birch bark peels in large sheets of paper; Yellow Birch bark peels in small curling strips; and Sweet Birch bark hardly peels at all.

Birch bark is extremely durable and often lasts long after the wood has rotted away. Some small birds take advantage of this fact by pecking through the bark and hollowing out nest cavities in the rotted wood. Hollow cylinders of White Birch bark lying on the forest floor can be used as kindling for fires, the resin in them burning even after a heavy rain.

Look for catkins growing on the tips of the upper branches; they are small oblong growths occurring in one's, two's, or three's. In spring they will open and produce pollen to fertilize the female catkins. The clusters of seeds, which mature by fall, often last into winter. They are tightly

*Birch seeds*

packed into a conelike form; birds use them as a valuable winter food, and the wind disperses them over the snow's crust, making them appear like small stars in a snowy sky.

There are basically four Birches in the North. Two — White Birch and Gray Birch — have whitish bark. Gray Birch is also known as "Old-Field Birch" because of its habit of reforesting old abandoned fields. White Birch is also

*White Birch bark*

*Yellow Birch bark*

known as Paper Birch because of the quality of the bark, which can be written on and which peels off in large sections. These big pieces of bark were used by American Indians for canoes and by early settlers in their roofs. Yellow Birch has silvery bark, and its wood is the most valuable

*Sweet Birch bark*

commercially; it is favored for fine furniture because it is strong and takes a good finish. Sweet Birch has black bark and is named for the oil of wintergreen in its twigs. A mildly flavored tea can be made by steeping the young twigs in boiling water.

Birches are valuable winter food: Rabbits and Deer browse the twigs, Grouse eat the buds, and numerous small birds feast on the seeds.

## Buckeye (*Aesculus* species)

At the tips of Buckeye's sinuous branches are the largest end buds of all our northern trees. Their upward pointing betrays the habit of the tree's lush flowers, which in late spring are borne on upright spikes. Inside the brown, shiny bud

*Horsechestnut*

you will also find miniature palmate compound leaves, five leaflets radiating from the tip of a single stem like the fingers of your hand (thus the word "palm"-ate). A sticky substance on the buds' surface may help protect them from

*Buckeye bud*

insect invasion. The side buds are opposite each other, making Buckeye one of our four trees with opposite buds.

Perhaps the most familiar feature of Buckeyes is their shiny mahogany-colored seeds. Normally three of these are produced in each green husk. When it drops in autumn, the husk splits into three parts, revealing the seeds. On each seed there is a round gray scar called the "hilum." It marks the place where nourishment was passed between the seed and the tree, and its shape reminded someone of a buck's eye — thus the tree's name. (Acorns also have conspicuous hila where they were attached to their caps.) The Buckeye seeds can be found beneath the tree during fall and winter thaws.

Although it is obviously rich in starch, the seed is rarely eaten by wildlife, possibly because it contains esculin, a glucoside (plant sugar) poisonous to most animals. People

*Buckeye nut and husk*

have been known to use the seeds for ground meal after extensive leaching in water, and I have noticed Squirrels peeling them, eating only the area around the hilum. Although inedible for humans, they certainly are attractive, so smooth to the touch and shiny to look at. It is hard to leave the tree without a few of them in your pocket.

There are at least three species of Buckeyes in the north. The Yellow Buckeye (*Aesculus octandra*) and Ohio Buckeye (*Aesculus glabra*) are two native trees that grow near the southern Great Lakes. Horsechestnut (*Aesculus hippocastanum*) is an alien member of the Buckeyes, native to Asia and introduced here from Europe. It is often planted as a shade tree and is now common in the eastern half of North America.

## Cedar (*Juniperus virginiana, Thuja occidentalis*)

Neither Eastern Red Cedar nor Northern White Cedar is actually a Cedar, nor are they in the same genus. Nevertheless, they are often grouped together because of their names and outward similarity. Both are evergreens, are shaped like spires, and have small scalelike leaves distinct from those of our other evergreen trees. But this is where the similarity stops.

*Red Cedars*

Eastern Red Cedars, *Juniperus virginiana,* are sun-loving trees that soon die when overshadowed. Their small blue berries are eaten by mice and birds, which then disperse the seeds as undigested remains of their droppings. Therefore, Red Cedar is found scattered across fields where mice have runways and placed along fencerows where birds often perch. Once dispersed, the seeds take two or three years to germinate. Cedars grow slowly and are most often seen dotting the poorer soil of neglected fields.

The male and female "flowers" of Red Cedar are often on separate trees. The female flowers produce light blue fleshy cones, which look like berries and are fragrant when crushed. The cones last through fall, forming an important source of winter food. Grosbeaks, Finches, and various mice eat them; the Cedar Waxwing even gets its name from its love of the fruit.

The foliage of Red Cedars is of two kinds: square scales pressed close to the twig and short projecting sharp needles.

*Red Cedar needles and berries*

In open sunlight the foliage is dense and forms a thick cover for many animals. Mockingbirds, Sparrows, and Robins nest in its cover. These nests are then reused as winter homes for Deermice, which cover them over with soft plant fibers. The foliage is also excellent for roosting. Juncos or Sparrows may stay there during the night or through severe winter storms.

Red Cedars can live to be three hundred years old. Their longevity is usually explained by the resistance of their wood to insect attacks and fungal decay. The red wood has a fragrance familiar to those who have stored clothes in cedar chests or spread cedar chips in the bottom of a hamster cage. Pencils used to be made only with Red Cedar, but the tree is now so scarce that manufacturers have switched to the Western Incense Cedar.

Red Cedar is very susceptible to fire, for it has a shallow root system that is easily hurt by the heat, and its thin bark is very flammable. The bark, easily pulled from the tree in long thin wisps, makes an excellent kindling for campfires, and if only the outer layers are taken, the tree is not damaged. In the Northeast, Red Cedars are often found with large areas of their trunk bark shredded off. The culprits are Red Squirrels, which use the peeled bark to insulate the inner layer of their leafy nests.

In contrast to the Red Cedar, the Northern White Cedar, or Arborvitae (*Thuja occidentalis*), often forms dense stands, especially at the borders of swampy land. It is more common than Red Cedar in the North and an important member of the rich and varied northern conifer forests. Its foliage, rich green sprays of flattened scales, creates a dense form, shaped much like the spade on a deck of cards. The needles, when crushed, give off a strong pungent odor. White-tailed Deer browse these leaves and twigs so heavily that often the trees are trimmed clean as high as a deer can reach.

Arborvitae is also a slow-growing tree, but it has a tough fire-resistant bark that is easily distinguished from that of Red Cedar. Since the wood resists rotting and splits easily along growth rings, it is used for roof shingles. The Indians used to use it for the frames of their canoes.

*Northern White Cedar*

In further contrast with the Red Cedar, White Cedar has a cone with winged seeds. These cones are produced in

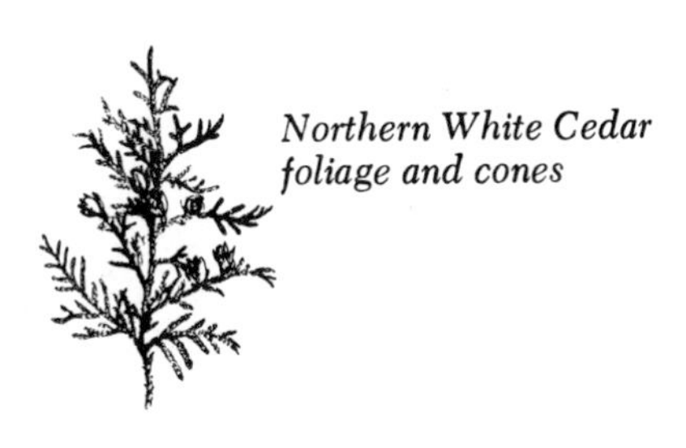
*Northern White Cedar foliage and cones*

large numbers every three to five years, and are extensively eaten in winter by Finches.

## Cherry (*Prunus* species)

Horizontal lenticels, so characteristic of Birches, are present on the bark of Cherry trees also. Cherries can be told from Birches in winter by the lack of catkins on their upper branches and by their straight rather than zigzag twigs.

Two other phenomena aid in identifying Cherry trees: the old webbed nests of leaf-eating caterpillars and a fungal distortion of the twigs. Both the Tent Caterpillar and Fall Webworm eat the leaves of Cherries, building protective webs as they do so. By winter these nests appear as disheveled masses of webbing, and from a distance they are often mistaken for birds' nests. The growth called Black Knot is also common; it appears as a black warty mass surrounding twigs or branches. It is caused by a fungus whose growth kills cells and distorts the branches.

Cherries vary widely in form, depending on their habitat. Reaching for sunlight within forests, they produce tall, branchless trunks, whereas in open fields their growth is stunted, the trunk dividing into many gnarled branches.

*Cherry*

There are basically three species of Cherries found in the area covered by this guide: Chokecherry, often only a shrub, favoring forest edges; Pin Cherry, which grows to 50 feet in height; and Wild Black Cherry, a forest tree, which grows the largest of the three.

*Black Cherry bark*

Wild Black Cherry is the woodworker's delight; its strong, fine-grained wood, with a red color that darkens with age and a surface that takes high-quality finishes, is rivaled among American hardwoods only by Black Walnut. Up to 1900, Cherry was still plentiful and used for common objects, but now the best lumber trees have been methodically cut from the forests, making good-sized Cherry trees scarce, so that Cherry wood is used only in expensive items.

*Black Cherry twig and two Pin Cherry twigs*

In summer, Cherry trees produce hundreds of fruits, each usually with a large pit and thin layer of surrounding flesh. Birds, including Robins, Waxwings, Crossbills, and Grosbeaks, seem to cease all other eating habits in order to gorge themselves on the barely ripened fruit. The combination of a fruit so attractive to wildlife and the indigestible quality of the pit adds up to a foolproof method of seed dispersal. Birds fly away and disgorge the pits, while mammals excrete them in their feces. With varying amounts of work and sugar, the fruits of all three varieties of Cherries can be made into fine jams and preserves.

## Dogwood, Flowering (*Cornus florida*)

The distinct and upturned flower buds on Dogwood in winter are a promise of the delicate, subtle beauty the tree puts out in spring, lining the borders between fields and woods with a fringe of white. Flowering Dogwood always favors these woodland margins as well as the understory of open forests. The tree is not as common in the North as most would wish it to be, being replaced by numerous shrubby relatives.

The flowers develop into bunches of red berries by late

*Flowering Dogwood*

fall, which are an important wildlife food, some of them lasting into the winter. Squirrels, Grouse, Turkeys, Cardinals, and Grosbeaks are the main northern consumers. The twigs and bark are eaten primarily by Rabbits.

The wood of the Flowering Dogwood is one of the hardest and heaviest woods in North America; it has the special quality of becoming very smooth with continued use. These qualities, plus the fact that the trees are rarely large enough for board lumber, created the custom of using Dogwood to

*Dogwood leaf and flower buds*

make shuttles for weaving. When weaving machines began to be used, Dogwood was even more valuable, for it could withstand the increased impact stress the machines inflicted on the shuttles. The same qualities made the wood useful for pulleys, sled runners, and hayforks. Today plastic shuttles and metal replace its former uses.

## Elm (*Ulmus* species)

Few trees have as close an association with summer's ease as the American Elm; its tall trunk divides 20 feet above the ground into many large arching branches, providing a huge area of filtered shade as well as plenty of space beneath the

*American Elm*

tree in which to enjoy it. These features, along with the graceful sway of the Elm's branches, has earned it a place in thousands of parks and along even more town and city streets.

But actually there are two other Elms that do not have this form and are thus often neglected: they are the Rock, or Cork, Elm (*Ulmus thomasii*) and the Red, or Slippery, Elm (*Ulmus rubra*). Of the two the Slippery Elm has received more attention, because of the properties of its light-colored inner bark. This slippery but pleasant-smelling bark used to be stripped off the trees in spring, dried in the sun, and ground up. The powder was then applied to reduce inflammation from cuts and sores. The inner bark also was chewed.

The Cork Elm gets its common name from the corky ridges of bark that often run the length of its inner twigs.

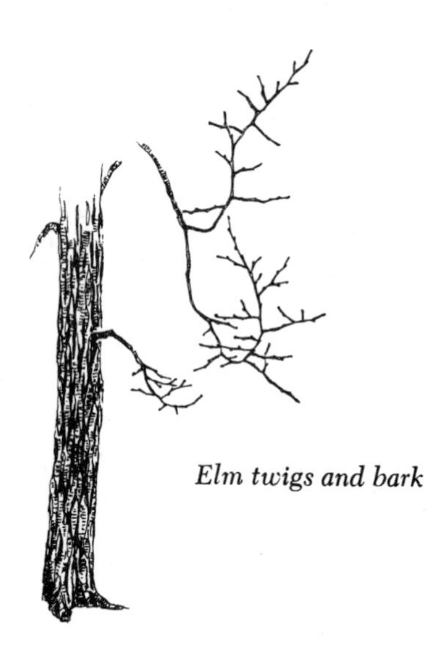

*Elm twigs and bark*

The tree has markedly drooping branch tips. It is not common on the East Coast, but it is frequently found on uplands from Western New England into the Great Lakes area.

Elm seeds are an important early spring food for birds and squirrels. Deer eat the twigs and buds in winter. The strong pendant tips of Elm branches are a favorite spot for Orioles to construct their hanging nests.

*Dead Elm*

In the 1930s a fungus, already known in Europe as *Ceratostomella ulmi,* found its way to this continent. It grew on Elms, killing them, and came to be known as Dutch elm disease. It is spread by a native engraver beetle, which feeds on Elms. As the beetle flies to new trees, it carries the fungal spores with it, facilitating their entry into the wood by its own habits of boring holes through the bark. Despite attempts to stop the fungus, it spread rapidly and wiped out thousands of Elms throughout the continent. Since Elm was the only planted tree on the streets of many towns in New England, the disease had a particularly devastating effect on these streets — once covered and kept cool by grand arcades of Elms, now bare and baked by the summer sun.

So common are the dead or dying trees that a particular woody mushroom, *Polyporus conchifer,* that lives on them has also become common. It is pure white and about the size and shape of a bottle cap. You can often find it on a fallen twig on the sidewalk, and in that setting it is like a symbol, pointing to both the Elm's popularity among humans and the wild tree's potential extinction.

## Hawthorn (*Crataegus* species)

The word "haw" is Anglo-Saxon for "fence" or "hedge" and is certainly well placed in the name of Hawthorns, for not

*Hawthorns*

only have the trees been used for centuries in Europe as hedges between fields, but they also tend to grow along fences, for birds void the seeds there after eating the bright red berries. The tree also typically grows in old fields because of further distribution by birds.

What makes Hawthorns valuable as hedges are their strong and dangerously sharp thorns, which line the branches. Birds find the trees ideal for nesting, well protected from Raccoons, Squirrels, snakes, and other egg eaters. Why some trees develop thorns and others don't is certainly a good question. Thorns don't protect the berries from birds, nor do they keep Rabbits from eating the bark, Deer from browsing on the twigs, or insects from eating the leaves. Thorns would keep Squirrels, Raccoons, and other

*Thorns and Rabbit-chewed bark of Hawthorn*

medium-sized mammals from climbing the tree for the berries or leaves, but this is about all. Thorns may have evolved when the tree had different needs and may now remain simply as a vestige.

There are hundreds of varieties of Hawthorns in eastern North America. There is a great deal of variety in the taste and quality of Hawthorn berries; some are considered edible right off the tree, others, by far the majority, inedible. In any case, it is commonly agreed that most, when boiled down and sweetened, make some of our best wild fruit jellies and marmalades.

## Hemlock (*Tsuga canadensis*)

Hemlocks are shade-loving trees, often found on north-facing slopes along river gorges. In mature stands, they create such dense shade that only their own seedlings can

*Hemlock*

survive. These groves remain nothing but Hemlocks until man, disease, or fire alters their condition enough to enable other trees to invade. This is one type of climax forest — a forest that will normally regenerate itself and will not allow the invasion of new plant types.

The underside of every Hemlock needle is marked with two white lines, composed of hundreds of tiny openings into the leaf. These openings, called stomata, close and open as they regulate the flow of air and water vapor in and out of the leaf. All leaves have stomata, but in Hemlock they are grouped in such a way as to be visible.

Hemlock trees are not what poisoned Socrates. There are

a number of unrelated plants of the carrot family, also called Hemlock, which are highly poisonous, but this tree's buds and needles are edible, and although not very tasty, can be used to make a weak tea. Grouse and Rabbits eat these buds and needles; Deer also strip young saplings of their greenery, depending on it as a winter staple when other food is covered by snow.

Hemlock cones are another source of wildlife food. Growing at the ends of twigs, they are less than 1 inch long and contain two winged seeds under each of their scales. They open in dry, cold weather and close at other times. Both Red Squirrels and Deermice chew off the scales to get at the

*Hemlock needles*

*Hemlock cones*

seeds; the Red Squirrel scatters the scales as it eats, while the Deermouse leaves them in a neat little pile on the snow. Many birds depend on the seeds for food in winter.

A common winter resident in Hemlock trees in certain localities is the Porcupine. It may climb a Hemlock and stay there for weeks, eating the bark and chewing off large twigs. These twigs strewn over the snow are a sure sign of the animal's presence; they are also valuable to Deer as winter browse which they otherwise could never have reached.

Because Hemlocks like shade, their lower branches live for many years. Even after they die they remain on the tree, collecting sap where they join the trunk. These pitch knots are so hard they can chip saw blades, making many Hemlocks useless as lumber.

In the 1800s Hemlock bark furnished the raw material for an entire industry. It contains great amounts of tannin, an oil used to tan leather. Large 4-foot squares were stripped off the trees, girdling them and causing them to die. Since Pine, which was abundant, was a more serviceable wood, Hemlocks were left to rot by the hundreds of acres. Today, with the development of synthetic tanning agents, Hemlock bark is no longer used.

## Hickory (*Carya* species)

The most distinctive and prevalent Hickory is the Shagbark. Its trunk bark splits off in large, gray arcs, making the tree clearly shaggy in appearance. Once you have seen it, there is no mistaking it thereafter.

*Shagbark Hickory*

The forces that cause its bark to split are common to all trees. Trees grow new bark under the old, pushing it outward. Every species of tree reacts differently to this outward pressure, depending on the structure of its bark. Shagbark

*Shagbark Hickory bark*

Hickory sloughs off its outer bark at a very young age and in larger pieces than any of our other northern trees. Its common name is obviously well chosen.

There are basically four types of Hickories in the area of this guide: Shagbark, Pignut, Mockernut, and Bitternut, each having a distinctive end bud and all having large shield-shaped leaf scars. As their names imply, they all produce nuts. These nuts are characteristically enclosed in a four-part husk, which splits when the nut is ripe, unlike walnuts, which have a leathery husk which doesn't split. The smooth shell of Hickory nuts varies in thickness with the different species, Shagbark having the thinnest shell as well as a tasty and edible nut. The other species are thick-shelled, so they are less valuable to wildlife.

*Shagbark Hickory bud and leaf stem*

*Shagbark Hickory nut and husk*

Perhaps one of the best-known uses of Hickory wood is in smoke-curing ham products such as bacon and ham. The green, unseasoned wood is used, but the dry, seasoned wood is also an excellent fuel wood, and it is claimed that a cord of Hickory is equal to a ton of coal in the amount of heat energy it can produce.

## Hop Hornbeam (*Ostrya virginiana*)

Hop Hornbeam is probably a tree name that few have heard of before, yet the tree is common in the areas included in this guide. It usually grows as an isolated tree under the canopy of taller Maples, Beeches, and Birches,

*Hop Hornbeam*

and is easy to recognize by its bark and small size. The bark is composed of thin rectangular overlapping strips, slightly curving outward at their bottom ends.

Also distinctive on the tree in winter are its male flowers,

*Hop Hornbeam bark*

called catkins. Their presence shows the tree's relationship to Birches, which also have winter catkins, although Birch bark is very different from that of Hop Hornbeam. In spring the catkins release pollen, fertilizing the female catkins. Hop Hornbeam's unusual seed cases develop in the fall and look somewhat like Hops — thus that part of the tree's name.

*Hop Hornbeam seeds and catkins*

The seeds are encased in separate light tan envelopes and dispersed by being blown across the snow's surface.

Although the wood is one of the hardest and strongest known, the tree is never large or common enough to be used for its wood. The seeds are also too few to be of value to wildlife.

Hop Hornbeam is a beautiful tree in winter; its finely divided bark, dark red twigs, and lanternlike seed casings that ornament the lower branches always make it a rewarding find in the winter woods.

## Hornbeam (*Carpinus caroliniana*)

Between the canopy of leaves formed by tall hardwood trees and the shrub layer that is close to the forest floor is the understory. It is an ecological niche to which the American Hornbeam is perfectly adapted. It loves moist soil, and its trunk branches freely close to the ground, forming a crown that is flat-topped and spreading. This branching pattern distributes its leaves laterally so that they can make the most of the dappled light that filters through the forest canopy.

*Hornbeam bark*

This understory, also filled in with Dogwoods and shade-tolerant saplings of other trees, is a protected environment — sheltered from the heat and drying action of the sun,

*Hornbeam seeds and twigs*

from pelting rainstorms, and from wind. It is an ideal place for birds' nests and insect development; it also provides berries, seeds, browse, and leaves for mammals, birds, and insects.

Hornbeam, Birch, and Hop Hornbeam all belong to the Birch family (*Betulaceae*). They have similar twigs, but the seeds and bark of all three are very different. Hornbeam seeds are in a cluster, each having its own wing, like those of Maple seeds. Its bark, hard and smooth, lacks the horizontal lenticels of Birch and the vertical strips of Hop Hornbeam, and of the three it is the only one without catkins in winter.

## Larch (*Larix laricina*)

All summer, the Larches have looked like evergreens, covered from top to bottom with bunches of soft gray-green needles. But in fall the trees turn a golden yellow and drop all their needles as if they had been hit by a blight. Since we are used to coniferous (cone-bearing) trees being evergreen, the Larch looks dead — but it's not. The Larch is our one deciduous (leaf-shedding) coniferous tree.

The needles in summer grow in bunches out of stubby twigs similar to the fruit spurs of Apple trees. These spurs are very visible in winter, so they make identification easy. The small cones, when they have opened to release seeds, look like woody flowers, growing upright along the branches.

Larch displays an ordered pattern of growth in winter. It has a single excurrent (undivided) trunk off which grow

*Larch grove*

long shoots, the main structural branches. Off these grow short shoots, the fillers, and off these the spurs and then the needles. Excurrent growth makes it well suited for lumber. Larch is durable, too, when in contact with earth or water.

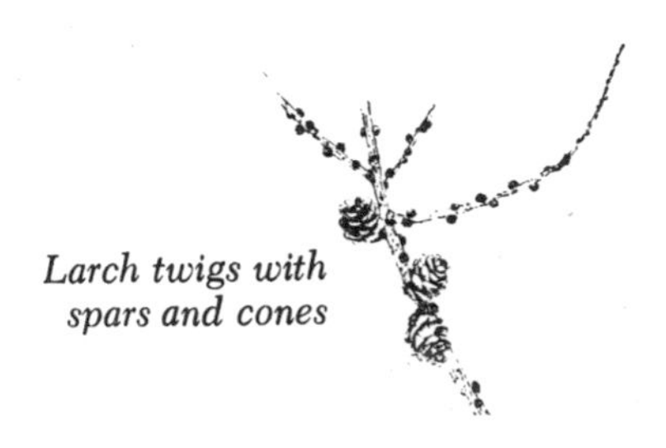
*Larch twigs with spars and cones*

It has been commercially used for posts, railroad ties, doorsills, and boat keels.

In the coniferous forests of the northern woods, Larches often form tight groves, especially around moist, boggy areas. As winter comes and they drop their needles, these groves seem like holes or vacuums in the dense fabric of the impenetrable evergreens.

## Locust (*Robinia pseudoacacia, Gleditsia triacanthos*)

Even though they are not directly related, Honey Locust and Black Locust are grouped together here, because they are the only arboreal (tree) members of the Legume family in the area of this guide. Legumes are mainly characterized by their production of pods containing seeds. Of course, all

*Black Locust*

of the vegetables we call beans are in the Legume family, too. The pods of Black Locust are 3 to 4 inches long and

*Black Locust seedpods*

contain 4 to 8 small black, poisonous seeds. The pods of Honey Locust are up to 18 inches long and have large round seeds surrounded by a sweet-tasting gummy pith. The pods of both Locusts hang on the trees in winter, the Black Locust pods lasting till spring, the Honey Locust pods littering the ground on early winter. Black Locust is insignificant as wildlife food, and Honey Locust pods and seeds are eaten only by cattle and a few squirrels.

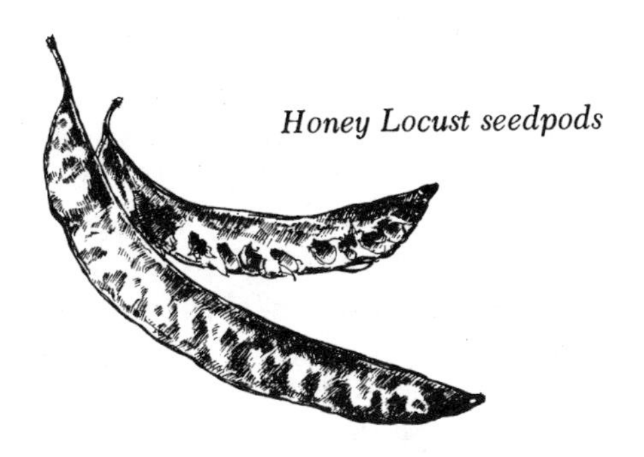

*Honey Locust seedpods*

The Black Locust is very important, however, as a reclaimer of strip-mined areas and other ravaged land. Its extensive fibrous root system and ability to send up suckers after its first five years of growth enable it to hold run-off water effectively and prevent erosion. It also attracts certain bacteria, which, in cooperation with the roots, absorb nitrogen from the air within the soil and incorporate it into the plant matter. This is an important process for all living things, for although nitrogen is the major constituent of the atmosphere and an essential part of every protein and amino acid, we, along with most higher plants and animals, have no way of directly absorbing nitrogen, so we depend on these bacteria to absorb nitrogen and make it available to plants, which in turn make it available to us.

In the process of absorbing nitrogen, the Black Locust rejuvenates soil in which nitrogen compounds have been leached away. Honey Locust, however, does not have this ability.

Both of these trees have scientific names that honor fa-

*Honey Locust trunk thorns*

mous botanists associated with them. Both were named by Linnaeus around 1750, *Robinia* for Jean and Vespasien Robin, who had been botanical explorers for the kings of France in the previous century and who introduced Black Locust into Europe, *Gleditsia* for Johann Gottlieb Gleditsch, a well-known botanist in Germany at the time of Linnaeus.

Both Locusts have spines, but you have to look closely to see the small, often opposite, thorns on Black Locust twigs. The thorns on Honey Locust are huge and forked, covering the branches and often lining the trunk in a gruesome manner.

## Maple (*Acer* species)

Almost every part of the Maple is used by wildlife as food. Beavers and Porcupines chew the bark. Rabbits and Hares, Deer and Moose browse the twigs and winter buds. Buds as well as flowers are eaten by Grosbeaks, Purple Finches, Nuthatches, and Grouse; and the seeds are stripped of their wings and stored as winter food by Squirrels and Chipmunks. Besides these food uses, the stalks of the seeds and leaves are used by birds in the construction of their nests.

As food for people, the Maples are not half as productive, but what they do produce is well-known to people of all ages. It is, of course, maple sugar and syrup, made from the

*Sugar Maples with maple syrup buckets*

spring-rising sap. The sap is water absorbed by the roots and mixed with some of the stored sugars of the trees. Sap runs best on warm days that are preceded by freezing nights; depending on the latitude, these conditions can occur at any time from the first of the year to late spring.

It was the American Indians who first taught the early settlers about taking sap from trees. Since water from the roots travels up the outer portion of the trunk, a hole ½ inch in diameter must be drilled 3 inches into the tree. The hole must slant downward, so that the sap will flow out. A short length of pipe is placed snugly in the hole, and a bucket is hung beneath it. An average tree can easily feed two taps; they will release more than 20 gallons of sap in one spring. That amount will boil down to about two quarts of syrup, and, with more boiling, about 3 or 4 pounds of sugar. All maples can produce good sap in some quantity; there is as much variation in sugar content within one species as there is between species. Even so, 90 percent of the trees tapped are Sugar Maples.

Maple lumber is traditionally divided into two types:

hard maple, from Sugar and Black Maples, and soft maple, from Red and Silver Maples. The hard Maples are by far the most important commercially. Wood from Sugar Maple is even lighter, stronger, and stiffer than that of White Oak, and has been used extensively since early colonial times for tools, furniture, floors, and musical instruments. Some Sugar Maples have a curving grain which produces the highly prized bird's-eye, or curly, maple. Wood of the soft Maple group is less resilient and splits easily, so it is not used commercially.

*Red Maples*

The most common Maple of eastern and central northern America is the Red Maple. Thriving in low swampy areas and near lakes and streams, it often forms pure stands. It is well-named, for in early spring it puts forth clusters of red flowers followed by leaves with red stems; then in fall the leaves turn a brilliant scarlet and, after dropping, reveal red twigs and red leaf and flower buds. Their color lasts all winter and somehow symbolizes a promise of their blooming and the distant return of spring.

## Oak (*Quercus* species)

No other tree provides as much for as many as do the Oaks.

Their rich fall harvest of acorns feeds many of our north-

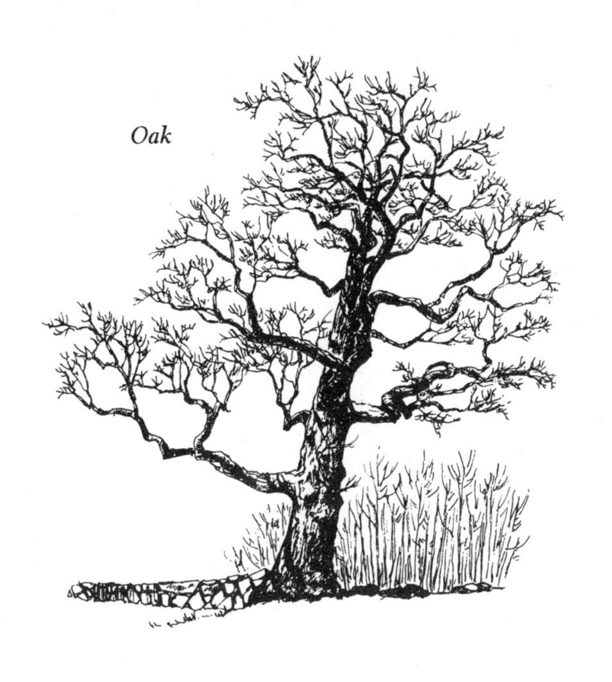
*Oak*

ern animals. Most birds, including the Ruffed Grouse, Blue Jay, Nuthatch, and Titmouse, just eat the nut after pecking open the shell, but the Wild Turkey eats them whole, consuming up to 50 in one meal. Large mammals such as Bears, Deer, and Raccoons also depend on acorns in winter, but the real consumers are the Squirrels. The Red, Gray, and Fox Squirrels all store tremendous hoards of acorns in the fall as winter reserves. The Gray Squirrel's habit of burying nuts singly and forgetting to eat some of them places the

*Acorns*

seeds in a perfect position for germination, protected from freezing in winter, and planted a few inches under the soil. It is suspected that a considerable number of our northern Oaks have grown from plantings such as these.

Numerous kinds of insects also find food and protection within the Oaks. Insects produce over 300 types of Oak galls, many easily seen in winter on the buds, twigs, and dead leaves. Looking like a tan Ping-Pong ball, the Oak Apple Gall hangs on the tree through the winter. It is made on the vein of a leaf by a wasp. Bullet Galls are another common winter sight — small, hard, gray spheres attached to the new twigs. (See Chapter 4.)

*Young Oak with dried leaves remaining on it*

While living Oaks are quite resistant to fungi, dead Oaks are havens for the hungry roots of wood-destroying fungi. Dead trunks and isolated limbs are frequently lined with the colorful concentric rings of the Turkey Tail fungus, or the purple gills of *Polyporus pergamenus*, or the mazelike pattern of *Daedalia quercina*. (See Chapter 6.)

Where Oak limbs fall off, insects and fungi eat into the heartwood, forming soft cavities. These are then hollowed out by Woodpeckers searching for insects or making nests. After being abandoned by the Woodpecker, these holes are reused either by other birds such as Owls, Starlings, and Chickadees, or by Squirrels as their winter home.

We also have come to the Oak for many of these same reasons. The Indians harvested the acorns to grind into flour; the early settlers used the galls and bark to make ink and dyes, while also using the bark's tannic acid to tan leather. And of course, to this day, the wood of the Oak has been one of our most valued and durable, extensively used for boats, floors, barrels, tools, and furniture.

The Oak, whether living or dead, seems to attract life to itself by its ability to produce food and homes for a large range of living things, from humans to animals to birds to insects to fungi.

## Pine (*Pinus* species)

The Pine is one of the first seed-bearing trees to have evolved; pines existed before the age of dinosaurs. Today they grow in many parts of North America, their form relatively unchanged for over 250 million years. This consistency is due to a flexibility in adaptation that has enabled

*Pines*

Pines to survive the changing climates and natural catastrophes that are so much a part of geologic time.

Their needle-shaped leaves are among their adaptations. Minimized surface area and wax coating cut down on evaporation and shed the weight of snow, helping the tree to survive in cold climates. The needles stay on the trees for 3 to 5 years and are replaced by new ones that grow at the tips of the branches.

Some species of Pine have adapted in relation to fire. The

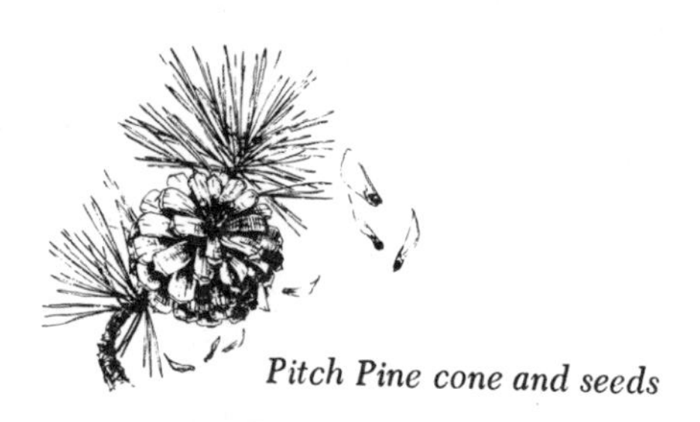

*Pitch Pine cone and seeds*

White and Red Pines both have a thick outer bark, which insulates the sensitive growth cells within the trunk from the killing heat. The Jack Pine, and to a lesser extent the Pitch Pine, produces cones that remain closed and on the tree for many years. Only after the extreme heat of a forest fire will the Jack Pine open its cone and release its seeds. They fall on the open burned land and establish themselves before most other trees do. In this way, large stands of Jack Pine have developed around the western Great Lakes.

*White Pine needles and cones*

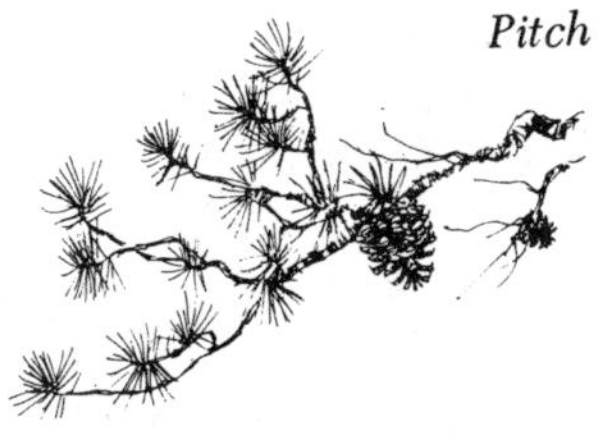

*Pitch Pine needles and cones*

The growth of Pines is termed "excurrent," which means that small branches grow off the sides of a single central trunk. Excurrent growth is controlled by a dominant terminal bud at the top of the trunk. Through the release of plant growth hormones, called auxins, this bud regulates the lower growth of the tree. When the apical bud is injured, as by lightning or insects, the nearest side branch or branches will turn upward and resume the function of the apical bud. This distortion is a common occurrence in Pines; look for a trunk split into two main parts, or one with a sharp curve. There is an insect, the White Pine Weevil, that attacks the apical bud of White Pines. It is considered a real pest by lumbermen, who are looking for the straight wood normal excurrent growth produces.

Pine branches grow in whorls around the trunk, in many species, one group for each year of development. In forest growth, only the upper branches stay alive; the lower ones die back, breaking off near the trunk.

Among trees, Pines are second only to Oaks in providing

*Jack Pine needles and cones*

food for wildlife. In the northeastern quarter of the continent, the White Pine is most important in terms of food production. Numerous birds — including Chickadees, Crossbills, Grosbeaks, Nuthatches, and Siskins — feed on the nutritious seeds. Small mammals that eat the seeds are the Chipmunk, Red and Gray Squirrels, and the White-footed Mouse. Large mammals such as the Rabbit, Porcupine, Beaver, and Deer tend to eat only the bark and foliage.

The Pines are trees of pleasant sensations: the soft mat of their fallen needles, the faint smell of their resin in the sun, and the whistling of the wind through their topmost branches. Perhaps because of their picturesque form, evergreen color, or continued usefulness to humans, Pines have become a special tree in myths and legends. They are a symbol for the unchanging aspects of life.

## Poplar (*Populus* species)

There are four main trees in the north that belong to the Poplar genus: Aspen, Eastern Cottonwood, Balsam Poplar, and Lombardy Poplar. Aspens have been described separately because of their prevalence, importance, and distinctive winter buds. What the other three have in common are the size and shape of their winter buds, their flowers borne on catkins, and the male and female flowers growing on separate trees. After these similarities, they are so distinct in habit that it is better to deal with them individually.

*Balsam Poplar buds*

The Eastern Cottonwood, *Populus deltoides*, gets its common name from the cottony fluff that surrounds its seeds and seems to fill the spring air wherever the trees are plenti-

*Balsam Poplar*

ful. Cottonwoods inhabit a niche similar to that of Willows, growing along streambanks and spreading roots toward the water. They are a fast-growing tree and are harvested for pulpwood, packing crates, and veneer. Early settlers and pioneers frequently settled or camped near Cottonwoods in the Midwest, for the trees provided shelter from weather as well as firewood for themselves and browse for their livestock. Although the wood warps as it seasons, it was good for constructing temporary homes.

The Balsam Poplar, *Populus balsamifera*, loves the cold, growing farther north than any of our other native deciduous trees. It is similar to Aspens in shape and growth habits, but differs in one delectable way: its winter buds, when rubbed, give off a strange, deep scent, like some sweet oriental incense. It is a real treat to come across and I never

*Lombardy Poplar*

leave it without carrying away some of its fragrance in my lungs.

The Lombardy Poplar, *Populus nigra* of the variety *italica,* was originally imported from Italy, where it forms a characteristic part of the landscape. It is extensively used in landscaping, its tall spire of leaves providing an interesting form and a touch of greenery while not creating shade. The tree is also planted in long rows to act as windbreaks in open farming areas.

A strange aspect of this species is that only its male form is known, an identical tree with female flowers never having been found. Since it cannot be reproduced by seed, it is either planted from cuttings or from the suckers that spring up from its roots.

## Sassafras (*Sassafras albidum*)

Don't leave Sassafras without tasting the bark of its distinctive green twigs; it has a sweet lime flavor. In fact, just about every part of this tree has either a pleasant smell or taste. The leaves in summer and fall taste much like the

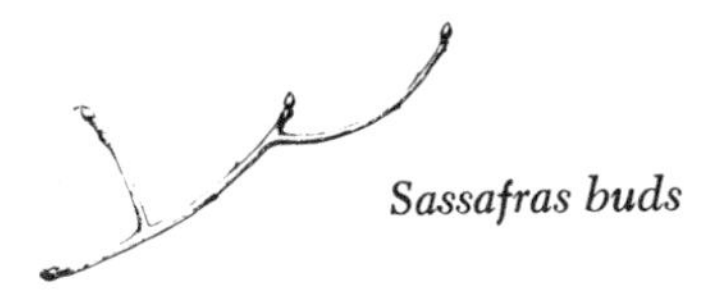
*Sassafras buds*

winter twigs, the wood has a pleasant odor, and the outer bark of the roots reminds one of old-time root beer.

These odors and tastes impressed early European explorers of North America, giving them hope of the discovery of a new wonder medicine. Exaggerated reports began to get back to Europe, and by 1625 there was a large profitable market for the import of Sassafras roots as well as the lumber. Although it was, and still is, used to make a rich-tasting tea, its powers as a panacea soon came into question and the demand for Sassafras diminished accordingly.

The aromatic wood is durable and was believed to repel insects. This led to its being used for floorboards, storage

*Sassafras clone*

barrels, and bed frames. There is little or no use of Sassafras lumber today.

Sending up new saplings from the parent rootstock, Sassafras often forms whole groves. In a group of this kind every member is identical in gene content to the parent plant, since no sexual reproduction has taken place; groups of this kind are called *clones*.

Male and female Sassafras flowers grow on separate trees. When these are in the same area, the female flowers are fertilized and produce a hard blue fruit in the fall. Neither the fruits nor the leaves are a significant source of wildlife food, although the twigs and buds are occasionally eaten by deer and the fruits eaten by birds.

## Spruce (*Picea* species)

After a storm the accumulation of snow under a stand of Spruce is only half that of deciduous forests. For Spruce trees, because of the placement of the needles, hold more snow on their branches than any other tree. The dense foliage of Spruce forests also lessens the full force of winds. These two factors cause many mammals to stay near Spruce groves during winter, for they provide warmth and freedom of movement in the shallow snow. Animals especially at-

*Spruces*

tracted to them are Deer, Snowshoe Hares, Bobcats, Lynx, and Fishers. Grouse roost in the trees, and small birds and Red Squirrels feed on the seeds.

To distinguish Spruce from Hemlock and Fir in the wild, simply take a bough in your hand and turn it over. If the underside is not distinctly lighter in color than the top side,

*Red Spruce needles and cones*

then it is Spruce. If it *is* distinctly lighter, then the tree is Hemlock or Fir. The needles of Black Spruce (*Picea mariana*) were once used in brewing a backwoods beer, and those of White Spruce (*Picea glauca*) have a bad odor when crushed. Spruce needles remain on the tree for 7 to 10 years.

Red Spruce grows fastest of the three types in the northern area and is the most valuable commercially. Its long wood fibers make it an important paper pulp tree, and large tracts of Spruce Forests in North America are owned by paper companies. One specialized use of Spruce is for the sounding boards of musical instruments. If it is especially clear of knots and imperfections it resonates better than other woods.

## Sycamore (*Platanus occidentalis*)

The Sycamore, best known for the mottled appearance of its bark, is the most massive American tree east of the Rockies.

*Sycamore bark*

In the open it produces a huge crown, over 100 feet across, with large branches spreading low and parallel to the ground. It grows in rich bottomlands, often lining the banks of rivers and streams.

Although Sycamore wood is hard, it has a tendency to rot inside the trunk, leaving the tree supported by just the outer layer of the trunk. Such hollows are ideal homes for animals such as Opossums, Raccoons, and Skunks, as well as for hibernating Bats, or day-resting Swallows. The outside trunks of some of the largest trees enclosed empty areas of up to 125 square feet, the size of a regular bedroom, and Sycamores of this size were used by early settlers as barns and even as homes.

Sycamore also has the largest leaf of all our deciduous trees with simple leaves. Since the tree is also particularly resistant to smoke and exhaust fumes, Sycamore is good for planting as a city shade tree.

Seed clusters, called buttonballs, hang on the tips of its zigzag branches in winter. Each is a spherical packing of over 200 seeds around a hard central core. The seeds are

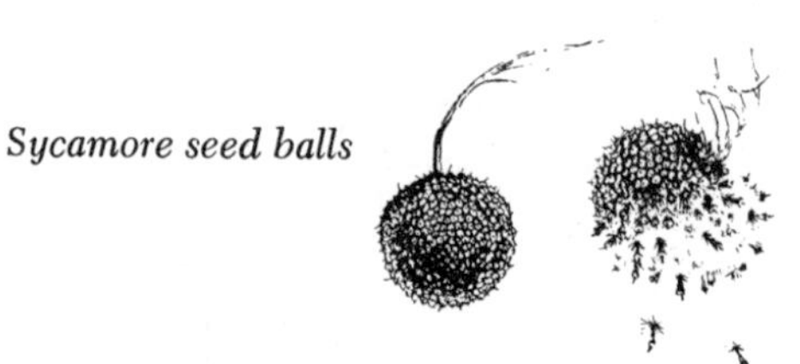
*Sycamore seed balls*

slightly conical, and each has its own parachute of filaments. In winter the buttonballs break apart and the seeds float to the ground or onto the water, where they are carried to new muddy areas suitable for growth.

The wood of the Sycamores, when not rotted, is fairly light, tough, and hard to split. It has been used in the past for dugout canoes, solid wagon wheels, boxes, furniture, and butchers' blocks. The hollow trunks of branches were also used as barrels; one simply cut a length and nailed a bottom on it.

The Sycamore is one of the loveliest trees in the winter

*Sycamore*

woods, easily recognized by the marvelous rounded shapes of green, white, and tan created by the peeling of its inelastic bark. Unfortunately, the tree needs rich soils to grow on, and humans continually cleared those soils for farming. So now the Sycamore, although common in the cities, is less often found in its native habitat and seldom grows to the immense size of its ancestors.

## Tulip Tree (*Liriodendron tulipifera*)

The Tulip Tree grows to be one of the tallest broadleaf trees in eastern North America. In forests, it produces a straight trunk free of branches for most of its height. This straightness and lack of branches, along with wood that is light, strong, and easily worked, have made it a valuable lumber tree.

*Tulip Tree*

The Tulip Tree is a member of the Magnolia family and as such has beautiful, large blossoms in early summer. These develop into seeds with attached wings, arranged on the twigs like the petals of a flower. They are one of the best signs by which you can identify the tree, for they last into winter, their light beige color shining out into the sunlight. But to get a closer look at them, you may need binoculars, because of the height of the tree. What little value these seeds have as wildlife food is due mainly to their being present in winter.

Another good way to recognize the winter tree is by its flattened end buds. They are shaped like a duck's bill, and the twig adjacent to them tastes at first like Sassafras, then seems slightly bitter.

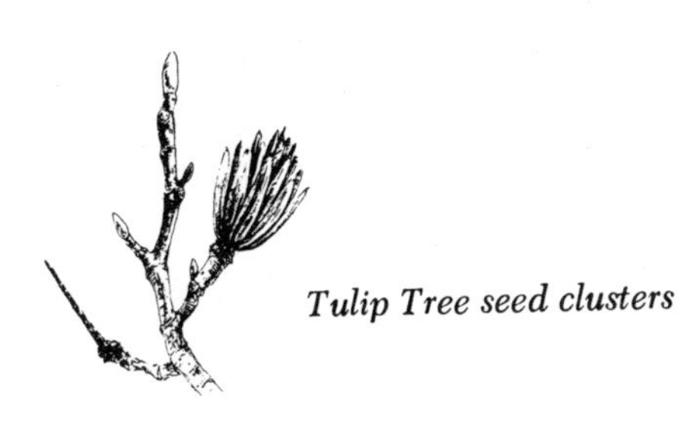

*Tulip Tree seed clusters*

The Greek genus name, *Liriodendron,* means "lily tree," and the species name, *tulipifera,* means "tulip-bearing." Linnaeus, when he named this tree, was obviously emphasizing the tulip-shaped leaves and the large summer blossoms, and maybe even the flowerlike design of the winter seeds.

## Walnut (*Juglans* species)

If you come upon a Walnut tree, consider yourself lucky, for it is rare to find one growing naturally in the woods and more common to find Walnut trees growing around houses

*White Walnut*

*Black Walnut nuts, some opened by Squirrels*

or in city parks. Before white settlers arrived, the Walnuts were common in our deciduous forests, and the American Indians used the nuts for food and the husks for dye. But the European settlers, discovering the great qualities of the wood, methodically cut almost all Walnuts from northeastern North America. The tree should now probably be protected by law.

There are two Walnuts native to this area: Black Walnut, *Juglans nigra*, and Butternut, *Juglans cinerea*. Black Walnut ranges farther south than Butternut, is the more valuable lumber tree, for it produces a tall massive trunk, and has dark heartwood, which turns a rich red-brown when oiled. The tree must be 20 to 30 years old before it produces walnuts, and even then good crops occur only every third year. The nuts of Black Walnut may be found beneath the tree in winter; they are round and about 1½ inches in diameter. The husk is leathery and has no divisions, unlike the Hickory nut husk, which is woody and comes off in four parts. The meat of the Black Walnut is hard to extract but well worth the effort; in fact usually you will find that a forest rodent has already taken the effort, leaving the shell behind.

Butternuts are so named because of the oil that can be extracted by boiling the split nuts in hot water. The oil and the nutmeats float to the top and, scraped off and mashed together, they can be used as a vegetable butter. The husks of both types of Walnut contain a yellow-brown stain that can be used as a dye. Butternut has also been called White Walnut, for its heartwood is a lighter color than that of Black Walnut. Butternuts, however, are typically short-trunked, spreading trees that are not as suitable for long-dimension lumber. Because they are spared cutting, the trees are more common, but their fruit is still often neglected.

*White Walnut twig and buds*

The leaf scars of both kinds of Walnut tree are large. A large leaf scar is usually left by a large or long leaf that needs extra support. The Walnuts have the largest compound leaf of our northern trees; its main stalk is 1 to 2 feet long, bearing from 11 to 23 leaflets. The Butternut is particularly easy to recognize by its twigs, for it has a furry "moustache" between its leaf scar and leafbud.

## Willow (*Salix* species)

Willows are especially well adapted to colonizing the edges of streams and rivers. Their seeds, carried by the slow-moving water, will germinate in less than 2 days when washed up on a muddy bank. After germinating the plant may grow to a height of 7 feet during the first year, while at the same time developing an extensive fibrous root system. This rapid and extensive growth insures its survival in the variable and easily eroded environment of river edges. Besides seeds, the mature tree produces flexible twigs that break off easily from the main branch. If these break off during floods and later wash up on muddy banks downstream, they quickly sprout roots and start new trees.

For many years Willows have been planted by humans to control erosion and preserve the banks of waterways. Only

*Black Willow*

one Willow of tree size is native to our North: the Black Willow, *Salix nigra*. It is the largest of the Willows and has upward-pointing, orange twigs grouped at the ends of its branches. The twigs of other Willow trees are yellower and hang downward, like those of the Weeping Willow, *Salix*

*Weeping Willow*

*babylonica*, a native of China. Both of these trees are often planted near farm ponds or park lakes for their graceful summer foliage.

Like Dogwoods, the Willow genus has many species that are shrubs in the North; and also like Dogwood, these shrubs have buds that are distinctive and similar to those of the tree variety. These Willow shrubs often dominate the moist land surrounding meadow streams, forming dense,

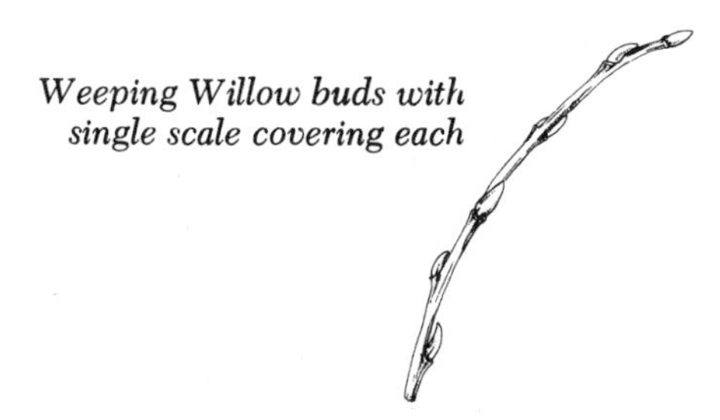

*Weeping Willow buds with single scale covering each*

impenetrable thickets. Some of the most beautiful insect galls, such as the Willow Petaled Gall and Willow Pine Cone Gall, are formed on these shrubs. The best known of these shrubs is, of course, the Pussy Willow, *Salix discolor*, which is collected in late winter for its attractive furry flowers.

IV

# *Evidence of Insects*

I HAVE ALWAYS THOUGHT that one of winter's strongest points was its lack of "bugs." Not bothered by mosquitoes, black flies, gnats, or ticks, I could go where I wanted; I was free to explore the swamp and no longer had to avoid the river's edge. And yet it was the "bugless" winter that first introduced me to insects. While exploring the winter woods, I saw more and more evidence of their summer feeding and winter homes. With the leaves gone, I saw insect tunnels in trees and insect homes in plant galls, and the marvelous nests of wasps and hornets could be explored without danger. The evidence of insects in winter is everywhere — on plants and buildings, in fields and woods, in city and country. Once spotted, it becomes increasingly evident, and the closer one looks the more one can learn about the habits and life histories of its makers.

One of the dominating facts in the study of insects is the tremendous diversity of the class. There are nearly one million species of insects now known and up to five thousand new species discovered each year. Because there are so many, we can't approach them as we do birds or mammals. The names and habits of all the larger mammals of a given area can be easily known. But considerably more effort would be needed to recognize even one hundredth of the local insect species. Clearly our emphasis must change from the species level to that of orders and families, and even then we are dealing with staggering numbers. The life histories of these insects are extremely diverse, yet some generalizations can be made which can help create a framework for further knowledge.

One such generalization, essential for any understanding of insects, concerns their stages of development. Unlike mammals, which have generally the same appearance all through their lives (if you know what a squirrel looks like you can recognize it whether it's young or old), insects undergo radically different stages in their lives. Some have as many as four stages, each distinct from the others in appearance. Other insects have a gradual development, which from beginning to end changes greatly but in which each consecutive stage is only slightly different from the one before and the one after.

In the latter type of metamorphosis (transformation), called *gradual*, the insect starts as an egg. Then a series of growth stages take place, in which the young insect molts its skin, becoming larger and slightly different with each molt. During the changing stages the insect is called a *nymph,* so gradual metamorphosis can be summarized as egg–nymph stages–adult. In the adult stage, the insect no longer molts; it is involved in reproducing.

The other type of development is known as *complete* metamorphosis; it consists first of the egg stage, from which hatches a small caterpillar or grub, known as the *larva*. The larva spends all its time eating food and growing, then it forms a coating (a pupa or cocoon) around itself and slowly changes into an adult. This is called the *pupal stage*. When the insect leaves this stage, it is an adult. So, complete metamorphosis can be summarized as egg–larva–pupa–adult.

Complete metamorphosis is considered the more recent type, and the majority of our insects undergo it, including moths, butterflies, wasps, bees, ants, and beetles. Bugs, dragonflies, crickets, and grasshoppers tend to have gradual metamorphosis.

But where are insects in winter? What do they do, where do they go, and why aren't we bothered by them?

All insects are cold-blooded. This designation simply means that their bodies are not internally regulated to a constant temperature; their temperature is generally that of their surroundings. Colder weather slows them down, and winter temperatures bring most of them to a standstill. In order to survive thermal changes, insects have adapted so that during the cold period of our temperate climate they enter a resting stage, in which they cease their life activities and development, until spring, when they reemerge and continue their development. This stage is called *diapause;* it occurs also in insects that experience dry and wet seasons. In general, diapause occurs during any season that is harsh to the normal activities of insects.

A good question is: what triggers the onset of diapause? Clearly, if an insect merely waited for the weather to get cold, it might be slowed down to the point where it could not complete its preparation for winter. It must prepare for winter while conditions are still good, long before the cold and the lack of food set in.

During the last hundred years it has slowly become apparent that many insects are sensitive to light and that their preparation for diapause is controlled by the changing ratio of day to night in late summer and fall. In the laboratory, caterpillers that normally build cocoons in late summer have been kept in their active feeding stage for up to 10 years by artificial lengthening of the day. Aphids that give birth to live young all summer but in fall change to laying eggs can be kept in their summer habits. Time and again light-to-dark ratios have been shown to be the starter of winter preparations in insects.

Preparation for diapause is generally accomplished in either or both of two ways. One is apparently intended to minimize the effect of the harsh environmental conditions. To do this many insects migrate, not north to south like birds but up to down; from the above-ground environment of trees, shrubs, and plants to areas beneath the ground, such as roots, fallen logs, rock crevices, burrows, or under leaf litter. Other insects migrate from above water to below it, still others go from shallow to deep water. In all cases, the winter environment is warmer and more stable than the air.

The other way an insect may prepare for diapause is to enter a different life stage, one that will best enable it to survive the winter. For many insects, this means the egg stage. Many adults lay their eggs in late summer and fall, and then die. The eggs start their development again in the spring and then hatch. Other insects are in the larval stage as caterpillars or grubs in summer and fall, feeding on the abundant vegetation. They enter their pupal stage for winter and emerge as adults in spring. Still others are able to acclimate themselves slowly to the cold and spend the winter as adults in protected environments. In fact, insects live through winter in all stages, but each species has a specific pattern which it always follows.

The next problem for the insect is when to emerge from diapause. This is slightly more complex, for many insects over-winter in total darkness and therefore cannot use light-dark ratios to time their emergence. Emergence is also complicated by the fact that their food sources — plants, other insects, or mammals — may not be ready in spring when warmth returns.

It has been theorized that in the heads of insects there are light receptors that, when exposed to the light-dark ratios of fall, produce a chemical. This chemical induces preparation behavior and diapause. During winter it gradually breaks down, possibly aided by the cold. When the chemical has finally disintegrated, the insect resumes its normal body processes and emerges. Each species would produce its own amount of the chemical in order to time its emergence to coincide with optimal life and food conditions.

These theories have been proven for only a minute percentage of all insects and are therefore quite speculative, yet the general principles of light-dark ratio as the starter of the winter clock and the chemical breakdown as the timing have been shown to operate also in other animals and plants. This would lead us to believe that these are general occurrences functioning in many life forms.

# *Chart of Evidence of Insects*

## *GALLERIES AND CARVINGS IN WOOD*

Bark Beetles
Carpenter Ants

## *GALLS ON PLANTS*

on Blueberry — Blueberry Stem Gall
on Goldenrod — Elliptical Goldenrod Gall
Goldenrod Ball Gall
Goldenrod Bunch Gall
on Oak — Oak Apple Gall
Oak Bullet Gall
Oak Twig Gall
on Spruce — Spruce Pineapple Gall
on Willow — Willow Petaled Gall
Willow Pine Cone Gall

## *ACTIVE WINTER INSECTS*

Springtails
Stoneflies

## *WASP NESTS*

Paper Wasp nest

Hornet nest
Mud Dauber nest

*WEB NESTS IN TREES*

Eastern Tent Caterpillar
Fall Webworm

# *Natural History Descriptions*

## Bark Beetles (Family *Scolytidae*)

Bark Beetles are small, inconspicuous insects that spend most of their lives under the surface of tree bark. They seem an unlikely candidate for a book on the common natural sights of winter, but the reason for their inclusion is the prominence of the adult and larval tunnels that appear like engravings on the surface wood of dead trees. Many of these engravings form delightful patterns that record the fascinating life habits of the beetles.

Bark Beetles can be either monogamous, bigamous, or polygamous. Among the monogamous beetles, the female starts the egg tunnels herself after mating, being sometimes later helped by the male. Among bigamous or polygamous beetles, the male first bores through the bark and creates an enlarged cavity, called a *nuptial chamber*. Two or more females will enter this chamber, mate with the male, and dig their egg tunnels leading off from the chamber.

After this, the beetles' life histories are similar. The female digs an egg tunnel in the wood surface, depositing eggs in small niches at either side. The larvae hatch and eat their own tunnels through the wood; each of these "larval mines" increases in size as the larva grows. When finished with eating, each hollows out a chamber, where it pupates

Bark Beetle

(forms a cocoon) and transforms into an adult. As adults, the beetles emerge through the bark and fly to new host trees.

Bark Beetles winter over as larvae, pupae, or adults. Peeling away the bark of an infested tree will reveal them, but chances of seeing the insect are slight, since it is only about $\frac{1}{10}$ inch long. And when the beetles are in a tree it is hard to guess at their presence. Even so, they have many predators, chiefly Woodpeckers, which feast on the beetles all year and especially in winter.

The Bark Beetle family, *Scolytidae*, is divided into three groups, distinguished by their habits: True Bark Beetles bore between the bark and the wood, Wood-eating Beetles bore into the wood, and Ambrosia Beetles bore into the wood and live off fungi that grow in their galleries.

Only True Bark Beetles are included here, for their galleries are most evident. There are many genera, some of the more important being *Scolytus*, *Dendroctonus*, and *Ips*. No genus is consistently represented by one type of egg tunnel, so that to label each type with only one or two genera would be misleading. I have therefore left the generic names out and stressed the construction of the tunnels and what they reveal about their makers. However, each species builds its tunnels in only certain types of trees, and often consistently on a certain part of that tree — for example, the lower branches, the upper branches, or the trunk. With continued observation you will soon be able to guess where certain patterns are likely to be found.

## SIMPLE EGG TUNNELS

These tunnels are formed by a single monogamous female. They may be bored with, across, or regardless of the grain, depending on the species. They may be winding or straight, 1 inch to more than 1 foot long. There are almost always

*Simple egg tunnels*

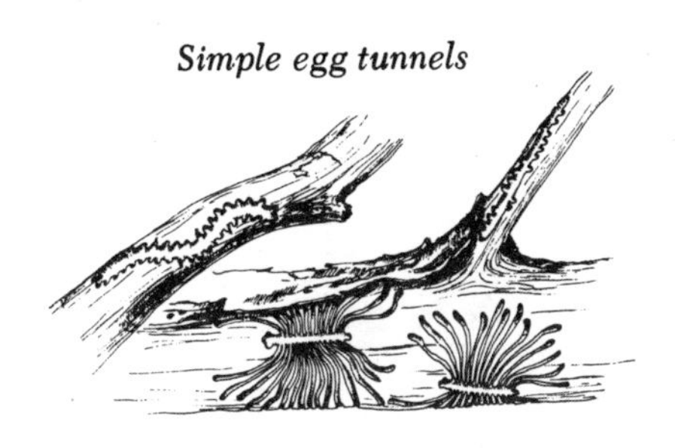

egg niches carved in their sides. Larval mines, radiating from the tunnels, may show in the wood or may have been bored in the bark and thus may not show on the wood surface.

## FORKED EGG TUNNELS

These tunnels are made by either monogamous or bigamous beetles. They have an extended entrance tunnel that forks

*Forked egg tunnels*

off in opposite directions or in the same direction. They most commonly go across the grain of branches. Sometimes larval mines and even egg niches are bored in the bark and do not show on the wood surface.

## *RADIATE EGG TUNNELS*

These are formed exclusively by polygamous beetles. The egg tunnels may be in a star pattern, either with the grain or

*Radiate egg tunnels*

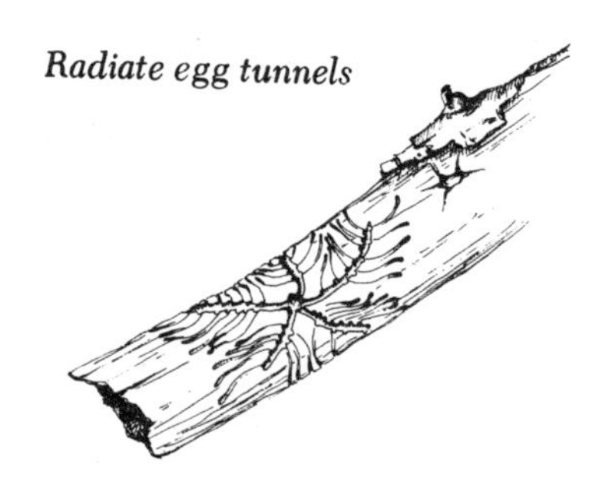

across it. Sometimes the nuptial chamber is bored in the bark and does not show in the wood surface.

## *CAVE EGG TUNNELS*

These tunnels are considered the most primitive form; they are made by either monogamous or polygamous beetles.

*Cave egg tunnels*

They are enlarged cavities in which all the eggs are laid in a group. The larvae eat together around the walls of the chamber, making it a large irregular shape.

### *IRREGULAR EGG TUNNELS*

This category is given just to admit that Bark Beetle behavior is not as neat and simple as the first four examples would

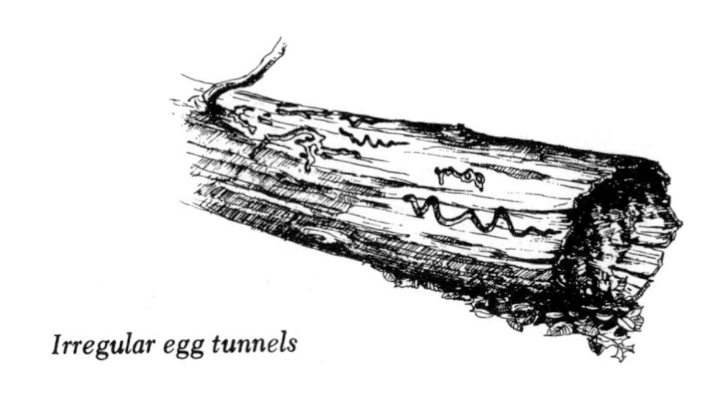

*Irregular egg tunnels*

suggest. Many of the Bark Beetles' tunnels are crisscrossing mazes with varying amounts of regularity.

## Carpenter Ants (*Camponotus* species)

Evidence of Carpenter Ants as well as the ants themselves are frequent sights in winter. Often, in standing dead trees, you will find the carved galleries of these ants. They excavate into the dry wood of dead trees, and some species even burrow into living wood. Alive or dead, the wood must be in contact with the ground in order to allow for tunneling in both dry and moist conditions. The tunnels are used to protect the colony and raise the young. Both moist and dry areas are needed in order to keep the eggs, larvae, and

*Carpenter Ant galleries*

pupae at the proper temperature and humidity for healthy growth.

Unlike termites, Carpenter Ants do not eat the wood of their tunnels, but they carefully carry each particle of sawdust and drop it outside the nest. In dry wood the nest takes on a smooth sculptured look, like an intricate latticework.

Like that of most ants, and similar to that of the social

*Carpenter Ant; female worker, queen, and male drone*

wasps, a Carpenter Ant society is made up of a fertile queen, which in Carpenter Ants may live as long as 15 years, males, which are short-lived and die after fertilization, and infertile females, which are the workers and soldiers. The workers are sometimes divided into two divisions, major and minor, depending on their size. The main job of the colony is to reproduce itself, which necessitates excavating the nest, rearing and protecting the young, and establishing new colonies. As winter approaches, egg laying ceases and the young are brought to maturity. The colony heads for the center of a log or to the underground part of their nest in order to minimize the rigors of winter. Here they hibernate in clusters and are often found in logs that have been split for firewood. They become active at anytime in winter when the temperature rises well above freezing.

An enemy of Carpenter Ants' in winter is the Pileated Woodpecker, which pecks huge holes in trees in order to feed on the ants. Often the empty galleries of Carpenter Ants are reused by other genera of ants as well as by other insects. The openings in the wood also enable moisture and fungi, which help speed the process of decay, to enter.

## *GALLS*

Galls are deformations of plants caused by insects and used by them for food and protection while developing. There are over 1,500 insects in North America that cause gall formations. Most likely everyone has seen galls, but few may have recognized them as such. Many are evident in summer as swellings, growths, or discolorations on the leaves of trees and plants; still others are more clearly seen in winter as deformations of twigs.

Galls have received scientific attention for three main reasons: they often interfere with agricultural productivity, particularly that of wheat; believed to be examples of tumorous growth, they are studied from the viewpoint of cancer research; and the life histories of the gall-makers are often unusual and intriguingly complex.

But even with this interest and study, the process of gall formation is still unclear and the life histories of the majority of gall-makers remain a mystery. The closest we can come to explaining gall formation is to say that the insect disrupts the normal growth of a plant either through physical irritation or chemical secretion. Around the insect, the plant grows a deformity, which the insect then uses for food and protection while developing.

Some galls have just one maker, others harbor many individuals. A number of insects use galls made by others. Those that do not hurt the gall-maker are called *inquilines*; those that kill the gall-maker are parasites. Even after a gall is left by its maker it is used as shelter by many other insects, especially in winter. These galls are in turn opened by birds and mammals seeking the insects inside. As you look for the galls included here you will certainly find many others, and will begin to realize what a common phenomenon gall formation is.

## Blueberry Stem Gall

The advantage of knowing this gall is that it enables you to identify Highbush Blueberry, one of the most common shrubs in the winter woods. In many books this gall is called Huckleberry Stem Gall, but it is most common on Blueberry bushes. A gall wasp, or Cynipid (*Hemadas nubilipennis*), causes it to grow.

The gall starts forming in early summer and is initiated in the cambium, the active growing layer, of young twigs. Its growth deforms the twig by making it bend downward. By fall, the gall is red-brown and kidney-shaped. In spring it will become riddled with holes bored by emerging adult wasps, showing that the gall is polythalamous — containing more than one chamber. Some flies are also known to inhabit this gall as inquilines.

*Blueberry Stem Galls: left is young, right is old.*

In winter you may find both this year's and last year's galls, the former brown and smooth, the latter gray, riddled with holes, and farther back on the twig.

## Elliptical Goldenrod Gall

This is one of the most widespread and common galls found in winter. It is formed by the larva of a moth (*Gnorimo-*

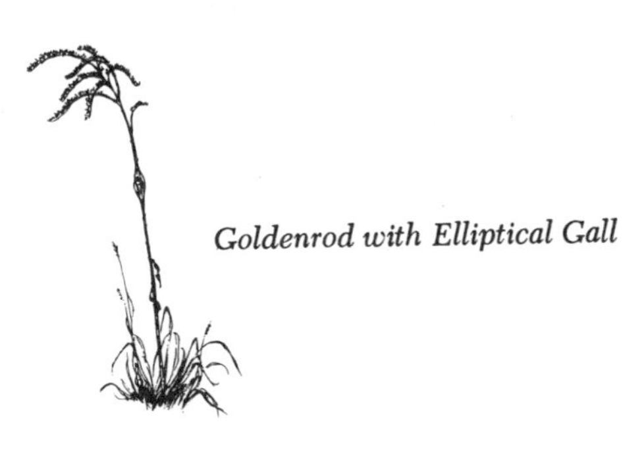

*Goldenrod with Elliptical Gall*

*schema gallaesolidaginis*), an unusual situation, for very few moths cause galls. In fall the adult moth lays its eggs singly on the lower leaves and stems of Goldenrod. The egg develops to a prehatching state in fall and overwinters in that stage. In spring the larva hatches, crawls toward new Goldenrod shoots, burrows into the end buds, and travels down inside the stem. When it has gone a few inches down, it stops and continues to feed in that place. At this point the plant begins to form the gall around the insect. The larva continues to feed until late July, then bores an exit hole in the upper end of the gall, so that when it is a nonboring adult it will be able to emerge. Before pupating, it plugs up the hole with a mixture of silk and plant material. It then pupates, emerging later in August and September as an adult.

*Elliptical Goldenrod Gall*

Thus, the normal Elliptical Goldenrod Gall will not contain its maker in winter — it will have an open exit hole at its top and a shed red-brown pupal skin arranged inside with the head up. But there are many parasites of this moth and you will often find evidence of their work in the winter galls. A common parasite is the Ichneumon wasp, *Calliephialtes notandus.* The Ichneumon wasp has a long ovipositor (egg despositor), which it can insert into the gall in order to lay an egg on the larva. The intruding insect eats the larva, spins a long thin brown cocoon in which to pupate, and emerges as an adult in late summer.

Another wasp, known as *Copidosoma gelechiae,* deposits

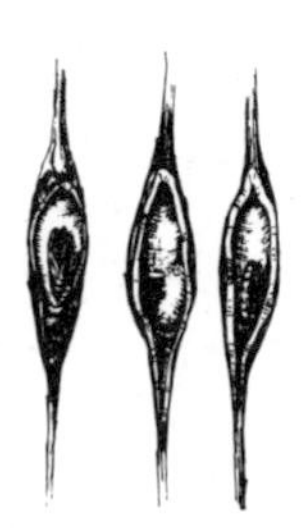

*Interior of Elliptical Goldenrod Gall. From left to right: shiny brown pupal skin of original maker, then white cocoon and brown cocoon of parasites*

its egg in the egg of the moth that makes the Elliptical Goldenrod Gall. The moth larva develops normally until pupation, then dies. The larva of the parasite hatches, develops, and pupates in the moth larva. The wasps emerge in late summer. Evidence of their work is a larval skin riddled with holes, lying inside the winter gall. There are others that overwinter in the gall as adults or pupae, either in a brown and white cocoon or naked in the gall.

Besides these parasites there are numerous Arthropods that reuse the empty galls. In particular, many spiders use them for shelter or for a protected spot in which to place their egg cases. Also reported present in empty Elliptical Goldenrod Galls are bees, ants, beetles, and thrips.

## Goldenrod Ball Gall

The Goldenrod Ball Gall is an abrupt round swelling on the plant stem. It is common; sometimes it will be present on most of the Goldenrod of a given field, occasionally with more than one on a single stem.

*Goldenrod Ball Gall*

The gall is caused by the larva of a small spotted-winged fly (*Eurosta solidaginis*). After mating, the female fly lays its eggs on the new stems in late May and June. The egg hatches, and the larva burrows into the stem. Here it continues to hollow out a chamber slightly larger than its body size, while the plant forms the gall around it. It is mature by the onset of winter and overwinters in the larval form. In spring the larva resumes activity by eating a tunnel just as far as the outside layer of the gall. It then reenters its chamber, where it pupates. The adult fly crawls out the hole and bursts through the outer skin of the gall.

Thus, normally the Goldenrod Ball Gall contains its maker in winter. But there are many other insects that regularly take advantage of the helpless larvae. In this case small beetles often enter the galls and eat the larvae before hibernating in the galls themselves.

## Goldenrod Bunch Gall

This is another of the more common and easily recognizable Goldenrod galls. It is formed by a midge, *Rhopalomyia*

*Goldenrod Bunch Gall*

*solidaginis,* and is reportedly found only on Canada Goldenrod (*Solidago canadensis*). Initiated in the leaf bud, it creates a stunting of stem growth along with a proliferation of leaves, so that the final gall appears like a flower with many woody petals. Occurring always at the tip of the winter stalk, it is easily spotted in a grove of Goldenrod plants.

Each Bunch Gall appears to be caused by a single larva, since there is generally one cavity at the center of the gall;

some other midges from the same genus are known to be inquilines. The specific name for the gall-maker, as with those of the other Goldenrod galls mentioned, is derived from the generic name for Goldenrod, *Solidago*.

## Oak Galls

Oaks host more types of gall-makers than any other plant. Of the nearly 1,500 North American galls so far discovered, over 800 have been found on Oaks. Galls seem to form on all parts of Oaks: the roots, trunk, branches, and twigs, leaves, flowers, and fruit (acorns). By far the greatest number form on the leaves, the next largest on the twigs. Once you become aware of these galls you can often recognize Oaks in winter just by noticing the number of deformities on the branches.

Almost all Oak galls are formed by a family of wasps called *Cynipidae* or Cynipids, or sometimes gall-wasps, because so many members utilize galls in different stages of their development. Many of these wasps are known to have alternating generations — one generation without males, the other with both sexes. But the life histories of the majority of these Cynipids, even the most common, still remain completely unknown. Study of them is made difficult by the fact that the generations of a single insect may form different galls, even on different host plants.

Below are shown three of the most common types of galls seen on Oaks in winter. For simplification of identification, many books on insects state that certain species are responsible for each of these types. But this oversimplification hides the astounding diversity of the galls and their subtle differences, for each of these three types of gall has many variations, each made by a different species of insect.

## Oak Apple Galls

Oak Apple Galls appear as small tan balls, between 1 and 2 inches in diameter. They are formed on the leaves, frequently on the leaf mid-vein or the leaf stem (petiole), and often initiated in the leaf bud itself. There are two groups: the ones that form in spring on the growing leaf, and the ones that form on the matured leaf in late summer and fall. The spring ones tend to be soft; the late-summer galls tend to have harder shells and to develop more slowly. Obviously the late-summer galls will be more common in winter. You may find them on the ground or hanging on the tree like Christmas ornaments. Sometimes a small sapling will be covered with twenty to thirty galls, looking quite festive in the winter woods.

These galls are divided into two categories depending on their internal structure: full and empty. Full Oak Apples

*Oak Apple Galls: one pecked open by a bird, the other split in half to show interior*

contain spongy growth between their hard center chambers and their outer shells, whereas the empty Oak Apples have just minute radiating fibers connecting the chambers with the shells.

As is the case with other galls, Oak Apples may contain many inquilines, parasites, or reusers. Opening up galls can be enjoyable, for you are never quite sure what you are going to find. In summer I once opened an Oak Apple, only to find a group of over a hundred eggs, with as many ants, who streamed onto my fingers from inside the gall. Another time I found mud nests of wasps inside.

*Amphibolops* and *Cynips* are two of the more common genera of insects that cause Oak Apple Galls. There are at least one hundred different types of Oak Apples, varying in size, shape, surface texture, and the part of the leaf on which they form.

## Oak Bullet Galls

As their name suggests, these are small hard round galls about the size of marbles. Unlike the Oak Apples, which grow on leaf parts, these are produced only on twigs. They

*Oak Bullet Galls*

can be found singly, in groups of two or three, or in clusters of twenty or more depending on the specific type of Bullet Gall. So far there have been over fifty types of Bullet Galls discovered in North America, the most common gall wasps forming them being members of the genus *Disholcapsis*.

## Twig and Branch Galls

This is a very general category, included here because its varied members are so commonly seen in winter. Oak Bullet Galls are actually also in this category, but have been mentioned separately because of their distinct shape. The other

*Oak twig and branch galls*

members included here tend to be irregular swellings and deformities growing at the ends of Oak twigs. Unlike both the Bullet and Oak Apple galls, each gall contains many larvae.

They have been given such common names as Oak Potato Galls, Gouty Oak Galls, and Oak Club Galls. Members of the genera *Neuroterus* and *Plagiotrochus* are among the most common causes of these galls.

## Spruce Pineapple Gall

Spruce Pineapple Galls form at the tips of Spruce branches where new growth is occurring and remain on the tree until the branch is shed. They look like miniature pineapples, between ½ and 1 inch long; often spines of old needles protrude from them.

The gall insect (*Chermes abietis*) belongs to the aphid

*Spruce Pineapple Gall*

*Spruce tree with galls*

family, a group that tends to have extremely complex life cycles involving what is called "alternation of generations." Parent A lays eggs, which develop into parent B. Parent B lays eggs, which in turn develop into a new parent A. The two generations may resemble each other or may be totally different in appearance. Therefore, it is often difficult to trace the life histories of aphids. Some other aphids are even more difficult to follow since they may have as many as five distinct generations before a return to parent A.

The Spruce Gall maker has only two generations, which complete their cycle in a single year. But, as if to offset this simplicity, *Chermes abietis* has no males in its species; all reproduction is parthenogenetic (partheno=virgin, genetic =birth). The cycle starts in fall with a winged female, parent A, which flies to a Spruce and lays eggs at the base of the needle buds. These eggs hatch into wingless female nymphs, parent B, which eat the Spruce needles in fall and overwinter at the base of the spring needle buds. In spring they resume feeding, and the needles swell and grow together, forming the gall. Soon the nymphs lay eggs, which hatch, feed on the needles, enter the gall, and emerge as winged females. These are parents A, which fly to new Spruces and start the cycle over. Thus the galls are not occupied in winter, but are used in spring by generation A.

## Willow Petaled Gall

One of the most beautiful winter galls, the Willow Petaled Gall, looks like a gray flower at the tip of a Willow shrub. These galls are often numerous, frequently seen on the same plant as the lovely Willow Pine Cone Gall. The Willow Petaled Gall is believed to be caused by the gall midge *Rhabdophaga rhodoides;* it starts forming in late spring and early summer when the plant is actively growing. Little is known of the gall's life history, except that the loose petals undoubtedly harbor many hibernating insects during winter.

*Willow Petaled Gall, both whole and split open*

This gall, along with the Willow Pine Cone Gall and Goldenrod Bunch Gall, is believed by some to be composed of modified leaves bunched together with no stem elongation in between. Cutting these three types of gall in half reveals their similar internal structure.

## Willow Pine Cone Gall

This gall appears only on Willow shrubs and is more common in the Great Lakes area than in the East. One of the most beautiful, it is shaped like a small, tightly closed pine cone and forms only at the tips of branches. A small gnat, or midge (*Rhabdophaga strobiloides*), just two tenths of an inch long is its maker. The family this insect belongs to, *Cecidomyiae*, contains many other gall-producing gnats.

The gnat's life cycle is refreshingly simple for a gall-maker. During winter it is a larva in the center of the gall.

*Willow Pine Cone Gall, both whole and split open*

In spring it pupates and emerges as an adult. The fertilized female then lays eggs on the new growth at the Willow branch tips. The larvae hatch, stimulate gall growth, and spend the winter in the gall.

What has attracted attention to this gall, besides its beauty, is the tremendous number of other insects that use it for overwintering and breeding, some as inquilines, others as parasites. For one study 23 galls were collected and 564 insects were reared from them. Only 15 contained the original host gnat, but in addition there were 6 wasp parasites, 169 other guest gnats, and 384 eggs of the Meadow Grasshopper (*Xiphidium eusiferum*). Clearly, the overlapping scales of this gall have proved to be extremely valuable to other insects that have adapted to taking advantage of this gnat's gall-causing ability.

## *ACTIVE WINTER INSECTS*

### Springtail (*Achorutes nivicolus*)

If you continue to explore nature in winter you are bound to come across "Snow Fleas." At the base of a tree on warmer winter days or where the sun has melted through to a patch of leaves, you may see the surrounding snow darkened with small black dots. It may at first appear to be soot on the surface of the snow, but as you look closer you will see

*Springtails peppering the snow at the base of a tree*

thousands of tiny gray insects hopping about. These are the "snow fleas," which are actually called Springtails, or *Achorutes nivicolus*.

They belong to a primitive but widely distributed order of wingless insects called *Collembola*. Members of this order generally inhabit the surface of the soil, but they also live on the surface of ponds and in tidal zones. They inhabit both temperate and tropical climates and are most often vegetarians, feeding on algae, pollen, and leaf mold. They are so prevalent that they often number well over ten million individuals per acre.

Their common name, Springtail, refers to the two ap-

*Springtails*

pendages they have on their last body segment. These are like two modified legs, which are normally folded against their abdomen and held in place by two clasps. When the clasps open, these two appendages spring against the ground, propelling the insect a few inches away. This flea-like leaping motion has given them the misleading name, "snow fleas."

Species *Achorutes nivicolus* comes out to feed in winter, taking advantage of microclimates in the sun that may be much warmer than air temperatures. Once you spot them you will begin to notice them more and more, for although they are inconspicuous at first, they are quite common.

## Stonefly (Order *Plecoptera*)

The Stonefly is another insect that is often active in winter. In fact some species of stoneflies have adjusted their cycle to

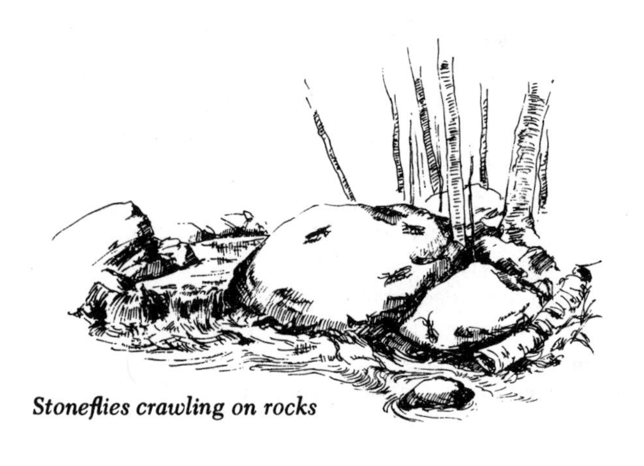
*Stoneflies crawling on rocks*

the exact opposite of those of most other insects. Their larvae, which live in streams, start feeding and growing in fall and early winter. The adults emerge from the water in midwinter and mate on the shores; then the female lays her eggs back in the water.

When they fly slowly through the air they appear like

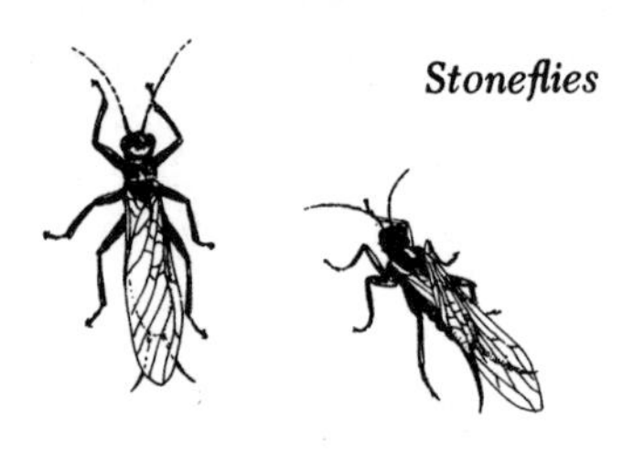
*Stoneflies*

large gray mosquitoes. But they are more often found crawling over rocks and snow at stream edges, where as adults they come to feed on algae. These insects live in only clean rushing water, the larvae living and feeding under stones at the river's edge.

## *WASPS*

### Paper Wasp (*Polistes fuscatus*)

The nest of this wasp is just a single layer of comb made with paper, with as few as 10 to as many as 150 cells. This layer is usually placed under the eaves of buildings or sheds or under large branches. It is hung with the cell openings

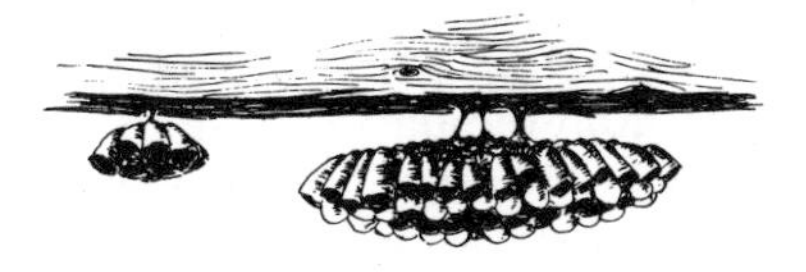

*Paper Wasp nests: one aborted, one completed*

facing downward and is attached by usually a single thread-like pedicel (stalk).

You need a simplified life history of these wasps in order to interpret all that you might see in relation to the nest. Male and female wasps mate in the fall, and both go into hibernation in rock crevices and rotting logs. Only the queens live through the winter, emerging in the first warm days of spring to fly around and seek out a good nesting site. Once one has been found, the queen starts building a few cells and lays an egg in each one. At this time, other queens, which for some reason did not complete their nests, join our queen and become subservient workers for her, finishing cells that she initiates and feeding the larvae when they hatch from the eggs. After the larvae are full-grown

*Paper Wasp on nest*

white grubs, they seal off their cells and pupate, emerging later as more female workers.

At the end of summer the queen lays more eggs, some that are fertilized and others that aren't. These eggs are fed extra amounts of food and develop into idle males and queens. These two types hang around the nest and are fed by the female workers. Soon the original queen stops laying eggs and the nest starts to break up. The workers stop working so hard; sometimes they eat the partially developed grubs. In fall the males and new queens leave the nest, mate, and hibernate. And the queens with extra reserves of fat stored in their bodies live through the winter to start the cycle over.

The nest itself reflects a great deal about the wasps' lives. It is made with dried wood and plant fibers, which are gathered from fenceposts, old buildings, and dead trees. Bits of wood are ripped off while held fast in the wasp's mandibles (mouth parts). They are taken to the nest, chewed, mixed with a saliva, and applied as paper pulp in circular additions to each cell. On some nests you can see the variation in color of these additions, reflecting the different sources of the wood.

The queen initiates the building of all cells with a small basal outline. The other workers complete them. You may find that some of the outer cells are half as long. These are queen-initiated but unfinished. You may also find a nest of just a few cells — this was started by a queen in spring but for some reason she left it and became a worker for another queen.

The single thread that attaches the nest to the limb or eave is believed to be a protective adaptation. With just one source of access by crawling parasites, the nest can be defended more easily, and in some species the queen coats this thread with a substance repellent to ants. The top of the cells are also usually coated with a shiny substance that makes the paper water-resistant.

The cells are built and filled concentrically, and when the first grubs are hatched, the initial cells are sometimes cleaned and used again. Some of the cells may have remains of larvae still in them; others may be sealed off and when opened found to contain dead but developed wasps. The lives of the workers are short, and there are rarely as many wasps as there are cells at any given time.

Often the nests are found on the ground in winter, blown there by the wind. Other good spots for seeing them are in abandoned sheds, garages, barns, and under the eaves of wooden buildings.

## Hornets, Yellow Jackets (*Vespula* species)

The paper nests of Hornets and Yellow Jackets (*Vespulae*) are considered more advanced than the open nests of *Polistes,* for they afford more protection from enemies and harsh environmental conditions. Basically their life cycle is the same as that of *Polistes* except that only a single queen starts the hive and she is never joined by other queens. She makes a few cells attached to a branch, lays eggs in them, and proceeds to surround them with an envelope of paper. She then feeds the larva until they pupate and emerge as adult female workers. After that the workers do the food gathering, nest building, and brood tending, while the queen lays eggs. In fall the queen will lay eggs that will hatch into males or fertile females; the adult insects will mate, and the fertilized females will winter over, emerging in the spring to start new nests.

The nests are abandoned in winter and can be safely collected and inspected after below-freezing weather has definitely set in. They can be built at almost any level from 2 to 40 feet off the ground. They are often in trees or shrubs and sometimes under the eaves of house roofs. They also vary in size from 8 to 18 inches in depth, those of Yellow Jackets often being the smaller ones.

After the first workers hatch they start to build new cells and enlarge the nest, chewing away the inner layers of the

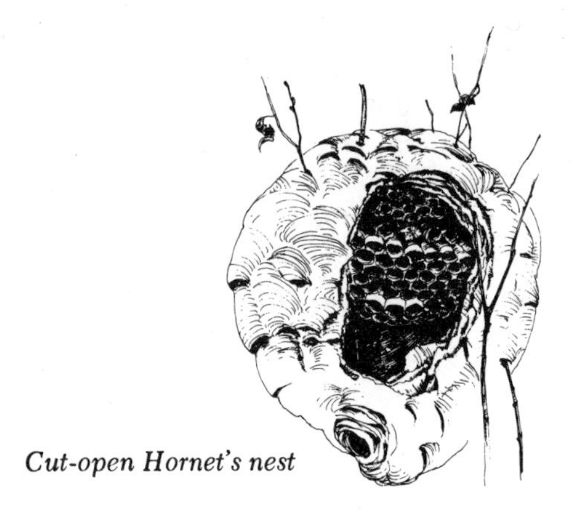

*Cut-open Hornet's nest*

envelope and adding new layers to the outside. Paper is made by collecting strips of dried wood, chewing them, and adding a fluid that acts like a glue to hold the paper together. If you examine the outside of the nest you can see the wood of different colors, added on in arcs that curve away from the hive. This makes the layers "quilted" and holds them apart so that their insulating affect is maximized. Most nests have between 6 and 8 layers of paper, the total covering averaging 2 inches in thickness.

It has been proven that Hornets can regulate the temperature of their nest. In one experiment it was shown that where outdoor temperatures varied as much as 40 degrees F. over a week, temperatures inside the hive varied only 5 degrees. Much of this consistency is due to temperature regulating by the wasps, but some of the evenness is certainly caused by this efficient insulation of the nest.

If you cut open part of the nest you are likely to see two to four tiers of egg cells arranged one beneath the other. Some of the outer cells may be short, which means they were never finished; some cells may contain dried larvae, which means the nest was abandoned before they matured. Other cells have an added white layer of paper. These cells were going to be used a second time. The first time, the larva excreted its feces in the bottom of the cell, and since this makes the cell too short for the next larva, the workers, instead of cleaning it out, just add an extension to the cell. If you poke into the bottom of these cells you will find the excrement packed there.

*Yellow Jacket and Hornet*

The entrance to the hive is a hole usually placed on one side of the base of the nest. Although the wasps abandon this nest in winter, it is still an excellent winter home, and many other types of insects and spiders spend the winter within it.

These same nests also are built underground by both Hornets and Yellow Jackets. Usually placed in a mammal burrow or natural cavity, they are often found in fall, ripped open by Skunks or Raccoons, who were seeking the grubs when the insects were slowed by the cold.

## Mud Daubers (Family *Sphecidae*)

Mud Daubers are solitary rather than social; they have no caste system, just males and females. After mating, the females build nests, provision them with paralyzed insects, lay their eggs in them, and seal them off. The young larvae feed on the living but paralyzed flesh of the stored insects. The Mud Daubers overwinter in the stage of larval growth that just precedes pupation. In spring they pupate and emerge as adults.

*Yellow Mud Dauber on nest*

In the *Sphecidae* family there are two common wasps which build mud nests and a third which reuses these nests. The nests are built on bridges, house eaves, and in sheds, garages, and barns. The wasps prefer to build in places that are dry, warm, and well supplied with especially spiders.

The Yellow Mud Dauber, *Sceliphron caementarium,* collects mud on warm days from the edges of ponds, puddles, and streams. It first lays down a mud foundation on its building surface, then adds half-arcs of mud, alternating from right to left to form a chamber. About thirty trips to collect mud are needed to make one cell, and each cell takes one to two hours of constant building to complete. After the cell is packed with paralyzed spiders and a single egg, the wasp seals it off with a mud cap. More cells are added to this one, and all of them may then be covered over with a layer of mud.

Old nests often persist for a year or two and another wasp, the Blue Mud Dauber, *Chalybion californicum,* cleans and repairs these nests for its own use. It carries water in its crop to the old nest. With this it dissolves old mud in order to make repairs and seal off the cells. The reuse of nests obviously saves time, allowing the wasp to do more food collecting and egg laying, with the result that these wasps are often more numerous than the species that originally made the nest.

A second group of nest builders are in the genus *Trypoxylon,* a few species of which build long separate tubes. The shape of their nests has led to their being called Pipe-Organ

Wasps. Unlike those of the Yellow Mud Dauber, their nests are not covered over with an extra mud layer, and each tube consists of many cells. Each of these cells contains spiders and an egg and is separated from the others with mud dividers.

Sometimes you can carefully remove mud nests intact and scrap away a portion of the mud backing to reveal what is inside. Depending on the time of year and the condition of the cell, you may find spiders and a larva, a dormant larva, a pupa, or an empty cocoon.

## *WEB BUILDERS*

The two moths described below, though belonging to separate families, are related in habits through their use of protective web nests during their larval stage. The nests are not particularly attractive in winter, when they appear as ragged masses of webbing filled with dried leaves and crumbling excrement, but they are so common a sight with the leaves gone that they bear some attention. Also, from a distance they can fool you into thinking they are birds' nests, and you should be able to tell the difference.

Since these insects are most conspicuous when they are larvae, both have been named for the larval stage: Tent Caterpillar and Fall Webworm.

### Eastern Tent Caterpillar (*Malacosoma americana*)

One type of webby mass hanging from trees belongs to the Tent Caterpillars. Their webs are built primarily in the crotches of branches and serve a very different purpose from those of the Fall Webworm. In spring, when the eggs first hatch, the caterpillars crawl down the branch to the first large joining of two branches. Here they build a web

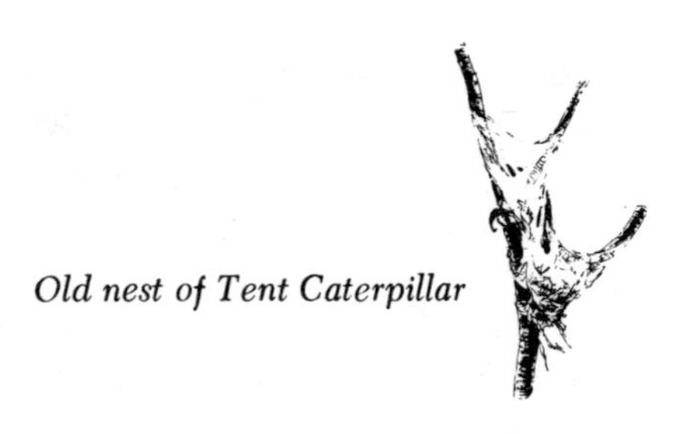
*Old nest of Tent Caterpillar*

for protection from such predators as birds and other insects. In order to feed, they leave the nest and crawl up the branches to the leaves.

The webbed nest is made communally and soon becomes filled with the remains of the caterpillar feces, as well as molted skins, for the larva, like insects in all stages of growth, must shed its skin as it grows. The caterpillars continue to add on layers of webbing, so that the final nest is

*Moth and larva of Tent Caterpillar*

made of many layers filled with excrement and molted skins. This stage lasts six weeks. At this point, after a certain number of molts or instars (periods between molting), they drop from the nest and spin cocoons in sheltered areas, leaving their former gregarious mode of life.

In three weeks they emerge as adult moths, then they soon mate and the females lay their egg masses on host twigs. These egg masses can also be found in winter. They

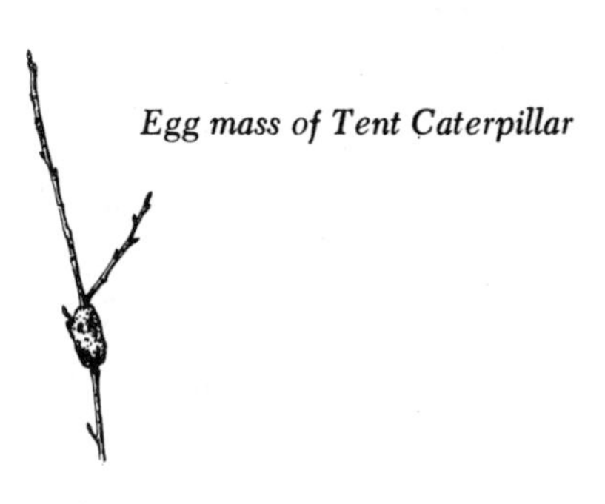
*Egg mass of Tent Caterpillar*

contain 100 to 300 eggs and are surrounded with a shiny, waterproof, foamy material. A group of Black Cherry or Chokecherry trees with webs hanging from them is an excellent place to spot the egg cases.

## Fall Webworm (*Hyphantria cunea*)

The Fall Webworm, like the Tent Caterpillar, builds a communal nest of webbing. But it is built in late summer and is more likely to last into fall and winter. The nests differ in location from those of Tent Caterpillars, reflecting their different use. Fall Webworms start to build their nest at the branch tips and enclose leaves with the webbing. As the leaves are enclosed the caterpillars eat them and extend

*Old nests of Fall Webworm*

the nest over new leaves as they are needed. Thus the finished product is not a triangular web in the crotch of branches, but a long loose web that encases the end of a twig. In winter these can mislead one into thinking they are the nest of the Baltimore Oriole, which is a similar color and hangs from branch tips. But an Oriole nest contains no leaves and is spherical at the base.

Another interesting contrast with the Tent Caterpillar is the life history of the Fall Webworm. Its eggs hatch in summer rather than spring, often being attached to the

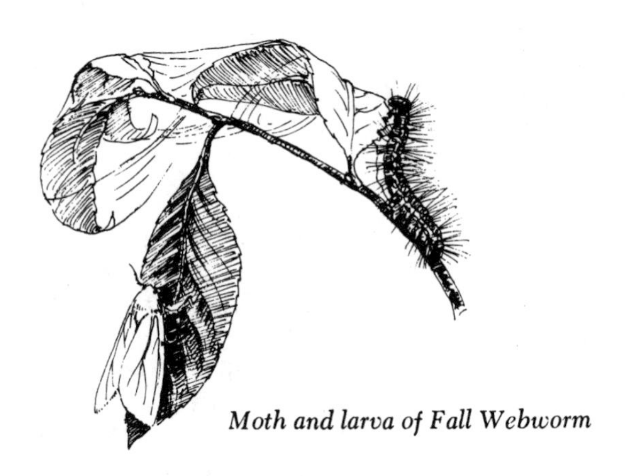

*Moth and larva of Fall Webworm*

underside of leaves of host plants. The larvae feed, never leaving their nest. As fall approaches they leave the web and head for bark crevices and leaf litter. Here they weave cocoons and stay in the pupal form throughout winter, in striking contrast to the long period the Tent Caterpillars spend as eggs. In May the adult Webworm moths emerge from the pupa, mate, and lay eggs.

The webs, like the Tent Caterpillars', are similarly filled with excrement and molted skins, but in addition contain skeletonized leaves.

V

# *Winter's Birds and Abandoned Nests*

Ever since the melting of the last glacier that covered much of North America, animals and plants have been slowly advancing to the North to claim unutilized habitats. Most birds can live comfortably in the North during summer, but in winter only a relatively few species are sufficiently adapted to survive. Probably the most important factor influencing which birds can remain North and which birds must return South, is a bird's ability to acquire food.

Two major aspects of winter substantially alter the availability of food; they are the cold and the snow. Cold most affects the food sources of water birds. It causes much of the water plant life to die back and makes many water animals recede into the mud to hibernate. The cold also freezes over lakes and streams, making what food still exists inaccessible. This lack causes inland water birds such as Herons, Ducks, Rails, and Sandpipers either to fly south to open water or to live by the sea, where more food is available.

Cold also affects another important source of food — airborne insects. Many birds depend solely on catching insects in the air and are specifically adapted to doing so. Insects cannot withstand the cold and are generally dormant throughout winter. Birds such as Flycatchers, Swifts, and Warblers must fly south in order to find aerial insects.

Snow, the other factor of winter that limits food sources, restricts those ground-feeding birds that eat insects or small animals — birds such as Robins, Thrashers, and Towhees. Snow also hides the movements of small rodents in fields, making it harder for some Hawks and Owls to catch their prey. These birds must move south to where snow cover is at most intermittent.

Birds that stay north in winter or come south from the arctic tundra are the ones that can live off the available food sources. Two sources are primary in winter: insects and seeds.

Hibernating insects are especially available on trees, where they overwinter in bark crevices, on buds, within the wood, or on needles, and about half of our small winter birds live off them. You will always find these birds in woodlands, often in mixed flocks, flitting among trees, searching above or beneath trunks and limbs for insect eggs, larvae, pupae, or adults. These birds include the Chickadees, Creepers, Titmice, Kinglets, Woodpeckers, and Nuthatches.

The other main source of winter food is the marvelously abundant fall harvest of tree and weed seeds and shrub berries. Almost half of all our winter birds use these as their primary source of food in winter. The number of plants that provide food of this kind are too numerous to begin to name; coniferous trees are particularly important, as of course are hedgerow shrubs and winter weeds. Birds that utilize this winter food include the Finches, Sparrows, Mockingbirds, and Grosbeaks, as well as Chickadees and Nuthatches.

The third main source of winter food is available to scavengers: birds such as Crows, Pigeons, and Gulls, which are not particular about what they eat and are not overly specialized in their feeding habits. These birds live off human refuse through most of the winter, frequenting dumps and city parks, using street litter and road kills. They are not shy of humans and seem to live and prosper on what we throw away.

Popular interest in birds during the last fifty years has centered on identification; amassing a "life list," which puts the emphasis on new species and encourages neglect of and disdain for the most common. This approach poses a problem for both the beginning and advanced bird-watcher in winter, for there are only twenty to thirty land bird species commonly present in winter, and they are already known by the experienced and easily learned by the beginner. So, after you know the name of a bird, what next? This is a serious and difficult question, and within its answer lie our deepest beliefs on the value of nature to humans. The question must be continually asked in order to avoid the empty naming of objects in nature.

One suggestion of an avenue of further involvement with birds is to take the time to observe their behavior — the relationship of birds to their environment and to other birds. And actually, winter is a particularly good time in which to do this, for with leaves gone, birds are more easily seen, and many join together in flocks, making them even more conspicuous. Now is the time to take birds you may have dismissed all summer as "just a Mockingbird" or "only another Chickadee" and relate to them on a deeper level of interest.

There are four areas of bird behavior to look for in winter: feeding, territorial, social, and breeding.

Eating enough food to keep warm is the main activity of birds in winter. The quantity and distribution of a bird's food determine most of its daily movements. Knowing what, how, when, and where a bird eats quickly involves you with the bird's physical structure and relationship to its environment. A bird's feet, bill, and feathers are primarilly adapted to feeding. How and in what way for each bird? Stop and watch birds feed in the wild; begin to learn the plants birds feed on, which are most favored and therefore lose their berries or seeds first, which ones aren't eaten all winter. Observe the variety of ways birds utilize food. A Cardinal may eat a Red Cedar berry whole, but a Chickadee will hold it in its feet, peck out the seeds, and let the fleshy part fall. Nuthatches can open nuts, often wedging them in tree bark and then battering them. Woodpeckers will peck into Oak Apple Galls to get insects that are inside. Nothing ties together a knowledge of nature as well as observing feeding habits, for they underlie and structure the larger parts of animal life.

Territorial behavior is also easily observed in winter, for two of our most common birds establish and maintain clearly defined winter territories. The Mockingbird, with a variety of displays and calls, establishes a territory in late fall which contains adequate food for the winter. When more than one Mockingbird settles on an area in fall, the displays are easily seen and the stages of territorial development are exciting to follow from week to week. Chickadees also establish territory in winter, each area lived in by a flock rather than by individual birds. Through observation in winter, you can estimate the extent of their territories and locate their favorite feeding areas.

Territory is generally defined as an area defended against intruders. But many other winter birds live in well-defined areas they do not defend. These areas are called ranges. Titmice and Juncos as flocks, and Woodpeckers and Nuthatches as pairs or single birds, all inhabit defined ranges. Once you begin to notice one of these birds in a particular area, you can expect to see it there all winter, and the Woodpecker and Nuthatch may also remain there through the summer to breed.

The social behavior of birds is in some ways more easily observed in winter than summer since many birds gather into flocks for the winter. Social behavior within species includes the huge roosts of Starlings and Crows; the feeding behavior of Crows, with their sentinel posted; the coveys of Bobwhites, which roost in circular formations, and the order of dominance within Chickadee flocks. Social behavior also occurs between species, especially in the common mixed flocks of Titmice, Kinglets, Chickadees, and Woodpeckers, usually led by the Titmice or Chickadees. Mockingbirds and Jays interact with other birds that might compete for their winter food, and Crows mob Hawks and Owls whenever they spot them.

Most people believe that all things associated with breeding behavior happen in spring, but this is far from the case. The breeding of most mammals and the courtship of many birds occurs in the middle of winter. Particularly obvious and easily observed are the displays of Mallard and Black Ducks. The ducks are common in small park ponds and can be watched from close by. They have a large vocabulary of gestures which, once learned, are not hard to spot. The ducks display in varying amounts all winter, hitting their peak of activity in November and December. Hairy Woodpeckers also begin courtship displays in December, and their "drumming" on resonant trees starts to be heard at that time. Jays gather in early spring to engage in a strange group display during February and March.

All of these types of bird behavior can be enjoyed even by the beginner; there is no need to learn the names of all the birds before you begin to be involved. Relatively little is known about the winter behavior of many of our birds, however. Where studies have been made, I have selected the most observable aspects and included them in the natural history descriptions. For readers who want more detail, they should seek out the journals listed in the Bibliography.

## *Key to Winter's Birds*

### *LARGE BIRDS (OVER 12 INCHES LONG), THE SIZE OF A CROW OR GULL*

GULL, SPECIES — Large whitish bird with gray or black wings; frequently soars over coast, rivers, lakes, and dumps; immature birds are mottled brown and white. Illustrated: Herring Gull.

DUCK, SPECIES — Large flattened bill; large heavy body; webbed feet; often swimming in water. Illustrated: male Mallard.

CROW, COMMON — Large all-black bird; often in small, wary groups; frequently feeds on ground.

HAWK, SPECIES — Large or medium-sized bird; generally brownish in color; usually soaring overhead; sharp pointed down-curved bill. Illustrated: Rough-legged Hawk.

OWL, SPECIES — Heavyset bird, large or medium-sized; large circular patterns around eyes; large rounded head; generally roosts in trees during day; often chased by crows. Illustrated: Great Horned Owl.

PHEASANT, RING-NECKED — Good-sized, ground-feeding bird; long pointed tail, which trails behind when bird is in flight; generally brown, but male has white neck-ring and dark head with red surrounding eye. Illustrated: male.

GROUSE, RUFFED — Large, brownish, ground-feeding bird with fan-shaped tail; head feathers often ruffled into a crest; tail brown with black terminal band.

GROUSE, SPRUCE — Similar to Ruffed Grouse, but extremely tame; has black tail with brown terminal band; male is black on chin and breast. Illustrated: Ruffed Grouse.

## *MEDIUM-SIZED BIRDS (12–16 INCHES LONG), SIZE OF A ROBIN OR PIGEON*

BOBWHITE — Medium-sized, brownish ground-feeding bird; black stripe through eye; short stubby tail.

LARK, HORNED — Black bib; black vertical stripe on light cheek; feeds on ground in open, barren areas; usually in flocks.

STARLING — Black medium-sized birds, speckled with white on breast and back; long, thin, pointed bill; by spring, speckles wear off and dark winter bill turns yellow.

GROSBEAK, EVENING — Black wing on yellowish bird; large whitish conical bill; patch of white on top of black wing; feeds in flocks, eating large seeds from trees; male has yellow forehead. Illustrated: male.

CARDINAL — Medium-sized bird with crest; male all red, female olive; both have reddish conical bill; frequently give a loud "chip . . . chip" call when disturbed.

JAY, BLUE — Medium-sized crested bird; bluish with white and black markings on wings; black bib from crest to around neck; in small, loose groups; often raucous.

JAY, GRAY — Medium-sized bird with a black patch on back of neck; no crest; common only in Canada and northern states. Illustrated: Blue Jay.

MOCKINGBIRD — Sleek, gray bird with long tail; light-colored underneath; shows large, obvious white patches on wings when flying; frequently gives a "chewk" call when disturbed.

DOVE, ROCK — Common street Pigeon; colored with shades of gray and iridescent green; when they take off, the sound of their wing tips hitting together can be heard.

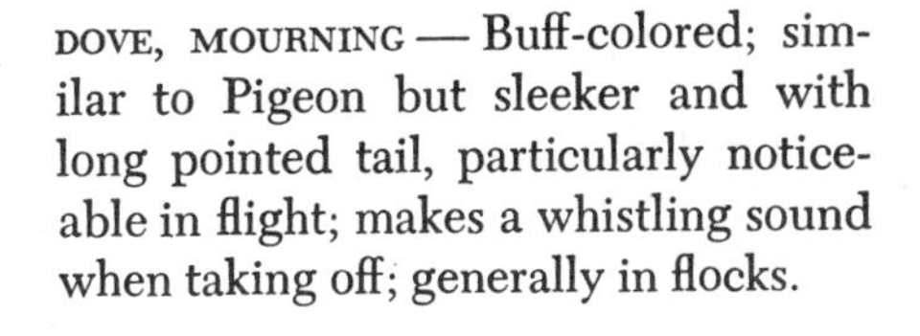

DOVE, MOURNING — Buff-colored; similar to Pigeon but sleeker and with long pointed tail, particularly noticeable in flight; makes a whistling sound when taking off; generally in flocks.

GROSBEAK, PINE — Dark wing with white wing bars; short, heavy black bill; male reddish, female olive-green.

WOODPECKER, HAIRY — Climbs up tree trunks; black and white patterned; white stripe down back; bill is almost as long as depth of head; male has red patch on back of head. Illustrated: Hairy Woodpecker.

## *SMALL BIRDS (LESS THAN 6 INCHES LONG), SIZE OF A SPARROW*

WOODPECKER, DOWNY — Same as Hairy Woodpecker, but smaller; bill only half as long as depth of head.

NUTHATCH, WHITE-BREASTED — Climbs up *and* down tree trunks; dark cap and black; white underneath; white face setting off dark eye.

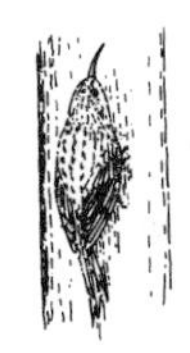

CREEPER, BROWN — Climbs only up tree trunks; small; brown streaked on top, white underneath; long, thin, down-curved bill; seen singly in mixed flocks.

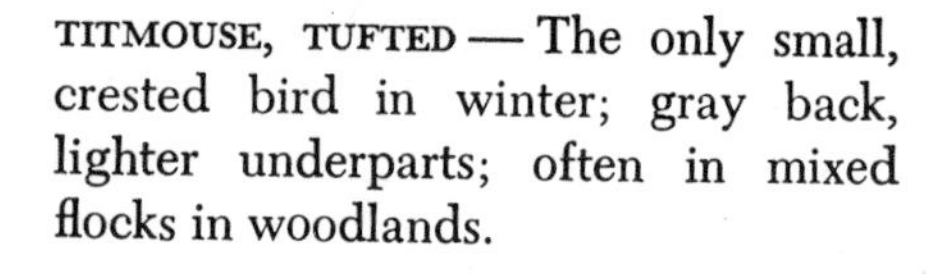

TITMOUSE, TUFTED — The only small, crested bird in winter; gray back, lighter underparts; often in mixed flocks in woodlands.

JUNCO, DARK-EYED — Dark gray bird with lighter underparts; light, pinkish bill; when Junco is in flight, sidetail feathers show two bands of white.

CHICKADEE, BLACK-CAPPED — A black-capped, black-chinned bird with white on cheek; small; often hangs upside down when feeding; tame and in flocks.

KINGLET, GOLDEN-CROWNED — Smallest bird of winter woods; olive- to brown-colored body with thin white wing bars; broad yellow stripe on top of head; short, thin bill.

GOLDFINCH, AMERICAN — Dark black wing on olive- to yellow-colored bird; small; thin white wing bars; short, light-colored bill; always gives a slight twittering call as it flies.

SISKIN, PINE — Heavily streaked, sleek, brown bird; patches of yellow on wings and tail (displayed best in flight); thin pointed bill; sometimes flock with Goldfinches.

FINCH, PURPLE — Female is brown-streaked; told from Sparrows by short, heavy, conical bill; male is reddish on head, back, and rump. Illustrated: female.

REDPOLL, COMMON — Brown-streaked bird with red patch above bill and black patch on chin.

SPARROW, SPECIES — Small brown birds with streaked backs; breast may or may not be streaked; comparatively small bill; none of the distinguishing features of our other small winter birds. Two common winter Sparrows have a dark spot on their breast: Song Sparrow on a streaked breast, Tree Sparrow on an unstreaked breast. Illustrated: Song Sparrow.

SPARROW, HOUSE — Common in the city; male told from other Sparrows by black chin patch; female is less streaked, with a buff throat and breast.

CROSSBILL, RED — Dark wings without crossbars; comparatively large bill crossed at its tip; male brick red, female olive green; moves like a parrot, using bill to grasp branches while climbing.

CROSSBILL, WHITE-WINGED — Same as Red Crossbill, except that dark wings are marked with two broad white wing bars. Illustrated: Red Crossbill.

# *Birds' Nests in Winter*

Birds' nests are more obvious in winter than in any other season. What were leafy forms and dense thickets are now merely a few branches, often revealing the once secret spot where a bird built a nest and raised its young.

Birds build nests in the ground, on the ground, in shrubs, in buildings, on and within trees, and on cliffs. The nests we see in winter are only those sturdy enough to last through summer and fall storms, and those not covered by autumn leaves or winter snow. This eliminates by far the majority of nests, which are either built on the ground or are so flimsy that they soon break apart.

Nests most commonly seen are those built below 20 feet above the ground, since we usually concentrate our vision on that range. Good places to look for nests are along the edges of fields and clearings, and among shrubs and low trees. Nests can be spotted by scanning for dark clumps or bunches of material among trees and shrubs. Fresh tree-hole nests can be spotted by finding wood chips on the forest floor, and older tree-hole nests by examining dead standing trees.

Identifying nests in winter has certain drawbacks. One is that neither the birds nor their eggs are present. Another problem is that many of the nests are considerably changed by weathering. This makes certain nests impossible to "pin down" to one particular maker. But there are certain categories of nests which can be easily distinguished from others, and knowing these may lead you to finer distinctions in the future.

Below I have outlined seven characteristic types of nests and in many cases narrowed down to species under each type. The types of nests listed are only those commonly found in winter and do not represent the tremendous variety of summer nests.

## *General Categories of Nests Commonly Found in Winter*

### *NESTS CONTAINING A LAYER OF MUD; INSIDE DIAMETER ABOUT 4 INCHES*

*Robin:* Lined with grasses, no leaves or sticks in the foundation.

*Woodthrush:* Lined with rootlets, with leaves in the foundation.

*Common Grackle:* Lined with grasses, with weed stalks or sticks in the foundation.

### *LARGE BULKY NEST WITH TWIG AND BARK STRIP FOUNDATION; THICK INNER LINING OF DARK ROOTLETS*

*Catbird, Mockingbird, Brown Thrasher:* These are all similar in foundation and lined with dark rootlets. Brown Thrasher nests are larger than the other two and contain foundation twigs 12 inches long or longer. The Catbird has a tendency to put cellophane in its foundation.

*Cardinal:* Like the Mockingbird's, not found very far north. It can be distinguished from the others by having no leaves in its foundation and by its lining of grasses instead of rootlets.

These nests are seen most often in shrubs, and frequently used by mice as winter homes, in which case they are lined with Cattail or Milkweed down.

*SMALL NESTS NEATLY FORMED OF GRASSES, USUALLY LOWER THAN 3 FEET OFF THE GROUND*

*Sparrows:* Song, Chipping, and Field Sparrows all make small, neatly cupped grass nests, often placing them on the

ground but at other times a few feet off the ground. They are often in the winter weed, Spiraea, and some may be lined with horsehair or, in these days, nylon fishing line.

### *SMALL NEATLY FORMED NESTS OF MILKWEED OR THISTLE DOWN AND GRASSES, OFTEN IN THE CROTCHES OF SAPLING TREES*

*Redstart, Yellow Warbler, Goldfinch, Flycatchers:* Downy materials show as gray or white in nest foundation. Rain

and weathering greatly alter these nests, making their distinguishing characteristics less clear. Some have quite thick, sturdy walls.

### *HANGING NESTS SUSPENDED FROM THE TIPS OF BRANCHES*

*Northern Oriole:* Woven of yarn, plant fibers, hair, etcetera, grayish in color, and often hanging from the drooping

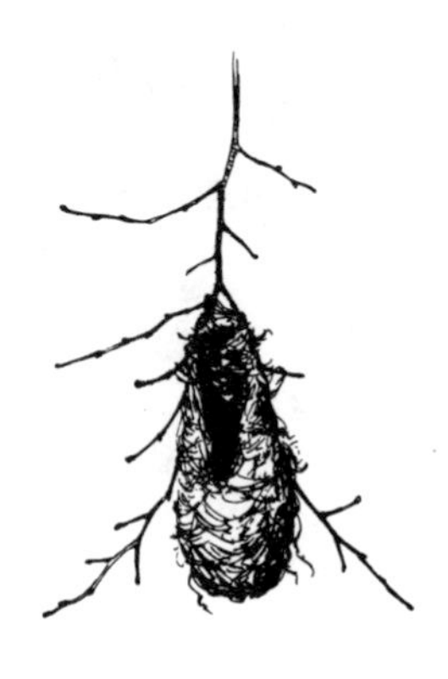

branch tips of Elm trees. Outside diameter about 4 inches.

## *SMALL NESTS NEATLY SUSPENDED AT THEIR RIM TO A FORKING BRANCH*

*Vireos:* Open at the top and built below the branch; outside diameter about 3 inches. Woven with plant fibers and spider silk, lined with pine needles and fine grasses. Nests can be found at any height. More common in woods.

## *NEST HOLES IN TREES*

*Chickadees* and *Woodpeckers* are known to excavate holes in trees, but many other birds live in these durable homes in following years, such as Titmice, Nuthatches, Wrens, Creepers, Tree Swallows. In larger holes, American Kestrals, Screech Owls, Saw-whet Owls, and Wood Ducks

may nest, as well as Squirrels and Mice. Studies of smaller Woodpecker holes shows that they tend to face east or south and be on the lower side of sloping branches or trunks. These two features enable them to receive the warmth and light of the morning sun and keep rain out.

# *Natural History Descriptions*

## Bobwhite (*Colinus virginianus*)

The family life of Bobwhites in summer is close-knit, the young and parents staying together as they roam their territory and feed. In fall, however, the families gather into larger groups, members of families dispersing among the groups. This time is often called the "fall shuffle" and probably insures against too much inbreeding during the coming summer. The larger groups then divide into smaller ones averaging 15 individuals. These are called "coveys"; they remain the social grouping for the rest of the winter.

Each covey eventually establishes its own area or range for feeding. It is a mixed social group of adults and juveniles of both sexes. At night the Bobwhites of a covey arrange themselves into a circular formation, their tails touching in the center, their heads facing outward. Each bird lifts its wings slightly in order to allow warmth to pass between birds. Each night is spent this way, usually in one of several favorite locations. Its function seems to be in protecting the group from cold. Sometimes coveys group into this formation during particularly cold days to conserve warmth and energy. Coveys utilize one of several favorite roosting locations, which can be identified by the ring of droppings the birds leave behind.

It has been shown by experiments that the degree of cold Bobwhites can withstand at night is directly related to the number of birds in the circular formation and that the optimal number is 14 or 15 birds. Often, when a covey becomes reduced by mortality, it will join another in order to increase its number.

Bobwhites, along with Pheasants, Grouse, and Chickens, are gallinaceous birds, a family characterized as ground-feeding, having short beaks and stout bodies, and preferring to walk rather than fly. Bobwhites are ill suited to the cold

*Bobwhites*

and snow of the north, and yet they are still quite common in the southern half of our snow belt. Their feeding habits are not as adaptable as those of some other northern gallinaceous birds, such as the Ruffed Grouse. During the year Bobwhites feed entirely on insects and seeds, and in winter 95 percent of their diet is seeds. Even a slight snow cover hampers their ability to locate seeds. There is a direct relationship between Bobwhite mortality and the number of consecutive days snow remains on the ground.

Bobwhites prefer a very specific habitat: they need open areas for foraging and brushy areas for cover. Ideal locations are at the edges of fields or pastures, where both situations occur. The size of their winter range depends on the suitability of the environment and the abundance of food — ranges vary from 5 to 75 acres and may overlap slightly with the ranges of other coveys.

As spring comes, individuals pair up and leave the covey.

At this time breeding territories are established, and the familiar "ah-bobwhite" call of the male is commonly heard and enjoyed.

As with each gallinaceous bird, you are more likely to see the tracks than the bird itself. The tracks of Bobwhite will usually be plentiful, for the covey stays fairly close together during the day, and following them may lead you to a winter roosting site. The size and shape of the tracks are shown in the key to the chapter "Tracks in the Snow."

## Cardinal (*Cardinalis cardinalis*)

During fall the male Cardinal may not seem as red as usual; he is not. For in late summer Cardinals molt, and many of the male's new feathers are tipped with light gray. As winter wears on, the tips of his feathers wear off, revealing his bright red breeding color beneath.

*Female and male Cardinal*

Since the 1900s and possibly earlier, the Cardinal has steadily moved north. This gradual migration has been ascribed to the clear trend toward warmer winters recorded over this time. Once strictly a southern bird, now the Cardinal is common in southern New England and parts of southern Canada.

The Cardinal is generally nonmigratory, and records from banding have shown adults to be rarely more than a few miles from their place of birth. Like many of our winter birds, Cardinals gather together in fall, forming loose flocks that stay and feed together. During this time males treat females the same way they treat other males in the flock, but in the second half of winter, males begin to solicit females with song. In late winter the females answer, and as pairs join together, the winter flocks break up.

Cardinal song, like that of most other birds in the Grosbeak family, consists of clear whistles. Both male and female participate in song, sometimes answering each other. Up to 28 distinct calls have been recorded, but among these only a few are commonly heard. The most common is described as "whoit-whoit-whoit-tear, tear, tear." The two parts of this song may be heard separately or together, slowly or extremely fast. Knowing this may help you to identify many of its calls. Another of its common calls is a short "chit . . . chit . . . ," which it seems to use when it is disturbed by another bird or an intruder. Cardinal song may be heard anytime during winter, but especially in late winter and spring, as the breeding season approaches.

The Cardinal's large bill is especially efficient at opening seeds. Attracted to the sunflower seeds at feeders, it takes them in its bill and neatly splits the husk, eating the kernel inside. In the wilds it uses this agility on the seeds of Ashes and Tulip Trees as well as eating seeds in the fruit of Grape, Sumac, and Dogwood berries.

Although most Cardinals join into flocks in winter, some pairs stay alone in their breeding territory. The average size of a flock is about 12 birds, but in the southern part of the Cardinal's winter range the flocks often contain over 50 birds. Flock size depends mainly on the abundance of food and how many birds a certain area can support. This is probably why there are smaller groups in the north, where food is less abundant during winter.

### Chickadee, Black-capped (*Parus atricapillus*)

Chickadees are some of the best birds to study in winter. They have interesting behavior and are present all winter in noisy and conspicuous flocks. However, these flocks are not like the loose-knit, free-roaming winter flocks of other birds; they are stable in membership and have rigid social structure. The flocks average 6 birds and form around a dominant pair which bred the previous summer. Other members may be juveniles that may or may not be the young of the dominant pair, as well as a few stray adults. While watching

*Chickadees*

the flock you may see one bird usurp another's feeding perch by scaring it away. This is a common expression of dominance among birds, and in this case it is an expression of the hierarchical structure of the Chickadee flock.

When out walking you may repeatedly find a Chickadee flock in the same place. This is because a flock will have three to five favorite foraging sites among which it circulates during the day. At these spots the birds feed more intensively than at other areas. These sites define the territory that is defended against other Chickadee flocks, an area that is often an extension of the dominant pair's summer breeding territory. A flock generally has a roosting area within its territory to which the birds return each night; it is often in dense evergreens, but individual birds may roost in small tree holes nearby.

Chickadees have a number of calls which make them easy to locate in the woods. Each call is more or less associated with a certain function. Their most frequent call is their "contact note." This is a high pitched "tseet-tseet" and is continually given by members of the flock in order to keep the flock together. When a bird has strayed farther away it may give the well-known call "chickadee-dee" to locate the flock. A scolding call is given to express dominance within the flock or between flocks; it is just "dee-dee-dee-dee," and is often given when a dominant bird is displacing another from a feeding perch.

The Chickadee has an extraordinary ability to maneuver on branches. It is as comfortable hanging below as it is perching on top. In winter, half of its diet is small eggs or larvae of insects and spiders which are nestled in bark crevices. The rest consists of seeds from Pines and Hemlocks. It has been suggested that the Chickadee's acrobatic ability is an adaptation to winter feeding — when snow covers the tops of evergreen branches, Chickadees can still hang beneath to gather seeds and insects.

In September and October local flocks of Chickadees are augmented by migrant Chickadee flocks. But by November only a few are left, and you have to travel over a number of woodland acres to see or hear a flock. But at this time the flocks begin to be joined by other species, such as Nuthatches, Woodpeckers, Kinglets, Brown Creepers, and Titmice. These are only loose associations, with each species coming and going at different times of day.

## Creeper, Brown (*Certhia familiaris*)

The Brown Creeper has been described as a "rather characterless and uninteresting bird," but I find it just the opposite. Unlike the Chickadees and Nuthatches, with their noisy

*Brown Creeper*

gatherings, the Brown Creeper is inconspicuous and often alone. It is always a treat to discover one as it quietly and industriously hitches itself up a tree trunk, scrutinizing bark crevices for wintering insects.

Its bill is long, thin, and curved, and although unsuited for pecking like the beak of the Nuthatch, it is perfect for reaching around and under bits of bark to glean insect eggs and cocoons. The Brown Creeper is almost completely insectivorous, but by its manner of feeding, reduces its competition for food with the Chickadees, Nuthatches, Kinglets, and Titmice, with whose flocks it is often associated. It is interesting to note that although all of these birds look for food on trees, each one's feeding habits are slightly different from those of the others so that they are not competing as much as one might imagine.

The Creeper climbs trees much as Woodpeckers do, holding onto the bark with its toes and leaning back on its long stiff tail feathers. This way of supporting itself enables it to move easily up the tree. Its characteristic foraging behavior is to alight at the base of a tree and spiral around it as it travels up. Upon reaching a point high up on the tree, it flies to the base of the next tree. Creepers roost either in holes in trees or clinging to bark on a protected area of a tree trunk.

The bird is not much affected by human presence, but when predators such as hawks are near, it flattens itself against the tree trunk, where its brown and white mottled feathers render it practically invisible against the coloring of the bark. In late winter it is not uncommon to find two or more Creepers together, spiraling up trees one after the other, an activity that may be part of their prebreeding display.

## Crossbill, Red (*Loxia curvirostra*)<br>White-winged (*Loxia leucoptera*)

This is one bird which you will see either commonly or not at all, for Red Crossbills are birds of the far North, which move south when cone crops fail.

The crossed bill is an obvious adaptation for prying cone scales apart while the bird's tongue gathers the seeds. The bill would seem to be overspecialized to the point where the birds are at the mercy of the irregular cone crops, but this is not the case. Time and again, observations have proven that Crossbills can adapt to eating both insects and other types of seeds.

The flocks, which are generally large, often feed together

*Red Crossbills*

in one tree, creating a crackling sound throughout the tree as each bird pries apart cone scales. Then the flock leaves together and moves to the next tree while giving their distinctive call notes. Sometimes they associate with other winter flocks of other birds and, since they are feeding on the ends of the higher branches, they become the "sentries" of the conglomerate flock, warning of approaching danger. Although Crossbills have been observed to be aggressive and competitive in captivity, they are noted for their lack of these characteristics in the wild.

Since the birds always seem to be busy feeding, their distinctive crossed bills may be hard to see, but their feeding habits should help you identify them, for they often use their bills to grab branches as they move, much like a parrot. The Red Crossbill male is brick-red and the female is a mottled greenish yellow. The other species, the White-winged Crossbill, is similar in habits and coloring except that both male and female have two white wing bars.

## Crow, Common (*Corvus brachyrhynchos*)

A spectacular feature of Crows in winter is their nightly communal roosts, which in some areas of North America may contain over 200,000 birds apiece. Roosts near you can be located by watching the direction toward which groups of Crows are flying in late afternoon or the direction from which they come at dawn, for every morning the birds disperse from their roost in small groups to feed, and then return at sunset in the same way. Why they roost together in such huge flocks is unknown. The roosts are usually located near good winter feeding grounds, such as by the ocean at river deltas, or near large inland lakes, but availability of food does not explain the size of the roosts.

Most Crows that summer in Canada or northern New England migrate south, for the northern snow cover makes feeding difficult. But many still remain and may drift to roosts by the sea or the Great Lakes or near large city dumps. These northern roosts are much smaller than those found farther south and will most likely contain between 500 and 10,000 birds.

*Crows*

Crows are seasoned omnivores, and will take advantage of any food source. At least 50 percent of Crows' winter diet is corn, the kernels that remain in the fields after harvesting. About 25 percent is other grains, weed seeds, and wild fruits, and the last 25 percent is animal matter collected near water, carrion found along roadsides, and garbage from town dumps. What remains undigested in the Crow's stomach is collected into a pellet and regurgitated. These pellets can be easily found under the roosts and are often clues to the bird's diet. In one study of a winter roost, it was found that the pellets consisted mostly of seeds. They averaged 36 seeds from either poison ivy or poison sumac, and many other seeds from Sumac, Grape, Dogwood, Hackberry, and Buckthorn.

As Crows feed in small groups, often one or more will stay on a perch and warn those feeding of approaching danger. Crows are extremely vocal and will always harass Owls or Hawks that they have spotted. If you see Crows swarming around a tree, it is worthwhile approaching, for you may locate an Owl or Hawk.

Since Crows do most of their feeding on land their footprints are a common sight. They sometimes hop, but more usually they walk. Their track pattern is easily identified and often has a characteristic mark where the bird drags the toe of its foot between each print and the next. At the landing or takeoff point of the trail you may see the beautiful imprint of the bird's wings at either side of its feet. Good places for Crow tracks are in cultivated fields and the snow-covered surfaces of frozen lakes.

### Dove, Mourning (*Zenaida macroura*)

The Mourning Dove is a ground feeding bird related to our domestic Pigeon. During winter, the doves gather in large flocks, which feed and roost as units. Seeds from grasses, corn, and weeds, and the berries from Pokeweed are important items in its strictly vegetarian diet. The birds are not

*Mourning Doves*

strong enough to scratch through crusted snow for their food, therefore most migrate south; but many others still manage to remain as winter residents in areas of intermittent snow cover.

When you approach a flock, they will all fly up into trees nearby; they can be recognized by the whistling sound their wings make as they take off. In level flight, they are spectacular fliers, their wings bending back after each powerful stroke and their pointed tails streaming behind.

Their name, which until seen in print is often thought to be "Morning Dove," refers to their song, which consists of five "coos," the second one rising and falling in tone; it is definitely a mournful sound. The call, so common at other times of year, most likely won't be heard in winter. But in spring, as the flocks break up and pairing begins, the call is often heard.

### Dove, Rock (*Columba livia*)

The Rock Dove, or Pigeon, is an excellent and beautiful flyer. It seems awkward at times on land, but once it is in

*Rock Doves, or Pigeons*

the air, its agility is remarkable. In flocks, Rock Doves display a marvelous ability for simultaneous flight as they circle and rise in unison. Strong flight is undoubtedly an adaptation to their native habitat, which is on the edges of cliffs by the sea. Here, with their nests on ledges and within caves, the birds had to be excellent flyers both to land on their perches and to contend with the changing gusts of wind so common along ocean cliffs.

The birds are not native to North America but were brought here as domesticated birds by European settlers. In time, many of the birds escaped or were released and started breeding. As cities grew up, Rock Doves were comfortable with the tall buildings that were so similar to their rocky cliffs; they now commonly place their nests on window ledges and air conditioners and among the crannies of bridges.

In the cities Pigeons feed mostly on garbage and human handouts. When near parks they feed on grass and weed seeds, never scratching the ground for them but only gleaning those that are in plain sight. During breeding season they are often in pairs, but for the winter months they simply gather in large flocks.

## Ducks, Mallard (*Anas platyrhynchos*) Black (*Anas rubripes*)

Almost everyone has had an occasion to watch Mallards or Black Ducks swim lazily around a park pond, but how many have seen their fascinating courtship displays, which occur most frequently during the months of November and December, continuing at a lower intensity throughout winter? Here is a chance for even experienced birdwatchers to discover new things about old birds, and of all places, in the local duck pond.

Different displays are done by females and males. The most common display of females is called "inciting." The female swims after the male of her choice and repeatedly nods her head back over her shoulder. This display has been called an "avowal of love" and may signify her choice of a mate. To see this, watch pairs where the female is following.

The bulk of the rest of the displays is done by groups of males toward each other. First the males do "preliminary shaking." A male floats with his head compressed down on his neck, so much so that on a Mallard the white ring on the neck does not show. After holding like this for a minute or two, the male lifts its head slightly and tentatively shakes it. It stops and repeats the shaking two more times, each time shaking more vigorously. Other nearby males usually do this also.

This display is not striking and may go unnoticed at first.

*Male and female Mallard*

It may occur as an isolated incident or may be followed by a series of other displays.

After preliminary shaking, a female may swim quickly around and among the males, jerking her head up, then down and stretched out flat along the water. This is "nod-swimming" and tends to stimulate the males to continue with other displays. It is very obvious and may help draw your attention to the following more subtle behavior of the males.

After the nod-swimming of the female the males may do one of three different displays, each of which is accompanied by a short whistle easily heard on a still day. One of these male displays, the "grunt-whistle," consists of the duck lifting the back of its neck high in the air while keeping its bill and tail in the water; at the same time it gives a grunt and whistle, but only the whistle is easily heard.

Mated pairs also display together. The male and female ducks face each other and alternately jerk their heads downward. This is called "pumping" and can be preliminary to mating, where the male swims onto the back of the female and holds the feathers from the back of her head in his bill. Mating can be followed by male nod-swimming.

These displays are best seen on a still day when the ducks are through with intensive feeding. Sometimes a slight disturbance, such as shooing those on land into water, can stimulate certain displays to occur.

## Finch, Purple (*Carpodacus purpureus*)

A common bird at suburban feeders in winter is the Purple Finch. You may at first mistake the bird for a sparrow, but the raspberry-colored feathers on the head and breast of the male and the large conical bill on the brown and white streaked female clearly distinguish it. The Purple Finch breeds in northern Canada and joins others in flocks to mi-

*Male and female Purple Finches*

grate south for the winter. Often females will arrive a few weeks ahead of the males.

Although gregarious in winter, it is quite aggressive toward its own species when feeding, but still Purple Finches roost together at night, generally in dense evergreens. In the wild they are often seen with groups of Goldfinches, feeding on the seeds of winter weeds. When seeds are scarce they eat Maple and Birch buds and the fruits of shrubs. In fact, their generic name, *Carpodacus*, means "fruit-biting" and may refer to their habit of eating buds off fruit trees as well as pecking at the fruit in fall.

Purple Finches are well-known for their song, which is a long, rich, and variable warble.

## Goldfinch, American (*Spinus tristis*)

After breeding in late summer male Goldfinches molt their bright yellow feathers, replacing them with muted yellow-green plumage that resembles the female plumage. In winter, they typically gather in flocks of from 5 to 100 birds, feeding on the grass and weed seeds of fields. Some of their more favorite foods are the seeds from Ragweed, Thistles, Goldenrod, Evening Primrose, and Mullein. Goldfinches often are joined by flocks of other birds that have similar feeding habits, such as the Tree Sparrows when in fields and Pine Siskins and Common Redpolls when feeding among conifers.

Goldfinches have a characteristic flight, which resembles the line created by a loose wire draped between telephone poles. The bird flies up, then, holding its wings against its body, swoops down, then again flies up. It characteristically gives a twittering call as it flies.

The Goldfinch is one of our latest breeders, waiting until late summer or early fall, when it uses the down from the matured thistle seeds to construct its nest. As a result the nest is often in better shape in winter than those of birds

*Goldfinches*

that bred in early spring and whose nests may have already been torn apart by summer and fall storms. See the key to bird's nests for help in identifying it.

## Grosbeak, Evening (*Hesperiphona vespertina*)

The Evening Grosbeak is a beautiful winter bird that is becoming more and more common in eastern Canada and northeastern states. Originally it was only a northwestern bird, but has extended its range eastward in the last forty years. When you spot Evening Grosbeaks in the wild, they will either be in calling flocks overhead or feeding on seeds in the tops of Maple, Locust, or Ash trees. Later in winter they frequent the ground, looking for fallen seeds, or come

*Evening Grosbeaks*

to feeders, where they are often belligerent toward their own and other species.

Like all Grosbeaks, they have bills that are particularly well adapted to feeding on seeds and are even strong enough to crack cherry pits to get at the nourishment inside. Although they eat some insects in summer, they are strict vegetarians in winter.

Their colors are particularly striking. The white and black patches of their wings, the yellow area on the male's forehead, and their large whitened conical bills are all easily seen, as the birds are not generally frightened by human presence.

## Grosbeak, Pine (*Pinicola enucleator*)

Although not as blatantly red as the Cardinal, the Pine Grosbeak is our largest red winter bird. But the two are not likely to be confused, for while the Cardinal is a southern bird extending its range to the north, the Pine Grosbeak is

*Pine Grosbeaks*

decidedly northern and barely makes it as far south as the United States in winter. Not until after December does it regularly cross Canada's southern border. But in the provinces it is locally common, and quite tame, feeding especially on Pine and Maple seeds and the berries from Mountain Ash.

The Pine Grosbeak is one of our winter birds that have worldwide distribution, for this same species is common in northern Europe, European Russia, and Siberia, and its range in North America extends across the continent all the way to Alaska.

## Grouse, Ruffed (*Bonasa umbellus*)<br>Spruce (*Canachites canadensis*)

Two species of Grouse live in the area covered by this guide: the Spruce Grouse and the Ruffed Grouse.

The Ruffed Grouse spends most of its time on the ground,

*Ruffed Grouse*

and you will probably see its tracks many times before actually seeing the bird. Its feet are physically adapted for travel on snow. In fall, small comblike projections grow on either side of the toes, doubling the surface area of the feet and supporting them on soft snow. Their growth is believed to be stimulated by the photoperiod of the fall days; the combs are shed again in the spring.

The tracks of the Ruffed Grouse may lead you to one of its winter roosts. When the snow conditions are right, the bird takes advantage of the insulating qualities of snow by burrowing beneath it for the night. It either scratches out a cavity or dives from above into soft snow, then tunnels a short distance and remains there for the night. The tunnels can be clearly recognized, for the bird always leaves droppings, small cylindrical scats about one inch long composed of plant fibers. Often tracks and wing imprints of the bird's landing or taking off can be seen around these snow roosts.

Unlike our other gallinaceous birds, the Bobwhite and Ring-necked Pheasant, Ruffed Grouse prefer to stay in the woods and in winter eat only plant material, mostly tree buds from Aspen, Oak, Hawthorn, and Beech, but also beechnuts, acorns, and the leaves from Mountain Laurel.

In contrast to this diet, the Spruce Grouse eats almost entirely buds from Pines, Spruces, and Firs. It is also a more sedentary bird, often spending a day or two in one evergreen tree, eating in daytime and roosting there at night. The Spruce Grouse is extremely tame, allowing humans to approach within a few feet and still remaining unconcerned. It lives farther north than the Ruffed Grouse and in southern latitudes will be found only in the mountains.

To distinguish Grouse tracks from those of Pheasant and Bobwhite, consult the key in Chapter 7.

## Gulls (*Larus* species)

Although many Gulls (largely immature) migrate south in fall, the adults tend to shift to river valleys, the seacoast, and the Great Lakes region. By spending winter in these areas the Gulls can continue to find food at the water's exposed edge. Besides these natural areas, Gulls also congregate at town and city dumps, where they eagerly await the tidbits of food that arrive in the new refuse.

But Gulls were well adapted to the omnivorous diet of the scavenger long before dumps became as large as they are today, for their natural habitat skirts the edges of two radically different environments: the land and the sea. In order to exploit the coastal edge, the Gull has become generalized in physiology and adaptable in habit. Its wings are neither as large as those of true sea birds nor as agile as land birds'. Its feet are webbed and it can swim, but it also walks easily and does most of its foraging on land. And compared to other birds', a Gull's bill is quite unspecialized.

These all enable the Gull to take advantage of many sources of food. Gulls feed on such varied items as earthworms, fish, rodents, mollusks, insects, and other birds' eggs. The Gull has a huge crop, which easily contains whole rats or fish that they might catch, and like many other large birds they regurgitate the undigestible parts of their food, in the form of small pellets about one inch long.

*Herring Gulls*

Gulls are generally gregarious at all times of the year. In winter they are most often seen in flocks that are traveling between roosting grounds and feeding sites. The roosting grounds are usually in open areas such as the centers of coastal bays, or remote beaches along the coast. When coastal weather is bad, they move inland and roost in open fields.

There are three common winter gulls in the northeastern and north central area. The largest is the Great Black-backed Gull, easily recognized by its black back and wing tops. The next in size is the Herring Gull, undoubtedly the most common of all our Gulls. Its appearance is generally nondescript, gray and white. The smallest, the Ring-billed Gull, is similar to the Herring Gull except that it is smaller and has a black ring that encircles its bill just in from the tip. All of these Gulls when one or two years old have an immature plumage that is mottled white and brown. To distinguish immature species, either consult a more detailed bird guide or else be content to know that all brownish gulls are still immature.

A great deal has been discovered about the behavior of Gulls, especially regarding their particular postures and stances that communicate social messages. Unfortunately, this behavior is limited primarily to the breeding season and would only rarely be observed in winter.

### Hawks (*Circus hudsonicus*, *Buteo* species, *Falco* species)

If during the day in winter you see soaring overhead a bird that is neither a Crow nor a Gull, then you have most likely spotted a Hawk. Hawks are large day-hunting birds that kill prey with the talons on their feet. Since their main diet is the Meadow Vole, they are most often seen hunting over fields and large open areas.

Almost all small mammals and birds are instantly aware

*Red-tailed Hawk*

of the presence of Hawks. Birds seek the cover of trees, and mammals freeze or run to their burrows. By their hunting methods Hawks try to offset this awareness on the part of their prey.

There are at least four common ways Hawks hunt, and often a species can be recognized by observing the way it hunts. Marsh Hawks hunt low to the ground, soaring just over the tops of grasses and shrubs. They depend on coming suddenly upon their prey and catching it unaware.

American Kestrels and Rough-legged Hawks hover in midair over fields, waiting for their prey to reemerge; then they dive down on it. The Red-tailed Hawk and Red-shouldered Hawk also wait, but they sit motionless in dead trees by the side of a field, or circle high overhead. When they spot prey, they coast off their perch or dive to attack.

When circling overhead, sometimes Hawks soar so high that they are only specks in the sky. Their eyesight is still so good that they can easily spot mice below and dive down upon them at tremendous speeds.

Between 75 percent and 95 percent of Hawk prey in winter consists of Meadow Voles, depending on the species of Hawk. The next most common prey animal is the White-footed Mouse, and it averages almost 10 percent of the diet. The rest of the diet is made up of larger mammals and small birds. Hawks usually pluck the fur or feathers off their prey before eating pieces of it whole. Many of the bones are eaten, and these, along with some fur, are regurgitated in the form of pellets. These pellets often accumulate under a roosting perch. By breaking them apart you can often discover the complete skulls and teeth of the rodents the Hawks have eaten.

Since the availability of prey depends heavily on the amount of snow cover, most Hawks migrate south, to where snow cover is at least intermittent. Of those that remain in the north the most common will be the Red-tailed Hawk, Red-shouldered Hawk, Marsh Hawk, and the American Kestrel.

## Jay, Blue (*Cyanocitta cristata*)
## Gray (*Perisoreus canadensis*)

Even more than Crows, Jays seem to take on the role of sentinel in nature. It is a rare moment when you can watch

*Blue Jay*

a Jay going quietly about its activities, for at most times it will spot you and sound "alarm" or "assembly" calls, which cause other Jays to join in warning all the rest of nature of your presence. Jays are particularly aggressive toward natural predators of the Dog, Cat, or Weasel families as well as toward Hawks and Owls. Their typical alarm or assembly call is the familiar "jaaay, jaaay."

Throughout the year Jays are aggressive food gatherers. They eat whatever they can get and often store food either in the ground or in crevices of the trunks and branches of trees. Their storing habits are irregular: sometimes they collect acorns in a knothole only to take them out for eating a few minutes later; at other times, food is carefully stored and left to rot or for squirrels to steal.

The Gray Jay of Canada and the northern states has gen-

*Gray Jay*

eral habits similar to those of the Blue Jay — storing food, having a variety of social calls, and being aggressive toward intruders — but its winter flocking habits may differ substantially. They have not yet been carefully studied. The Gray Jay does start nesting earlier than the Blue Jay, often building its nest and incubating eggs while snow is still on the ground.

## Junco, Dark-eyed (*Junco hyemalis*)

Juncos breed in the northern coniferous woods but migrate south in fall, spending the winter anywhere between southern Canada and the Gulf of Mexico. They winter in parks and suburbs of the city as well as in the country and often feed in the company of other birds, especially House Sparrows in the city and Tree Sparrows in the country.

Juncos migrate in small flocks. Each flock upon arrival establishes four or five favorite foraging sites, usually no more than two to three hundred yards apart. Members of this flock feed only at these established sites; they may forage alone or with different combinations of members of their flock, but rarely as a whole group. As new Juncos arrive they may join this flock by participating in its circuit of feeding sites.

It has also been shown, by banding the birds, that many individuals return to the same winter area each year, showing an ability to home in on winter areas as well as to summer breeding grounds. The first winter arrivals are often birds that have been there in previous winters, birds already

*Dark-eyed Juncos*

familiar with the foraging sites. Later arrivals may be younger birds, which are then integrated into the habits of the older flock.

Juncos are lovely winter birds and relatively unafraid of humans. They are unmistakable as they fly away, for their gray tails are lined on either side with white feathers. They feed primarily on seeds, especially Ragweed in the city. Their paired tracks are common, since they do most of their foraging on the ground.

In late winter before the flocks break up and individuals migrate north, you will hear a new bird song in the air. It is a high sustained trill, and it is the song of the Junco, which hasn't done more than twitter all winter. The call is one associated with its breeding period and probably signals to us the imminence of their spring migration.

## Kinglet, Golden-crowned (*Regulus satrapa*)<br>Ruby-crowned (*Regulus calendula*)

The Kinglet is the smallest bird of the winter woods, from beak to tail only 3½ inches long. It migrates down from the

*Golden-crowned Kinglets*

north in small flocks, most often feeding in Pines or Spruces. Its thin pointed bill is a mark of its insectivorous habits as it flits about the trees feeding on insect eggs and wintering spiders. Kinglets are so tame that it is common to be within ten feet of their active feeding. The yellow strip on the top of the heads of Golden-crowned Kinglets is often visible and makes them like little jewels of the winter woods.

Their flocks are often accompanied by a Downy Woodpecker or two and Chickadees. Its relative, the Ruby-crowned Kinglet, winters more to the south, but the two may be seen together in the north along the coast. The Golden-crowned Kinglet flocks in winter utilize contact notes to keep the flock together. This note can be recognized simply because it is the highest and slightest note one can imagine.

## Lark, Horned (*Eremophila alpestris*)

After leaving the nest, immature Horned Larks join together into flocks. In August and September the adults join them,

*Horned Larks*

and these flocks of from 10 to 100 birds stay together for the winter. Horned Larks have a decided preference for open barren areas. In this habitat they both feed and roost during winter and will nest in similar areas in spring. Common places to see them are barren land by the shore, open fields, and the large median strips of turnpikes. They feed on grass seeds, and their flocks are sometimes joined by Lapland Longspurs, sparrowlike birds from the far north. At night they roost in the same barren areas, settling out of the wind under tufts of grass.

### Mockingbird (*Mimus polyglottus*)

You must get out in early fall to see the interesting behavior of Mockingbirds. The stages of territory establishment can occur very quickly, and once they have been completed, Mockingbirds are quiet and inconspicuous for the rest of the winter. In early fall, many Mockingbirds may gather in favorable winter locations, "favor" being determined by the amount of available berries and fruit. During this time there will seem to be interminable chasing of birds from one bush or tree to another with no apparent consistent dominance by one bird. All chasing and aggression is usually accompanied by a loud "chewk . . . chewk" call. Mockingbirds will also be heard singing their continuous imitations of other birds' songs, usually each phrase repeated three times.

Soon, Mockingbirds pick prominent perches on the tops of small trees or shrubs and claim a few of these perches as the border markers of their territory. If a stray Mockingbird enters the area, each of the settled birds will start singing and "chewk"-ing and will chase the stray bird away.

The final stage of territory marking is inconspicuous but should be looked for. Where two territories abut, the two "owners" will land on the ground at the boundary line. They face each other, their tails pointed up, and hop forward and backward and from side to side. At the conclusion, both

*Mockingbird*

birds fly off into their territories. In late fall Mockingbirds will also chase other species out of their territory, especially migrating Robins and Cedar Waxwings, which also eat berries.

After about two months of activity in fall, Mockingbirds radically change their behavior; they become quiet and secretive, no longer singing or using their perches but merely skulking within the cover of their territory, for after early winter the territories seem agreed upon and there is no need for display.

The territories may be held by a pair or a single male or female bird. Sometimes a pair that bred last spring will hold separate but adjacent territories in winter. In the south, Mockingbirds are known for inhabiting the cities. This is also increasingly true in the north. Suburbs are probably good wintering areas for the birds because of extensive planting of shrubs.

## Nuthatch, White-breasted (*Sitta carolinensis*)
## Red-breasted (*Sitta canadensis*)

Although Nuthatches are not numerous you will nonetheless probably see them in winter, for they are often in the company of noisy Chickadee flocks and they are relatively tame toward humans. The Nuthatch is our only winter bird that can climb down a tree. Other trunk climbers such as the Brown Creeper and the Woodpeckers generally rely on sitting back on their tail feathers for support and usually face upward. But the Nuthatch just holds on hard with its feet and wanders up and down tree trunks at whim. This may give it some slight advantage in finding insects that Creepers and Woodpeckers missed coming the other way.

But the main food of the Nuthatch in winter is nuts: acorns, beechnuts, hickory nuts, and the pits from cherries. It is able to break open many of these to get at the nut, often wedging them into tree crevices in order to peck harder at them. Closely related to this same behavior of bracing nuts in crevices is its habit of storing food. In fall, Nuthatches take Hemlock seeds and bits of nuts from their source and store them in among bark crevices for later use.

*White-breasted Nuthatch*

There have even been observations of Nuthatches "covering" these stores with bits of bark or lichens.

Both male and female Nuthatches remain in the same territory year round, and because they do, they tend to select the same mates year after year. The territories are large and may in part be extended by an even larger range. These tend to become established over the years, and this fact, along with their size, results in very little aggressive behavior over territory boundaries. Within the territory the male and female have separate roosts. These roosts are holes in trees, holes probably chiseled out by a Downy or Hairy Woodpecker. Downies have been observed to take over the roost of a Nuthatch and vice versa. But since the Nuthatch seems to prefer a larger roost-hole entrance, there is probably no serious competition between the two.

In late winter Nuthatches begin their courtship song and display. These take place mostly within an hour after the male leaves his roost hole in the morning. They are subtle and not easily seen and so not included in this account. But the common call of the Nuthatch is not subtle and is easily heard. It is a nasal "ank . . . ank . . . ank" and is the best way to locate the bird.

## Owls (Order *Strigiformes*)

Owls and Hawks are our two main birds of prey. While Hawks hunt only by day, Owls hunt mostly at night. They have large eyes, which help them see at night, but they also depend mostly on their ears to pinpoint the rustlings of small rodents among the grasses and leaves. Their flight is quieter than that of most birds because of the construction of their flight feathers, so no extra sound is made that might warn prey of their attack.

Owls eat primarily rodents and thus perform a valuable function in helping control mouse populations. The larger Owls also feed on small mammals such as Hares, Squirrels,

*Great Horned Owl*

and Skunks; the smaller Owls feed occasionally on small birds and in summer on insects. Birds are often plucked of their feathers before being eaten, but many mice are just eaten whole. The undigested remains of fur and bones are then coughed back up as dense pellets, similar to those of Hawks. The "castings" can be found under nests or places where the Owls roost during daytime. (Crows and Gulls also cough up castings.)

One of the largest and most commonly seen Owls is the Great Horned Owl. It has become adapted to living in suburbs. It usually sits quietly among evergreens during the day but is frequently mobbed by Crows, which force it to shift continually from tree to tree, trying to rid itself of their calls and attacks. Other Owls, such as the Short-eared Owl and Snowy Owl, prefer to nest and roost on the ground in open areas. The Snowy Owl is a spectacular bird that comes south from the Arctic in winter. It is mostly white and blends with the snow as it sits on the ground in open areas.

## Pheasant, Ring-necked (*Phasianus colchicus*)

The Pheasant is basically a ground-dwelling bird. It will skulk away from you into the underbrush if it can, but if you get too close it will flush into flight, climbing steeply for a short distance, then spreading its wings and gliding slowly down. You may have seen a pheasant gliding above you across a road or turnpike after it was flushed from one side.

Because of its terrestrial nature you are more likely to see its tracks than the bird itself, and through tracking you can observe some of the Pheasant's more interesting winter habits. Pheasants join together in fall and winter in flocks of anywhere from 4 to over a hundred birds, mostly averaging about 15 birds per flock. The ratio of females to males in these flocks is about 3:1, which reflects the "harem" breeding behavior of Pheasants in spring. The flocks feed and roost together. Roosts are usually in lowland swamps, where cattails and other vegetation provide both cover and insulation. The flocks feed in the morning and evening but are known to stay in their roosts if the weather is severe. Their favorite winter food is field corn, so Pheasants are most abundant in farm areas with scrub field edges.

The size of Pheasant flocks is dependent on the abundance of food and suitable roosting cover. During winter

*Male and female Ring-necked Pheasants*

thaws, and as spring approaches, the swamps melt and force the birds to find other roosting areas. There is minimal cover at this time, which makes them more vulnerable to predator attack, especially by Hawks, Owls, and Foxes.

Actually, the Ring-necked Pheasant is not a native of North America. It is a hybrid whose original strain comes from China. It was first introduced in New Hampshire in 1790 by the governor of the state. The Pheasants soon died, but in 1880 and 1890 Pheasants were sent from Shanghai to Oregon, where they were released and succeeded in breeding and adjusting. Today the Ring-necked Pheasant lives all across North America and has learned to take advantage of numerous habitats; I have even scared them up from railroad yards in city centers.

## Redpoll, Common (*Acanthis flammea*)

The Common Redpoll comes from its breeding grounds at the edge of the Canadian tundra south to the northern

*Common Redpolls*

states for the winter. It is usually in flocks of from 5 to 50 birds and, like its relatives, the American Goldfinch and Pine Siskin, feeds in ever-active flocks on seeds from weeds and trees. Common Redpolls are known to favor particularly Alder and Birch groves, both trees producing abundant supplies of seeds that remain in winter. The further north you go the more you can expect to see their isolated flocks, for they prefer to stay as close to the tundra edge as weather and food permits.

They are smaller than the Purple Finch and both sexes have a well-defined patch on their crown. The Redpoll's black chin clearly distinguishes it from the Goldfinch, Pine Siskin, or House Finch, with which it might be confused.

## Siskin, Pine (*Spinus pinus*)

The Pine Siskin is another of the winter finches with the winter flocking habits of its relative the Goldfinch. Large

*Pine Siskin*

flocks of from 10 to 100 birds fly and feed together in compact groups. Their food in winter consists of seeds from Hemlock, Alder, Birch, and various weeds. They sometimes feed with American Goldfinches or Common Redpolls.

Their appearance has no consistently striking features, but they can be told from other small brown streaked birds by their longer pointed bills. In flight yellow patches may show on the tops of the wings and base of the tail. Their call is helpful in identifying them and has been described as similar to the sound of "steam escaping from a radiator."

## Sparrow, House (*Passer domesticus*)

The House Sparrow is separated here from other sparrows because it is not a native of North America and not a relative of our native Sparrows. It belongs to a family of birds called Weaver Finches or *Ploceidae*. It was introduced into this country in 1850 and 1851 with the hope that it might control some insect pests. The birds were released in Brooklyn, New York, and now are widespread over North America, inhabiting all but the deserts and highest mountains.

They are aggressive little birds and many believe they have driven some of our native birds away from the city and countryside. They are particularly successful in the city, nesting in and on buildings and living off the crumbs of civilization as well as monopolizing our bird feeders at the expense of some of our small native birds.

The male after its fall molt has a mottled breast. But by late winter the tips of the feathers have worn off, revealing a sleek black bib underneath. The female is a soft brown in coloration.

House Sparrows feed together in winter in small flocks. They like to feed at the edges of fields or where shrubs are near, so that at the least sign of danger they can all fly up together into the shrubbery for protection. Then one by one they will begin to return to feeding. Sometimes the flock

House Sparrows

will stop feeding and just sit in nearby shrubs preening and chattering.

They often roost together in ivy-covered walls, but in colder weather they roost singly in the niches and corners of buildings.

## Sparrow, Song (*Melospiza melodia*)
## Tree (*Spizella arborea*)

Sparrows are small brown birds that feed on seeds in shrubby open areas. In summer the number of species and their similar coloring are discouraging to most beginners, but in winter almost all of these species fly south, allowing us to identify more easily those that remain. One of these, the Tree Sparrow, summers in northern Canada, and so the only chance to see it is in winter when it migrates to southern Canada and the northern states. It is easily recognized by the dark spot on the middle of its clear gray breast and by its rufous cap. It gathers in winter flocks, which are often seen feeding with Junco flocks. Their primary food in winter is grass seeds.

Another common sparrow living in the range of this guide

*Song Sparrows*

is the Song Sparrow. It, too, has a dot on its breast, but its breast is heavily streaked with brown, and the dot is irregular in shape. Most migrate south in winter, but a few remain, sometimes gathering in small groups near the coast, or by marshes or fields where food is abundant. They also feed on the seeds from grasses and weeds in winter.

Other types of Sparrows can be expected to be seen in the north along the coast, for the sea has a moderating effect on the environment and is a good source of food. These include the Field Sparrow, White-throated Sparrow, Swamp Sparrow, and Fox Sparrow. Most of them are found only along the coast north to Massachusetts and further inland in the south, starting at Pennsylvania.

## Starling (*Sturnus vulgaris*)

Like the Crow, the Starling also gathers in huge numbers, sometimes between 50,000 and 250,000 birds, to roost. The locations may be used for more than one winter, but usually the birds' droppings kill all vegetation and their weight on trees breaks the branches, so that the site is no longer suitable. Starlings start gathering for their roost about one or two hours before sunset, usually staying first in small groups near the roost. These small groups join others that are circling the area, and finally as a large group they fly over the roost and suddenly dive into its center. The birds, singing together in the roost, sound from a distance like a tremendous waterfall.

In morning the birds fly up by the thousands, and, sorting themselves into smaller flocks, then disperse to feed. As with those of Crows, these roosts can be located by noting the direction in which flocks of Starlings are traveling at dawn or dusk.

Over winter the Starling's appearance changes considerably. Around September the bird molts, and the new feathers, everywhere but on its back, are all tipped with white. The bird keeps this speckled appearance until midwinter, when the white tips begin to wear off and reveal the bird's glossy black plumage. Also at this time the Starling's bill, which has been dark since its molt, now changes to bright yellow. This latter change occurs just before breeding activity begins — usually in January or February.

*Starlings*

Starlings are among our most efficient predators of ground insects. They feed in flocks of a hundred or more birds in winter and prefer large open areas such as city parks, cultivated fields, and the borders of large turnpikes. They feed in a close group, all moving in the same direction. The ones at the back periodically fly to the front. When disturbed, they all fly up and in simultaneous flight wheel around, then again land to resume feeding. Studies of their feeding habits have suggested that they may have the ability to adopt the feeding habits of other species of birds that join them.

The Starling is not all beneficial, though, by any account. Introduced from Europe into Central Park, New York City, in 1890 and 1891, it quickly took over in the city and rapidly spread across the country. It is aggressive and nests in holes, depriving many of our native birds of their nesting and roosting sites. Its roosting in cities and feeding at airports have caused major problems in some areas. The numbers of Starlings have not stopped increasing since it was introduced. It will be interesting to see if there is some natural check on their population growth, for though humans introduced the Starling, we seem helpless to stop its spreading.

## Titmouse, Tufted (*Parus bicolor*)

The Tufted Titmouse is generally a permanent resident of the areas it inhabits. It is often seen in small flocks of from 3 to 6 birds, and these flocks generally stay within a given range, not overlapping with the ranges of other Titmouse flocks. The flocks often consist of parents with their young, which then split up in spring. Titmice are often part of larger mixed-species flocks in winter. Studies of these mixed foraging flocks show that either Chickadees or Titmice tend to be the leaders in directing the movement of the flock as a whole. Other birds seen in the flocks include Creepers, Nuthatches, Chickadees, Kinglets, and Woodpeckers.

*Tufted Titmice*

Titmice are some of the more vocal birds of winter. They seem to be continually chattering a series of unmusical notes, often sounding remarkably like Chickadees. Toward the end of winter you are more likely to hear their clear whistle of two notes slurred together, like "peter — peter — peter," and these, when slurred even more into "peer — peer — peer," resemble the notes of the Cardinal. By imitating this call, you can nearly always get the bird to stop what it's doing and come look for its competition.

Although their summer food is primarily insects, the winter food of Titmice is chiefly acorns, beechnuts, corn, and some wild berries. They also glean the limbs of trees for small wintering insects. Titmice have been known occasionally to store food in crevices much as the Nuthatches do but not nearly as often.

The Tufted Titmouse used to be a strictly southern bird, but with the apparent trend toward milder weather and the popularity of bird feeders, it is continually extending its northern range.

## Woodpecker, Downy (*Dendrocopos pubescens*)
## Hairy (*Dendrocopos villosus*)

Hairy Woodpeckers and Downy Woodpeckers are similar in appearance but differ widely in their winter habits. Hairy Woodpeckers can be distinguished by the size of their bills, which are at least as long as their heads from front to back. Downy Woodpecker bills are much smaller. The males of both species have red on the back of their heads; the females don't.

Hairy Woodpeckers do not migrate, and a mated pair will keep the same territory for life. They begin courtship display in midwinter and continue to establish their bond until mating. The male takes the initiative in the display.

Some Downy Woodpeckers migrate south, but many still remain north. The male is generally aggressive toward the female until late winter. In March and April the female takes the initiative in courtship display, attracting a mate, and choosing a territory.

Both species use "signal posts," particularly resonant trees

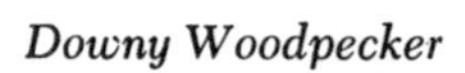
*Downy Woodpecker*

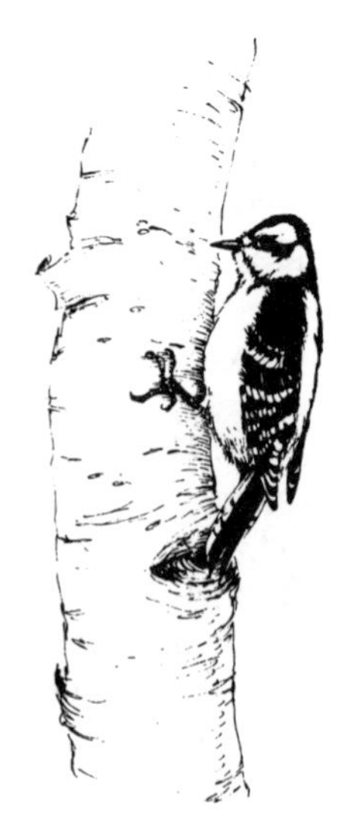

on which they "drum" to announce territory, attract a mate, or establish pair bonds. This drumming serves many of the functions song does in other birds. Usually both male and female have separate posts, each of which is strategically located within the territory. Locating these posts can help you to estimate the extent of a Woodpecker's territory. Near them there may also be good places to observe their behavior. Drumming may begin as early as December and it continues until summer.

Woodpeckers roost at night in separate roosting holes. These are found or excavated in fall and often vigorously defended against other hole-roosting birds. The larger range of the birds, averaging five to eight acres depending on habitat, is not defended but acts like a buffer zone around a roost or nest hole. Although each species does not nest near its own kind, it will tolerate other species of Woodpeckers within its territory. Thus the activities of Hairy and Downy Woodpeckers may overlap considerably.

Woodpeckers eat insects that live under the bark in the wood of trees. Each type of Woodpecker makes holes of a slightly different shape when looking for food. The two most conspicuous foraging holes are those made by Sapsuckers and Pileated Woodpeckers. Sapsuckers make rings of evenly spaced holes around a trunk. They drink the sap and eat the insects that are attracted to it. The holes are about ¼ inch in diameter and form easily recognizable geometric patterns. They are often seen on Apple trees.

The Pileated Woodpecker is huge for a Woodpecker, more than twice as large as the Hairy Woodpecker. The bird eats primarily carpenter ants inside trees. To get at them it chisels huge holes out of dead or living trees, holes that can be as much as 6 feet long, 8 inches wide, and 6 inches deep. The holes are always straight-sided and are far more conspicuous than the bird, which is shy and retiring.

VI

# Mushrooms in Winter

WHO WOULD THINK that, in winter, dead tree trunks, fallen logs, and rotting stumps could be exciting places to explore? But they are, for it is here that you will discover the many beautiful varieties of "Bracket" Fungi. It is a familiar theme in nature that where there is death there is likely to be a concentration of life, for in death the complex substances of a living organism are released and made available as nutrients to other plants and animals. This is also true of the Bracket Fungi; they grow on dead wood, using the nutrients that the roots and green leaves of the living tree once collected.

Bracket Fungi are a type of mushroom. But they don't look like the mushrooms we buy in stores or find growing in lawns. They are usually semicircular, tough, and leathery, and broadly attached to living or dead trees. In many cases they grow in clusters, one above the other, covering whole sides of trees.

There are only a few kinds that are really common in our area, and they can be distinguished quite easily. Some have beautiful upper surfaces, many have striking lower surfaces, some form spectacular groupings, others are impressive as lone forms. But, in any case, the part we see and identify is only a portion of the plant. The rest is within the wood, causing decay perhaps growing inside for many years before it produces the fruit part we see.

Mushrooms grow from spores. A spore is similar to a seed but simpler in structure. When a spore is in contact with wood, and conditions are right, small thread-like strands grow from this spore, ultimately branching out into the wood. At the tip of each of these strands enzymes are produced which break down the tough wood cells, making their substances available to the mushroom for nutrition. This process continues until many tubes exist throughout an area of the wood. Collectively these strands are called the *mycelium.* This is the vegetative and main part of the mushroom, hidden within the wood, and even when exposed often too small to be seen except where mycelia are massed together.

The mycelium is the most important part of the mushroom, for it is the chief cause of decay in the forest, and without decay our forests would be impenetrable. Consider how long wood can last when protected from fungal decay: hundreds of years in many of our buildings and constructions. If there were no fungi in the woods, all the trees that had died and the leaves that had fallen during recent decades would still be piled on the earth as if they had just fallen. But with the mycelium of mushrooms constantly at work, all this forest debris is broken down into soil on the forest floor and made available to new growing plants.

After the mycelium has matured and conditions are right it produces a growth that pushes its way through an opening to the outside of the tree. The function of this growth is to produce spores, which will land on new trees and disseminate that species of mushroom. This growth is called the *sporophore*, a name meaning "the bearer of spores." Sporophores are what we see when we see mushrooms. The sporophores of bracket fungi usually produce billions to trillions of spores on their lower surface. The spores are microscopic but can be seen when thousands accumulate in one spot. The spores are produced on many types of structures and each type is characteristic of a certain *family* of mushrooms. Some are produced on the sides of gills, others in pores, others on a smooth surface, others in tubes or on teethlike projections. In any case, in bracket fungi and mushrooms in general, in order that the spores fall freely, the sporophore must be exactly perpendicular to the force of gravity; otherwise the spores stick to the gills, pores, etcetera, on which they are produced. Because of this, the living sporophores will continually orient themselves to be perpendicular to gravity if for some reason the log or tree they are on shifts position. This phenomenon can cause many interesting forms of sporophores. Frequently mushrooms start on a standing tree; the sporophores orient themselves in relation to gravity. When the tree falls, the sporophores are out of alignment and often grow new sporophores from the old ones, again perpendicular to gravity but obviously in different positions from the first and older ones. You could even take a tree with living sporophores and tilt it differently; come back in a month and see the changes.

All mushrooms are plants, but they are different from most other plants in one respect — they lack the green pigment, chlorophyll, that would enable them to make their own food with the sun's energy. In this sense they are more like us than most plants are; we can lie out in the sun for hours but we won't get any food or nourishment that way. We have to use the sun's energy indirectly by eating green plants or eating animals, which in turn have eaten green plants. Mushrooms are the same way; it makes no difference whether they are in sun or shade, they must be only where they can get the sun's energy indirectly, by living off other plants. Therefore, mushrooms are found only where there is organic material to live off. The more organic material, the better; this is why so many fungi are found in forests — on trees, on the fallen needles or leaves below, or on the roots.

For this reason a certain mushroom cannot grow forever on a log, for at some time it will use up the substances it can absorb. Sometimes Bracket Fungi are divided into two classes, depending on the parts of wood they dissolve for nourishment. One group, the White Rots, decompose most compounds of the wood, including the two major constituents of the cell walls, lignin and cellulose. They leave the wood white, spongy, and fibrous. The other group, Brown Rots, use only the cellulose of the wood cells, leaving the wood brown and crumbly. These two general types of rot are easily observed in the winter woods; check the rotted wood of trees and you will see that some is whitish, fibrous, and spongy, while other trees have dry, brown rotted wood, often breaking into small cubes.

Brown Rot is sometimes called "Dry Rot," but this is misleading, for no fungus can grow in absolutely dry conditions. For optimum growth, mushrooms need moist conditions and temperatures around 60 degrees, which explains why most mushrooms on trees grow in the fall. Many ground mushrooms also grow in fall, but they soon deteriorate, not having the leathery toughness of the Bracket Fungi.

Most of the Bracket Fungi are termed nonpoisonous, rather than edible, which means suitable for eating. In other words, they could be a survival food if necessary but are otherwise about as desirable as shoe leather.

## *Key to Winter Mushrooms*

Common mushrooms growing on trees in winter can be divided into four categories depending on what they look like underneath. The four categories are listed below, and under each heading there are descriptions of common mushrooms you are likely to find. There are many others not included here, and some of the popular guides listed in the Bibliography may help you identify them if you decide you want to know more.

For most of these mushrooms there are no common

names; even their Latin names are continually changing as mycologists make revision after revision of groupings. The names used here are not the most recent classification but are nonetheless correct and represent a simpler grouping, one that I believe will be easier for the beginner to relate to.

### *MINUTE ROUND PORES COVER THE SURFACE UNDERNEATH*

—Top of mushroom is lacquered dark red, appearing shiny: *Ganoderma lucidum.*

—Growing only on White Birch; pores white or golden; thick lateral stem holds mushroom to tree; shaped like a piece of flattened bread dough: *Polyporus betulinus.*

—Smooth, concentric ridges on top; thick, hard as wood; white pores underneath, which show brown when scratched: *Ganoderma applanatum.*

—Hard as wood; concentric rings on top, each one lower than the next, older ones gray, newer ones biege; fine brown pores beneath; shaped like horse hoof: *Fomes fomentarius.*

—Brown pores; woody at base, thin at margin; showing a bright mustard brown inside when broken in half: *Polyporus gilvus.*

—White pores and white top; thin and papery; growing on dead Elm branches; sometimes shaped like little saucers: *Polyporus conchifer.*

—Light-colored pores; beautiful concentric zones of dark colors on top; downy hairs on top: *Polyporus versicolor.*

—Light-colored pores; concentric zones of different length hairs on top, some the length of velvet nap: *Polyporus hirsutus.*

*Polyporus versicolor* is similar but only finely downy; it is darker in color, and more common.

## *GILLS OR IRREGULARLY SHAPED PORES UNDERNEATH*

— White mushroom with large irregularly shaped pores; divisions between pores as thick as cardboard: *Daedalia quercina.*
— Concentric zones of gray hairs on top; creamy white gills beneath: *Lenzites betulinus.*
— Red-brown top with yellow margin; yellow-orange gills or irregularly shaped pores underneath: *Lenzites saepiaria.*
— Concentric lines of dull brown on hairless top; intricate design of mazelike pores or toothed gills beneath; paper-thin divisions between pores: *Daedalia confragosa.*
— White and downy on top; gray or lavender split gills underneath; small: *Schizophylum commune.*

## *HUNDREDS OF SMALL "TEETH" PROJECTING DOWN UNDERNEATH*

— Thin mushroom with faint concentric zones on top; small teeth beneath are lavender when fresh, turning golden brown with age: *Polyporus pergamenus.*
— White teeth projecting beneath, ¼ inch or more long; tends to grow in shelves along a branch: *Polyporus tulipiferae.*

## *MUSHROOMS THIN AND ABSOLUTELY SMOOTH UNDERNEATH*

— Projecting an inch or more from wood; concentric zones of beige on top; smooth beige surface underneath; wafer-like: *Stereum fasciatum.*
— Projecting less than a half-inch from wood; beige top

with some hairs; crinkled or extremely wavy margin: *Stereum gausapatum.*

# *Natural History Descriptions*

## *Armillaria mellea*

The vegetative portion of *Armillaria mellea* is commonly seen on trees that have lost their bark. It has a striking appearance and is included here to give another view of the biology of fungi. When the strands of the mycelium are

*Rhizomorphs of* Armillaria mellea

joined together into thicker strands they are called rhizomorphs. This is the case with *Armillaria mellea;* it has two types of rhizomorphs that are formed after the normal mycelium has lived in a decaying tree for some time. One type travels underground seeking out new hosts. The other type travels up the tree between the bark and sapwood. This kills the tree and the bark falls off and reveals the rhizomorphs: black tough strands of interlacing veins traveling up the tree. Their appearance has led some to call these mushrooms the "Bootstrap Fungi." When fresh, they are luminescent in the dark.

In fall the reproductive portion, or sporophore, of *Armillaria mellea* grows on the trunk or at the base of infected trees. It looks like a typical mushroom, and is quite edible. The fruit, not seen in winter, lasts only a week or so before rotting.

## *Cankers*

Cankers are localized deformations of trees caused by fungi. These fungi are related to mushrooms, in the same group. The fungi enter the tree through wounds or broken branches, where spores land and send in the beginnings of the mycelium. In Cankers the fungi attack mostly the bark and the cambial layer of the tree. Usually the bark is just locally roughened or deformed, but sometimes it is killed and sloughed off, revealing the wood beneath.

Cankers are common on all parts of trees, especially trunks and branches. Some Cankers are annual and have a limited effect; others are perennial and can be more destructive.

*Large canker on Oak*

A common Canker on Cherry trees is called Black Knot. It usually first infects twigs, causing black, gnarled swellings along the twig. It can kill the twig in a year and in that time start to spread to the trunk. Lumbermen are aware of Black

*Black Knot Canker*

Knot, since when it infests trunks it makes the wood commercially useless. It is caused by a fungus named *Dibotryon morbosum.*

Some perennial Cankers grow only during seasons when the tree is not growing and stop when the tree grows. Because of this alternation, some trees can heal the area deformed by the Canker each year. This process can cause a series of concentric lines in the bark of the tree because of each year's cycle of growth and healing. These patterns are sometimes called Target Cankers.

*Target Canker*

Other Cankers can deform trees so much that they substantially weaken the trees; then, during windstorms or with snow load, the trees break at the cankered point.

## *Daedalia confragosa*

The two common species of *Daedalia* are among our most beautiful winter mushrooms. Their beauty is mainly in the mazelike pores of their lower surface. The genus is named for this, referring to Daedalus, the Athenian architect of Greek mythology who built a labyrinth, or maze, for King Minos. The fruit bodies (sporophores) of these mushrooms

Daedalia confragosa

usually last only one year but may revive for another season. As they age, their lower surfaces change from a maze to a more gill-like construction.

*Daedalia confragosa* can occur in spectacular groups along logs or on branches. It is fairly thin, corky, and speckled light brown on top. When it is turned over you may find it partly gilled and partly mazelike, or all mazelike. The partitions underneath are thin as paper, presenting a delicate and intricate pattern, unlike the bold, thickly divided pattern of *Daedalia quercina.*

It is most often found on hardwoods, especially Willow, Yellow Birch, and Oak. It grows on only dead wood and is an important destroyer of slash timber that remains after lumbering. Its vegetative part causes a soft white rot of the wood, sometimes with zone lines at the outermost edge of its progress. The sporophores at times can completely encircle fallen branches or twigs.

## *Daedalia quercina*

*Daedalia quercina* is heavier-set than its cousin *Daedalia confragosa.* Its mazelike pores are formed by thick dividers,

Daedalia quercina

more like cardboard than the papery divisions of *Daedalia confragosa.* Its underside pattern is therefore less intricate and more simple and bold. It is generally stark white when young, but it may turn to brown or black with age. The sporophore, being tough and corky, may persist for several years.

Its species name, *quercina*, means "of oak" for this is where it is generally found, although it can also occur on other hardwoods. It prefers large areas of wood such as logs, stumps, and trunks rather than branches or twigs. It grows all over the northern hemisphere.

*Daedalia quercina* causes a brown rot. In advanced stages of decay, the wood breaks into small cubical fragments, which can be crumbled between your fingers. Of the two species of *Daedalia*, this one seems to be the less common in the area of this guide.

## *Fomes fomentarius*

*Fomes fomentarius* is distinctive, for it is shaped like a horse's hoof. The upper surface is crusty, in shades of light

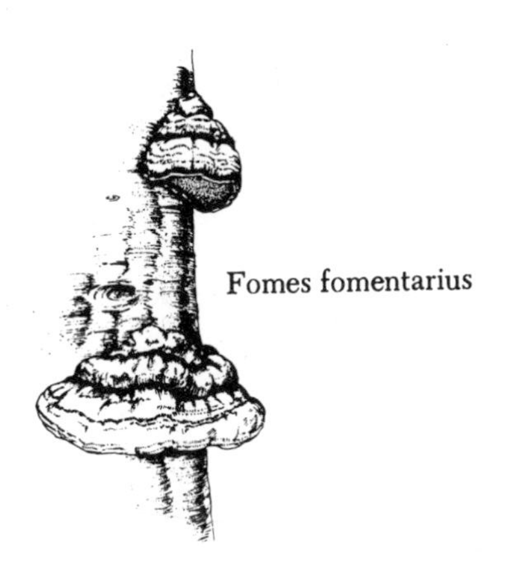


to dark gray, and composed of a series of concentric rings, each larger and lower than the previous one. A new ring is added during each favorable growing period. The undersurface is chocolate or rich brown, somewhat waxy, and covered with fine pores.

*Fomes fomentarius* rarely grows over six inches in diameter but, being common, is still easily seen on standing tree trunks. It is particularly obvious when it grows on the smooth bark of Beech, Birch, or Poplar trees, which it favors. Often several sporophores occur on a tree.

The spores of the mushroom probably enter the tree

Fomes fomentarius, *cut in half to show annual layers of pores*

through broken limbs and wounds. Inside the tree, the root-like mycelium forms straw-colored mats in the cracks of the wood, attacking both the heartwood and sapwood of dead or live trees.

## *Ganoderma applanatum*

*Ganoderma applanatum* grows to be the largest of the common winter fungi. It can grow to 2 feet in diameter, and live for over fifty years. It has a flat upper surface, with concentric rings showing as slight rounded ridges. The upper surface is generally some shade of light beige or gray. The lower surface, when the fungus is living, is white, but scratch marks on it appear brown. Some people have

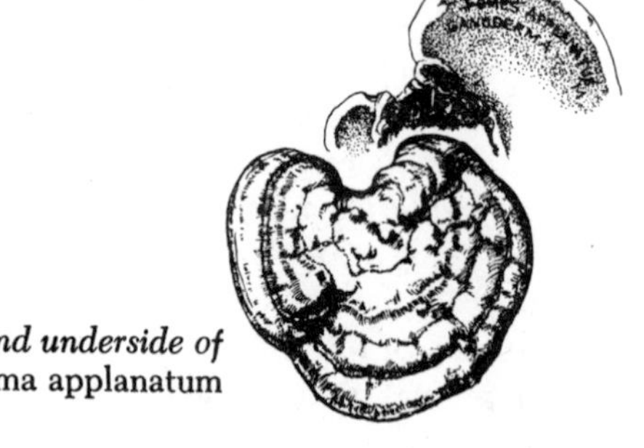


*Top and underside of* Ganoderma applanatum

scratched whole drawings onto this mushroom's lower surface and have kept the fungus or sold it as a curio. Because this can be done, it is often called the Artist's Fungus. The sporophore can be as hard as wood and impossible to remove from a tree without tools.

*Ganoderma applanatum* is commonly found all across North America; it also exists in Europe. It produces a white

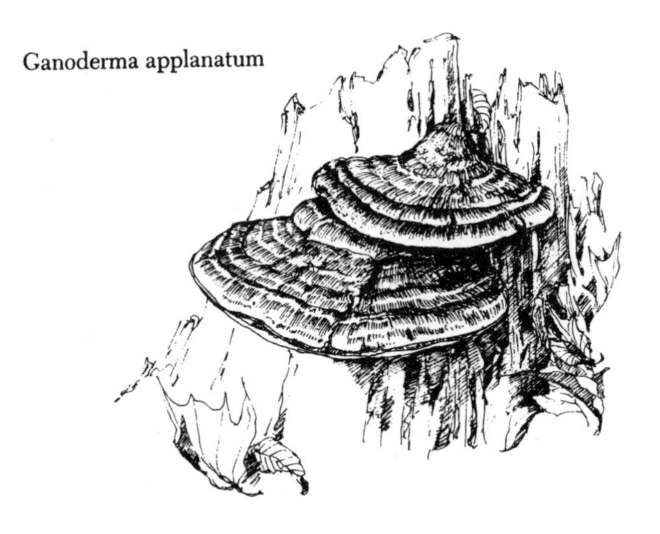
Ganoderma applanatum

rot that leaves the wood firm for a long time. It attacks both heartwood and sapwood and is found mostly on hardwoods although occasionally on conifers.

## *Ganoderma lucidum*

*Ganoderma lucidum* has a dark, red-brown, shiny top, as if it were covered with varnish. The undersurface, at first white, may change to yellow-brown in color, depending on the age of the sporophore. Sometimes this species has a lateral stem, also a varnished red on top, holding the sporo-

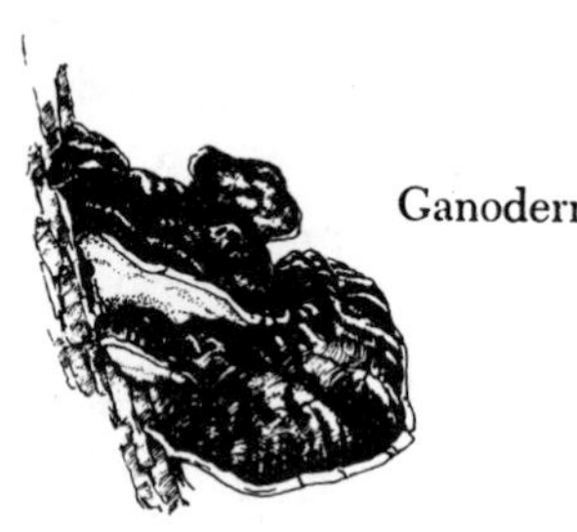
Ganoderma lucidum

phore away from the tree. At other times when there are no stems, the fungi can grow so closely together, one above the other, that they become fused into one group. The upper surface is often very bumpy and wrinkled and always keeps its maroon lacquered quality.

*Ganoderma lucidum* is found mostly on stumps and at the bases of hardwood trees, often Silver Maple. Another very similar species, *Ganoderma tsugae*, grows only on Hemlock.

## *Lenzites betulina*

*Lenzites betulina* is covered with concentric rings of gray velvety hairs on top and has large creamy white gills be-

Lenzites betulina

neath. The gills, though sometimes they run together irregularly at the margin, usually are separate. Its species name means "of Birch," but it is also found on other hardwoods and occasionally on conifers. The mycelium attacks mostly sapwood.

### *Lenzites saepiaria*

*Lenzites saepiaria* is a lovely small yellow-brown mushroom seen mostly in early winter. It is usually found growing on conifers, and as you look closely at it you will find its under-

Lenzites saepiaria

side covered with small firm, plate-like gills. Its upper surface is plainer, with concentric zones of muted color variation and often with a pale yellow band at its margin.

*Lenzites saepiaria* is found all over the world and is an important destroyer of the discarded conifer logs and limbs left after lumbering. It also grows on processed lumber, such as railroad ties and building timbers. Its color, intricate lower surface, and small size make its discovery as exciting as finding a small jewel.

### *Polyporus betulinus*

The species name *betulinus* ("of Birch") is the key to identifying this mushroom. *Polyporus betulinus* grows only on

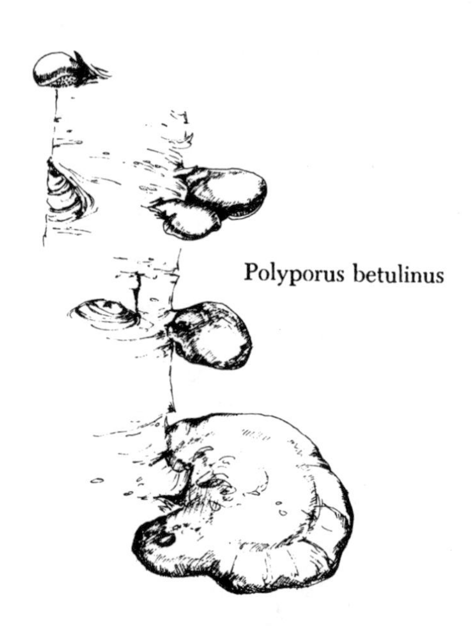

Polyporus betulinus

Birch, usually on White or Gray Birch. The sporophore looks like a thick puffed-up pancake on top. This upper surface is any shade from beige to white and it often has slight pits in the skin. The edges curl under and extend over the pores at the cap's rim.

The underside at first has white pores, which change to tan with age. The whole sporophore is spongy and moist when fresh, but dry and tough when old. Last year's sporophores are usually turned to dust by the quick work of insects. If you look closely, you will see that the sporophore

Polyporus betulinus *cut in half to show pore structure*

is growing out through the lenticels in the Birch bark. The vegetative mycelium attacks the sapwood and sends out sporophores wherever there is an opening. The mycelium causes a white rot, turning the interior of the tree into a spongy white mass of fibers.

## *Polyporus conchifer*

*Polyporus conchifer* is a common sight in the city, for it attacks especially the dead branches of Elms. Since the Dutch elm disease started killing Elms, I am sure this mushroom has increased in abundance.

*Large fertile sporophores and small sterile cups of* Polyporus conchifer

Two types of sporophores are produced by *Polyporus conchifer*. One is shaped like a tiny dollhouse saucer and is sterile, not producing any spores. The other sporophore is fertile and shaped more like a thin rounded shelf. Both types are pure white, very thin, and dainty. Sometimes the fertile sporophore will grow around the cup-shaped sterile one.

This mushroom can occur also on Maple, Birch, and Cherry.

## *Polyporus gilvus*

*Polyporus gilvus* is best identified by its color; it is mustard-yellow to brown throughout. When it is old, break it apart

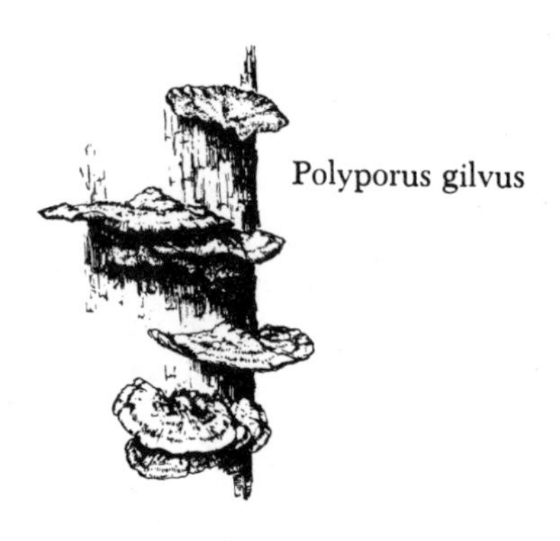
Polyporus gilvus

and the mustard color will still be fresh inside. The young sporophore is fairly spongy, and the upper surface is rough, with little rounded bumps. It is about ½ inch thick at its

*Back of* Polyporus gilvus *where it was connected to the tree*

base and tapers to a thin margin. *Polyporus gilvus* causes a white rot in the sapwood of hardwood trees.

## *Polyporus hirsutus*

*Polyporus hirsutus* is named for the dense small hairs that cover the sporophore's upper surface. Some other Polypores are also somewhat fuzzy, but once you find *Polyporus hirsutus* you will see how much longer the hairs on it are; they

Polyporus hirsutus

are about the length of velvet nap. The upper surface also shows concentric zones of gray, the hair in each zone slightly different in length from those in other zones. The bottom surface is porous and can be white, yellow, or light gray.

This is a common mushroom in winter; it occurs mostly on hardwood trees.

## *Polyporus pergamenus*

*Polyporus pergamenus* is the most common winter mushroom in our area. On top it looks like many other Polypores,

*Top and bottom of* Polyporus pergamenous

but underneath it has tiny pores which tend to elongate into toothlike forms; they are purple when living and tan or

Polyporus pergamenus

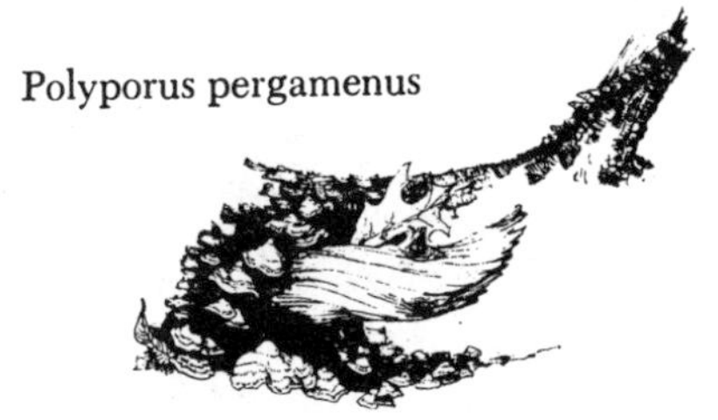

brown later. The small, thin sporophores usually occur in groups of fifty or more, and from a distance their tops look like white scales covering scars in dead wood. They often form in fire scars at the bases of trees. A common sight is the white tops of the sporophores covered with green algae at their bases.

### *Polyporus tulipiferae*

*Polyporus tulipiferae* is distinguished from other Polypores by the long teeth or tubes, rather than pores, that make up its undersurface. The teeth are about as long as toothbrush bristles and are colored white to creamy yellow. The upper surface is also white, turning yellowish as it dries. *Polyporus tulipiferae* usually grows in long narrow shelves on fallen

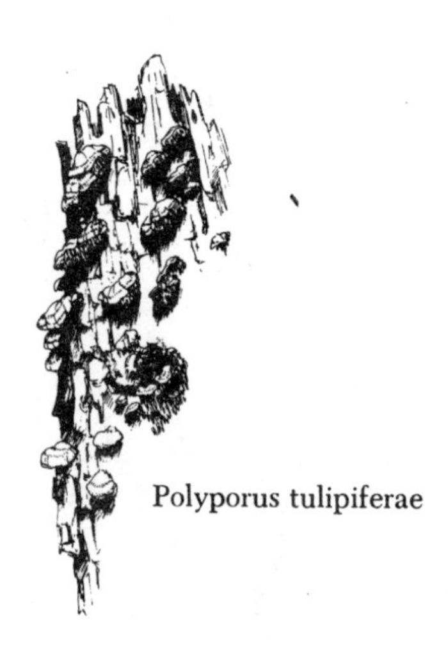
Polyporus tulipiferae

hardwood trees, and causes a white rot in the dead sapwood. It sometimes occurs on conifers. In winter it is an interesting study in black and white, appearing as irregular ribbons spreading across black stretches of fallen logs.

## *Polyporus versicolor*

If you learn how to recognize *Polyporus versicolor* and *Polyporus pergamenus* you will know about 30 percent of the winter mushrooms you come in contact with. Of the

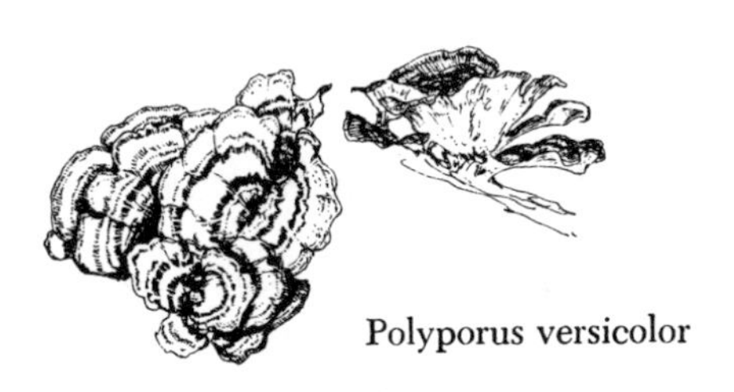

Polyporus versicolor

two, *Polyporus versicolor* is by far the more spectacular. On its upper surface are found beautiful concentric zones of tan, brown, gray, dark red, and dark green. Often the sporophores grow in whorls at the ends of logs, so that some have called them "Turkey Tails." The lower surface may be white, yellow, brownish, or light gray; it is uniformly covered with a thin layer of pores. Some people collect whorls

Polyporus versicolor *growing on Beaver-chewed tree stump*

of *Polyporus versicolor* for decorations around their houses; if you do this, be sure there are no insects in them or you will find little piles of white powder under each one in a few weeks. I once discovered an area long since chewed over by Beavers; on the top of each stump top were whorls of this lovely mushroom, as well as those of *Lenzites betulina.*

## *Schizophylum commune*

*Schizophylum commune* is a small, fairly inconspicuous, mushroom, but it is common and easily identified when you turn it over. Its genus name, which means "split kind," refers to its unusual gills, which are small but neatly split down their centers. The gill surface is typically a very pale

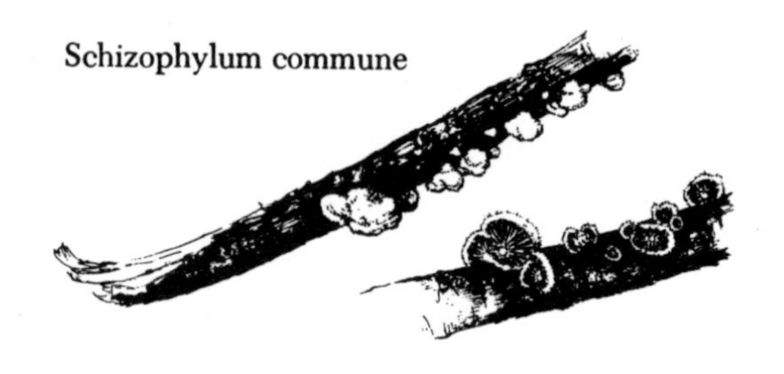


blue when fresh. The upper surface is white frilled and covered with little tufts of cottony material. You will often find the sporophore on dead branches or on an old log that has attracted your attention because of other more conspicuous mushrooms.

## *Stereum fasciatum*

*Stereum* is easily distinguished from all other mushrooms by its absolutely smooth underside, which shows no pores, gills,

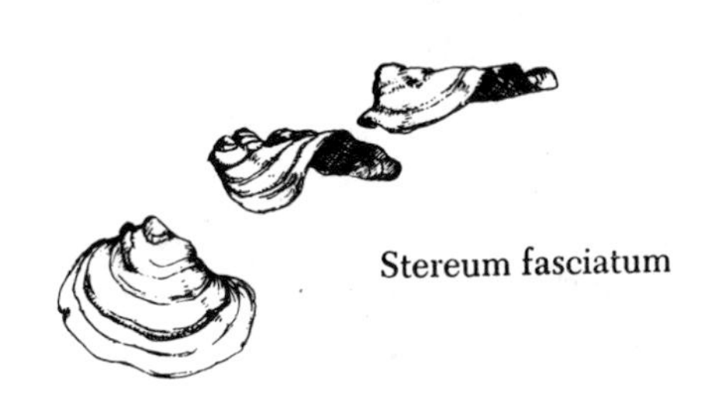

Stereum fasciatum

or teeth. *Stereum fasciatum* is a thin waferlike mushroom, with some concentric zones on its clay-colored upper surface; its lower surface is usually pale tan and absolutely smooth. Sometimes the sporophore is narrow at its base, at other times broadly attached. Nearby sporophores may be joined together along their sides.

This mushroom attacks both sapwood and heartwood of

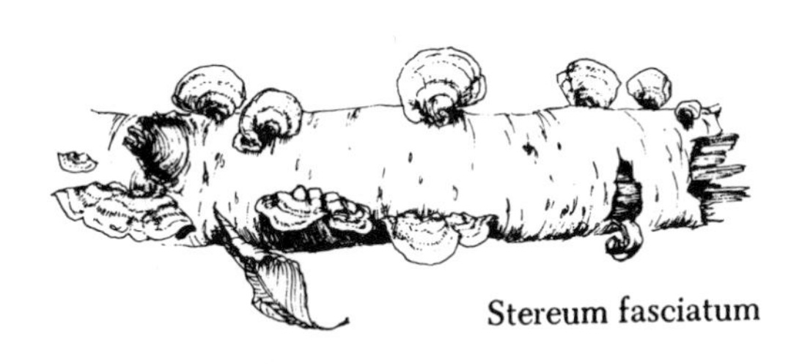

Stereum fasciatum

Oaks especially and is important as a decayer of slash wood left behind after lumbering. *Stereum fasciatum* is a common mushroom and resembles *Polyporus pergamenus* on top, but its poreless undersurface distinguishes it from the other fungus.

## *Stereum gausapatum*

*Stereum gausapatum* is a small but common mushroom, especially on recently felled Oak. It is recognized by its ex-

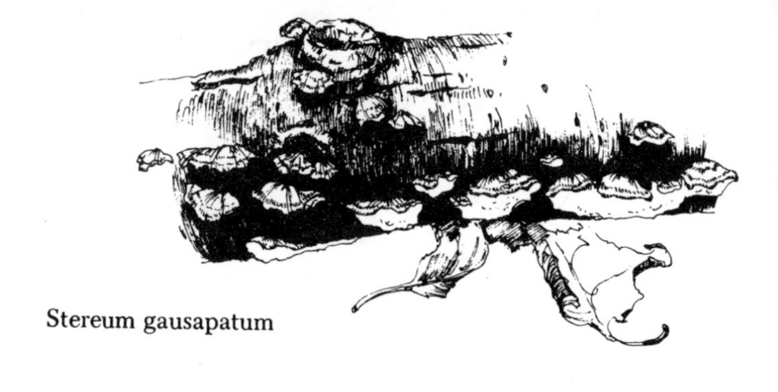

Stereum gausapatum

tremely wavy margin and lack of pores or gills underneath. It often grows in long ridges with the grain extending rarely more than ½ inch out from the wood surface. It may have matted hairs on its coppery, yellow-brown surface. The lower surface is often purple-brown and is absolutely smooth.

It produces a white localized decay of Oaks and is particularly successful at invading young sprouts that grow up around an infested older tree.

VII

# Tracks in the Snow

It is hard to equal the excitement of searching for the magical trails of animals imprinted in the snow's surface: the Fox's night wanderings, the Crow's landing in a field, or part of the Mink's circuit. To see an animal requires the gift of coincidence, you and it meeting at the same place at almost the same time. But the chances of meeting its tracks are much greater, for up to three or four days of its travels may be recorded, and you need to cross them at only one point.

More than just an impression in the snow, a trail is like a rope connecting disparate moments of time — both a record of the past and a connection to the present, for back on the trail are sketched the encounters of a living being, while ahead is the present animal continually leaving its life experience one step behind.

When looking at animals, we often miss the secrets of their private lives, since the animals have invariably seen us first and are reacting most to our presence. But the trail records the animal when it was alone in nature and brings us closer than ever before to its normal habits and perceptions of the world.

Besides the track itself, other signs should be looked for: stray feathers, a drop of blood, urine markings or a scat, twigs chewed, bark gnawed, kills stored, wood lodges, bank dens, tree dens, diggings in the ground, holes in the ice, torn-open hornets' nests, and countless others. Anything unusual in nature was affected by something or some one. What did it and why was it done?

Animal locomotion is extremely complex; the number of different ways four feet can move is astounding. But for the tracker it is valuable to be aware of at least the five basic modes of four-footed travel: two kinds of walking, plus trotting, bounding, and galloping. If you are limber there is no better way to understand these movements than by getting down on all fours and recreating them yourself, or watching someone else do it.

The simplest type of movement is the walk. In a walk a quadruped (four-footed animal) always keeps at least two feet on the ground. Doing this, it moves in one of two ways: either by moving both limbs on the right side, then both limbs on the left (pacing), or by moving hind left leg and front right leg, then hind right leg and front left leg (diagonal walking). Pacing makes the whole animal sway from side to side in a waddling gait. Diagonal walking is more balanced, since there is always support on both sides of the body. A child who has learned to crawl uses the diagonal walk of a quadruped.

Trotting can be similar to the diagonal walk, except that the whole body is lifted off the ground at one point. It is like the difference between our walking and jogging; in both, the feet alternate in the same way, but in the latter there is a moment between steps when the body is suspended in air.

In the fourth type of movement, bounding, the front feet reach out together and the hind feet follow as a pair, landing just behind the front feet or almost in the front prints. This movement is typical of members of the Weasel family.

The fifth common type of movement is galloping. It is

similar to bounding except that here the hind feet land to either side or ahead of the front feet. This is typical of Rabbits and Squirrels, and also all long-legged animals when they are trying to move fast. The human body is not made for this type of movement, and it's easy to pull a muscle trying to imitate it. If you ever have occasion to look further into animal locomotion, you will see how oversimplified this account is, but it is still valuable as a framework for interpreting tracks.

The ways in which most of even our common animals move has not yet been studied, and the effects these movements can have on track patterns is even less known. As you begin to notice the common patterns of tracks, musing over what type of locomotion created them can be a real challenge, especially in a number of the medium-speed patterns usually grouped under the term "loping."

I was once confronted with a particularly confusing track: a long trough 2 inches wide and 20 yards long. It began and ended abruptly with no sign of tunnels or further tracks. But, most curious of all, it proceeded directly through a fine wire-mesh fence with no sign of pausing or leaping over, as any animal larger than a mouse would have had to have done.

While puzzling over it I was momentarily distracted by a bird alighting on an electric line directly overhead. Suddenly it occurred to me — the electric line, the bird, the track! A wet snow had built up on the line and had been knocked off by the wind or a perching bird. From this anecdote it is clear that other things besides animals can make impressions in the snow. Blowing leaves or small cones form sketchy trails across meadows and frozen lakes; snow fallen from trees makes convincing prints beneath them, sometimes rolling as small snowballs down hills, leaving a clearly directed trail (surely they must be from an animal); and the drops from the snow melting off roof eaves mimic the trail of a scampering mouse.

So for especially mysterious prints always check above you for the possibility that bits of snow may have dropped from trees, telephone wires, or roof overhangs.

Good tracking conditions depend on the quality of the snow as it fell, the weather conditions after it fell, and the ways in which these two affect the movements of animals. Generally animals stay in dens or protected areas during bad storms and for a few hours after. They then come out only if it is their time of activity. So if a storm ends in the morning or middle of the night you will have to wait through one more night before the majority of tracks will be present, since most animals are active at night. Clearly, the longer the snow remains unmelted or undrifted after a storm, the more chances you will have to find tracks.

A dry drifty snow leaves few prints, and a wet snow will gather on branches and drop to the ground in the wind, leaving the forest floor pockmarked and impossible for tracking.

Tracks can be found anywhere, but they are often most common at the edges of habitats, such as where a forest and field meet, and particularly near water, as by lakes, along streams, or at the edges of swamps. When following a track, don't step into it, but walk alongside it; you may want to go back over it for measurements or photographs. Besides, a track is an exquisite, though fleeting, creation of nature, and others after you may want to enjoy it.

## *Key to Animal Tracks*

When a track has been discovered there are two approaches to identifying it.

(1) The first is to follow the trail until you find a clear print, one that shows the shape of the foot and number of toes. In this case, use the Key to Prints.

(2) If you cannot find a clear print, then you must use the pattern of the track for identification. In this case, use the Key to Patterns.

In most cases both methods are used, as well as knowledge of other signs and habits of the animal. Often tracks will not be clear in either pattern or print and you must use a range of knowledge to guess who the maker was. Reading through the natural history descriptions of the animals as well as becoming familiar with the keys will help you in these situations, and enable you to make at least an educated guess.

All the animals in our north can be divided into four groups based on the number of toes on their hind and front feet. Those in the first three categories have the same number of toes on each foot. In the last category, the animals have four toes on their front feet and five toes on their hind feet.

Measurements for length and width of prints are given. When both hind and forefeet are different, the distinctive one has been included and labeled. All measurements are merely guidelines, since print size varies with sex and age of animal and depth of snow. Prints are measured from one side of the toe pattern to the other, rather than by the general impression in the snow, which will invariably be larger.

Prints in each of the four groups are proportionately scaled.

*TWO-TOED ANIMALS*

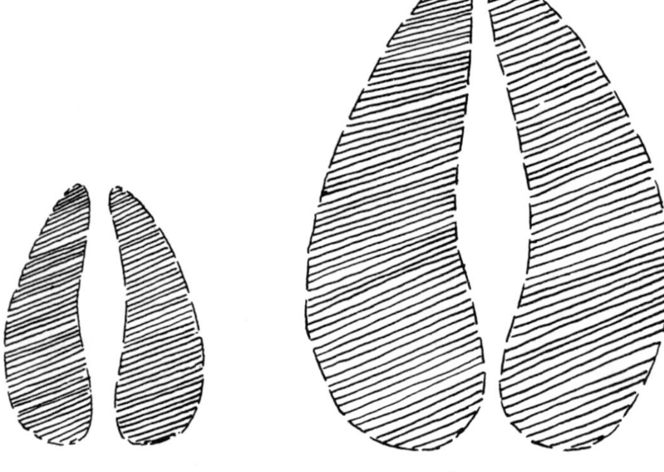

*Deer*
L. 3½ inches, W. 2½ inches

*Moose*
L. 7 inches, W. 5 inches

Often the front part of the toes is spread apart when the animal is supporting itself on soft surfaces. Also two small toes, called "dewclaws," may show in deep snow as two circular marks behind each foot.

*FOUR-TOED ANIMALS*

*Dog*
*variable*

*Coyote*
L. 2¾ inches,
W. 2¼ inches

*Fox*
L. 2½ inches,
W. 1¾ inches

All canines have four toes in an oval print with claws showing. All three are difficult to distinguish and one must rely most on other signs and the character of the trail. Read the natural history descriptions of Fox and Coyote, and see Key to Patterns.

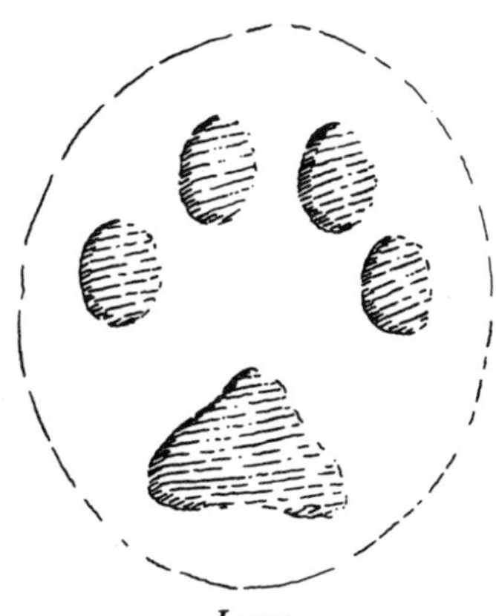

*Lynx*
*L. 3½ inches, W. 3½ inches*

*Bobcat*
*L. 2 inches, W. 2 inches*

*Cat*
*L. 1 inch, W. 1 inch*

All felines have four toes in a circular print with no claws showing. Their prints are easy to distinguish by size alone. The Lynx has stiff hairs over its feet, which obscure its toe pads. Sometimes house cats are born with extra toes on one or more feet.

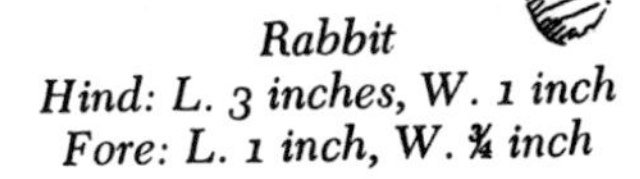

*Rabbit*
*Hind: L. 3 inches, W. 1 inch*
*Fore: L. 1 inch, W. ¾ inch*

*Hare*
*Hind: L. 5 inches, W. 3½ inches*
*Fore: L. 1¾ inches, W. 1½ inches*

The front feet of Rabbits or Hares could be confused with other prints, but their long hind feet and common galloping pattern distinguish them. The Hare print is particularly large and obvious. See Key to Patterns.

*FIVE-TOED ANIMALS*

*Weasel*
*L. ¾ inch*
*W. ¾ inch*

*Skunk*
*L. 1¼ inches*
*W. 1 inch*

*Mink*
*L. 1¼ inches*
*W. 1¼ inches*

*Marten*
*L. 1¼ inches*
*W. 1½ inches*

*Fisher*
*L. 2½ inches*
*W. 2½ inches*

*Otter*
*Hind: W. 3½ inches*
*L. 4 inches*

All of the Weasel family above have five toes, but the small fifth toe may not show in the print, in which case the pointed shape of the toe pad and claw together helps distinguish them from four-toed animals.

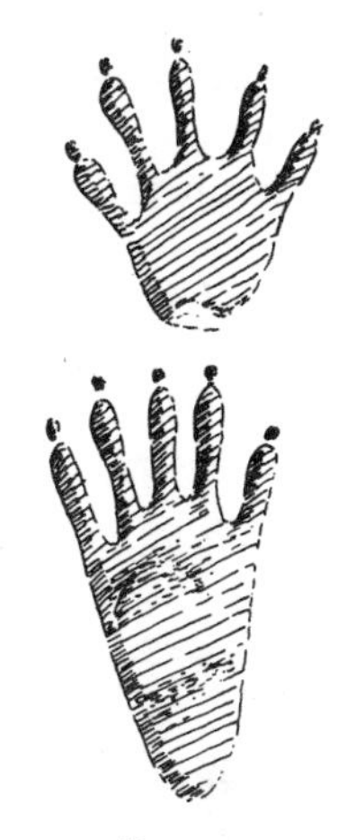

*Raccoon*
*Fore: L. 2½ inches*
*W. 2½ inches*
*Hind: L. 4 inches*
*W. 2¼ inches*

*Opossum*
*Fore: L. 2 inches*
*W. 2 inches*
*Hind: L. 3 inches*
*W. 1½ inches*

*Muskrat*
*Fore: L. 1½ inches*
*W. 1½ inches*
*Hind: L. 3 inches*
*W. 2 inches*

Raccoon prints have five clear toes on both hind and forefeet, while Opossum prints show four toes and a thumb on hind foot, and those of a Muskrat show primarily four toes on a small front foot.

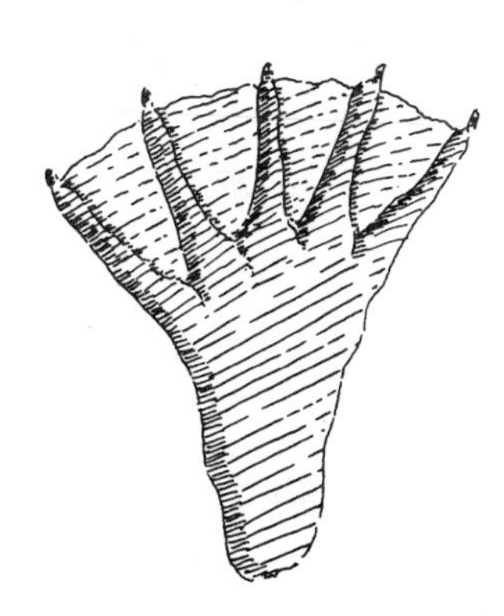

*Beaver*
*Hind: L. 5 inches*
*W. 4½ inches*

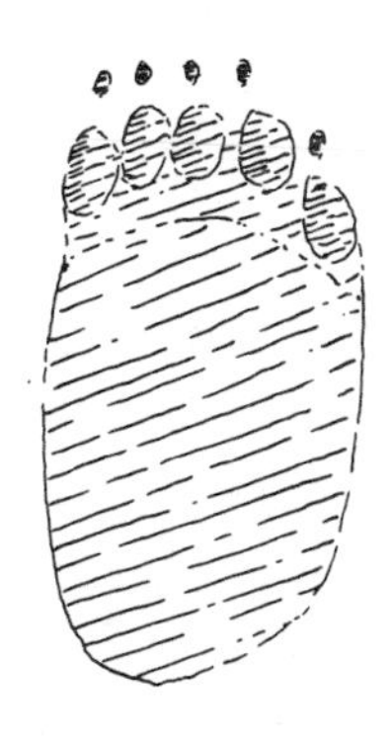

*Porcupine*
*Hind: L. 5 inches*
*W. 2½ inches*

The large-fingered and webbed hind foot of Beaver is distinctive. Toe pads of Porcupine rarely show up in prints, but the large oval print and the pattern of the trail are distinctive (see Key to Patterns).

*ANIMALS WITH FOUR TOES ON FRONT FEET AND FIVE TOES ON HIND FEET*

*Mouse*
*L. ¼ inch*
*W. ¼ inch*

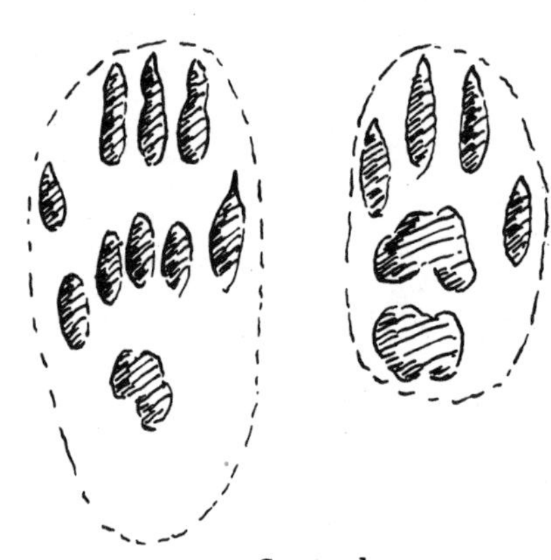

*Squirrel*
*Fore: L. 1½ inches, W. 1 inch*
*Hind: L. 2 inches, W. 1 inch*

See also five-toed animals: Muskrat and Opossum.

## *Key to Track Patterns*

All animals can move in a variety of ways, but each also has a characteristic normal gait it uses most often. We can walk, leap, or run, but we most often walk; a Rabbit can walk or gallop, but it almost always gallops. Our northern animals can be divided into four groups, based on their most common gaits and the patterns of tracks they create. Below is an outline of these four divisions, followed by a detailed discussion of each division and the animals within it.

Familiarize yourself with these basic patterns, so that when you find a track you can make a good guess as to which of four groups it belongs to; then use the detailed descriptions to make a more accurate identification.

## *FOUR BASIC TRACK PATTERNS*

*A.*

A track that appears to be nearly a straight line of single prints is characteristic of all canines (Dog, Fox, Coyote), felines (Cat, Bobcat, Lynx), and ungulates (Deer and Moose). It is produced by walking or trotting — the most common gaits of these animals.

*B.*

Evenly spaced pairs or bunches of prints are the characteristic pattern of all members of the Weasel family except the slower-moving Skunk; this pattern includes the Weasel, Mink, Marten, Fisher, and Otter. It is created by bounding, a gait well suited to animals with short legs and long bodies.

When moving at slower speeds, they all tend to show the same variations; these are the faster gaits of the Skunk.

1. 2.

This pattern is a gallop, produced by the landing of the hind legs ahead of the front legs. It is the most common gait of the Rabbit, Hare, Squirrel, and Mouse.

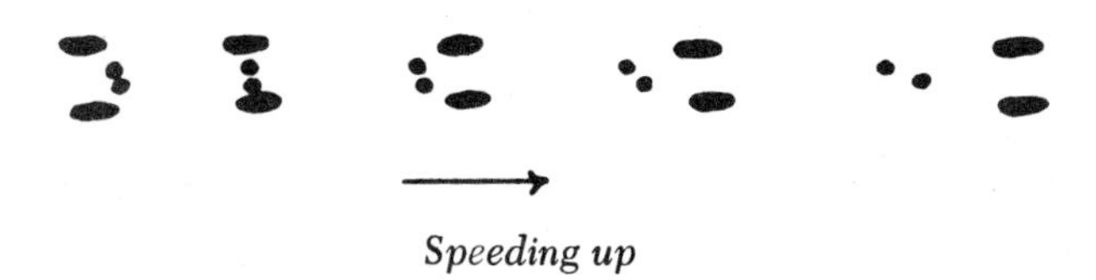

*Speeding up*

Shrews and Voles are also included in this division, for they sometimes gallop; their tracks are best compared to those of the Mouse, since all three make very small tracks.

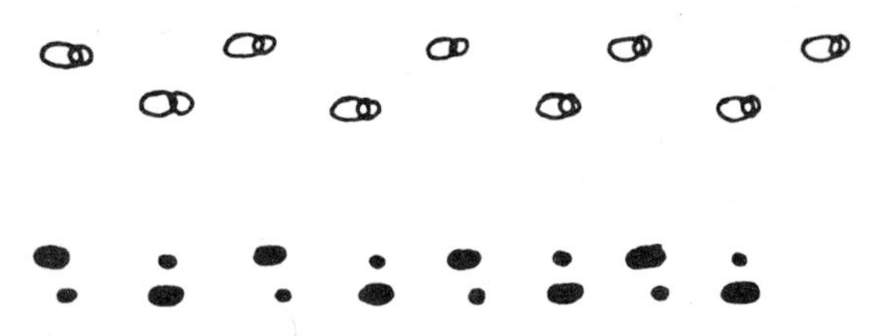

These are two types of walking created by wide, heavyset animals as they waddle along. This is the characteristic track of the Raccoon, Muskrat, Opossum, Porcupine, and Beaver.

# *Detailed Descriptions of Track Patterns*

In each of the detailed sections is a chart, which shows what animals you can expect to find in the city, suburb, country, or wilderness. All identification relies on eliminating those choices which are unlikely, and these charts will help you do that.

Two measurements are often used in the descriptions: *stride* and *straddle*. Stride is the measurement from the center of one print or group of prints to the center of the next one in the trail. This is extremely variable, depending on the speed of the animal, and is listed here only as an average for the most common gait of each animal. When it is too variable, it is omitted.

Although stride is only of minimal importance for idenfication, straddle is very important and far less variable. Straddle is the width of the trail, and in cases of similar track patterns often is the key identifying factor. Nevertheless, it is still variable and only to be used as a guideline.

*AA.*

All two-toed, and most four-toed, animals make this pattern. When walking they place a hind foot directly in the print of the front foot. Sometimes the hind foot lands behind or to the side of the front foot, making these two variations:

1.

2.

Notice that the paired prints in the second variation do not form a straight line like those of the Weasel family in pattern B, but are placed to either side of an imaginary line drawn down the center of the trail.

All of these animals display gallop patterns also, but they never gallop for very long in winter before changing back to more normal gaits.

What to expect where:

CITY SUBURB COUNTRY WILDERNESS

Cat

Dog

Fox

Deer

Coyote

Bobcat

Lynx

Moose

CAT Distinguished from others by small circular print (1 inch in diameter) and short stride. Average stride: 6–8 inches. Average straddle: 3 inches.

BOBCAT Circular print twice as large as that of Cat, and found mostly in wilderness. Average stride: 10–14 inches. Average straddle: 4½ inches.

LYNX Circular print almost twice as large as Bobcat's; toes seldom show through thick hairs on bottom of foot. Found only in Canada and northern border of United States. Average stride: 10–14 inches. Average straddle: 7 inches.

DOG Dogs vary so in size that no generalizations of stride or straddle are useful. Oval shape distinguishes Dog prints from those of all Cats, but it is still easy to confuse Dog with Fox or Coyote. In general, their tracks show large feet, often being dragged, and their trail expresses a playful attitude toward their environment, rather than the keen awareness and stealth expressed in Fox and Coyote trails.

FOX Straight lines of neat, oval prints, often following prominent aspects of the landscape: for example, a stone wall, the side of a woods road, a swamp edge, or a ridge. It expresses careful curiosity rather than the abandoned curiosity of a Dog. Travels long distances between hunting areas at a constant trot. Average stride: 12–15 inches. Average straddle: 3–4 inches.

COYOTE Difficult to distinguish from Red Fox prints, for the size of the oval print and the length of the stride are similar. The straddle when walking or trotting tends to be larger. The prints are distinguished from those of the Dog by awareness and cunning expressed in the trail. Average stride: 12–15 inches. Average straddle: 4–6 inches.

DEER Deer and Moose almost always leave some indication of their two-toed hoof at the base of their print. Since these animals are heavier than any of the canines or felines listed above and have thin, long legs, their feet penetrate the snow's crust and leave a deep wedge-shaped mark. Sometimes the foot drags between steps.

In deep snow other deer will follow in the same steps, forming even deeper wedges. Average stride: 14–16 inches. Average straddle: 6 inches.

MOOSE Extremely large prints, sinking deep into the snow. Found only in Canada and northern border of United States. Average stride: 24 inches. Average straddle: 10 inches.

*BB.*

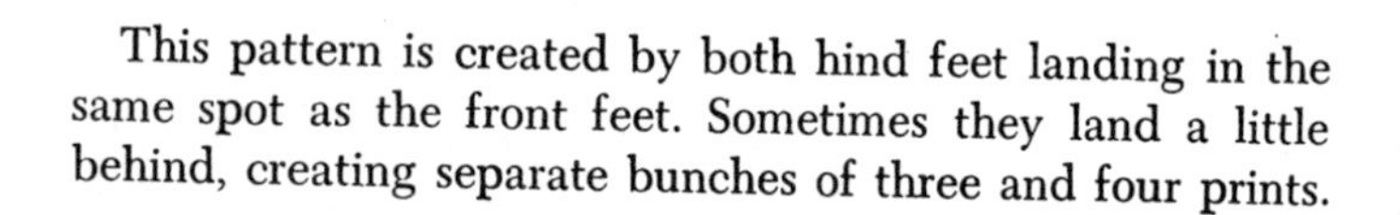

This pattern is created by both hind feet landing in the same spot as the front feet. Sometimes they land a little behind, creating separate bunches of three and four prints.

When the pattern forms pairs of prints, they are usually on a slight diagonal, rather than directly opposed.

What to expect where:

| CITY | SUBURB | COUNTRY | WILDERNESS |
|---|---|---|---|
| Skunk ———————— | ———————— | ———————— | ———————— |
| | Weasel ———————— | ———————— | ———————— |
| | | Mink ———————— | ———————— |
| | | Otter ———————— | ———————— |
| | | | Fisher ———————— |
| | | | Marten ———————— |

SKUNK

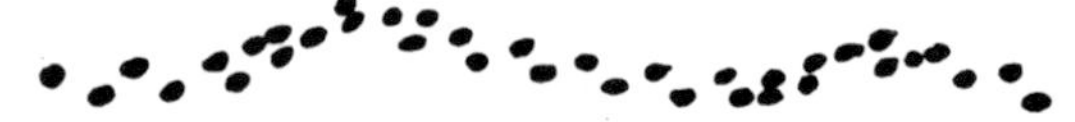

A slow animal that leaves a meandering trail of small, round prints as it searches for hibernating insects, fruit, or small rodents. The skunk is included in this group because when moving faster it has the same variations of gait as the rest of the Weasel family does when moving more slowly.

1. 2. 3.

Skunk tracks always end at a ground den or similar lodging. Average straddle: 2½–3½ inches.
Note: Since all members of the Weasel family, except the Skunk, have similar patterns, you must use habits and size of straddle to distinguish between them.

WEASEL The Weasel is the smallest of the Mustelids, but it varies most in size, since the Least Weasel is only half the size of the Long-tailed Weasel. Nevertheless, Weasel tracks and straddles are substantially smaller than those of the Mink, with whose track it might be confused. The Weasel often tunnels, stays away from directly entering water, and its body sometimes makes a connecting impression between prints. Average stride: 10–16 inches. Average straddle: 2 inches.

MINK Mink hunts in and near water, and its straddle averages an inch larger than that of the Weasel. Weasel tracks can be minute, but Mink tracks are slightly larger than those of a House Cat. The only other Weasel family print near water would be that of the Otter, but the Otter's is over three times the size of the Mink's. Mink have large hunting circuits and frequently travel overland. Average stride: 18 inches. Average straddle: 3 inches.

MARTEN Found only in Canada, and near the northern border of the United States — an unlikely print to find. The Marten lives in the forest and climbs trees as well as a Squirrel does. If a paired diagonal print leads to or from a tree, it may be that of a Marten. The Fisher also can climb trees but does not do so as frequently, and its print is almost twice as large. Mink and Marten could be difficult to distinguish except by habits, one entering water, the other climbing trees; but the Marten is so rare that in most areas it should not even be considered. Average stride: 24 inches. Average straddle: 3½–4 inches.

FISHER The Fisher exists only in Canada and near the northern border of the United States. Its tracks are not rare in wilderness areas, and they are easily recognized by their large size. The tracks are often found in the mountains traveling cross-country. They could be confused with those of the Otter, since Otters also travel overland at times, but the Otter track is larger and the animal slides regularly in traveling. Average stride: 28 inches. Average straddle: 6 inches.

OTTER

Otter is the largest of the Weasel family and its track is easily recognized, since it slides with its body on the snow whenever doing so is easier than bounding. The slides are 8 to 10 inches wide and start and end with prints. Otters hunt primarily in water, but their tracks are so much larger than Mink's that there is no possibility of confusing the two. Otter tracks are not rare and may be found far from water. Average stride: 36 inches. Average straddle: 8–10 inches.

*CC.*

What to expect where:

| CITY | SUBURB | COUNTRY | WILDERNESS |
|---|---|---|---|
| Squirrel ——— | ——— | ——— | ——— |
| Mouse ——— | ——— | ——— | ——— |
| | Shrew ——— | ——— | ——— |
| | | Vole ——— | ——— |
| | | Rabbit ——— | ——— |
| | | | Hare ——— |

SQUIRREL Squirrel tracks begin and end at trees and rarely differ from the gallop pattern. In deep snow the hind and fore print on each side make one impression, resulting in this track:

Squirrel tracks often lead to diggings in the snow where nuts were buried in the ground. The strides of Squirrels vary greatly but their straddles may be some clue to different species. Chipmunk — Straddle: 2–3 inches. Red Squirrel — Average straddle: 3–4 inches. Gray or Fox Squirrel — Average straddle: 4–5 inches.

MOUSE, VOLE, SHREW These three types of animal make the smallest prints in winter. The Mouse typically gallops, sometimes leaving a tail drag.

It can leap long distances, and its track can be told from the Chipmunk's by having a straddle less than 2 inches and by the occasional tail drag.

Vole and Shrew also may gallop, but they usually run. The main distinction from Mouse tracks is that these tracks vary between galloping and different types of running.

The two are distinguished from each other by the size of the straddle — the Shrew's is smaller. Mouse — Straddle: 1½–2 inches; mostly gallops. Vole — Straddle: 1½–2 inches; varying gait. Shrew — Straddle: less than 1½ inches; varying gait.

RABBIT, HARE

Rabbit and Hare always gallop, and tend to place their smaller front feet one behind the other, rather than paired like the Squirrel and Mouse.

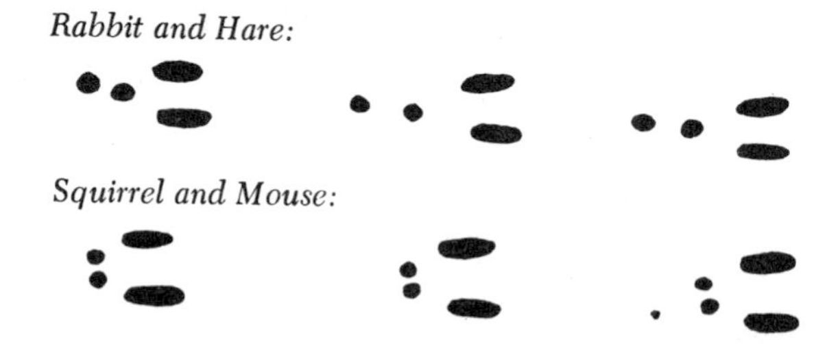


The hind feet of Rabbits and Hares are typically much larger than the front feet, and in the case of the Snowshoe Hare, they are so large that they are unmistakable (see Four-toed Prints). On the other hand, the Cottontail in shallow snow may show only the toes of its hind feet, making its trail look like the gallop of a House Cat.

In deep snow, the Cottontail may place both hind and front feet close together, making an impression where only its

body and tail show. Rabbit — Average straddle: 4–5 inches. Hare — Average straddle: 7–8 inches.

*DD.*

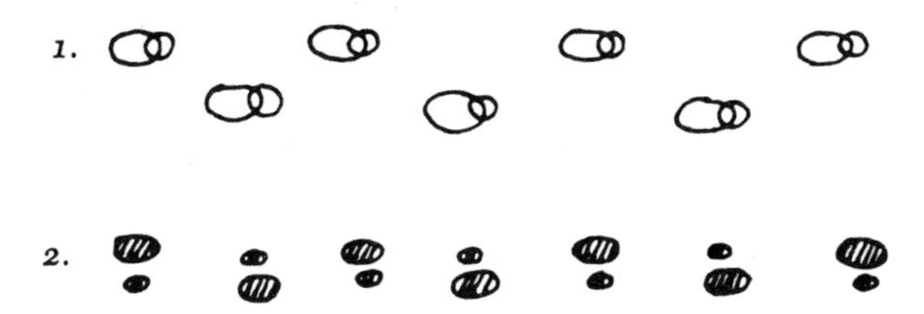


This pattern is seen only for heavyset, slow-moving, wide-straddled animals. All five of these animals spend a lot, or even the majority, of their time moving in other environments: the Beaver and Muskrat in water, and the Raccoon, Opossum, and Porcupine in trees. Hind feet are always larger, their print showing either on top of or overlapping with the front print (1, above), or alongside the smaller front print (2, above).

If these animals gallop, it will be for only short distances, and the spacing between gallops will be small, indicating a slow and lumbering movement.

What to expect where:

CITY SUBURB COUNTRY WILDERNESS

Raccoon ______________________________

Muskrat ________________________

Opossum __________________

Beaver ____________

Porcupine _______

RACCOON

Raccoon tends to place its larger hind foot beside the smaller front foot, as shown above. The pattern may be difficult to distinguish from the Opossum's, for the latter frequently walks with the same gait. But the Opossum trail sometimes has a tail-drag, while the Raccoon's never does. Details of hind prints easily distinguish the two (see Five-toed Prints). Average stride: 8–12 inches. Average straddle: 3½–5 inches.

MUSKRAT

Muskrats typically overlap their hind and fore prints and their tails may or may not make marks. Their prints are distinguished from those of the Raccoon by smaller front feet, occasional tail-drag, and by entering deep water or plunge holes. When the Muskrat is in its lumbering gallop, the tail mark shows irregularly between sets of prints.

The Muskrat, of course, does not climb trees as do the Raccoon and Opossum. Average stride: 3–4 inches. Average straddle: 3–4 inches.

OPOSSUM Opossum gaits vary, making patterns similar to those of both Muskrat and Raccoon. Their stride is larger than that of the Muskrat and usually smaller than that of the Raccoon. Average stride: 6–8 inches. Average straddle: 4–5 inches.

BEAVER

The hind foot of the Beaver makes an impression that is easily recognized, even when obscured by melting. The large webbed area and narrow heel distinguish its prints from those of the other four animals in this category. A Beaver track will not be far from water, and the animal does not leave the safety of water except for a good reason, so look for evidence of gnawing nearby. Average stride: 4–6 inches. Average straddle: 6–8 inches.

PORCUPINE

Porcupines make a wide distinctive trough or series of prints. The prints are large and rounded, and they always alternate. Often arcs to either side show where the animal is lifting its feet around while waddling along. Its quilled tail usually drags over the trail, making a winding pattern over the prints. The trail usually ends at trees or dens before very long, at which point you may see evidence of chewed bark, or scats.

Many other animals will use a Porcupine trail also, since in deep snow it packs down a nice trough. Certain Porcupine trails between trees may be repeatedly used and worn down. Average stride: 5–6 inches. Average straddle: 8–10 inches.

# *Key to Bird Tracks*

The tracks of birds are common and are often confused with those of other animals. Five prints are shown below. The first is a generalized print of all small or medium-sized birds that occasionally feed on the ground, such as Juncos, Sparrows, Starlings, Pigeons. The second is the Crow print, which is common and distinctive. The last three belong to our large ground-dwelling birds: Bobwhite, Grouse, and Pheasant. Note how all three have a short fourth toe.

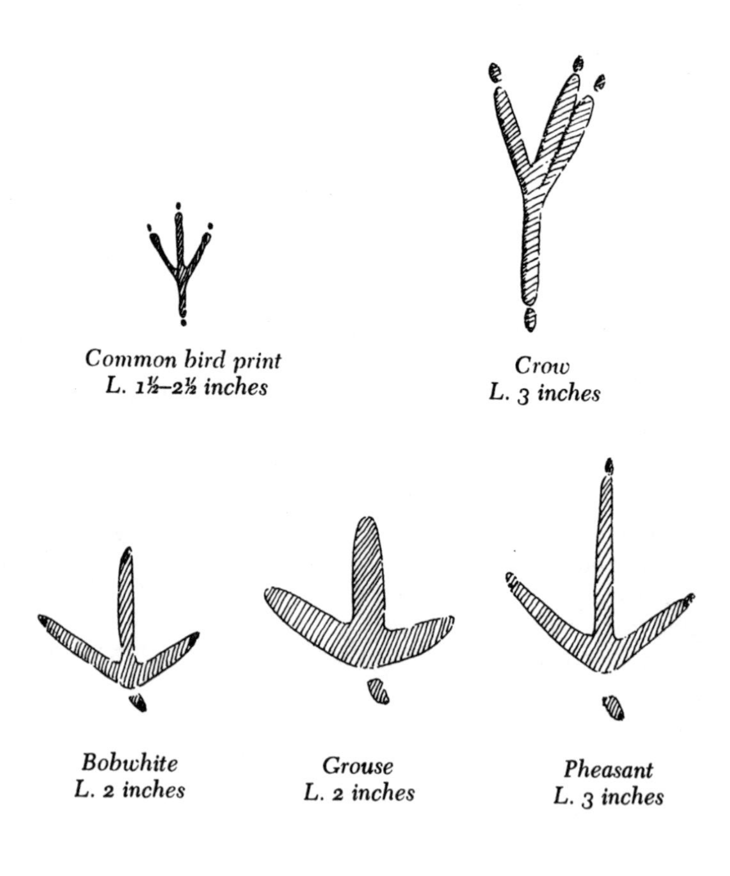

*Common bird print*
*L. 1½–2½ inches*

*Crow*
*L. 3 inches*

*Bobwhite*
*L. 2 inches*

*Grouse*
*L. 2 inches*

*Pheasant*
*L. 3 inches*

Bobwhite and Pheasant are distinguished by the size of the print; Grouse is distinguished from the other two by the width of its toes.

## *Bird Track Patterns*

Small birds either hop or walk. Their patterns are easily confused with those of Mice or Voles. Bird tracks, however, are longer and thinner and don't end at holes or trees, but just stop when the bird takes off. Wing marks in the snow are common and are a good clue.

Note how the hind toe drags when a small bird hops; this helps distinguish its track from those of Mice.

*A small bird walking*

*A Crow walking from shallow to deep snow.*

A Crow walks long distances in search of food, and in shallow snow its middle toe makes a drag mark.

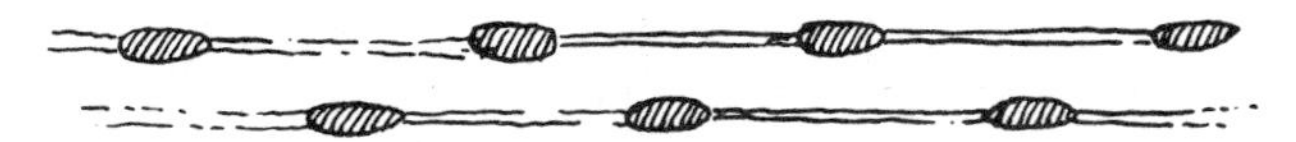

In deep snow the Crow, Bobwhite, Grouse, and Pheasant all make a track similar to this.

The tail makes a mark as a bird lands, and its wings make a mark as it takes off.

## *Natural History Descriptions*

### Beaver (*Castor canadensis*)

Beaver tracks are rarely seen in winter, but evidence of the animal's presence will be abundant. Signs of Beavers include dams, lodges, ground dens, gnawed trees and wood chips, twigs and saplings stripped of bark, and water channels.

Beaver dams are infamous, as well as famous, as being some of the largest structures built by animals. Their function is to create an area of water that will provide the Beaver with safety and ease in transporting food and building materials. Although the Beaver is vulnerable on land, its main food, tree bark, exists on land. The pond allows the Beaver to reach its food source without ever being far from the safety of water. When Beavers eat away the food from around the dam, they either extend the pond by raising the dam or dig channels from the pond into good foraging areas. The pond also provides protection for the rest of the Beaver's activities, for the animal builds a lodge in the pond and is thus shielded by a moat from its predators.

*Beaver with dam and lodge*

The Beaver is not quite the master engineer it is made out to be. Dams are often built in difficult locations when only half as much effort might be needed to build one nearby. But once a Beaver chooses a location, it seems determined to make that location work. Shrubs are cut and placed trunk-end upstream in a line across the waterway. Rocks, mud, and branches are then piled on until the dam is sufficiently high and watertight. Dams may vary from a very few to 8 feet high. They are generally extremely sturdy and can be used by animals as bridges.

A Beaver lodge is made by piling up a mound of sticks and mud and then gnawing out a chamber inside. Beavers continually pack fresh mud on the outside but leave the top uncovered, possibly for ventilation within the lodge. Fresh mud is a sign that the lodge is actively used; in winter it will freeze up, making an impenetrable fortress at a time when predators can approach on the ice. Within the lodge, Beavers enjoy considerable warmth. A study in Canada showed the average minimum temperature of the air outdoors to be −30 degrees F. while average minimum temperatures inside the lodge were 34 degrees F.

The lodge usually has two underwater entrances, which

converge onto a feeding platform. A few inches higher and off to one side of this platform is a resting area covered with shredded wood (rather than grasses, which might rot).

Before winter the Beavers cut saplings and store them under the water near the lodge. In winter they leave the lodge and bring some of this food back to eat. Thus the Beaver rarely has occasion to leave the lodge or the protection of the pond in winter.

Beaver-felled trees are easy to recognize, for no other animals except humans cut trees. You may find felled trees at quite a distance from the dam or in an area where there are no dams, in which case the Beavers may live in bank dens similar to those of Muskrats or build their lodges in a river backwater. Beavers cut down trees for three reasons: to get food, to get construction materials, and to keep their teeth worn down. They do not eat the wood of the tree but only the young bark and so must cut down large trees to reach the young bark of the upper branches. These peeled branches are in turn used in the lodge and dam. Beavers cannot direct the fall of a tree they are cutting; their trees simply fall the way they are leaning. But even if a Beaver has enough food, it must chew, for its front incisors continually grow. If they are not worn down, they may grow so large that the animal won't be able to feed.

A lodge in winter may contain a number of Beavers. A pair tend to mate for life, and young Beavers stay with the adults for two years, so a winter family would contain two adults, two or more yearlings, and two or more kits born in the last spring. In the coming spring the yearlings are driven from the area and must start a life on their own.

## Bobcat (*Lynx rufus*)

The Bobcat is the most common and widespread wild cat in North America. It ranges south into Mexico, and north into southern Canada.

*Bobcat*

As with most predators the Bobcat spends the majority of its time hunting. It is our only wild predator in the East that regularly kills Deer. This occurs mostly in winter, when the Deer are more vulnerable because of deep snow. Bobcats hunt at night and generally stalk Deer near the latter's bedding areas. Another of their methods of hunting is to lie waiting in areas where they know Deer will come, and then to bound onto them in a surprise attack. Bobcats kill Deer by attacking them on the back of the neck and biting through important veins. A Deer killed by a Bobcat is characteristically lying in the snow with its head bent back. There is often very little evidence of attack. The Deer is eaten, starting with the hind quarters; it is partly covered over with snow and debris when the cat leaves. Often a kill is used only for one meal, but the remainder provides important carrion for smaller predators, such as Foxes and Fishers, that would never attack a Deer themselves. Bobcats also regularly feed on smaller game such as Porcupines, Gray Squirrels, Cottontails, Rodents, and small birds.

The Bobcat is extremely wary of the snow. Although it is roughly the same size as the Lynx, the Bobcat has feet that are not as densely covered with hairs and so don't have as much surface area as those of the Lynx. In snow under 6 inches deep the Bobcat roams freely for distances of many miles a night. But if it encounters drifts or areas of snow deeper than 6 inches, it either avoids them or bounds through. When the whole snow cover is deep, a Bobcat restricts its movements, stays nearer to cached kills, and utilizes that food more. It rarely expends much energy chasing prey through snow; if prey is not caught within a few bounds it is given up.

The Bobcat beds down during the day. It beds under upturned stumps, in cavities among rocks, or on sunny knolls, depending on the weather. As it travels it explores all possible bedding sites within its range. Doing this serves the dual purpose of possibly finding prey in them and also being familiar with their locations so that the Bobcat can head for the nearest one after hunting.

Bobcats range over areas 25 miles or more in diameter, depending on the availability of prey. They mark their ranges with scats, urine, and scent excreted from scent glands. Although cats in general are believed to cover their feces, this is true only about 60 percent of the time with Bobcats, mostly younger cats doing so. Once a range is established by a Bobcat, other Bobcats seldom remain long within it but intrude only when passing through.

The track of the Bobcat is a larger version of the house cat track, being round, with four toe pads on each foot, and showing no claws. Cats use their claws for hunting, and retract them into their feet to keep the claws sharp. Canines kill mainly with their teeth, using their claws for traction and digging; their claws cannot be retracted and almost always show in prints. The trail of the Bobcat wanders considerably, as the animal explores all unusual objects and checks out all dens.

### Cottontail (*Sylvilagus floridanus*)
### Snowshoe Hare (*Lepus americanus*)

The winter habits and activities of Cottontails and Snowshoe Hares are easy to detect in the snow. Both animals eat

*Cottontail with scats and chewed twigs*

mainly the buds and twigs of sapling trees or shrubs in winter. These twigs are easily recognized, for they are cut at a neat 45 degree angle about 1 or 2 feet off the ground.

Rabbits also chew bark off the branches of Apple, Hawthorn, and other trees. Near where they feed there are often scats on the snow surface. These are slightly flattened spheres of chewed plant material, light brown in color; none of our other animals has a scat like this. Since the woody fibers these Rabbits eat in winter are hard to digest, such nutrition still exists in their scats. Therefore, when food is scarce, they may eat their own scats in order to absorb more of their nutritive value.

Rabbits and Hares forage at night and during the day often rest in "forms." Forms are small hollows among grasses and leaves, preferably under shrubs, where the snow is shallow, where there is protection from wind, and where the sun's warmth can penetrate the cover. In forms Rabbits rely on their ability to remain motionless and on the camou-

*Snowshoe Hare*

flage of their fur for protection. The Snowshoe Hare's winter coat is white, which makes it ideal protection in the Hare's northern range of constant winter snow. The Cottontail remains brown in winter, a color that is perfect for the patchy snow of its more southern range.

None of our Rabbits live permanently in underground dens or "warrens" as do European Rabbits; rather they build an above-ground nest of plant fibers when breeding and at other seasons use forms. Cottontail tracks may lead to the entrance of a woodchuck den or similar burrow, but the Rabbit is just remaining within the entrance. A Cottontail may even rest beneath soft snow and, when frightened, actually burrow through it.

Both animals keep to winter ranges of only a few acres, depending on the availability of food. In this range they reuse their trails so often that the snow can become packed along them. This familiarity with their range gives them an important advantage over their predators, which, generally having larger ranges, cannot know the nooks and crannies peculiar to smaller areas. The main winter predator of the Snowshoe Hare is the Lynx; for the Cottontail it is the Fox.

The Snowshoe Hare track is unmistakable from any other. It is only commonly seen in the northern states and Canada. A Squirrel track can resemble that of a Cottontail, but the fact that it sooner or later ends at a tree distinguishes it.

An unusual print of the Cottontail occurs in deep snow. Here it places hind and forefeet together, so that the whole body makes an oval impression, with a small mark at the back where the tail has hit the snow.

### Coyote (*Canis latrans* variety)

The Coyote, which has always thrived in the West and Midwest, is now extending its range to the East. It is already present in the western sections of New England and

*Coyotes with dead Deer*

is believed to be expanding its range at about 15 miles per year. The Coyote of the East may be a new species from the western variety; it is slightly larger.

The reason for Coyote expansion is the extreme cunning and adaptability of these animals. They are able to live quite close to humans and still go unnoticed. They are feeding primarily on small rodents, carrion Deer, the unfinished prey of other predators, and fruits and berries. Often at the outskirts of cities they can find prey and carrion around dumps.

Their print is not much larger than the Red Fox's and indistinguishable from that of a small dog, except that it tends to be narrower than the print of the domestic dog. Like the Fox, it can best be distinguished from dogs by the keen awareness represented in its trail. It will approach points of interest cautiously, not making wasted movements, nor dragging its feet, and it will circle to smell the wind before bedding down for the day.

Coyotes often hunt the margins between two habitats and sometimes hunt in parallel pairs or loose groups of three or four. They move rapidly between known carcasses or favorite hunting areas, then slow down at those areas to search more intensively. Their ranges may be between 20 and 50 square miles in winter and may overlap with those of other Coyotes. They hunt open land most thoroughly and tend to avoid upland hardwood forests. Their trails often follow those of other animals, so as to conserve strength and avoid unaltered snow. Feral dogs (domestic dogs gone wild) are always an increasingly common animal of the woods, and their tracks and trails may be difficult to distinguish from those of the Coyote.

Coyote scats are larger than those of Fox but similarly pointed at the ends; they often contain much hair. Like other canines and cats, Coyotes place the scats at strategic locations within their territory. These "scent posts" may have scats of varying ages, possibly reflecting the frequency of the animal's visits.

## Deer, White-tailed (*Odocoileus virginianus*)

To help them survive the winter, Deer stay within a limited area with which they become familiar, packing down a network of trails throughout it. The trails enable them to escape predators and get through deep snow to reach areas containing winter food. When these trails become particularly concentrated and the Deer remain in that location, it is

*Deer rising from bedding area*

termed a "yard," or "Deer yard." This is rarely a uniformly packed down area but rather a maze of small trails.

Where Deer stay in winter is mostly a function of the vegetation and topography. They generally bed during the day and feed at night. The bedding area must be warm, protected from sight, and not too far from food. In the South, this means on south-facing slopes, where they are protected from prevailing north winter winds and receive increased warmth from the hill's sloping toward the sun. In the North, they stay in Cedar swamps, which are generally lowlands protected from winds, or in Spruce groves, which also protect them from wind as well as from snow accumulation, since Spruces hold so much snow in their branches. In general, Deer try to take advantage of all the environmental factors they can to keep warm and conserve energy.

Winter food is a problem for Deer. Snow soon covers grasses except on south-sloping hills, where it may have melted, so most Deer switch to feeding on the buds of deciduous trees and the foliage of evergreens. They chew sapling trees down to nubs and eat the buds off all branches they can reach. Hemlock and Cedar needles are some of their favorites to browse. Deer-chewed twigs can be told from those chewed by Rabbits, for the Deer bite them off in their molars, making a ragged cut, whereas Rabbits use their sharp front teeth, making a neat 45-degree slice in the stem.

Most of the Deer's natural predators have long since disappeared from our area, so the Deer population is often too large for the winter food supply. As a result, many Deer starve or become too weak to defend themselves or manage in deep snow. But these dead Deer in turn are eaten by many of our smaller predators, such as Fox, Opossum, Coyote, Raccoon, Mink, and Fisher, which would not try to kill Deer themselves.

Two other signs of Deer are their beds and their scats. When Deer rest during the day or through a storm at night, they shelter the ground underneath them. You can frequently find these Deer beds as leafy areas surrounded by snow or as packed snow showing the outline of the resting Deer. Deer scats are distinctive, being dark black pellets each with a small point at one end. Their presence near the track, nibbled twigs, or a bedding area help make your identification positive.

When a Deer walks it places its hind foot directly in the print of its front foot; sometimes the footprints overlap slightly, making the print not quite clear. Patterns of White-tailed Deer movement are generally either walking, as described above, or galloping where the hind feet land ahead of the front feet.

Deer tracks may be of slightly different sizes, since does and yearlings are smaller than bucks. The front feet of Deer are larger than the hind feet, because they need to support the weight of the head and neck. Deer can spread the front parts of their hooves quite far apart when trying to support themselves on soft surfaces.

The track of the White-tailed Deer varies considerably, depending on the depth of the snow. In light snow, it is unmistakable, for the Deer is the only two-toed animal in this area, with a foot at most 3 inches long. The Moose also has a cloven hoof, but its feet are 5 to 7 inches long. As snow gets deeper, Deer's hooves sink all the way through, leaving a thin wedge-shaped impression slanting in the direction of travel.

### Fisher (*Martes pennanti*)

The Fisher is a large member of the Weasel family. It is dark-furred, about the size of a Raccoon, although thinner, and has a long bushy tail. Its population and range have definitely been increasing over the last twenty-five years, so the chances of seeing the track or the animal are quite good now in the northern United States and Canada.

The best way to identify the print is to get a close view of the toe prints; there should be five, each with the mark of a

*Fisher*

claw. The print can be confused only with that of the Mink or Otter. Mink prints are much smaller and almost always neatly paired. Otters have larger tracks, with marks of webbed hind feet, and Otters frequently slide where the terrain allows. Both Otter and Mink enter water, but a Fisher will avoid it if possible. The Fisher's track, though sometimes paired, regularly shows a variety of patterns as the animal ranges freely across-country, from wooded mountainsides to lowland stream edges.

Fisher food is entirely different from that of the Mink or Otter. It eats Snowshoe Hare, Porcupine, Grouse, rodents, Raccoons, Deer carrion, and Shrews. It has a reputation for eating Porcupines, and studies show that Fishers do in fact feed on them, but Porcupines are only about 20 percent of a Fisher's diet. Carrion Deer are an important winter food, and Fishers will remain near a Deer carcass to feed on it for as long as it lasts. At other times Fishers are constantly moving on a circuit that may cover as much as 10 square miles. Fishers have been known to travel up to 15 miles in a single day. They are active during day or night and generally rest in caves or old dens.

## Fox, Red (*Vulpes fulva*)
## Gray (*Urocyon cinereoargenteus*)

Foxes are among the most exciting and accessible of all northern mammals to track.

Although secretive, they are common and prefer areas with both fields and woods, frequently making a habitat of suburbs and farmland. You are not likely to see evidence of a Fox in other seasons, but a thin layer of snow can boldly announce its presence.

What makes tracking Foxes most exciting is that you can see the mind of a predator in the wild. A Fox is always hunting in winter, and its kills and attempted kills are all

*Red Fox walking from cache in foreground*

revealed in its track. Since the Fox is seeking out other animals, following its trail will bring you in contact with other game also, so that you can spot their tracks and learn of the interaction.

Although Foxes hunt primarily at night, they may extend this activity into daytime during winter, since prey is harder to catch. They sleep in the open during the midday, curling up on the snow in some spot protected from wind but exposed to the sun, often on a slight rise of ground. They seldom sleep deeply but, more often, just doze off for a few seconds at a time.

A Fox must kill as much game as it can, for hunting conditions may be poor the next day. When game is available the Fox captures it; when it is not, the Fox can return to previous kills. Many kills are stored in caches: a pit is dug into the snow, the prey is placed in it, then covered over. Caches occur along the Fox's trail and appear as small areas of disturbed snow 6 to 12 inches across. Even old caches are repeatedly visited by a Fox, for they attract other animals that come to feed on the carrion, and the Fox may be able to catch them.

Another sign frequently seen along Fox trails is their scats or urine. These are odor communications to other Foxes and are usually placed at strategic points within a Fox's range. The scats are twisted, 2 to 3 inches long, and pointed at one or both ends; they usually contain hair or berries, unlike the scats of domestic dogs. Scats are often left at small physical landmarks, such as a break in a wall, a large rock, or a mound of earth. They may be of varying ages in a pile that shows that the Fox has repeatedly visited this spot. Like domestic dogs, Foxes leave urine markings along their trail. These may be used to help relocate a cache or may be to outline a territory.

Foxes tend to pair up in mid-December as a preliminary to breeding. From this time on, their trails may be seen in pairs, traveling parallel at one or two hundred yards apart or even following one another in the same prints. Mating occurs in January and February, and after this the two seek out and explore all dens in their range. Two or three are enlarged and cleaned out, but only one of these will be used. The Fox can dig its own den but more often will make over a Woodchuck den. The den openings can be obvious, for there is usually a large mound of excavated earth, there may be more than one entrance, and parts of prey animals may be scattered nearby. Den entrances average 10 inches wide and 15 inches high. Kits are born between mid-February and mid-March.

The home range of a mated Fox is about 1½ square miles; a solitary Fox may roam much farther. Ranges of Foxes sometimes overlap considerably, so that dens of different pairs could be quite close together.

Because the Fox often lives near humans, its tracks can be confused with those of the domestic dog. The best way to distinguish the two kinds of prints is to observe the overall pattern of the trail, for the realities of the two animals are totally different. A dog does not need to catch food, therefore it needn't be cautious, or alert to game; it can squander energy, romping through deep or shallow snow, and basically it has no enemies. The Fox is faced with the reality of winter survival; it must spot food and approach it carefully enough to catch it. It must always be on the alert for its prey and its enemies, and in winter it must conserve energy by walking in shallow snow, staying out of the wind, and getting the sun's warmth whenever possible.

The tracks vary accordingly. A dog track tends to be sloppy, often showing that the dog dragged its feet in the snow; a dog will explore, but without caution, and it will often gallop and romp without immediate purpose. A Fox track expresses extreme alert concern for every part of the animal's environment. The most common pattern is an almost straight line of neat prints. Objects explored are approached from downwind; galloping is used when the Fox is actually chasing prey. The Fox often walks along prominent aspects of the vegetation and topography — like following the woods' edge, or a stone wall, or a slight ridge. It has been generalized that a Fox's track is straight when the animal is traveling between areas, wandering when it is hunting, and circling when it is about to bed down.

Two species of Fox are present in northeastern and central North America: the Red Fox and the Gray Fox. The Red Fox is the larger and more common one, generally found closer to human activity. The Gray Fox is smaller, with a very delicate print, prefers more secluded areas, is able to climb trees, and frequently walks up fallen logs.

## Lynx (*Lynx canadensis*)

The Lynx is strictly a northern cat and is not likely to be seen except in Canada and northern Maine. It is only a few inches larger than the Bobcat, but its feet are proportionately much larger. They are 3 to 4 inches in width and in winter are totally covered with hairs, which then help create a snow print 4½ to 5 inches in diameter. This print characteristically shows very little evidence of toe pads.

About 70 percent of the Lynx's diet in winter is the Snowshoe Hare; the rest is carrion and game birds. The Lynx and

*Lynx*

Snowshoe Hare seem to have a battle of snow adaptations going on, each developing larger feet, which support them more on the snow. The Lynx prefers to hunt from hunting beds, areas where it lies in wait for the Hares. When the population of Hares is great, the Lynx can do this more often; when Hares are scarce, it must travel more to find food.

A Lynx averages about one kill every other night. Although this figure remains constant for the Lynx, the distance it has to travel varies with the Hare population. Success in hunting is also intimately tied to the bearing strength of the snow cover: certain types of crust may support the Hare but not the Lynx; others may support neither or both.

The patterns of the track will be similar to those of dogs and cats — a straight line when walking or trotting, and a gallop when moving faster.

## Marten (*Martes americana*)

The Marten is a relatively unknown mammal, which has become rare because of trapping. Of the tracks included in this guide, those of the Marten and Lynx are probably the ones least likely to be seen. Yet efforts are being made in Canada to preserve the Marten and enable it to increase. They have been partially successful, and so, with the hope that the Marten will increase its range, as has its cousin the Fisher, I have included it. Its track is not likely to be seen except in Canada and just into the northern edge of the United States.

The Marten is midway in size between the larger Fisher and smaller Mink. It displays track patterns typical of the Weasel family, but it is more arboreal than any of the other members, being as comfortable in trees as Squirrels are. It is one of the few predators on Squirrels, particularly the Red Squirrel, since the latter lives within the area of the Marten's distribution. Martens are also known to eat the Red-

*Marten*

backed Vole and Meadow Vole. The Marten hunts within a more restricted range than the Fisher and often intensively searches small areas of overlapping territory on successive days.

Obviously a track similar to but smaller than a Fisher's and one that ends or starts at a tree might be clues to a Marten.

## Mink (*Mustela vison*)

Tracks of the Weasel Family can be difficult to distinguish. Weasel tracks are very small, Otter very large, but in between are the Mink, Marten, and Fisher. Each of these animals overlaps with the others in size, because females in each species are significantly smaller than the males. Therefore the way to identify them is to find which two or three animals your print fits in size and then to use habitat and habits to make the final estimation. Unfortunately the latter can also overlap.

The Mink, like its cousins the Weasel and Otter, is not a rare animal. It is widely distributed, and once you are away from cities and in good habitats, you have more than a good chance of spotting its tracks.

The animal is smaller and more common than the Marten, but larger than the Weasel. It will not climb trees like the Marten and it won't be found frequenting barns and fields in search of mice, as will Weasels. The Mink's favorite habitat is at the edge of lakes and streams, for its main food includes fish, crayfish, frogs, and Muskrats. In winter it feeds through a hole in the ice, digging into the mud to get the smaller hibernating animals. Larger prey, such as Muskrats, Cottontails, or Ducks, is often brought back to the den to be eaten or stored. Dens are situated near water, under

*Mink*

are: two native Mice, the Deermouse and the White-footed Mouse, and an introduced Mouse, the House Mouse. All three types may be found in human habitations but only our native mice readily survive in the wilds. Their main food is seeds and nuts but when they are living in buildings, they will eat any scraps.

Mice are considered strictly nocturnal but in the wild will feed in broad daylight. Mice eat all kinds of food: berries, buds, bark, nuts, seeds, greens, insects, and even carrion if it is available. They also prodigiously store food in a number of areas within their territory, such as under logs or among rock crevices. Their territories are rarely more than a quarter-mile in diameter, but their trails will often be longer, as they frequently explore all over their territory, checking out every small hollow and burrow.

Mice have an amazing ability to leap and climb, which enables them to get to many spots that you would think they could never reach. Because of this agility, they can nest just about anywhere. A Mouse nest is composed of some soft material gathered together into a mass, within which the Mice create a small chamber. Often more than one Mouse lives in a nest, and since they leave their scats within the nest, it soon becomes fouled; at that point they move out and make a new one. Nests can be found within walls, in logs or stumps, beneath tree roots, or even in birds' nests. As a matter of fact, it is quite common for Mice to use birds' nests for homes, so when you see a birds' nest that seems particularly bulky, carefully open it apart. You may find three or four mice huddled together in a Cattail down lining. Some Mice also nest in old Woodpecker or Chickadee treehole nests; they have been found as high as 50 feet up in the trees.

Mouse tracks can be found anywhere, especially around barns, swamps, and field edges, and in woodlands. The most common gait of a Mouse is galloping, the hind feet landing ahead of the forefeet, forming a miniature track similar in pattern to that of a Rabbit or Squirrel. During warm spells, Chipmunks emerge onto the snow, forming a similar pat-

*Deermouse with nest in background*

tern, except that their straddle is greater than 2 inches whereas the straddle of Mice is less than 2 inches.

Two other tracks of similar size are those of the Shrew and Vole. Because these animals live mainly in tunnels, their characteristic track is running rather than galloping, but they may also gallop. The clue is to follow the trail: if it continually gallops it is probably a Mouse; if it varies a lot or is not a gallop it is probably a Shrew or Vole.

## Muskrat (*Ondatra zibethica*)

Muskrats are fairly well prepared for winter in their water environment, so they may not even show their tracks on land, but if they do, it will always be near a source of water, whether it be a lake, swamp, stream, or road ditch. They feed in winter primarily on rootstocks of water plants such as Cattail or Arrowhead. They also eat crayfish, snails, freshwater clams, and some fish. If an orchard is especially close, they will roam on land for the fallen fruit, but generally they stay right near the water, for they are slow on land and vulnerable to a variety of predators.

Muskrats build two types of homes, one of which is particularly evident in winter: a lodge shaped like a miniature Beaver lodge and made of Cattails, mud, and small water plants. The Muskrat builds up the mound of plant material and mud and then, like the Beaver, eats and digs out an entrance from underwater and a chamber inside. The area inside is linear, with a number of enlarged spaces for sleeping, depending on how many Muskrats stay in the lodge. The lodges may be up to 4 feet in height and 8 feet in diameter, but are generally smaller. Water birds sometimes build nests on top of them, water snakes may bask on them and hibernate in their walls, and Snapping Turtles sometimes lay their eggs inside abandoned ones.

*Muskrat with snow-covered home in background*

The other home Muskrats make is in the bank of a lake or stream. They dig an underwater entrance and then an enlarged chamber above water level. Sometimes there are other entrances directly down through the ground above the chamber. These are called "plunge holes" and are used for quick escape from danger when foraging on land. Bank homes are sometimes taken over by Mink, or enlarged and used by Beavers.

Muskrats that live in swampy areas often excavate extensive channel systems radiating from their lodges or burrows; when water is low, these remain filled and provide protection as the animal feeds. Sometimes these are dry in winter, and the Muskrat's tracks will show in them.

The tracks are quite small, and often will show where the tail dragged, although it can also be held above the snow. Typically a Muskrat puts its hind foot close to where its front foot went, but variations in this pattern will be seen. In its running gait, the hind feet land ahead of the front feet in a pattern similar to the gallop of many animals. The Muskrat's long toe prints could be confused only with those of the Raccoon or Opossum. The Raccoon's prints, however, are easily distinguished, for they are almost twice as large. Those of the Opossum can be distinguished by also being larger, by having an opposable thumb at a weird angle, by ending at trees, since the Opossum regularly climbs, and by not entering into plunge holes or deep water.

## Opossum (*Didelphis marsupialis*)

The Opossum is slowly extending its range to the north even though its body is ill suited for the cold. Its ears and tail are hairless and very often bits of them freeze and break off. Nevertheless, some force is pushing them north, and they are surviving.

Opossums regularly climb trees, and their opposable thumb, as well as their tail, which can support them from branches, undoubtedly helps them. They eat fruit and ber-

*Opossums*

ries off trees, also feed on small mammals, insects, reptiles, and amphibians.

Opossums stay in dens for most of the winter, usually as lone individuals. They readily use the network of dens also used by Raccoons and Skunks, though rarely at the same time. Tree dens and building foundations are also used for daytime resting areas. They come out to feed mostly at night and their home range may be up to 50 acres.

## Otter (*Lutra canadensis*)

Otter tracks are usually found at the spillways of lakes where fish gather, or along sections of streams too shallow for the Otter to swim in. It prefers water habitats, for its diet is primarily fish, crayfish, turtles, and frogs. But Otters also frequently travel overland to hunt small rodents, and move to other areas of water for fishing. They may travel up to 3 miles overland in search of food or new waterways.

Their track is unmistakable, for they have adapted to snow travel by combining bounding and sliding. They typically take two to four bounds and then slide 5 to 15 feet. The slide is wide and looks as if someone had pulled a toy toboggan over the snow; it starts and terminates with a group of prints. Otters usually slide down slopes, and also when going up a slight incline, they may slide by pushing with their hind feet.

An emphasis on the playful character of the Otter is misleading. The fact that animals raised in captivity are playful with humans is also true of Mice, Squirrels, Skunks, and Raccoons, among others; and Otters' repetitive use of a single slide is the exception in nature. A more realistic look has shown that they prefer to walk down slopes into water and that sliding in snow is an important adaptation to the restrictions of snow travel, enabling the animal to forage on land in times of winter food scarcity.

When fishing in winter, the Otters keep a hole or two

*Otters*

open in frozen lakes. They dive into the water, chase the slower fish in toward shore, where they catch them in their mouths; they emerge from the water and eat the fish nearby.

Otters use dens for winter protection; these may be up to 500 feet from water, in a Woodchuck burrow, or under upturned tree roofs. But more often they are in the bank of the stream or lake — underground burrows that are frequently old bank dens of Muskrats or Beavers.

## Porcupine (*Erethizon dorsatum*)

It is hard to follow a Porcupine track for more than a quarter-mile without coming upon some sign of the animal's activities, for Porcupines are relatively sedentary creatures and find it hard to walk in deep snow. The tracks are distinctive in themselves and in combination with evidence of the animal's activity are unmistakable.

Three signs of the Porcupine's activity are easily spotted: its tree or cave den, its scats, and evidence of its feeding. Often you will find the animal's tracks leading to a den among rocks or a hole in a tree. If these homes have been at all used by a Porcupine they will have the animal's scats covering the floor, for Porcupines defecate in their dens all the time and don't seem to mind the filth or stench. They seem to use the den until it is so filled with scats that there is no room left for them. The scats are distinctive: they are oval, mustard-brown, composed of wood fiber, and have a somewhat sweet smell.

If a Porcupine is not in its den it will be in a tree feeding. Porcupines eat the inner bark primarily, and favor coniferous trees. Their chewing is easily distinguished from that of Beavers, both because it occurs high on the tree and because it never penetrates the wood. A few scats may be present at the base of a feeding tree. A common habit of Porcupines is to chew the tips off Hemlock branches, discarding the last foot of the branch on the ground. An area

*Porcupines*

of snow covered with these pruned branch tips is a sure sign of Porcupine; this litter also aids White-tailed Deer, providing them with winter browse they could otherwise never reach.

In the case of the Porcupine, evidence of its presence is more common than sight of the animal itself. But if you find either fresh scats or tracks, and then look hard in the tops of feeding trees you may spot it. It is often less conspicuous than you might think.

If snow cover is 6 inches or more, Porcupines must plow through the snow, forming a trough about 8 inches wide. The prints alternate and are slightly pigeon-toed. The trail usually ends at a den or a foraging tree.

## Raccoon (*Procyon lotor*)

Raccoon tracks are likely to be found at the edges of cities as well as in the country, for Raccoons are opportunists, able to take advantage of human refuse by raiding backyard trashcans and staying near town dumps. Being omnivores, they eat whatever is available, but in the wild they prefer nuts and berries, eat frogs, clams, snails and crayfish along streams, and an occasional bird or small rodent.

Raccoons are not as active in winter as they are in other seasons. They build up some fat reserves in fall which enable them to stay holed up in their dens during deep snow or very cold weather.

In some areas Raccoons, along with Opossums and Skunks, may use a number of particularly good dens over the year. All of these animals have similar intermittent periods of activity during winter. Many of them frequently switch dens after a night's ramblings. Because they do this, they all get to know the best dens over an area of many hundred acres, and one den may be inhabited by Skunk one night and Raccoons the next. Skunks tend to use ground dens, Opossums tree dens, while Raccoons use both. By

*Raccoons*

following trails you may be able to locate dens, but since the animals can wander over a mile at night you may have to follow them for quite a distance. Since these three animals may use an area for several generations, sharing dens and eating similar foods, trails become worn in the forest and can be seen as a winding impression even with autumn leaves on the ground. When snow falls, the prints of one or more of these animals will be along the trails.

Raccoons often spend the warmer days of winter resting high in the branches of trees. Tracks that lead to a tree may help you to spot the animal; Raccoons may not rest in the same tree on two consecutive days. Frequently their scats can be seen at the bases of trees they have climbed. The scats are about ¾ inch in diameter and have flat ends; they are crumbly and often contain bits of insect or crayfish shells and, possibly, hair.

Raccoon tracks are distinctive. They have five clear long

toes on each foot, and the long hind foot comes to a blunt point at its heel. Claws may or may not show. The pattern is typically in pairs, one hind foot next to one forefoot. This may represent a style of movement called "pacing," where both left feet are moved, then both right feet. Raccoons often walk on fallen logs or travel along the edges of streams and wet areas.

Raccoons tend to feed in small groups at night, and being part of a group gives a Raccoon dominance over solitary individuals. When one group is feeding in an area, they may keep a solitary Raccoon away or, if another group approaches, allow them to stay after appropriate signs of dominance or subordination have been exchanged.

## Shrew (Family *Soricidae*)

Shrews are the smallest and most common mammal in North America, inhabiting almost every country habitat,

*Shrew*

from fields to woods to swamps. But for all this they are rarely seen, for they live just under the soil surface, sharing with Moles and Voles a network of tunnels and nests.

Shrews eat insects, earthworms, nuts, and berries, and occasionally kill small Mice or other Shrews. To gather these foods they travel in both surface and subterranean tunnels. A Shrew's own underground tunnel has a short vertical section of a few inches, then may travel horizontally for a few feet. But these tunnels are probably more for protection than feeding, since the tunnels of Voles and Moles are readily available.

Shrews are active only for short periods at anytime, day or night. The rest of the time they sleep in their tunnels, sometimes huddled together for warmth. Their eyesight and sense of smell are poor, but their hearing is well developed and probably relied on for protection in the wild. There are many species of Shrews, of varying sizes and habits. Those that live in swamps even readily take to water and may be seen swimming.

In winter, Shrews often tunnel through the snow. Their tunnels are about 1 inch in diameter and frequently come to the surface at a tuft of grass or the base of a shrub. It may be that the snow is softer at these points, so that the Shrew can penetrate surface crusts. The Shrew's track shows a variable running gait with a straddle about an inch wide, never more than 1½ inches. This straddle size distinguishes it from the Vole's track, which is similar in its evidence of variable running gaits but which shows a straddle of 1½ inches or greater. The Vole's tail will not show in the track, but the Shrew's will leave a mark about 50 percent of the time.

### Skunk, Striped (*Mephitis mephitis*)

The Striped Skunk is active in early and late winter, but during midwinter is more or less dormant. Skunks prefer

*Striped Skunk*

areas of mixed woodlands and fields; their winter food consists of fruit (apples, shrub berries), small mice, shrews, carrion, garbage, nuts, seeds, and grains. This winter diet is in marked contrast to its largely insectivorous habits of spring, summer, and fall.

Skunks spend most of winter holed up in underground dens. The dens are often old Woodchuck, Squirrel, or Badger homes refilled with new grasses and dried leaves and stoppered with a plug of similar material. Up to twelve Skunks may be in a single den, usually with many more females than males; this proportion has led some to believe that they are polygamous. The dens are frequently on the sides of hills, where drainage is best, or along fencerows, where farm equipment won't damage them. Skunks can be found from the wilderness right on into the edge of the center city.

Skunks are members of the Mustelids or Weasel family, which includes Mink, Otter, Marten, Fisher, and Wolverine. But they are nowhere near as speedy as their relatives and prefer to wander slowly across the land, eating more vegetable matter and using scent rather than speed for defense. The Striped Skunk will spray only as a last resort. First, it will try to gallop away, then if that fails, it will turn to face you while stamping its front feet. If this does not make you retreat, it will turn and spray its scent. It can spray up to 8 feet away, usually in an arc so as to be sure to hit its target.

Striped Skunks come out to forage only at night. As yet there is no conclusive evidence that weather determines their activities. It is also unclear how far they may forage. Some people have followed Skunk tracks up to 3 miles long; most are much shorter, and it is believed that females range less far from the den than males do. A foraging Skunk will check most dens it comes across and may switch dens a number of times during the winter. The dens it uses may be used at other times by Opossums and Raccoons.

The track is usually seen coming from a den, where the fresh earth from inside will darken the snow at the entrance. As Skunks look for food they wander here and there, the foot pattern varying tremendously. It is this meandering trail of varying prints that is often a good clue to the Skunk. Its track varies with increasing speed, forming patterns similar to those formed by the medium gaits of other members of the Weasel family.

## Squirrel (Family *Sciuridae*)

Squirrels, because they are adapted to many environments, including the city, are some of the most successful animals in North America. In the West and Midwest most Squirrels, chiefly ground-dwellers, hibernate through winter. In the north central and northeastern regions most Squirrels are tree Squirrels; they are active all winter. These include the Fox Squirrel, *Sciurus niger,* in the central United States, the Gray Squirrel, *Sciurus carolinensis,* in the eastern United States, and the Red Squirrel, *Tamiasciurus hudsonicus,* in Canada and the northern United States.

The Red Squirrel is the smallest of the three and, unlike the other two, is almost always associated with coniferous trees. It stores cones and nuts in large caches under tree roots or in underground burrows. Near these caches are

*Gray Squirrel*

often piles of discarded shells or scales chewed off Pine or Spruce cones. These piles, called "middens," are a clue to its presence. The Red Squirrel also tunnels through snow to search for nuts on the ground or to have safe and easy access to a shrub or tree that has fruits. The tunnels measure 2½ inches in diameter and have double grooves in their floors, caused by the Squirrels' running. They can be up to 100 feet long.

Red Squirrels make leafy nests in the treetops and often line them with Red Cedar bark as insulation. If you find Cedars stripped of their bark, you can guess that a Squirrel's nest is nearby. Red Squirrels will also live in tree dens or dens underneath the ground. A single Squirrel may have all three of these types of home. The range of a Red Squirrel is small, rarely more than 400 feet in diameter.

Unlike Red Squirrels, Gray Squirrels and Fox Squirrels bury nuts and other food, each piece separately, in the ground. They dig a small pit, place the food in it and tamp it down. In winter they go to the areas where nuts were cached and rely on smell to locate them. One attempt to check their ability to do this found that out of 250 nuts stored, only two were uneaten by spring and one of those was rotted.

Gray and Fox Squirrels, like Red Squirrels, live in tree dens or leaf nests. When using tree dens, they often seek out old Flicker homes or places where a limb has broken off and the wood rotted out. Squirrels sometimes gnaw back the bark to enlarge the entrance — seeing evidence of this may help you decide if a tree den is in use. Gray and Fox Squirrels invariably line their tree dens with leaves and plant material.

The Gray Squirrel lives in Oak or Beech woods, and its range may be up to 7 acres, depending on food availability. The Fox Squirrel is more apt to live in woods mixed with farmland. It spends more time on the ground than the other two and often nests in lone trees out in fields.

In December and January, male squirrels get more aggressive toward each other and start to chase females through the trees as a preliminary act to breeding. Young are born in March, at which time the female becomes fiercely protective of her young and keeps the male away.

Squirrels move on land very much like rabbits, their larger hind feet landing ahead of their forefeet, except that with Squirrels the front feet are usually paired, whereas Rabbits' are placed one behind the other. Squirrel tracks can also be distinguished from those of Rabbits by the fact that they start and end at trees. Squirrel prints are also distinctive: when visible, they show small delicate toe pads — four on front feet and five on hind feet. Rabbits show four furry pads on all feet.

The Eastern Chipmunk, *Tamias striatus*, although dormant through most of winter, occasionally comes onto the snow surface. Chipmunk tracks are slightly smaller than the Red Squirrel's and larger than the Deer Mouse's. The track of the Flying Squirrel, *Glaucomus* species, is also occasionally seen. The animal is nocturnal and doesn't often land on the snow, since it glides between trees. But when it bounds through snow, its prints are connected on either side with lines where the large flaps of skin used for gliding leave their imprint.

## Vole, Meadow (*Microtus pennsylvanicus*)
## Redback (*Clethrionomys gapperi*)

Voles and Mice are the smallest members of the Rodent family. Voles differ from Mice by having small ears and eyes, blunt profiles, and short tails, and by living in tunnels under leaf litter or within meadow grasses. They are the most important source of food for our birds of prey and many carnivorous mammals. Ninety-five percent of our eastern Hawks' and Owls' winter food consists of the Meadow Vole, *Microtus pennsylvanicus*, and to the North and West the Boreal Red-backed Vole, *Clethrionomys gapperi*, is equally important. Both animals are prolific and

*Meadow Vole with tunnels*

create an essential link in the food chain between grasses and carnivores.

Because Voles move mostly in tunnels, their tracks are not commonly seen. But as the snow melts their tunnel network in the lower level of the snow cover becomes obvious; the tops of the tunnels melt first and expose rows of tracks worn down inside. Sometimes Voles dig holes from under the snow to the surface for ventilation among their subnivean burrows. When their tracks are seen, they can be recognized by evidence of varying gait, changing even over short distances; Voles tend to run rather than to gallop. The tracks are distinguished from those of Shrews by having a straddle greater than 1½ inches and from those of Mice by the fact that they don't show a tail mark or evidence of consistent galloping.

Most Meadow Voles live in meadows, while the Boreal Red-backed Vole lives in woods; both prefer moist areas, and their tracks can often be found near marshes. A common habit for them in winter when food is scarce is to gnaw the bark off shrubs and fruit trees. At the base of these trees or shrubs you may find sections stripped of bark and with many tiny indentations from the animal's two front teeth.

Voles make nests among the grasses; these are woven bits of rootlets and grass fiber formed into a spherical nest with a chamber inside. Unlike Mice, they do not leave their droppings in the nest but deposit them in piles at crossroads in the tunnel network. These can be found by lifting the grasses from over the tunnels until you come to a large intersection.

## Weasel (*Mustela* species)

The Weasel is adapted primarily to catching Mice. Its small head and sleek body enable it to enter Mouse runways and Vole tunnels. About 75 percent of its diet is small rodents; the larger Weasels also eat Rabbits, Squirrels, Rats, and Shrews. Because of their food preferences, the tracks of Weasels are frequently seen near barns and sheds, where mice spend the winter. Weasels seem to be distributed fairly evenly over the country, in woods, fields, around farms, and at the edges of cities. In winter they live in dens, which may be underground, in woodpiles, or under buildings. Weasels are active at night and characteristically hunt by smell, zigzagging over the snow in search of a scent. When they locate prey they chase or burrow after it. Weasels kill by biting through the back of their prey at the base of the skull. They are scrappy fighters and can capture animals much larger than themselves. They rarely feed on carrion.

Weasels are the smallest member of Mustelidae, the Weasel family. The Least Weasel, *Mustela rixosa,* measures a mere 5 to 6 inches in length, while the largest, the Long-tailed Weasel, *Mustela frenata,* is still only 10 inches long (neither measurement includes the tail). Their size is important in distinguishing their tracks from those of the

*Short-tailed Weasel*

larger Mink and Marten, which create similar patterns and are in the same family. Weasel prints can be very small, single prints generally being less than 1 inch wide. They have five toes on each foot, hind and front, but these will show only in an exceptionally clear print.

Weasel movement is typically bounding, which creates pairs or bunches of three and four prints. Since the animal is so short-legged, its body can make a connecting mark between prints in deep snow. Distance between sets of tracks depends on the speed. The straddle of Weasels is generally less than 3 inches, while that of Minks is equal to or greater than 3 inches.

VIII

# Woodland Evergreen Plants

During the fall months, when summer greenery has died back and winter snows have not yet arrived, numerous small evergreen plants become conspicuous in the woods, their dark green leaves contrasting strongly with the brown leaf litter. These plants form a natural category in our winter experiences, but they represent such a wide variety of classes, orders, and families in the plant kingdom that it is difficult to generalize about them. Nonetheless, they are all hardy plants even during freezing weather, and it is worthwhile to see how most have adapted to the northern environment.

Two conditions particularly hard on plants are a lack of water during winter and a short growing season in summer. Water is unavailable to plants in winter, since it is frozen. Most of the evergreen plants have developed woody stems and waxy coatings on their leaves, both of which cut down on evaporation. Protection from drying winds is especially important, and many northern evergreen plants remain short and close to the ground, where wind speeds are substantially less.

The short growing season in the North puts limits on the amount of energy available to each plant. Many, therefore, rely more on vegetative reproduction than on reproduction by seed, since growing a flower and maturing a seed require more energy and time. Vegetative reproduction, either by underground rootstocks or trailing stems, creates small colonies of plants, a common feature among woodland evergreens.

Evergreen leaves may also aid plants during short growing seasons, for photosynthesis can continue longer into fall and start sooner in spring. They also eliminate the need for growing a whole set of new leaves each year, allowing that energy to be channeled toward reproduction.

Most plant leaves are killed by frost, for water within their cells freezes, expands, and ruptures the cell walls. Evergreen leaves are believed to overcome this handicap in at least two ways. One is to channel most of the water from within the cell walls to spaces between cells; here its expansion through freezing does less damage. Another adaptation is to increase the sugar content of the cells, thus lowering the freezing point of the remaining water.

Two other plants are included in this chapter, for they are closely related to the evergreens and also grow in woodlands. But, in total contrast to evergreens, these plants are never green; they have given up the green pigment chlorophyll and, with it, their ability to produce their own food. Instead they live in association with fungi, which dissolve organic material and make it available as nutrition for the plant. The two plants are Indian Pipes and Beechdrops. They appear more like winter weeds, but unlike the weeds, are found in the woods.

# *Key to Woodland Evergreen Plants*

## *SHRUBS OVER 1 FOOT TALL*

— Obvious white or brown hairs covering bottom of leaf:
Labrador Tea and Bog Rosemary

— Sharp-pointed needlelike leaves with one side white:
Common Juniper

— Leaves opposite or in whorls of three:
Pale Laurel and Sheep Laurel

— Leaves 2–5 inches long bunched near end of twig; usually 6–10 feet tall, can grow much taller, found on hillsides:
Mountain Laurel

— Leaves 1–2 inches long and pointing upward all along the stem; grows to 4 feet tall and invariably near acid bogs or cedar water streams:
Leatherleaf

## *FERNS*

— Leaflets undivided, rounded at their tips, and broadly attached to the stem:
Common Polypody

— Leaflets undivided, attached at a single point to the stem:
Christmas Fern

— Leaflets much divided, attached at a single point to the stem:
Woodfern

## *TRAILING EVERGREEN VINES*

— Small leaves in pairs along stem; leaves with a smooth edge and light colored midvein; red berry:
Partridgeberry
— Small leaves in pairs along stem; leaves with several rounded teeth along edge; no light midvein and no berry:
Twinflower
— Leaves in groups of threes along stem; thin thorns or bristles on stem:
Bristly Dewberry
— Large oval leaves of different sizes densely clustered on a woody trailing vine; leaves 1–5 inches long; stem often brown and hairy:
Trailing Arbutus
— Small alternate leaves on slender, hairless stems; grows mostly in acid bog habitats:
Cranberry

## *SMALL EVERGREEN PLANTS GROWING SINGLY OR IN GROUPS*

— Light-colored veins on green leaves; leaves with a few teeth on their margins:
Spotted Pipsissewa
— Light-colored veins all over green leaves; leaves with smooth margins; grows as rosette close to ground:
Rattlesnake Plantain
— Leaves grouped in threes; leaves paper thin, and with toothed edges; golden colored rootlets; no berries:
Goldthread
— Round or oblong shiny green leaves in a rosette; plant has no main stem; leaves have long stems:
Pyrola
— A few rounded leathery leaves on each plant; leaves

smell or taste of wintergreen when crushed; leaves barely toothed on margin; frequently has red berry:
Teaberry

— Dark green, shiny, toothed leaves; leaves in whorls on the stem:
Pipsissewa

### *SMALL EVERGREEN PLANTS GROWING IN GROUPS WITH NEEDLELIKE OR SCALELIKE LEAVES LINING THEIR STEMS*

— Clubmosses
For plants that are "nevergreens," see Beechdrops and Indian Pipes in the natural history descriptions.

## *Natural History Descriptions*

### Arbutus, Trailing (*Epigaea repens*)

Trailing Arbutus always seems luxuriant, even in winter. Its bright green leaves are the largest among our trailing evergreen plants, and their waxy edges and loose arrangement seem casual in light of winter rigors. The plant grows on rocky or sandy soil by setting down roots only in one place. Its woody stems, lined with small hairs, then trail across the rocks and grow new leaves. The roots of Arbutus are often associated with fungi that live on decaying plant matter

*Trailing Arbutus*

underground. The fungal roots, called "mycorrhizae," secrete enzymes that may break down the newly decaying material of rocky areas and make its nutrition available to the plant. Trailing Arbutuses are difficult to transplant or cultivate because of this association.

Arbutus is best known for its late winter and early spring flowers, which are among the most fragrant in our woods. If you find Arbutus in the fall, return there as the snow melts, and you may find the flowers already in bloom. The flowers used to be picked and sold for their fragrance, but now they are scarce because of overpicking, and are protected by law in many states.

Both the generic and species name refer to its growth habits: *Epigaea* means "on the earth" or "near the ground" and *repens* "creeping."

## Beechdrops (*Epifagus virginiana*)

Beechdrops is one of the common "nevergreen" flowering plants. It rarely grows more than a foot high, and even

For millions of years tremendous deposits of these Clubmosses accumulated on the earth's surface. They were covered over and compressed with new growth and eroded sediment. Today we dig them up as coal and burn them for heat, releasing the sun's energy they absorbed over a quarter of a billion years ago.

The Clubmosses spread by underground rootstocks, and

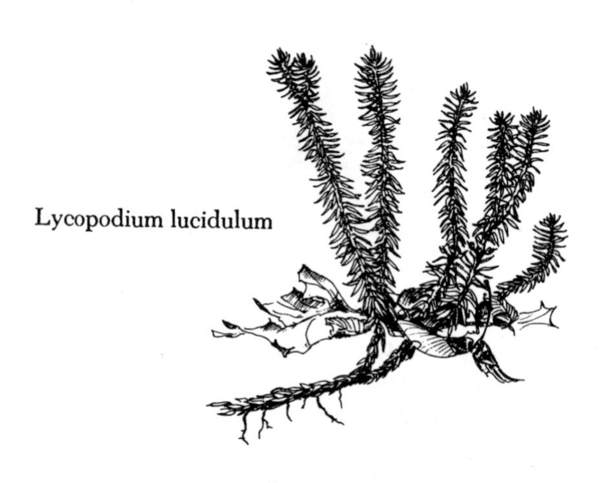
Lycopodium lucidulum

form small colonies of plants. The rootstocks differ in each species; some grow 6 inches under ground, others only an inch or two, others at the soil surface. As the rootstocks spread, the older plants die back.

Some species also reproduce by small vegetative growths that drop off their upper leaves, much like the bulbets of Wild Garlic. Clubmosses start new colonies of plants from spores, which are grown either at the base of the leaves or on long spikes called "strobili." If you knock these spikes in early winter, you can see clouds of yellow spores released into the air. The spores land on the soil and grow into a different style of plant, shaped like a minute single leaf. These are rarely found, partly because some lack chloro-

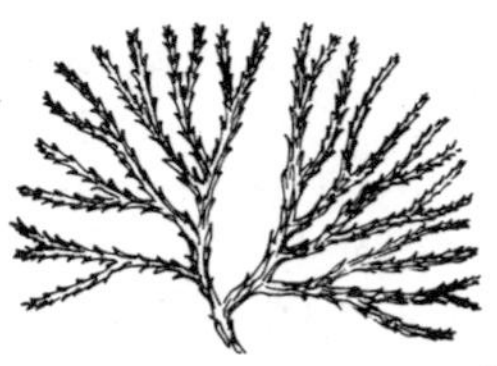

*Leaves of* Lycopodium complanatum

phyll and live in association with fungi underground. These small plants produce both male and female cells, which unite and grow into the Clubmosses as we see them. This life cycle is very similar to that of ferns.

Great numbers of spores are produced. They have been commercially gathered for fireworks and "flash powder" for old-time cameras. They ignite quickly and cause a small explosive flash.

## Cranberry (*Vaccinium* species)

Cranberry is found in the acid soil of bogs. It is a trailing plant with shallow rootstocks that continuously send down roots and send up branches. The branches can grow to one and a half feet long and are generally low-lying. They have small, rounded, alternate evergreen leaves, and sometimes

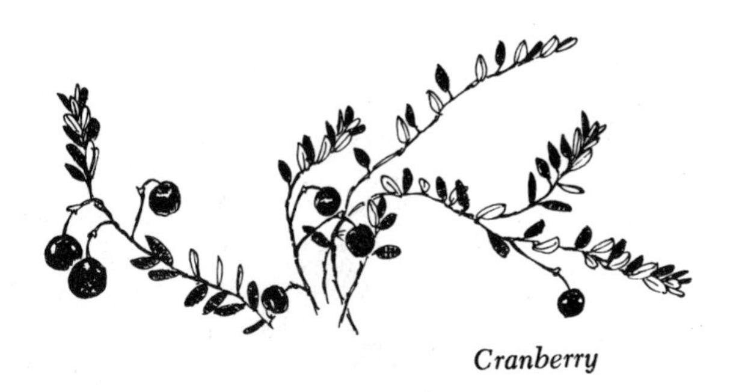

*Cranberry*

bright red berries will be present along or at the tips of the stems.

There are three common varieties in our area each with a different size leaf and berry. The Small Cranberry, *Vaccinium oxycoccus,* is a very delicate plant with pointed leaves, unlike the other two species. The Large Cranberry is much larger and produces a fruit over ½ inch in diameter. Its specific Greek name, *macrocarpon,* means "large fruit." This is the variety of cranberry you buy in stores. The third variety is Mountain Cranberry, *Vaccinium vitis-idaea;* it grows only in the North or in the mountains of the mid-Atlantic states. It is midway in size between the other two and its leaves have black dots beneath.

Cranberries are a great fruit and can be gathered during fall and into winter. They are sour when eaten raw, but with cooking and sugar they make a good jam or jelly to accompany meat. Cranberries grow over much of North America but are only found locally where their habitat of acid bogs exists.

## Christmas Fern (*Polystichum acrostichoides*)

Christmas fern is the largest of our evergreen ferns. It is easily recognized by the shape of its pinnae (leaflets). The

*Christmas Fern*

fronds lie flat on the ground in winter but are easily spotted when the snow melts because of their luxuriant dark green color. The fern is very similar to our cultivated Boston Fern, which many people keep in their houses.

Some of the fronds have smaller leaflets at their ends; these bear the fern's spores. They often die back in winter, leaving the fronds with a cut-off appearance. Christmas Fern is used in winter by florists for flower arrangements; this is probably the origin of its name — simply being used near Christmas. New fronds start growing in late winter as the snow melts.

### Dewberry, Bristly (*Rubus hispidus*)

Dewberries are the trailing member of the Raspberry and Blackberry genus, *Rubus*. They are similar in appearance to

*Bristly Dewberry*

wild Strawberries, having three toothed leaflets joined together and, in spring, an almost identical flower. But their main difference is that Dewberry is a trailing vine; just pick up a part of the plant and you will find it connected to the other Dewberries nearby.

Dewberry typically grows in woodlands and woodland margins. It often covers a whole area, its shiny green leaves poking through the fall leaf litter. In farther northern areas it may not be evergreen, and in other areas the leaves may be green mixed with a reddish color caused by the formation of anthocyanin, the pigment present in the leaves of other evergreen plants. Small thorns or pliable bristles line its stems, and roots grow at points where erect stems and leaves emerge from the trailing vine.

Being related to the Blackberries and Raspberries, Dewberries produce a small many-seeded berry in summer. The berry is black and does not detach from the stem as do other berries. It is slightly sour, but with sugar added it can be used interchangeably in recipes calling for its sweeter cousins.

## Goldthread (*Coptis groenlandica*)

Goldthread is a lovely evergreen plant with dark shiny green leaves. It loves cool climates and is often found along

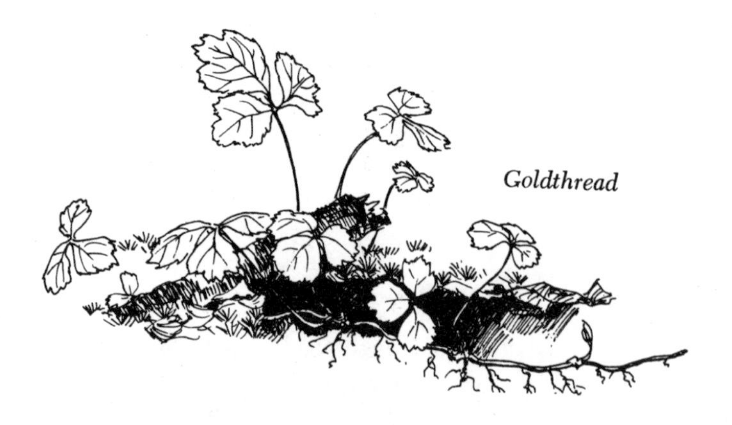

*Goldthread*

wet mountain paths or moist shaded woods. It is easily recognized, for it has three small leaves joined together. The leaves are rounded and toothed along their edges. Our only other common evergreen with three toothed leaves is Dewberry, and that is larger and has thorns.

The common name comes from the plant's bright golden roots; by digging slightly at the base of the plant you can reveal them. The roots, when gathered and steeped in hot water, produce a bitter to stimulate the appetite or a mouthwash that may help sooth cankers and other mouth sores. It has also been called Canker Root.

### Indian Pipe (*Monotropa uniflora*)

Indian Pipe is one of the two common "nevergreens," included here because they grow in the same woodlands as the evergreens, and because they are a common and puzzling sight. Indian Pipe appears as a small group of black stems four to ten inches tall, topped with urn-shaped seed

*Indian Pipes*

cases. The plant is a waxy white color in summer and has no leaves, except for small bracts along its stem.

In summer its white flowers droop down off the top of the stem, but as the seeds ripen in fall they turn up, as we find them in winter. The genus name means "one turn" and may refer to this turning.

Indian Pipe belongs to the same family as the evergreens Pyrola and Pipsissewa, but it has no chlorophyll — the green pigment in most other plants that enables them to manufacture food with energy from the sun. Therefore it must live off organic material, but since it can't absorb this directly, its roots associate with a fungus that can dissolve the organic matter and make it available to the plant.

There is another similar species, called Pinesap, *Monotropa hypopitys*, which has many flowers on each stem and also grows in dry woodlands. Its specific name means "under pine."

## Juniper, Common (*Juniperus communis*)

Juniper is an aggressive colonizer of old fields, cutover woods, and rocky mountaintops. It is a shrub, rarely grow-

*Common Juniper*

ing more than 2 feet tall but spreading its tough stems to either side. Its needles grow in whorls of threes, and each has a clear white stripe on one side. They are evergreen and very sharp-pointed; they provide valuable winter cover for small animals, protecting them from both predators and weather. Deer browse the needles and birds eat the berries as well as nest in the foliage.

The berries are blue and are commercially collected both in North America and Europe for use in flavoring gin. The fruits are similar to those of Red Cedar, for the two plants are close relatives. Juniper's persistent growth on mountain slopes and old fields helps prevent erosion.

### Labrador Tea (*Ledum groenlandicum*)

Labrador Tea typically grows in the cold bogs and swamps of the North. It can be easily recognized as a shrub about 2

*Labrador Tea*

feet tall, whose leaves have brown wool on the underside and leaf margins rolled under. The leaves are aromatic when crushed and can be gathered at any time of year for use as a tea substitute. The leaves should be dried thoroughly in the sun or near a heater before being used in tea. Bog Rosemary, *Andromeda glaucophylla,* is another small shrub often found in bogs along with Labrador Tea. It could be confused with Labrador Tea since its leaf margins are also rolled under; this similarity is important, since Bog Rosemary leaves are considered poisonous. However, Bog Rosemary leaves are very narrow, bluish-green on top, and distinctly white underneath. Also, they are not strongly aromatic, as are those of Labrador Tea.

The rolled-under, narrow, and woolly leaves of these two plants are believed to be adaptations to conserving water, for although the plants live in water, it is often too acidic for them to use, so they reduce their water needs by these adaptations.

## Laurel, Mountain (*Kalmia latifolia*)

Mountain Laurel is our most luxuriant northern evergreen shrub. It can grow up to 12 feet tall and cover the understory of whole mountain hillsides. The leaves are large,

*Mountain Laurel*

shiny, and dark green all through winter, forming a striking contrast with the snow-covered forest floor.

Sometimes Mountain Laurel grows in dense thickets, its twisting stems creating winter shelter for small mammals, its leaves browse for Deer. The wood is hard and fine-grained

*Dried seeds of Mountain Laurel*

but of such small dimension that it has been used only for small articles such as spoons and pipes. The dried flower-parts and mature seeds are clearly visible at the tips of the stems throughout winter. The leaves are often collected in winter for Christmas wreaths and decorations. In spring the plant bursts into bloom with clusters of pink blossoms.

The genus is named after Peter Kalm, a Swedish botanist and naturalist who came to America in the early 1700s. He traveled extensively in eastern North America, exploring the natural history of the land and keeping complete journals of his experiences. Linnaeus was a good friend of his and named this genus in his honor.

## Laurel, Sheep (*Kalmia angustifolia*)
## Pale (*Kalmia polifolia*)

The Laurel is the primary northern evergreen shrub of our woodlands. There are only three kinds in our area, one of

*Sheep Laurel leaves and seeds*

which, Mountain Laurel, grows tall and has large shiny leaves. It is dealt with separately above. The other two are similar in size and habitat.

Both Sheep Laurel and Pale Laurel grow to between two and three feet in height. They have narrow pale green leaves growing in whorls of three. They generally grow in small groups. The two can be easily distinguished, for Pale Laurel has two-edged twigs and produces flowers at the tips of the stems. Sheep Laurel has round twigs and produces flowers along its stems. In winter, the remains of flower parts as well as seeds may still be present on the plant.

*Sheep Laurel*

Laurels belong to the large family of Heaths, *Ericaceae*, which includes the Rhododendrons and a number of evergreens. The leaves are thought to be poisonous to livestock, but wild animals such as Deer and Rabbits seem unaffected by them.

## Leatherleaf (*Chamaedaphne calyculata*)

Leatherleaf is the third evergreen shrub, along with Labrador Tea and Bog Rosemary, that is likely to be found at the edges of acid peat bogs. Unlike the other two it has leaf

*Leatherleaf*

margins that are not rolled in but flat. The leaves are broad and shiny on top and often point up along the stem. The shrub can grow to 4 feet in height but is more likely to be between 1 and 2 feet tall. In spring or even late winter, white bell-like flowers are borne along the tips of the twigs. In winter the resulting seeds are eaten by Grouse. Cottontails are known to eat the leaves. Leatherleaf is often found along with Cranberry.

## Partridgeberry (*Mitchella repens*)

Partridgeberry is a very common ground cover of almost all areas. The leaves are dark green with light midveins showing through on top, and they line the trailing stems in pairs. Where leaves are produced, roots also often form if the

*Partridgeberry*

conditions are favorable. Partridgeberry seems to favor moist woodlands, especially under stands of White Pine.

In summer it grows paired flowers that are merged at their bases. These two flowers produce one fruit that is composed of two parts. It is red and berrylike and lasts up to a year on the vine, if not eaten by mice or grouse. The fruit is not poisonous to humans but is usually termed "barely edible," being dry and containing lots of seeds.

The common name is derived from the fact that "Partridge" or Bobwhites may eat the berries. The genus is named after John Mitchell, a man who moved to Virginia around 1725. He was most famous for his maps of the colonies, but he also had a keen interest in plants and studied them as he traveled. He often corresponded with Linnaeus about his discoveries. The specific name, *repens,* means "creeping" or "crawling."

## Pipsissewa (*Chimaphila umbellata*)

Pipsissewa is a common inhabitant of the dry forest floor beneath Pines and Oaks. It appears as a group of individual plants that are usually connected by an underground root-

*Pipsissewa*

stock. The leaves are shiny and grow in whorls off erect stems which grow as tall as 12 inches. Some years, the plant produces a stalk protruding from its topmost whorl of leaves. This stalk divides at the top where flowers bloom in summer and seeds are matured by fall. Often these stalks and seedcases are all you will see sticking through the snow cover; dig beneath to find the evergreen plant.

Many books recommend the leaves as a pleasant trailside nibble, but anyone who has tried them knows that what little taste they have is rather unpleasant and takes effort to remove from your mouth.

## Pipsissewa, Spotted (*Chimaphila maculata*)

Spotted Pipsissewa is a close relative of Pipsissewa; it differs from it by having white pigment along the veins of its dark green leaves. It is not as common as Pipsissewa but is always a prize when found. Unlike the close groups character-

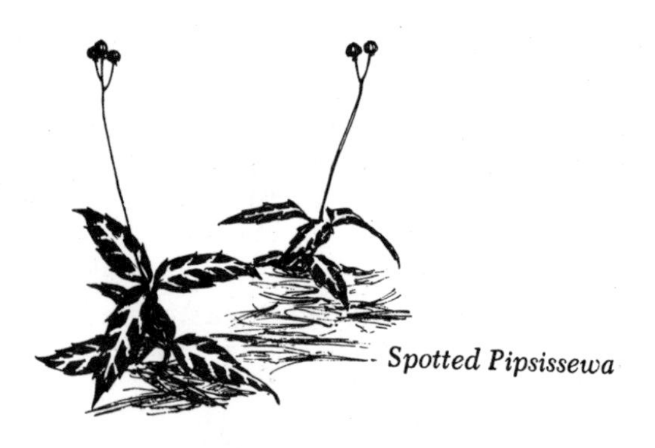
Spotted Pipsissewa

istic of Pipsissewa, Spotted Pipsissewas are more scattered, the extensive underground stems placing individual plants up to 10 feet apart. Spotted Pipsissewa also produces a flower stalk similar to that of Pipsissewa.

The common name *Pipsissewa* is believed to be of Cree Indian origin. The genus name means "winter-loving." It belongs to the Wintergreen family, *Pyrolaceae,* along with Indian Pipes and Pyrola.

## Polypody, Common (*Polypodium vulgare*)

Common Polypody is undoubtedly the most hardy of the winter ferns, standing erect and green at all times. It has

Common Polypody

also been called the Rock-cap Fern because of its marvelous habit of growing on the tops of rocks. Especially in the North, where the glaciers left huge boulders, these are now often covered with a carpet of the Common Polypody. Occasionally the plant also grows on trees or logs.

The fern is easily recognized, if not by this habit, then by the way the leaflets are broadly attached to the main stem. Also the leaflets' undersides often have their large round fruit dots in two rows, easily seen and creating a strong, clear visual pattern.

The plant spreads mostly by creeping rootstocks that travel over the rock surface. These have swellings at intervals, from which the fern fronds grow. The fronds are normally about 1 foot long, new ones being produced in early summer. The plant is found worldwide in the North Temperate Zone.

## Pyrola (*Pyrola* species)

Pyrola is a low-growing evergreen plant that may be partly covered by fallen tree leaves. Its leaves are generally round,

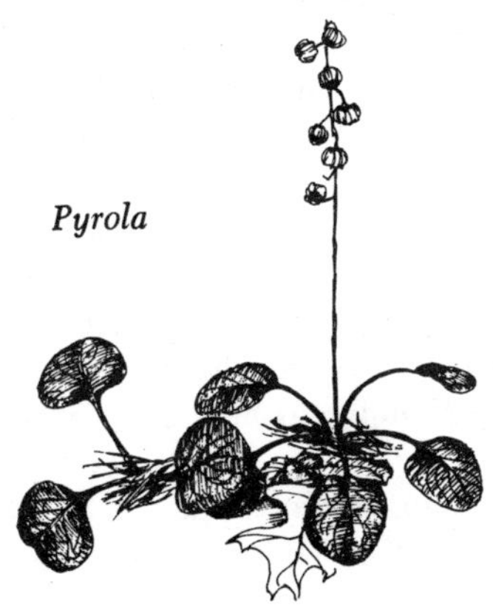

*Pyrola*

darker and shinier on top than underneath, and connected to a central root by a long weak reddish stem. The leaves grow as a rosette, and from its center the plant sometimes produces a tall stalk with bell-like flowers coming off its upper part.

These flower stalks may be all that first attracts you to Pyrola in winter, and you may need to clear away the snow and dead leaves to reveal the green plant. There are a number of species most easily distinguished by their flower stalks. One species, *Pyrola secunda,* has flower remains on only one side of its stalk; other species have flower remains on all sides. The common name often given to Pyrola is Shinleaf, which may be a corruption of "Shineleaf," for the upper surfaces of the leaves have a water-conserving waxy coating.

## Rattlesnake Plantain (*Goddyera* species)

Rattlesnake Plantain is always exciting to find, maybe because its name suggests something unusual or dangerous. It is certainly not dangerous, but it is unusual, being small, light-colored, and usually covered by dry leaves. However, its flower stalk may be up to 20 inches high and is lined at its tip with seeds and flower remains. Rattlesnake Plantain is not related to our Common Plantain, *Plantago major,* but is a member of the Orchid family and blooms in late summer.

If you dig down through snow and leaves to the base of the flowerstalk, you will uncover the plant's rosette. Its leaves are green with white veins which must have appeared like the scales of snakeskin to early discoverers. In old-time medicine, if something resembled an affliction it was believed to have power over it; therefore, Rattlesnake Plantain was thought to help cure snakebites or scaly skin diseases.

There are four common species of *Goodyera,* each with varying numbers of white veins. The genus is named in

*Rattlesnake Plantain*

honor of John Goodyer, an English botanist who lived in the early 1600s.

## Teaberry (*Gaultheria procumbens*)

Teaberry is a hardy little plant of the woods, a pleasure to know and find. I almost always pick a leaf or berry to chew as I pass by the plant. The bright red berries mature in fall and last all winter, but are almost always hard to see, being nestled beneath the shiny evergreen leaves.

The plant seems to thrive on acidic soil. It grows slowly by means of an underground stem, which periodically sends up small erect stems up to 6 inches tall. As with other members of the Heath family, Teaberry's leaves are well adapted for conserving moisture, their upper surface being coated with a thick waxy layer, which helps prevent evaporation and desiccation by winter winds.

Teaberry is eaten by Deer for its tasty leaves, and it is no doubt protected from extinction in late winter by suitable

*Teaberry*

snow cover that limits the access of Deer. Grouse and Mice may also eat the leaves or berries. The plant has long been known to contain oil of wintergreen in the leaves and berries. This is a familiar taste to us, being used in chewing gum, toothpaste, and medicines. The oil is no longer extracted from plants for commercial uses but is produced synthetically. The oil exists in Snowberry, *Gaultheria hispidula,* another plant in the same genus, but curiously it also exists in the bark of Sweet Birch, *Betula lenta,* to a greater extent than in Teaberry. The oil is tasted in Teaberry when the leaves or berries are chewed, and if equal amounts of boiling water and fresh leaves are combined and let sit for a day or two, a good tea results; just reheat the mixture. A very weak tea can be made by just steeping the fresh leaves in a teapot of hot water.

There are many common names for this plant, and each book uses a different one. I prefer Teaberry or Checkerberry, but complications arise with the name Wintergreen, for although the plant contains wintergreen oil, there is a family of plants called *Pyrolaceae,* the Wintergreen family, to which *Gaultheria* does not belong, its family being the *Ericaceae* or Heath family.

## Twinflower (*Linnaea borealis*)

Twinflower is a small trailing plant partial to the cold woods of the North, but it is found south as far as Maryland and Virginia. Its paired green leaves are similar to those of Partridgeberry, but instead of being attached directly to the trailing stem, they are on short stalks that grow off the trailing stem. Twinflower is a member of the Honeysuckle family and produces two nodding pink flowers on a long stalk.

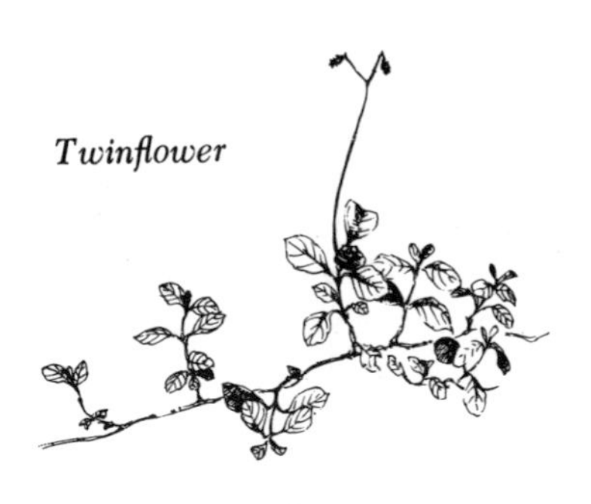
*Twinflower*

The famous Swedish botanist Linnaeus, who helped to stimulate great interest in collecting and naming plants in the 1700s, is often pictured with a sprig of Twinflower in his hand. The species name, *borealis,* simply means "from the north."

## Woodfern (*Dryopteris* species)

The genus *Dryopteris* includes a whole group of ferns, some of which are evergreen, others only occasionally so, depending on their location. The genus name comes from two words meaning "oak" and "fern" and refers to the plants' preference for woodland habitats. Swampy lowland woods are particularly favored. Like other ferns they spread pri-

*Marginal Woodfern*

marily by underground rootstocks that send up new clusters of leaves at irregular intervals. At the base of these leaves in winter you will find next year's leaves already formed as tightly curled bundles. They are called fiddleheads because of their resemblance to the neck of a fiddle as they uncurl in spring. Mice use fiddleheads as an extra source of food in winter.

Two species of Woodfern are most common and prominent in the winter woods. One is Marginal Woodfern, *Dryopteris marginalis,* so named because of the placement of fruit dots on the underside margin of the leaflets. Marginal Woodfern leaves are leathery and only twice-cut: in

*Leaflets and spore sacs of Spinulose Woodfern (left) and Marginal Woodfern (right)*

other words, there are leaflets and subleaflets but no further division.

The other species is called Spinulose Woodfern, *Dryopteris spinulosa.* In contrast to the above, this fern has fruit dots in from the leaflet margin and is often thrice-cut, making it appear very lacy. This fern prefers wetter areas than the ones in which Marginal Woodfern grows.

Another twice-cut Woodfern is called Goldie's Woodfern. It is similar in appearance to Marginal Woodfern but has fruit dots placed in from the leaflet margins.

# *Bibliography*

This is only a partial list of the sources used in writing *A Guide to Nature in Winter*. The books included are those that I felt would be enjoyable, useful, and accessible to people wanting to know more.


WINTER WEEDS

Brown, Lauren. *Weeds in Winter*. W. W. Norton Co., 1976.

Fogg, John M., Jr. *Weeds of Lawn and Garden*. University of Pennsylvania Press, 1945.

Gibbons, Euell. *Stalking the Wild Asparagus*. David McKay Co., 1962.

Hall, Alan. *The Wild Food Trailguide*. Holt, Rinehart and Winston 1973.

Martin, Alexander C., Herbert S. Zim, and Arnold L. Nelson. *American Wildlife and Plants*. Dover, 1961.

Palmer, E. Laurence. *Fieldbook of Natural History*. McGraw-Hill, 1961.

Peterson, Roger Tory, and Margaret McKenny. *A Field Guide to Wildflowers*. Houghton Mifflin, 1968.

Shosteck, Robert. *Flowers and Plants: A Lexicon*. Quadrangle, 1974.

Spencer, Edwin Rollin. *All About Weeds*. Dover, 1974.

SNOW

Bell, Corydon. *The Wonder of Snow*. Hill and Wang, 1957.

Bentley, W. A., and W. J. Humphreys. *Snow Crystals*. Dover, 1962.

Formozov, A. N. *Snow Cover as an Integral Factor of the Environment and Its Importance in the Ecology of Mammals and Birds*. Boreal Institute, University of Alberta, 1969.

LaChapelle, Edward R. *Field Guide to Snow Crystals.* University of Washington, 1969.
Nakaya, Ukichiro. *Snow Crystals.* Harvard University Press, 1954.

### WINTERING TREES

Betts, H. S. *American Woods.* U. S. Forest Service, Government Printing Office, 1945–1954.
Collingwood, G. H., and Warren D. Brush. *Knowing Your Trees.* Revised by Devereux Butcher. American Forestry Association, 1964.
Harlow, William M. *Trees of the Eastern United States and Canada.* Dover, 1957.
Huntington, Annie Oakes. *Studies of Trees in Winter.* Knight and Millet, 1902.
Peattie, Donald Culross. *A Natural History of Trees.* Houghton Mifflin, 1950.
Symonds, George W. D. *The Tree Identification Book.* M. Barrows and Co., 1950.
Watts, Mary Theilgaard, and Tom Watts. *Winter Tree Finder.* Nature Study Guild, 1970.
Wilson, B. F. *The Growing Tree.* University of Massachusetts, 1970.

### EVIDENCE OF INSECTS

Anderson, R. F. *Forest and Shade Tree Entomology.* Wiley, 1960.
Brues, Charles T. *Insect Dietary.* Harvard University Press, 1964.
Comstock, John Henry. *An Introduction to Entomology.* Comstock Publishing Company, 1947.
Evans, Howard E. *Wasp Farm.* Anchor Press/Doubleday & Co., 1970.
Felt, Ephraim Porter. *Plant Galls and Gall Makers.* Comstock Publishing Co., 1940.
Lanham, Url. *The Insects.* Columbia University Press, 1964.
Morgan, Ann Haven. *Field Book of Animals in Winter.* G. P. Putnam's Sons, 1939.
Swain, Ralph B. *The Insect Guide.* Doubleday & Co., 1948.
Teale, Edwin Way. *Strange Lives of Familiar Insects.* Dodd, Mead & Co., 1962.

### WINTER'S BIRDS AND ABANDONED NESTS

Current information on birds is found primarily in short research articles published in ornithological journals. The journals most useful were:
*Auk*
*Condor*
*Ibis*
*Wilson Bulletin*

Others include:
*Aviculture Magazine*
*Bird Banding*
*British Birds*
*Living Bird*
*Ornithological Monographs*

### MUSHROOMS IN WINTER

Boyce, John Shaw. *Forest Pathology*. McGraw-Hill, 1961.
Christensen, Clyde M. *Common Fleshy Fungi*. Burgess Publishing Co., 1967.
Krieger, Louis C. C. *The Mushroom Handbook*. Dover, 1967.
Overholts, Lee O. *Polyporaceae of the United States, Alaska, and Canada*. Revised by J. L. Lowe. University of Michigan Press, 1953.

### TRACKS IN THE SNOW

Cahalane, Victor H. *Mammals of North America*. Macmillan, 1947.
Jaeger, Ellsworth. *Trails and Trailcraft*. Macmillan, 1948.
Murie, Olaus J. *A Field Guide to Animal Tracks*. Houghton Mifflin, 1954.
Palmer, Ralph S. *The Mammal Guide*. Doubleday, 1954.
Rue, Leonard Lee, III. *Sportsman's Guide to Game Animals*. Outdoor Life Books, 1968.
Seton, Ernest Thompson. *Animal Tracks and Hunter Signs*. Doubleday, 1958.
The most current information on mammals exists as short articles in two leading wildlife journals:
*Journal of Mammalogy*
*Journal of Wildlife Management*

### WOODLAND EVERGREEN PLANTS

Clute, Willard Nelson. *Our Ferns: Their Haunts, Habits, and Folklore*. Frederick A. Stokes Co., 1938.
Cobb, Boughton. *A Field Guide to Ferns*. Houghton Mifflin, 1956.
Cunningham, James, A., and John E. Klimas. *Wildflowers of Eastern American*. Knopf, 1974.
Gibbons, Euell. *Stalking the Healthful Herbs*. David McKay Co., 1966.
Milne, Lorus, and Margery Milne. *Living Plants of the World*. Random House, 1967.
Symonds, George W. D. *The Shrub Identification Book*. William Morrow & Co., 1963.

# Index